FORUM
ANGEWANDTE LINGUISTIK
F.A.L. BAND 59

Hrsg. von der Gesellschaft für Angewandte Linguistik

Die in dieser Reihe erscheinenden Arbeiten werden vor der Publikation durch die F.A.L.-Redaktion geprüft sowie einem Double-Blind-Peer-Review-Verfahren durch mehrere Gutachter/innen unterzogen.

The quality of the work published in this series is assured both by the editorial staff of the F.A.L. and by a double-blind peer review process by several external referees.

Gesellschaft für Angewandte Linguistik e.V.

Gesellschaft für
Angewandte Linguistik e.V.

**Der Vorstand der
Gesellschaft für Angewandte Linguistik**

Prof. Dr. Markus Bieswanger
Prof. Dr. Karin Birkner
Dr. Patrick Voßkamp
Prof. Dr. Martin Luginbühl
Prof. Dr. Ines Bose

**Der Wissenschaftliche Beirat der
Gesellschaft für Angewandte Linguistik**

Prof. Dr. Michael Beißwenger
Prof. Dr. Albert Busch
Dr. Oliver Ehmer
Dr. Sven Grawunder
Prof. Dr. Elke Grundler
Prof. Dr. Stefan Hauser
Prof. Dr. Britta Hufeisen
Prof. Dr. Heike Jüngst
Jun.-Prof. Dr. Iris Kleinbub
Dr. Annette Klosa
Dr. Matthias Knopp
Dr. Dagmar Knorr
Prof. Dr. Markus Kötter
Prof. Dr. Beatrix Kreß

Dr. Lisa Link
Prof. Dr. Karin Luttermann
Dr. Bernd Meyer
Dr. Florence Oloff
Dr. Steffen Pappert
Dr. Monika Reif
Dr. Peter Rosenberg
PD Dr. Kersten Sven Roth
Steffen Schaub
Dr. Marco Schilk
Prof. Dr. Christoph Schroeder
Dr. Cordula Schwarze
Prof. Dr. Angelika Storrer
Prof. Dr. Eva Wyss

Das Redaktionsteam der F.A.L.

Prof. Dr. Hajo Diekmannshenke
Prof. Dr. Ulrich Schmitz
Jun.-Prof. Dr. Antje Wilton

FORUM ANGEWANDTE LINGUISTIK
F.A.L. BAND 59

Christian Ludwig / Kris Van de Poel (eds)

Collaborative Learning and New Media

New Insights into an Evolving Field

Bibliographic Information published by the Deutsche Nationalbibliothek
The Deutsche Nationalbibliothek lists this publication in the
Deutsche Nationalbibliografie; detailed bibliographic data is
available in the internet at http://dnb.d-nb.de.

Library of Congress Cataloging-in-Publication Data
A CIP catalog record for this book has been applied for
at the Library of Congress.

Printed by CPI books GmbH, Leck

ISBN 978-3-631-66797-2 (Print)
E-ISBN 978-3-653-05921-2 (E-Book)
E-ISBN 978-3-631-71320-4 (EPUB)
E-ISBN 978-3-631-71321-1 (MOBI)
DOI 10.3726/b11402

© Peter Lang GmbH
Internationaler Verlag der Wissenschaften
Frankfurt am Main 2017
All rights reserved.
Peter Lang Edition is an Imprint of Peter Lang GmbH.

Peter Lang – Frankfurt am Main · Bern · Bruxelles · New York ·
Oxford · Warszawa · Wien

All parts of this publication are protected by copyright. Any
utilisation outside the strict limits of the copyright law, without
the permission of the publisher, is forbidden and liable to
rosecution. This applies in particular to reproductions,
translations, microfilming, and storage and processing in
electronic retrieval systems.
This publication has been peer reviewed.

www.peterlang.com

Table of Contents

Christian Ludwig & Kris Van de Poel
Introduction 7

Christian Ludwig & Kris Van de Poel
Collaborative Learning and the New Media 13

Jozef Colpaert & Linda Gijsen
Ontological Specification of Telecollaborative Tasks in Language Teaching 23

Lienhard Legenhausen
Authentic Interactions and Language Learning – The Interaction Hypothesis Revisited 41

Theresa Schenker & Fiona Heather Poorman
Students' Perceptions of Telecollaborative Communication Tools 55

Maria Eisenmann
Differentiation and Individualisation through Digital Media 73

Saskia Kersten
Email Communication in the EFL classroom 87

Veronica dal Bianco & Lawrie Moore-Walter
Tools and Collaborative Tasks for Enabling Language Learning in a Blended Learning Environment 103

Thorsten Merse & Fiona Heather Poorman
Voices from the University Classroom: Using Social Media for Collaborative Learning in Language Teacher Education 129

Christine Fourie
Facing (and Facebooking) Authentic Tasks in a Blended Learning Environment: Metacognitive Awareness Demonstrated by Medical Students 151

Table of Contents

Kris Van de Poel & Jessica Gasiorek
Collaborative Academic Acculturation Processes in a Blended-Learning Approach 177

Stephan Gabel & Jochen Schmidt
Collaborative Writing with Writing Pads in the Foreign Language Classroom – Chances and Limitations 189

Judith Buendgens-Kosten
Writing for a 'Real Audience'? The Role of Audience in Computer-Assisted Language Learning 213

Simon Falk
"Let's Work Together" – How Mobile-Assisted Language Learning Can Contribute to More Collaboration and Interaction among Students 227

Bert Van Poeck
Critical Perspectives on the Collaborative Learning Potential of Digital Game-Based Learning in the Foreign Language Classroom 241

Dominik Rumlich & Sabine Ahlers
The Rich Environment of CLIL Classes as an Ideal Setting for Collaborative Learning 255

Jo Mynard
Investigating Social Presence in a Social Networking Environment 271

Elke Ruelens, Nick Van deneynde & Dieter Vermandere
A Preliminary Needs Analysis for Online Collaborative Language Learning 291

Christian Ludwig & Kris Van de Poel
Postscript 311

Christian Ludwig & Kris Van de Poel
Further reading 315

References 323

Editors/Contributors 373

Introduction

> "In this new wave of technology, you can't do it all yourself, you have to form alliances."
> (Carlos Slim Helú)

All quiet on the media front? Certainly not! New media, as Socha and Eber-Schmid (2014[1]) legitimately point out, evolve and morph continuously with the effect that "[w]hat it will be tomorrow is virtually unpredictable for most of us […]". In addition to this, the cornucopia of catchall terms such as new media, digital media, social media, social networking, and media tools, to mention but a few, causes lively discussions among researchers, practitioners, and students alike about their content, form, application and usability. Despite the fact that the field of "computer-assisted language learning (CALL) is changing so quickly and significantly that the only constant is change itself" (Egbert/Hanson-Smith 1999: ix), digital technologies show enormous potential to effect change in foreign language learning and prepare learners for the demands of an increasingly mobile and yet highly connected modern knowledge society. Yet, in order to take optimal advantage of this social potential –and help learners see the light in that they do not have to go the path alone– we need also to reflect on the traditional teaching methods and embed all in a sound and balanced approach of combined face-to-face and online learning to enable students to learn in a flexible and tailored way. Probably one of the greatest potentials of the 'new' technologies is the opportunity to facilitate and enhance the learning process by providing learners with the possibility to interact and collaborate with basically anyone, anywhere and anytime, and in doing so lowering the threshold for learning, making the learning content more relevant and motivational. The duality and need for dovetailing these demands have been aptly summarised by Thomas, Reinders, and Warschauer (2014: 6):

> extending the research on the collaborative potential of digital media will be a concern of CALL researchers over the next decade. While the various attempts to describe a generation of new learners, from digital natives to Generation X, remain flawed, digital media are more widely used than ever before.

This is exactly the anchor point where this book comes into play: at the nexus between research and teaching in a digital age. And as such it is a truly applied linguistic endeavour where the demands from the field critically inform the underlying methods and approaches; in short, they instigate theoretical reflections

---

1 http://www.newmedia.org/what-is-new-media.html.

and theory formation where terms have to be defined in this emergent research area taking into account the speed of change both of the stakeholders and the environment as well as the demands of society. And in good applied linguistic fashion the outcomes also have to be critically evaluated by the field at large in order to feed the theory underlying them.

To this end the present volume comprises 17 papers in which (action) researchers and practitioners share their experiences, case studies, empirical data and thoughts on different forms of interactive media and innovative strategies for using digital media tools and explore how these affect or can be effectively used to support collaborative learning in foreign language education.

The book will commence with a first part containing a detailed discussion underlying the theoretical framework of digital media and collaborative foreign language learning. In the introductory article, *Collaborative Learning and the New Media*, **Christian Ludwig** and **Kris Van de Poel** shed light on the jungle of scary-sounding jargon surrounding collaborative learning and digital media, advocating numerous potential benefits for foreign language learning. In the course of their argument, the authors particularly emphasise the fact that creating an interactive and collaborative learning environment takes more than 'just' technology, but has to be supported by careful curricular reflections. Their article is complemented by a theoretical essay on the *Ontological Specification of Telecollaborative Tasks in Language Teaching* by **Jozef Colpaert** and **Linda Gijsen**. They propose an educational engineering approach which defines task design as a process which is related to concepts such as meaningfulness and usefulness. In addition to this, the final theoretical review chapter by **Lienhard Legenhausen**, *Authentic Interactions and Language Learning – The Interaction Hypothesis Revisited*, based on Long's interaction hypothesis (1980), discusses various types of interaction and how they are influenced by classroom activities, but also have an effect on language learning processes.

The second and major part of the volume is of a truly applied nature –often resulting from action-research or critically presenting case-studies– and commences with an article by **Fiona Heather Poorman** and **Theresa Schenker** on *Students' Perceptions of Telecollaborative Communication Tools* which reports on a cross-cultural telecollaborative project between German and American university students. Following a nine-week virtual exchange via different communication tools, the authors investigated which tools students prefer for communication in telecollaborative exchanges providing implications for educators conducting telecollaborative projects.

The idea of differentiating between students through the use of digital media has gained centre stage in current discussions in the field of foreign language learning. This is exactly the focus of the contribution by **Maria Eisenmann** entitled *Differentiation and Individualisation through Digital Media*. Drawing on a number of examples such as Webquests, e-mail projects and Pod- as well as Vodcasts, the author shows how digital media support collaboration among students in a differentiated and individualised way.

Despite their image of being unfashionable within the Generation Y, emails are still among the most routinely used means of communication in people's lives. **Saskia Kersten**'s article *Email Communication in the EFL Classroom* looks at the role email exchanges can play in foreign language learning, discussing the main features of email communication and suggesting ways of making use of email communication in the classroom with special respect to its pragmatic dimension.

Adding to the plethora of tools available, **Veronica Dal-Bianco** and **Lawrie Moore-Walter** discuss in *Tools and Collaborative Tasks for Enabling Language Learning in a Blended Learning Environment*, how new media can effectively be employed to facilitate collaboration among students in a blended-learning context. By presenting a wide variety of tasks and corresponding tools, such as Skype, Vocaroo, wikis, and Padlet, to mention but a few, they show how students are encouraged to jointly construct meaning and take responsibility for their learning.

The ensuing chapter by **Thorsten Merse** and **Fiona Heather Poorman**, *Voices from the University Classroom: Using Social Media for Collaborative Learning in Language Teacher Education*, stresses that prospective teachers already use social media in their private lives. Proceeding from this assumption their article reports on a project in which two language teacher education courses from the University of Münster and Karlsruhe merged in a collaborative e-learning environment using social media applications such as a classroom wiki and blogs. The project's results form the basis for discussing the potential of social media for collaborative learning scenarios in higher education.

The following two contributions grapple with one of the currently most popular social networking tools but in very different environments: Facebook. More specifically, *Facing (and Facebooking) Authentic Tasks in a Blended Learning Environment: Metacognitive Awareness Demonstrated by Medical Students* by **Christine Fourie** reports on a study conducted within two consecutive years of a blended-learning intensive second language medical communication course which required students to collaboratively solve authentic tasks in a social media environment. The data offer intriguing insights into how to raise students' metacognitive awareness in the context of collaboration among students themselves and between students and the teacher.

Academic acculturation has become one of the catch phrases especially in higher education programmes. In *Collaborative Academic Acculturation Processes in a Blended-Learning Approach* **Kris Van de Poel** and **Jessica Gasiorek** report on a study investigating the role of Facebook as a space for collaboration in an academic writing course for first- and second-year English majors. Students were required to complete online tasks which encouraged them to actively engage with the specific discourse of their discipline and thus academically acculturate.

The next three articles continue on the topic of writing first with *Collaborative Writing with Writing Pads in the Foreign Language Classroom – Chances and Limitations* by **Stephan Gabel** and **Jochen Schmidt**, reverting to writing pads such as Titanpad. By turning text production into a collaborative endeavour, students are likely to experience a reduction of the complexity of the writing process. Analysing the asynchronous writing processes of EFL students by using Titanpad, the authors investigate whether the asynchronous production of texts yields similar results as synchronous writing. One of the alleged advantages of using new media in the context of foreign language learning is that students assume that they will have an audience other than just their teacher or peers.

Taking a critical stance, in *Writing for a 'real audience'? The role of audience in computer-assisted language learning*, **Judith Buendgens-Kosten** takes collaborative writing to a different level. By looking at how comments and corrections from blog readers in a language learning blogging community are taken up by blogpost authors in shaping the final form of blogposts, the author discusses what happens if feedback is used for revisions and what effect audience conceptualisations have on blog writers.

Apart from new ways of knowledge acquisition, mobile devices such as smartphones or tablets also offer additional opportunities of connecting with other people. In his essay, *Let's Work Together – How Mobile Assisted Language Learning Can Contribute to More Collaboration and Interaction Among Students*, **Simon Falk** takes readers literally beyond the four walls of the classroom. Following a brief introduction to the growing field of mobile-assisted language learning (MALL) and its potential for collaborative learning, the author concentrates on the results of an empirical study investigating impact of collaborative activities on mobile devices on students' language proficiency.

At first glance, it seems almost obvious that Massive Multiplayer Online Games (MMOs) are collaborative in nature and thus it should be possible to exploit their potential for foreign language learning. The article by **Bert Van Poeck** *Critical Perspectives on the Collaborative Learning Potential of Digital Game-Based Learning in the Foreign Language Classroom* questions this apparent reality by reviewing three exemplifying studies on the collaborative foreign language learning potential of

MMOs. Based on this, the author makes suggestions for an informed implementation of video games in the foreign language learning classroom.

The subsequent contribution by **Dominik Rumlich** and **Sabine Ahlers**, *The Rich Environment of CLIL Classes as an Ideal Setting for Collaborative Learning*, discusses the role of new media collaboration in a CLIL-environment. Arguing that CLIL and collaborative learning are strictly speaking two sides of the same coin, the article provides practical examples of collaborative methods in the context of CLIL geography classes; namely detective stories, mini books, and experiments.

The contributions to this volume argue that digital media tools can encourage students to collaborate and thus have a positive impact on students' performances. Convinced by the benefits of digital media and the ideal image of students as digital natives (Prensky 2001), digital residents (White, & Le Cornu, 2010) or the Generation Y, who make natural use of digital technology, we often seem to take for granted that our students not only have an encompassing positive attitude towards technological tools, but also possess the necessary skills for an informed use of digital media tools for foreign language learning purposes. Even though these issues have resounded in many of the previous articles, the following two articles pursue exactly this issue in more detail. *Investigating Social Presence in a Social Networking Environment* by **Jo Mynard** explores the nature of social presence in an online social networking environment. Students completed a range of online tasks on the social networking site Ning as part of a blended-learning course at a Japanese university. The results indicate that students are unaware of the conventions of social networking sites and needed greater preparation for beneficially participating in online discussions.

The ensuing contribution by **Elke Ruelens**, **Nick Van deneynde** and **Dieter Vermandere**, entitled *A Preliminary Needs Analysis for Online Collaborative Language Learning*, is similarly concerned with the effect of students' pre-knowledge on the success of online activities in blended-learning environments. The results of a needs analysis among Belgian university students indicate that they need to be prepared for the demands of online collaboration in blended-learning contexts.

This volume rounds off with a further reading section and a brief conclusion by the editors summarising the most cogent points made in the individual chapters and providing a glimpse into a possible future of collaborative learning and technology.

Of course, we are well aware of the fact that the articles in this volume only cover a limited section of the intersection between digital media and collaborative foreign language learning and that there is much more that one might want to explore. However, this volume tried to touch on some central points and issues in an exemplary fashion, at the same time keeping an open mind about other areas and potential applications. In all cases have we tried to make a strong plea for further investigating the nexus teaching/learning and research and we sincerely hope that you as a reader and thus a collaborator of this book will take it from here and dive into the range of fields that collaborative foreign language learning in the digital media age embraces.

Christian Ludwig & Kris Van de Poel
Karlsruhe & Antwerp (2017)

Acknowledgment

This book could not have been conceived without the help of many minds and hands. We would like to express our sincere gratitude to all contributors for helping to bring this edited volume to life and for being patient enough to engage in discussions with us. Without the support of the GAL, you would not be holding this book now. Sincere thanks are also due to the anonymous reviewers who have enhanced the quality of the argument. Last but not least, we would also like to thank Lars Salles and Raphael Röder for thoroughly proofreading and meticulously following up on the different versions of the manuscript and Kenneth McGillivray for bringing the references into shape.

Christian Ludwig & Kris Van de Poel
University of Education Karlsruhe, Germany
University of Antwerp, Belgium

Collaborative Learning and the New Media

"We do live in this age of new media."
(Seal)

This chapter addresses the ways in which new media can stimulate and shape collaborative learning in the foreign language classroom. New media have drastically changed the ways we interact and communicate in daily life and are gradually finding their way into foreign language classrooms. At the same time, in foreign language learning, the educational approach has shifted from learning by individual 'lone fighters' to collaborative learning involving groups of learners working towards a common goal. In the first part of this chapter the rationale and benefits of the collaborative approach will be scrutinised. This chapter further seeks to propose a definition for the term new media which appears to have remained elusive since its very conception. Finally, we will investigate the potential of new media to facilitate collaboration in the foreign language classroom.

Being able to collaborate with people in different spaces, contexts, and in multiple constellations is a substantial skill in our increasingly globalised world, especially with the changes and possibilities brought on by today's technologies. In the context of foreign language learning and teaching, collaborative learning has gained accelerating attention in recent years (cf. Smith/MacGregor 1992; Macaro 1997; Bruffee 1999; Barkley/Major 2014). It is not only seen as an important aim in itself, but also believed to increase communication skills in the target language, to build confidence, to lead to deeper learning and understanding as well as to stimulate students to be more actively involved in their own learning. Collaborative learning, however, is not clearly defined and often used as an umbrella term for a variety of educational approaches (Smith/MacGregor 1992) involving different kinds of organisation and tasks. The lowest common denominator of those frameworks is that in collaborative learning scenarios, learners work together to accomplish a common learning goal. Findley (1987), in his seminal and often quoted definition, states rather broadly that collaborative learning can be defined as "a situation in which a group of two or more learners learn or attempt to learn something together". This is a definition which can be interpreted in different ways (for a criticism of this definition see Dillenbourg 1999: 1). According to Gerlach (1994), collaborative learning "is based on the idea that learning is a naturally social act in which the participants talk among themselves". Smith and McGregor (1992: n.p.) take the social aspect slightly further and put most of the activity with the learners when defining collaborative learning as a joint intellectual effort by students, or students and teachers together. Usually students work in groups of two or more, mutually searching for understanding, solutions or meanings, or creating a product. Collaborative learning activities vary widely, but most centre on students' exploration or application of the course material, not simply the teacher's presentation or explication of it. A more recent definition by Dooly (2008: 21) focuses on the learners' responsibility and personal growth and stresses that collaborative learning

> requires working together toward a common goal. [...] More importantly, it means that students are responsible for one another's learning as well as their own and that reaching the goal implies that students have helped each other to understand and learn. [...] Collaborative learning [...] is aimed at getting the students to take almost full responsibility for working together, building knowledge together, changing and evolving together and of course, improving together.

While understandings of collaborative learning as well the different types of activities that come out of it vary, most definitions share the idea that the philosophy underlying collaborative learning is rooted in Vygotzky's theory of social constructivism. Vygotzsky advocates that learning is an active and constructive process which is mediated through interaction with others (Vygotzky 1978). According to Vygotzsky, students are able to perform at higher intellectual levels in collaborative situations than when working individually. In social interaction, new knowledge is actively integrated into existing knowledge by actively processing new information and creating something new. This requires learners to recontextualise knowledge, skills, and competences. Drawing on his social constructivist view of learning, Vygotzky developed the idea of a so-called zone of proximal development which is defined as the distance between the actual developmental level as determined by the individual's degree of independent problem solving and the level of potential development as determined through problem solving under adult guidance or in collaboration with more capable peers (Vygotsky 1978: 86). The process of support through adult guidance or collaboration with knowledgeable peers is often referred to as mediation or scaffolding, which can be defined as setting up "temporary supports, provided by capable people, that permit learners to participate in the complex process before they are able to do so unassisted" (Peregoy/Boyle 1997: 80).

Although collaborative learning can take different forms depending on the context, background, and traditions of learning, most definitions of collaborative learning are based on a set of assumptions about the learning process as proposed by Smith and MacGregor (1992: n.p.): (1) learning is an **active** process during which learners incorporate new knowledge into already existing knowledge, (2) learning needs a **challenge** that requires learners to engage with their peers, (3) learners benefit when **exposed** to diverse viewpoints from people with varied backgrounds, (4) learning flourishes in a social environment where **conversation** between learners takes place, (5) learners are challenged both socially and **emotionally** as they listen to different perspectives, and are required to articulate and defend their ideas. This socio-psychological orientation is sometimes taken a step further to include goal-orientation. For instance, Hu (2001) describes the features of collaborative learning as: (1) **interaction** including peer-to-peer and learner-teacher interaction, (2) learning **goal** which is pursued by all learners, (3) learner's own **responsibility** which is shared among and within groups, (4) a group **target** must be reached. However, sometimes a cognitive and metacognitive approach is also adopted: Panitz (1997) summarises the outcomes of collaborative learning in 38 merits, some of which are the development of higher level thinking, oral communication, and social interaction skills. Furthermore, collaborative learning creates an environment of active, involved exploratory learning.

Although cooperative and collaborative learning are often interchangeable, it is worth noting that collaborative learning, while similar to cooperative learning, is also distinct from it as cooperative learning represents "the most carefully structured end of the collaborative learning continuum" (Smith/MacGregor 1992: n.p.). In other words, cooperative learning is much more teacher-dependent and teacher guided than collaborative learning where "the lecturing/listening/note-taking process should not disappear entirely, but it lives alongside other processes that are based in students' discussion and active work with the course material" (*ibid.*). Here, students reach out to one another for knowledge sharing and problem-solving as they share the same goals of learning, while the role of the teacher changes according to the needs of the students; translating learning goals into tasks, and making sure that everyone is learning. Based on the preceding thoughts we can derive the following definition of collaborative learning which will form the basis for the remaining part of this article:

> Collaborative learning is an approach to learning that through enticing and stimulating activities encourages (but does not force) learners to work together towards a common goal by adding their skills and knowledge to establishing a goal-oriented process that empowers all team members as well as the group as a whole. In order to achieve this goal, learners need to actively engage in their own and others' learning and interact within and on behalf of their community as socially responsible people.

Collaborative learning has been more widely acknowledged, practiced, and researched with the arrival of the new (digital) media which are interactive in nature and have generated a shift from 'users as passive individuals' to 'users as an active community'. Collaborative learning seems to be adding something to media learning that it is missing and, vice versa, the new media provide incentives for collaborative learning which it has not encountered before. Both seem to marry well. One prominent example underlining the collaborative nature of the new media refers to the nature of its information exchange. In the early days of the internet, generally proprietary Web 1.0 applications simply enabled users to retrieve static information. In comparison, the Web 2.0, also referred to as the participatory web, motivates active participation and collaboration among its users. This paradigm shift from mere consumer to consumer-as-producer and the growing importance of user-generated content (UGC) and consumer-generated media (CGM) has led to a strengthening of the community where individuals and groups have become active participants in creating and recreating content. The shift from content-driven to user-driven has far-reaching consequences with members of the Web 2.0 community having numerous opportunities to make their voices heard simply because the vast majority of new media tools depend on active user involvement. Having identified some key concepts in the area of collaborative learning, we will now briefly review the term new media which, although equally difficult to define, has had a major influence on the accelerating success of collaborative learning in recent years.

The label 'new media' has found its way into everyday language to refers to a wide range of technologies such as website, blogs, video games, or social media. But what exactly are new media and what makes them different from 'old' media? In the 1950s most people would have referred to television as a new medium but does that mean that TV is still a new medium in the 21st century? If we classify TV as belonging to old media how do we then classify interactive digital television? Robert K. Logan in his *Understanding New Media: Extending Marshall McLuhan* suggests using "new media" (with quotation marks) to allude to digital interactive media, including digital television, and new media (without quotation marks) to denote media "that are new to the context under discussion" (Logan 2010: 5). This is a solution which emphasises the elusive character of the term.

Generally speaking, new media is a cover term often used to describe a rather vague, open group of digital tools used in the internet age. Or as stated by Socha and Eber-Schmid:

> **New Media** is a 21st Century catchall term used to define all that is related to the internet and the interplay between technology, images and sound. In fact, the definition of new

media changes daily, and will continue to do so. New media evolves and morphs continuously. What it will be tomorrow is virtually unpredictable for most of us, but we do know that it will continue to evolve in fast and furious ways.[1]

While such a broad definition enables us to easily add new emerging technological tools, it does not reveal the real nature of new media. Some authors even refer to new media as the "use of images, words, and sounds"[2]. Lev Manovich defines new media with reference to their carrier as:

> new cultural forms which are native to computers or rely on computers for distribution: Web sites, human-computer interface, virtual worlds, VR, multimedia, computer games, computer animation, digital video, special effects in cinema and net films, interactive computer installations. (Manovich as qtd. in Logan 2010: 5)

In his groundbreaking book *The Language of New Media* Manovich (2001: 27–48) proposes five principles of new media clearly delineating analogue from digital media: (1) Numerical Representation, (2) Modularity, (3) Automation, (4) Variability, (5) Transcoding. For Manovich, all new media are composed of digital codes; they are numerical representations (principle 1) which makes them programmable. They possess a modular structure which can be assembled and reassembled, but nevertheless continue to remain separate (principle 2). The fact that new media objects are numerical codes and structured in a modular and "fundamentally [...] nonhierarchical" (*ibid.*: 31) way allows "for the automation of many operations involved in media creation, manipulation, and access" (*ibid.*: 32). Manovich's fourth principle puts forward the idea that new media objects can exist in infinite versions. The fifth and last principle represents "the most substantial consequence of the computerization of media" (*ibid.*: 45). While technically, transcoding refers to the translation of a new media object from one format to another, it designates the ways in which media and culture are being reshaped and transformed by the logic of the computer.

Bolter and Grusin (1999: 45) suggest that remediation is the defining characteristic of new media: "We call the representation of one medium in another remediation and we will argue that remediation is the defining characteristic of the new digital media".

Attempts have been made to define new media by distinguishing them from old media as mass media "with the possible exception of the Internet and the World Wide Web" (Logan 2010: 5–6) which, according to Logan are too intimate to count as traditional mass media:

---

1 http://www.newmedia.org/what-is-new-media.html.
2 *ibid.*

Although the latter two media may be considered mass media because any one with a computer and a telephone or cable connection can access them, they are nevertheless "experienced on an intimate level, each user working alone with the screen and interface" (Wolf, 2003b, p. 11). Another point is that although millions of people access the Net and the Web every day, they are each accessing different material given that there are billions of pages already extant on the Net. (Logan 2010: 6)

Logan names 14 characteristics of new media, which were originally set-up to to identify the characteristics of new media in contrast to electric mass media dealt with by McLuhan (McLuhan 1964; cf. Logan 2010: 48). These 14 principles are:

1. Two-way communication;
2. Ease of access to and dissemination of information;
3. Continuous learning;
4. Alignment and integration;
5. Community;
6. Portability and time flexibility;
7. Convergence of many different media;
8. Interoperability;
9. Aggregation of content and crowd sourcing;
10. Variety and choice;
11. The closing of the gap between (or the convergence of) producers and consumers of media;
12. Social collectivity and cooperation;
13. Remix culture;
14. The transition from products to services

Some of Logan's principles overlap with Manovich's mechanics of how new media work which we already discussed earlier in this chapter. However, the principles put forward by Logan (2010: 48–49) differ from Manovich's propositions in that they attempt to conceptualise the effects, or "messages" (*ibid.*: 49) of new media.

It seems as if the term new media will always remain elusive and evasive as any medium at a given point in time will be new. In the 2010s, however, we are using the term new media to refer to digital media, "linked and cross-linked with each other, and the information they mediate is very easily processed, stored, transformed, retrieved, hyper-linked, and perhaps most radical of all, easily searched for accessed" (*ibid.*: 7).

After having established a theoretical framework for collaborative learning and new media, the ensuing part of this chapter will focus on the possibilities that new media offer for collaborative foreign language learning —in- and outside the walls of the classroom. Collaboration in the new/digital media age has been summarised under instructional frameworks such as 'Computer-Supported Collaborative Learning' (CSCL) or 'Collaborative Learning Supported by Digital Media' (CLSDM) a teaching/learning strategy with digital media collaborative tools (Cattafi/Metzner 2007). Furthermore, the new media literacies (see Appendix A for a complete overview) show a strong focus on community involvement, a process in which (social) skills are developed through collaboration within a network (Jenkins 2009). More generally, new media literacies, a complex set of competences and skills, are defined as:

> the core cultural competencies and social skills that young people need in our new media landscape. We call them "literacies," but they change the focus of literacy from one of individual expression to one of community involvement. They build on the foundation of traditional literacy, research skills, technical skills, and critical analysis skills taught in the classroom. If these New Media Literacies are learned –and they can be learned without computers in the classroom– they can form the building blocks for students' participation in new media.[3]

Among the skills there is collective intelligence, "the ability to pool knowledge and compare notes with others toward a common goal", networking, "the ability to search for, synthesize, and disseminate information", and negotiating as the "ability to travel across diverse communities, discerning and respecting multiple perspectives, and grasping and following alternative norms". This glimpse into the skills required to interact successfully in a global network of communities shows that forming and using groups effectively for collaborative learning is not an easy undertaking.

At first glance it may seem that the challenges of adding a digital media dimension to collaborative learning raises more questions than answers in relation to stakeholders, activities and goals. For example, creating positive interdependence between group members in a face-to-face learning scenario might become increasingly challenging if group members are recruited from different classrooms in different timezones and with different cultural contexts. Yet, the digital media landscape provides a scope for participation and community building, facilitating and challenging collaboration in foreign language learning.

The articles collected in this edited volume provide examples from different backgrounds and contexts of what types of collaboration new media can trigger, how learners can turn their own, individual learning paths into a collaborative learning path and what we as teachers can do to embed collaborative activities in curriculum and syllabus design. On a meta-level new media offer possibilities for

---

3   http://www.newmedialiteracies.org.

students and teachers to organise their collaborative endeavour as they can give all group members equal access to the same sources and materials, especially in an online community. New media unlimit students' access to materials and give them greater freedom of choice from an increasing variety (see Logan principle 10) of resources. The easy access to reliable information and materials makes learners less dependent on the teacher and course materials for information input and at the same time sharpen their critical attitude to the value of authentic sources. Information, ideas, and materials can be distributed in a matter of seconds. Students become their own publishers and become published which may add to their psychological well-being in a sometimes stressful learning environment. The downside of crowd-sharing may be that it is not a mutual activity within the collaborative context and empowerment is thus not achieved for all.

New media allow their users to interact not only with the information but also with the producer of the information. This two-way communication "makes dialogue and knowledge sharing possible through the medium of a shared visual or audio space" (Logan 2010: 52). Through the blurring boundaries between producer and consumer, learners are encouraged to participate and share content, moving to triadic or multi-way communication. Many-to-many communication (Warschauer 1996) with a wide variety of partners is possible. In addition to this, learners interact with others in hypertext. It goes without saying that interaction is not constant, even in collaborative learning environments. Students turn the interaction on and off depending on the needs of the moment and constantly re-evaluate their own and the group members' roles as do responsible citizens in any community.

In the last years, concepts such as extra-mural learning (see Sundqvist/Sylvén 2016) have become increasingly important in the field of foreign language learning to increase students' learning experience. Due to their portability (Logan 2010: 57), the new media have contributed to this development in the sense that they allow students to transcend the physical space of the classroom by accessing resources beyond the walls of the classroom. They can be used anywhere and at any time. Depending on the context, setting, and learning goals, different forms of interaction can take place: "face-to-face or computer-mediated, synchronous or not, frequent in time or not, whether it is a truly joint effort or whether the labour is divided in a systematic way" (Dillenbourg 1999: 1). Thus the boundaries between online and offline communities are becoming more and more blurred (Kafai/Fields 2013: 491); if the online/offline divide even still exists (cf. Leander 2008; Hine 2000; Kafai/Fields 2013: 491 for further discussion). By collaborating in the new media world, students learn to become members of different communities and interact within and beyond those communities. The formulation of collaborative learning and community building already put forth by Smith and MacGregor at the beginning of the 1990s is especially true for collaborative endeavours in the new media age:

> [...] students inevitably encounter difference, and must grapple with recognizing and working with it. Building the capacities for tolerating or resolving differences, for building agreement that honors all the voices in a group, for caring how others are doing — these abilities are crucial aspects of living in a community (1992: n.p.)

Closely related to this is the aspect of social identity as collaborative learning provides students with the opportunity to develop social skills (Johnson/Johnson/Holubec 1993). By using new media social skill training is not confined to the physical space of the classroom, but engages learners in social skills training in the virtual world as well. Here the question of which identities are possible in digital spaces and how those identities relate to those that occur in classroom spaces appears to be the most relevant one.

Successful collaborative learning requires a shift from the instructivist classroom to a learning environment in which both learners and teacher design instruction and learning. Especially with the new media, we "need to consider carefully how we examine collaboration as it happens between multiple participants and multiple spaces" (Kafai/Fields 2013: 490). Here, the teacher plays a vital role in guaranteeing the success of the collaborative endeavour by supporting the students in engaging in their own learning and reflecting on their learning experiences.

It is worthwhile noting that collaboration through new media is also an important topic in the field of teacher education in which the need for peer-to-peer interaction is becoming prevalent as teachers increasingly turn to communities of practice in order to organise their exchange of experience. Teachers can only teach what they have been taught and convincingly implement those collaboration strategies they have been exposed to themselves. The overview by Mercier *et al.* (2010: 1) shows that teacher collaboration does not end with successfully completing pre-service teacher training but is something that has to become part of a teacher's routine work: Collaboration is necessary between student teachers learning to teach, between teachers learning to teach, between teacher educators and classroom teachers, between teachers in professional development, between student-teachers and teacher-educators, and between teachers while planning and implementing lessons.

The aim of this introductory section was to shed light on two key concepts in today's pedagogical landscape, i.e. collaborative learning, as one of the most prevalent approaches to foreign language learning, and new media, an everyday phenomenon gradually finding its way into the foreign language classroom. We wanted to highlight how new media and collaborative learning increasingly intertwine in a world in which the meaning of geographic space is altered and opportunities for interactive and increasingly speedy communication are created. Taking the collaborative learning endeavour outside of the traditional classroom setting will, contrary to what some might fear, not loosen group dynamics, but contribute to real community building.

Any new media-driven collaborative learning endeavour in a foreign language context will eventually contribute to community building as it is driven by empowered and ever-evolving peers. It represents a low-threshold learning environment where exchanging foreign language content and providing feedback to reach shared goals and objectives are less threatening than in the confines of the teacher-geared traditional classroom.

Nicht nur in der Arbeitswelt, sondern auch in der Fremdsprachendidaktik ist ein Paradigmenwechsel von der reinen Wissensvermittlung hin zu kollaborativen Arbeits- und Lernprozessen zu beobachten. So geht man inzwischen verstärkt von einem dynamischen Wissens- und Kompetenzerwerb aus, im Rahmen derer Lerner, die räumlich und sozial auch weit voneinander entfernt sein können, an der Erfüllung gemeinsamer Lernziele arbeiten. Im ersten Teil dieses Beitrages wird der Ansatz des kollaborativen Lernens näher beleuchtet und unterschiedliche Verständnisse des Begriffs vorgestellt. Kollaboratives Lernen wird hierbei als eine Kombination unterschiedlicher Aktivitäten, wie das Festlegen von Lernzielen oder die Planung von Arbeitsprozessen, in der Gruppe verstanden. Der zweite Teil des Beitrages befasst sich mit dem Begriff Neue Medien, der trotz seiner vielfältigen Verwendung immer noch ein schwammiger Begriff ist. In einem letzten Schritt wird der Frage nachgegangen, ob und wie neue Medien zu erfolgreichen kollaborativen Lernprozessen beitragen können. Das direkte übertragen traditioneller Lernsituationen in die virtuelle Welt scheint hierbei nur bedingt eine Lösung zu sein. Es wird jedoch angenommen, dass Neue Medien gerade aufgrund ihres sozialen, interaktiven und kommunikativen Charakters vielfältige Möglichkeiten bieten, kollaborative Lernprozesse aufzubauen oder zumindest zu unterstützen. Neue Medien bieten jedoch nicht nur Fremdsprachenlernern Möglichkeiten zur Zusammenarbeit, denn auch Lehrkräften in allen Phasen des Professionalisierungsprozesses können vom interaktiven Charakter Neuer Medien profitieren.

Jozef Colpaert & Linda Gijsen
University of Antwerp, Belgium
Fontys Tilburg, Netherlands

Ontological Specification of Telecollaborative Tasks in Language Teaching

Collaboration is beneficial for learners. It should be included as such in the design of powerful learning environments, but its targeted effect largely depends on factors such as modality, activity type, task type, context and personal goals. Technology in the case of telecollaborative projects imposes its own limitations but also unexpected affordances if we take task-based language teaching (TBLT) as a starting point for task design. In this chapter, we propose an educational engineering approach which defines task design as process, a process which focuses on deeper concepts such as meaningfulness, usefulness and enjoyability. Effective tasks heavily depend on context and are the result of a methodological process which focuses first on willingness and acceptability for the learner and later on the other criteria mentioned by SLA and TBLT. The consequence of this approach is that it is impossible to suggest tasks as good examples or 'good practices'.

1. Introduction

In recent years language teachers worldwide have been confronted with a tsunami of new terms such as blended learning, digital pedagogy, flipped classrooms, twenty-first century skills, digital natives, MOOCs (Massive Online Open Courses), serious games, big data, VLEs (virtual learning environments) and BYOD (Bring Your Own Device). These terms have become *pervasive*, but also *persuasive* at the same time. They have probably been coined to name new and largely unknown phenomena, but very few remember their originally intended meanings, and many use these terms with different connotations in mind. These are fuzzy concepts with blurred ontologies that convey a hidden message. They convey a (mostly ungrounded) reason for using technology. They put pressure on teachers to use technology, without explaining why in terms of rationale or substantiated evidence. Any self-respecting discipline should work on a domain-specific terminology which reflects a coherent set of common concepts, principles and models. This is the case in the fields of law, medicine, technology and economy, but less so in 'softer' or younger disciplines such as pedagogy, instructional design and computer assisted language learning (CALL). We should ask ourselves to what extent other earlier educational trends such as learner autonomy, (social) constructivism and collaborative learning suffer from the same syndrome.

In this volume, collaborative learning is being presented as a valuable principle and instructional model. It is a multifaceted concept, involving activities such as peer feedback, peer evaluation, peer coaching, peer teaching, peer reviewing, group reflection, decision making and co-construction. In this chapter the focus will be on the rationale behind collaborative learning, to identify its key features, and to specify the affordances and limitations of technology in the context of foreign language learning and more specifically telecollaboration. We hope it will convince language teachers that more effective task design can yield a wide panoply of surprising, enabling and empowering functionalities which by far exceed their own expectations.

2. Collaborative learning

Collaborative learning has been used as a term in pedagogy for many years now, and in short it is seen as a situation in which two or more people learn or attempt to learn something together (Mitnik *et al.* 2009). The term is based on the instructional model that knowledge can be created within a population where members actively interact by sharing experiences and take on asymmetry roles (Bruffee 1993). Stemming from the ideology that students should be active participants in their processes of learning, collaborative learning is, for obvious reasons, used in student-centred settings. Collaboration is seen as a key feature of deeper learning as it contributes to students identifying and creating solutions to academic, social, vocational, and personal challenges. Up to date few studies have tried to question or criticize its acclaimed benefits when applied in the field of technology. Some frequently mentioned advantages, such as 'enhance critical thinking', 'engage students', 'enhance problem solving skills', 'increase student retention', 'build self-esteem in students', 'enhance student satisfaction with the learning experience', 'enhance shared-knowledge building', 'promote a positive attitude toward the subject matter' and 'develop higher level thinking skills' are vague and not always based on substantiated evidence. Most evidence supporting advantages of collaborative learning stems from research that has been conducted in traditional classroom-based settings and it is by no means a valid assumption that collaborative learning in a technology-mediated setting can trigger the same results. By technology-mediated settings –or blended language learning environments– we refer to settings where digital tools and media are being used together with more traditional non-digital forms of learning (Whitelock/Jelfs 2003).

Although quite a few respected researchers base their research in the field of technology-enhanced language learning on theories which proved themselves in face-to-face (FTF) task-based interaction, such as constructivism and sociocultural theory, there is, up to date, not enough evidence to support its acclaimed effects on collaborative learning in technology-mediated settings. According to Ellis, technology allows us to design and work with tasks in highly varied environments, but we cannot assume that tasks work in the same way as they do in the FTF classrooms (Thomas/Reinders 2010). Further research on the effects of collaborative learning on e.g. students' engagement or critical thinking skills is needed for teachers to make informed decisions in the process of designing collaborative tasks for their own learners. Meanwhile there is consensus among researchers that collaboration is beneficial for learners, and that it should be included in the design of powerful learning environments and with them many teachers have started exploring collaborative activities with their learners. Viewed from the teacher's perspective we could mention benefits such as fewer teacher-centered classrooms and the subsequent assumption of a reduced workload, which is an understandable rationale given the pressure many teachers are confronted with. When students work together on a task or project, teachers should have more time to spend on other obligations. Unfortunately, in practice this often turns out to be a major pitfall as students, from their perspective as active agents involved in learning, do not always see the benefits of collaboration or feel the necessity to work and learn together with their peers. Students can be largely disappointed when their teacher confronts them with a collaborative task that is ill-prepared, when they feel poorly supported, when they do not receive timely and detailed feedback, when they feel unable to solve interpersonal problems, or when the expected outcome is considered to be 'too vague'. So since the learner is the point of focus here, the question that remains is: do students really want to work and learn together? And why do we want them to collaborate? As the latter will be addressed later on, let us focus on the first question. The way learners perceive, work with and learn from a collaborative task depends on a number of factors. To start with there are several learner types: some prefer collaborative tasks over individual tasks; others do not. Especially when the emphasis switches from teacher-centered, large group instruction to a more individualized and learner-centered working environment, learners have to adjust to this change in context and not all of them will readily adapt to this new style of teaching and learning. Many learners associate collaborative learning with problems related to anxiety: lazy students might profit from the work of hard-working students, peer-evaluation might be less objective, the teacher might be too far away and not have an objective view on the situation, and conflicts or misunderstandings might arise, especially in intercultural settings (Belz 2002; Kramsch/Thorne 2002; O'Dowd 2003; O'Dowd/Ritter 2006).

What we have learned from theory, but even more so empirically in the last thirty years, here formulated as a research hypothesis to be validated, is that the need for and the effect of collaborative learning largely depends on factors such as modality, activity type, task type, context and personal goals. Modality is the way the proposed collaborative activity is being presented and implemented, in terms of pre-task, in-task and post-task events (Ellis 2003). Activity type refers to the nature of the collaborative activity: peer teaching, peer evaluation, peer coaching, peer feedback, co-construction, and group reflection (Ellis 2003). In the next sections, we will discuss more factors that have an effect on learners' collaboration such as task design in a technology-mediated setting and personal goals.

3. Technology and task design

For some time now Task-Based Language Teaching (TBLT) has been established as one of the main approaches to language learning and teaching worldwide (Van den Branden 2006; Van den Branden/Bygate/Norris 2009; Thomas/Reinders 2010; Ortega/Gonzalez 2014). TBLT is a fairly recent educational framework; it focuses on the use of authentic language and on real-world tasks using the target language with a view to developing target language fluency and building student confidence. Tasks can include visiting a doctor, conducting an interview, or calling customer service for help. A task has four main characteristics (Ellis 2003): it involves a primary focus on (pragmatic) meaning, it presents a gap to be bridged, it requires participants to choose the needed linguistic resources and it has a clearly defined, non-linguistic outcome. Assessment is primarily based on task outcome (in other words the appropriate completion of real world tasks) rather than on accuracy of prescribed language forms. TBLT has its own conference series (www.tblt.org) and a high mental acceptability factor with teachers and language learners. The role of technology in TBLT is significant as it has created a new series of real-world target tasks such as corresponding, engaging in web writing, playing online games or participating in online courses. One of the domains where technology, TBLT and collaborative learning meet is telecollaboration, resulting in a series of conferences and European projects. Telecollaborative projects have the potential to facilitate interaction and collaboration, enhance language learning and intercultural communicative competencies in a technology mediated setting. In language learning contexts, telecollaboration is understood to be: "Internet-based intercultural exchange between people of different cultural/national backgrounds, set up in an institutional blended-learning context with the aim of developing both language skills and intercultural communicative competence (as defined by Byram/Nichols/Stevens 2001) through structured tasks" (Guth/Helm 2011: 42). During these exchanges learners get a chance to engage online in authentic meaningful communication with new peers from other countries. Web 2.0, with synchronous (chat, videoconferencing, virtual worlds) and asynchronous (blogs, wikis, discussion fora) communication applications, allows for this interaction. The INTENT project (Integrating Telecollaborative Networks into Foreign Language Higher Education) which focused on the greater integration of telecollaborative exchange in university education, resulted in the creation of the Unicollaboration platform (www.unicollaboration.eu) and in the organization of the Conferences on Telecollaboration in University Education (León 2014; Dublin 2016). In addition the Erasmus+ TILA project (Telecollaboration for Intercultural Language Acquisition; www.tilaproject.eu) and more recently its follow-up, the Erasmus+ TeCoLa project have focused on meaningful telecollaboration among secondary school pupils. These projects have provided ample opportunity for teachers and learners to be involved in online intercultural collaboration.

It is clear that a TBLT approach in technology mediated environments holds promising developments for the future. However, we need to pinpoint three caveats here. First, TBLT views a task as a product with features, in the best case defined with pre-task, in-task and post-task events. The context in which the task is performed (think of choice of mode) and personal goals of the learner are not explicitly part of the design process. When assessing the potential of a task more attention should be paid to mapping the context and "the way in which learners interpret and engage with tasks (as plans and as outcomes), because it may reveal new learning opportunities in these processes" (Dooly 2011: 86). The research field is still in its infancy with few tested models for describing the process for designing tasks effectively, let alone the possible effect of collaboration on task performance and (language) learning. O'Dowd and Ware (2009) attempted to structure the wide variety of tasks being employed in telecollaboration and came to identify three main categories of tasks –information exchange, comparison and collaboration. This was followed by Guth and Helm (2011) who designed a model, Telecollaboration 2.0, which focused not only on the development of learners' linguistic and intercultural competence but also on other competences, such as e-literacies, opening doors for researchers and teachers who want to employ a more holistic approach to task design. More recently, González-Lloret and Ortega (2014a) identified five key definitional features of a task in the context of technology-and-task integration: primary focus on meaning, goal orientation, learner-centeredness, holism and reflective learning. Focus on features such as learner-centeredness and reflective learning set out to design more flexible and diverse tasks leaving more room for learners' needs and wants and offer more opportunities for reflective higher-order learning. In this buzzing field new frameworks emerge, all with collaborative learning as a pivotal element in task design. "CALL and Task Design" was the theme of the XVIIth International CALL Research Conference in 2015 (www.call2015.org; Colpaert *et al.* 2015) and as one of the presenters concluded in her paper on the effects of task design on students' collaboration, there is an urgent need for more information on the effects task design can have on students' collaboration when effectively co-constructing tasks. Secondly, TBLT advocates state that technology opens up a new range of possibilities, but until recently technology had not led to new types of activities, ontologically speaking. What one can observe is that technology made activities faster, easier, cheaper and more feasible. More recently, tasks that lead to activities such as online games, tours in virtual environments and synchronous collaborative writing, open up a completely new range of task types which still remain largely underexplored from a scholarly point of view: what is the exact role of technology and to what extent does it have an effect on collaborative learning? How to determine to what extent technology limits or enables task activities?

Thirdly, in most cases, even if the task complies with TBLT criteria, it may or may not appeal to the learner. An attractive real-world activity is not necessarily a meaningful, engaging activity for the individual learner. Why would a learner be motivated to prepare for a party that is never going to take place? It is not because a task is real-world that it suddenly becomes meaningful. "If tasks are the things that people do in real life, we need to find out what drives people to really engage in learning activities and the performance of tasks [...]" (Van den Branden 2015). So the process of task development needs to focus not only on TBLT criteria but also on psychological –motivational– factors. González-Lloret and Ortega (2014), in their review of literature on language teaching in general and TBLT in particular, insist on a more important role of needs analysis in task design. "[...] we encounter terms such as: aims, demands, needs, lacks, necessities, objectives, wants, wishes [...]" (*ibid.* 25). All come into play, but nevertheless the focus is on the targeted product and pedagogical goals. The first steps are taken, but little is said about the process and how to take into account learners' deeper lying motives to work together on a task. In 1997, Warschauer formulated a priority research question: "How does participation in CMC (*Computer-Mediated Communication*) work affect learners' motivation and sense of identity?' (1997: 478). How can we indeed make sure that learners engage with a task? How can we spend more time analyzing their 'wants and desires' before jumping to product features under pressure of the pedagogical goals to be realized? The motivation scale by Deci & Ryan (2000) shows different levels of regulation and identification which might prove useful to situate our learners and to monitor their progress. Self-Determination Theory is a universal approach, based on universal psychological needs of relatedness, competence and autonomy. The L2 SELF model by Dörnyei and Ushioda (2009) on the other hand is an individual approach which aims at identifying conflicting Ideal Selves and Ought-to-Selves which may regulate the extent to which the learner identifies him/herself with a task and by doing so is better able to collaborate with a peer on a shared need or goal. In the next section, an intermediate approach for designing tasks will be introduced demonstrating how collaborative learning could fit in.

4. An educational engineering approach

Teachers might be familiar with the various approaches and paradigms concerning language teaching. Some might have experimented with TBLT or have experience in participating in multimodal exchanges but do not know how to apply their knowledge and skills to their classroom practice. There is a need to develop 'new' pedagogy which will help to develop tasks for the available modes in such a way that they do not only support but also add to the quality of foreign language curricula. In 1997, Warschauer already warned that technology is not a panacea for challenges facing language teachers: "new technologies will not revolutionize, or even improve, language learning unless they are well understood and intelligently implemented. The Internet itself is only a tool, albeit a powerful one, in the hands of good or bad pedagogy" (Warschauer 1997: 9).

Educational engineering is a largely unpublished instructional design framework (Colpaert, in press) based on more than 30 years of experience with theory and practice, national and international projects, and presentations worldwide as part of its ongoing empirical and theoretical validation. A book on the topic is expected to appear around 2017. The framework has the potential to support researchers and teachers in their design processes when designing content for multi-dimensional contexts, such as in technology-mediated settings. At the macro level this could involve the design of language courses, at the meso level designing a lesson consisting of various tasks but also at the micro level the design of a single task. It is based on the idea that education has always been *l'art du possible*, and this for four reasons. First, by its very nature, education can and will never be perfect. Secondly, lack of time and resources often prevent us from duly implementing the required changes. Thirdly, any change, even the most justifiable one, entails some kind of resistance, often from stakeholders that are being misjudged. Last but not least, there is not yet enough knowledge available in terms of substantiated findings which enable teachers and/or policy makers to instantly improve education, solve complex problems or design solutions in a more systematic, methodological and justifiable way. Engineering is "the strategy for causing the best change in a poorly understood situation within the available resources" (Koen 1985: 23) or, in other words, the strategy to be used for devising the best possible real-world solutions when not enough knowledge is available for doing so. It is a line of thinking, applicable to education, that does not necessarily imply technology (Koen 2003). Engineering is about building knowledge through real-world implementations, in a systematic and verifiable way, using working hypotheses that should be empirically and theoretically validated. Hypothesis testing analyzes the effect of modified parameters, taking into account the specificity of the context. Engineering is about formulating and validating working hypotheses regarding the role, order, weight and intensity of these parameters. These hypotheses represent the best possible guess based on theory and practice and should be theoretically and empirically validated. Educational Engineering formulates the blueprint of an optimal artefact and tries to test real-world intermediate artefacts as hypotheses on the pathway to that optimal artefact.

Engineering seldom leads to proven facts in one project, but it often requires several iterations due to resistance, financial limitations, technological challenges or practical constraints in order to observe significant changes in the effect of the parameters in play (Bayesian epistemology). In the same vein, Educational Engineering is about building the best possible educational artefacts. These educational artefacts can be documents, tools, content, concepts, models and solutions such as textbooks, syllabi, lesson plans, curricula, graded readers, exercises, tests, applications, electronic learning platforms or, to narrow things down for the purpose of this chapter, collaborative tasks. Not only researchers, but also teachers who use technology in their classes, should become educational engineers by formulating and validating their own hypotheses.

The first author's research focuses on the theoretical and empirical validation of the following hypotheses, which have been grouped under the term Distributed Design referring to the idea that the design process should take into account as many actors and factors as possible. The four paradigm shifts stand for a radically new way of thinking about technology in education:

1) The Ecological Paradigm Shift: No technology has an inherent, measurable and generalizable effect on learning. Only the entire learning environment, seen as an ecology of interacting components, can have this effect.

2) The Process-Oriented Paradigm Shift: The targeted effect of a learning environment does not depend on product features, but is proportional to its *designedness*. Designedness stands for the extent to which the learning environment has been designed in a methodological and justifiable way. This methodological approach is universally applicable, but leads to polymorphous results.
3) The Psychological Paradigm Shift: In cases of problematic or lesser motivation, there is a tendency to insist more on pedagogical goals. This appears to be counterproductive and it is better to focus on personal goals first. Personal goals are defined here as subconscious volitions which hinder or stimulate acceptance and willingness to engage in the learning process. The problem with personal goals is that they are difficult to elicit (Colpaert 2010).
4) The Demand-Driven Paradigm Shift: Neither technology nor pedagogy is an appropriate starting point for design (Colpaert 2014a). The methodological design process creates a need, a strong demand for theoretical knowledge, content and technology. Technology, the pedagogical model (for teaching, learning and evaluation), the content types, etc. are results of the design process, not starting points.

These four paradigm shifts as hypotheses form the backbone of the educational engineering approach 'Distributed Design'.

5. Distributed design

Distributed Design can be considered an instructional design model for guiding the analysis, design, development, implementation and evaluation (ADDIE) of educational artefacts for learning, testing and teaching. As a typical ADDIE model it is staged, with every stage having its own importance and specificity, its own input and output, but it is not necessarily a 'waterfall' model. Distributed Design is holistic in nature: it first designs an optimal learning environment (OLE) before deciding on intermediate steps and artefacts to be developed. It defines a learning situation as the context, as 'what is', and the learning environment as what is being designed in our mind. The learning environment is defined as a collection of interacting components (ecology): actors (learner, teacher, parent), models (learning, teaching and evaluation model), content, infrastructure and technology.

5.1 Analysis

During the Analysis Stage, designers try to identify for each of these components which aspects are amenable to change which should and can be changed. The first step is to analyze the local context: to what extent is it different from other contexts (local requirements) and which differences (differential requirements) can one observe within the local context regarding the components of the learning environment? Designers identify which aspects can (italic) and should (bold) be changed.

Table 1: *The analysis stage in Distributed Design*

	LOCAL	DIFFERENTIAL
Learner		**Some learners are not motivated enough**
Teacher	**Local teachers are not innovative enough in their teaching methods**	
Other personas	Parents want to monitor the learning progress of their children	
Learning model	Learners are expected to prepare the lessons in advance	Different learning paths are offered according to the most suitable degree of autonomy
Teaching model	*Teachers see themselves as coaches rather than instructors*	
Evaluation model	**There is no spreading of evaluation over self-, co- and peer-evaluation**	Some students require specific forms of evaluation (written, oral, computer-assisted) due to psychological or physical limitations
Content	Students co-construct course content	Some students prefer textbooks
Infrastructure		**Classrooms should be more flexible and multi-functional**
ICT	Classrooms equipped with Interactive Whiteboards	*Some rooms do not have wifi yet*

5.2 Design

The Design Stage consists of three steps. During *conceptualization*, the main concept behind the learning environment is worked out as a compromise between conflicting personal and pedagogical goals (Colpaert 2010). This is the most difficult part of the design process, as there is, up-to-date, no procedure for reconciling these goals. Let us take, as an example, a learning situation, a context, where we encounter the following conflicts:

- students should learn how to collaborate, but they/some of them do not want to do so;
- students should acquire attitude based on insight, but they prefer knowledge transfer;
- students should learn how to speak up, but most of them prefer to remain silent in the classroom.

A good conceptualization has the following advantages: it reconciles as many goal conflicts as possible, and the resulting concept should be clear for all stakeholders involved (even content and software developers). In the best case, it can lead to a metaphor for the entire learning environment such as a beehive, a library, a city, a factory or a casino. A metaphor that reconciles most conflicts creates acceptance and willingness in the learner's mind. This is why this metaphor should be reflected in the first message the learner receives about the learning environment: the course description (which is mostly quite boring), the lesson schedule or the textbook used. During *specification*, this concept needs to be specified in detail in terms of what is needed. Pedagogical specification is the specification of what is needed in terms of theories and models (instructional design models such as 4C/ID) in order to be able to design a learning environment in a justifiable way. Theories and models about learning (degree of autonomy), teaching (the role of the coach) and evaluation (co-, self-and peer-evaluation). Content specification is the description of the content that should be added or created in order to make the best possible learning environment: off-the-shelf, Open Educational Resources, co-authored, MOOCs (Colpaert 2014b) etc. Architectural specification is the description of interactions that need to take place inside and outside the classroom between all learners, teacher and content. Finally, this leads to the technological specification, meaning the description of functionalities needed to guarantee these interactions. During the *prototyping* stage, designers test to see if their requirements can be found or if they need to be created/developed. This is the case for the teaching model, the learning model, the evaluation model, content, infrastructure and ICT.

5.3 Development

The Development stage is the actual elaboration of pedagogical approach, content and technology.

5.4 Implementation

During the Implementation stage designers observe and monitor phenomena which may be expected or unexpected, not immediately with a view on the product, but in order to adjust the design process parameters in place.

5.5 Evaluation

Although the Evaluation stage does not immediately try to measure or prove anything, it is the central tenet of the educational engineering approaching as it tries to validate the formulated hypothesis by comparing the expected outcome with the actual outcome ('I expect my students to be happier if [...]; I expect my students to be more active if my role as coach [...].') in order to formulate a new hypothesis for the next loop to be undertaken.

6. An engineering approach in (tele)collaborative task design

Task design is at the root of online intercultural exchanges as it is at the base of each rich learning activity teachers want to engage their learners in. If there is a shared objective that tasks should be much more than a set of required features in order to become acceptable, then task design should be the result of a systematic process and language teachers should not only pay attention to designing pre-, in- and post-tasks, but also follow a methodologically informed procedure to design tasks for their learners. The focus should lie on improving this process leading to polymorphous results which strongly depend on context. The learner should understand how and why the task fits. We can get inspired by tasks (good practices) we see in other contexts, but that does not mean they are effective as such in other contexts. This holds the implication that tasks are context-dependent. The conceptualization of tasks, unfortunately, is a complex and arduous process. We are currently analyzing where pedagogical goals conflict with personal goals (as defined in Colpaert 2010). Regarding collaborative learning, we might want our learners to learn how to collaborate, but they might prefer to work alone. In this respect, the three universal innate psychological needs as defined by the Self-Determination Theory can be relevant as are the Ideal Self Images as defined by Dörnyei and Ushioda (2009). The problem in FTF classroom context is that designers need to define a kind of common denominator for the entire group of learners, or define a set of *personas* or subgroups. One of the future challenges in telecollaboration is to research to what extent it is possible to focus more on the personal goals of the learner and his/her peer instead of adhering to group or class goals. The possibilities that telecollaborative projects offer in a learner-centered context should be explored, but how do we design tasks that lead to more identification, enhance collaborative learning and in doing so contribute to more learning effect?

When applying the EE/DD model repeatedly, we came to the point where we had to specify the most appropriate tasks (learning and teaching model). Much to our surprise, the best tasks, according to TBLT criteria, did not necessarily lead to the most identification, acceptance and willingness. In this respect, a more project-based approach within TBLT, to create an intermediate layer, has appeared to be effective to make tasks appear more coherent. It was more by accident that we discovered, later corroborated by indications in literature, that there were three other factors, as hypotheses, that appeared to play a preponderant role in the motivation of students to participate in tasks. There are three recurring aspects in this respect: meaningfulness, usefulness and enjoyability. First of all, *meaningfulness*, not related to linguistic meaning, but redefined as the extent to which the proposed task results in something valuable for the learner. The expected end result or outcome of the task should be something concrete, real and tangible. Something that represents a challenge for the learner so that (s)he will surpass him/herself. Preparing a fictitious or virtual party or trip to Paris hardly has any motivating value at all. Preparing a real trip to Paris, climbing the Mont Ventoux, staging a musical: these are examples of tasks (or projects) that –again depending on context– may be perceived as meaningful by learners. In language learning contexts, one could also say that tasks must have an authentic communicative purpose in order to be meaningful. Prabhu (1987) distinguishes between information-gap activities, reasoning-gap activities, and opinion-gap activities and he argues that when learners engage in these task types, ideal conditions for language learning are created. Prahbu's classification of tasks is interesting in this discussion because it "rests on the account of the kinds of cognitive operations that underlie the actual performance of different kinds of tasks" (1987) and a lesson we might draw from his work, although it is based on FTF classroom-based interaction, is that the type of task that works best may depend on the contingencies of individual teaching contexts (Ellis 2003). Secondly, *usefulness*, less mentioned by others, can be defined as the extent to which the result of the proposed task will be valuable to others: what will others be able to do with my work? What if the result of my task or project can be used by others? Thirdly: *enjoyability*. Not in the sense of fun, wrongly supposed to carry any effect on learning, but the real fun is in the realization of the two previous qualities. In this sense, collaboration in itself does not seem to motivate the majority of our learners. On the contrary, as described previously, many learners immediately perceive disadvantages and dangers. But it is not because there is a conflict that we need to give up on our goals. If we are convinced that collaborative learning is an educational goal, then we need to ask ourselves how we can make collaboration-oriented tasks both meaningful and useful for all learners involved. If collaborative tasks are geared towards a meaningful and useful result, they will become more acceptable and subsequently lead to more effective learning.

7. Ontological specification of telecollaborative tasks

So how should we proceed in order to specify meaningful and useful tasks in telecollaborative environments? The following iterative and cyclic process suggests globally applicable steps to be undertaken, leading to polymorphous results depending on context. Therefore, the examples given cannot be simply exported to other contexts as good practices. But hopefully they inspire teachers to apply the same procedure, provide feedback and in doing so contribute to their empirical validation. A *powerful task* is defined as a task which aims at creating acceptance and willingness in the first place by focusing first on meaningfulness and usefulness, and second by focusing on the other TBLT criteria.

Step 1: ANALYSIS
A powerful task addresses one or more of aspects in the learning environment which can and should be changed.

Step 2: DESIGN-conceptualization
A powerful task contributes to reconciling personal and pedagogical goals.

Step 3: DESIGN-specification
A powerful task fits within the needed learning model, teaching model, evaluation model (co-, self-, peer-), content, infrastructure and technology.

Step 4: DESIGN-prototyping
A powerful task is a task that can be tested first.

Step 5: DEVELOPMENT
A powerful task accurately describes pre-task, in-task and post-task activities, support and feedback.

Step 6: IMPLEMENTATION
A powerful task has some parameters which can be adjusted.

Step 7: EVALUATION
A powerful task is a hypothesis. We need to evaluate what worked well so we can reformulate the next hypothesis.

So a powerful task is not the collection of properties, of boxes to be ticked, but the result of a methodological design process. The result of such a process is a task ontology, a detailed description or task design template. In our case, what seemed to work quite well is co-construction. Co-construction of course content, knowledge clips, apps, virtual environments, fairy tales and musicals (with actual performance) but also collaboration on complex tasks which involved some kind of gap activity (Prahbu 1987). The tasks that we deem powerful are almost without exception tasks and projects that involve some kind of problem-solving. Within one project, there can be room for all kinds of tasks, even the most traditional ones, as long as their position in the syllabus, project or lesson plan is relevant for the learner's learning process.

8. What does this mean for technology?

The last few years telecollaborative projects have evolved from written and asynchronous communication to multimodal environments that offer both synchronous and asynchronous communication among learners (Guth/Helm 2011).
So where communication primarily took place by means of email and discussion forums, a shift has been made to oral, written, and media-sharing communication (Hampel 2006). In this context, researchers have looked into the affordances and constraints of various modes and the positive and negative effects of synchronous and asynchronous environments on collaborative learning. In the Distributed Design approach, the added value of technology is defined as the extent to which the affordances of a particular technology match the requirements of the learning environment. So it is very important not to implement a technology in order to measure something. We need to first specify the exact functionalities we need, and then evaluate to what extent existing technologies allow us to do that.

Table 2: *Functionalities and technologies in Distributed Design*

Task	Technology	Context
Co-construction of course content	*Wiki (PBWorks, Wikispace, Wikimedia), Google Docs, Evernote, OpenLearning …*	Tertiary education
Co-construction of knowledge clips	*Animoto, Powtoon …*	Secondary education
Co-construction of apps	*Github*	CLIL for secondary and tertiary education (e.g. informatics)

Task	Technology	Context
Co-construction of 'virtual' artefacts	*Open Sim, Second Life …*	Secondary and tertiary
Live staging of musical or play (during exchange visit)	*Microsoft Project (during preparations)*	Secondary and tertiary
Peer-teaching	*Edmodo, Google Classroom, Any Meeting*	Tertiary
Collaborative writing: e.g. fairy tale	*Google Docs*	Primary and tertiary

9. Conclusions

When designing powerful telecollaborative tasks, the need for technology becomes obvious. The choice of technology largely depends on the conclusions of the design process and is not its starting point. So there is no reason why one would try to measure the effect of technology in this respect. We need the readers of this volume to test the proposed task design process themselves, and in doing so, contribute to its empirical and theoretical validation. Once we have identified which parameters play which role, and we obtain some stability in their effect, only then can we start collecting data. We can indeed consider educational engineering as a research method that contributes to identifying the parameters, factors and variables and their potential co-dependency. Especially in foreign language education, where the ability to collaborate and communicate effectively with peers is a necessity, new pedagogies to support the implementation of meaningful telecollaboration practices in curricula are needed. "Considering the difficulties already inherent to teaching, moving from more common (classroom-bound) teacher-centred strategies into open learner-centred, peer-to-peer strategies such as those facilitated by telecollaboration requires a closer look into the blueprints teachers use for designing these exchanges" (Dooly 2011: 87). It can be a question of several years in one's trusted learning situation before discovering surprising effects in terms of willingness and acceptance. A collaborative task which makes learners surpass themselves and which produces a result that is useful for others appears to counter the perceived negative side-effects of collaboration. What we have experienced is that successful tasks are the result of a methodological process which focuses first on willingness and acceptability for the learner, and later on the other criteria mentioned by Second Language Acquisition (SLA) and TBLT. Learners appear to be more willing to identify themselves with a task if they perceive its meaningfulness and usefulness. The ultimate objective for further research should be to provide researchers and teachers with more insight in the processes of task design and collaborative learning in a technology-based intercultural setting.

Der Beitrag befasst sich mit dem Ansatz des telekollaborativen Lernens aus ontologischer Sicht. Kollaborative Lernprozesse werden allgemein als dem Lernerfolg zuträglich angesehen, ihr Erfolg hängt jedoch von einer Vielzahl von Faktoren wie Aufgabentyp, Kontext sowie individuelle Lernziele der Lerner ab. Telekollaborative Lernszenarien, bei denen Lerner gemeinsam in interaktiven, technologiegestützten Lernumgebungen an einer Aufgabe arbeiten, haben in den letzten Jahren im Rahmen internationaler Projekte und Praxisversuche eine immer stärkere Aufmerksamkeit erfahren, jedoch besteht in diesem Bereich immer noch Forschungsbedarf. Vor diesem Hintergrund schlagen die Autoren einen *Educational Engineering* Ansatz vor, der von Aufgabengestaltung als Prozess ausgeht. Educational Engineering ist noch ein relativ unbekannter Instructional Design Framework, der Forscher und Lehrkräfte bei der Entwicklung von Lerninhalten in multi-dimensionalen Lernkontexten, wie es in technologiegestützten Lernumgebungen oft der Fall ist, unterstützen kann.

Lienhard Legenhausen
University of Münster, Germany

Authentic Interactions and Language Learning – The Interaction Hypothesis Revisited

Although the Interaction Hypothesis was introduced several decades ago, basic issues are still controversially discussed today. These issues will be taken up one by one. It is claimed that some of the problems that arise have to do with the type of data collected in mainstream classrooms. It is here that the complex notion of authenticity plays a decisive role. Other problems call for more explicit models of comprehension and language learning in order to be able to relate the two. The focus of this article is an attempt to distinguish various types of interaction and to show how they are determined by different classroom activities, on the one hand, and how they might affect language-learning processes, on the other.

1. Introductory remarks

The observation that immigrants can learn a foreign language just by being exposed to it has given rise to Krashen's Input Hypothesis (1981), which postulates that all that is needed to acquire a language is "comprehensible input". It is based on the assumption that many features of a target language are acquired in a "natural sequence". However, it soon turned out that this theory was not powerful enough and lacked empirical evidence. Although recognizing that comprehensible input is an essential element of language acquisition, researchers such as Merril Swain saw the need to complement the Input Hypothesis with an Output Hypothesis. "The importance to learning of output could be that output pushes learners to process language more deeply (with more mental effort) than does input" (Swain 1995: 126). If learners use language productively, then this leads to their noticing linguistic gaps in their interlanguage. Furthermore, it provokes hypothesis testing, which, together with informative feedback, supports and speeds up the language-learning process (cf. Swain 2000). At one stage Swain (1997: 119) even claims that "the output IS the hypothesis" [capitals in the original]. Combining the Input and Output Hypotheses might lead naturally to the Interaction Hypothesis, although, historically speaking, Long's Interaction Hypothesis grew out of early ethnomethodological work that analysed communicative breakdowns, and it is also indebted to Evelyn Hatch's work on the role of discourse in the acquisition of formal features (cf. Hatch 1978).

Long's original Interaction Hypothesis (1980) was intensely criticised, which then led to an updated version (Long 1996). Critics saw a marked improvement:

> The updated version of the IH, with its emphasis on the contributions of negative feedback and modified output as well as comprehensible input and its recognition that interaction works by connecting input, internal capacities and output via selective attention, is obviously a major advance on the early version. (Ellis 1999: 14)

There can be no doubt that, especially in the wake of the discussions on the importance of output and the role of negotiation of meaning, the Interaction Hypothesis gained considerable weight. That is not to say, however, that the research problems in connection with the Interaction Hypothesis have been solved. Basic questions still remain that have not yet been satisfactorily answered. The most important issue remains: How does comprehension turn into acquisition? Incidentally, one of the many 'missing links' when it comes to research issues in language pedagogy (cf. *inter alia* Oxford 1990; Wright/Bolitho 1993). Some of the tentative answers to explain the relationship between comprehension and acquisition and thus "close the gap" will be addressed in the first part of this paper.

The second part will discuss some other weaknesses of the Interaction Hypothesis. The quality and nature of conversational interactions in learner-learner discourses varies greatly. However, so far no detailed attempt has been made to distinguish between various types of conversational interaction within the Interaction Hypothesis, and elaborate on their impact on learning processes. It has to be assumed, for example, that certain types of interaction have a differential effect on language-learning processes. This issue will be taken up in the last part.

2. How does comprehension or interaction turn into acquisition?

Swain and Lapkin (1998: 320) quite pertinently ask the question: "What are the mechanisms by which comprehensible input is converted into L2 knowledge and use?". The answers are as manifold as they are vague. Long himself, as indicated above, claims that the learners' "selective attention" and negotiation of meaning activate attentional resources which lead to gap-noticing. In combination with negative feedback, it sets the scene for acquisition (Long 1996: 414). Swain and Lapkin's answer to the puzzle is that language as a cognitive or a mediational tool brings about the conversion.

Although comprehension processes were focused upon in the early days, the emphasis soon shifted to linguistic processing in general. If learners engage in collaborative dialogue and outperform their competence, then "language is learned as it is used" (Swain 1997: 17). Rod Ellis (1994: 365) claims that "the way language is learnt is a reflection of the way it is used". In similar vein, David Little (1995: 176) assumes that "language learning and language use engage the same underlying mechanisms". Although this hypothesis has an immediate and plausible appeal, as yet there has been no attempt to explain these mechanisms. Small wonder, then, that Mitchell and Myles (1998: 133) claim that "stronger theoretical models clarifying the precise nature of the supposed link between interaction and acquisition" are needed.

If it is accepted that in communicative interactions and acquisition the same underlying mechanisms are applied, then ideally we would have to resort to explicit models both of interactive linguistic processing and of acquisition in order to be able to define those features they have in common. One has to admit, however, that the research communities have not yet reached consensus with regard to either type of model, but there are tentative ideas about how modelling processes could explain the relationship between interaction and acquisition.

The crucial question is: What happens when linguistic data are processed? The hint of an answer might be found in the models of linguistic processing as proposed by Dieter Wolff. The point is that when processing linguistic data, concept-driven processes and data-driven processes (or top-down and bottom-up processes) interact when working out a cognitive representation of linguistic utterances. This type of interaction between stored concepts or schemata (old information), on the one hand, and new data or incoming linguistic stimuli, on the other, seems also to be happening in acquisition. The main difference would be that the new cognitive representation in the acquisition process would lead to a more permanent restructuring of schemata (or linguistic knowledge), and thus to learning (cf. Wolff 1986). Figure 1 was given a more complex representation in Wolff (cf. 2002: 182, 294).

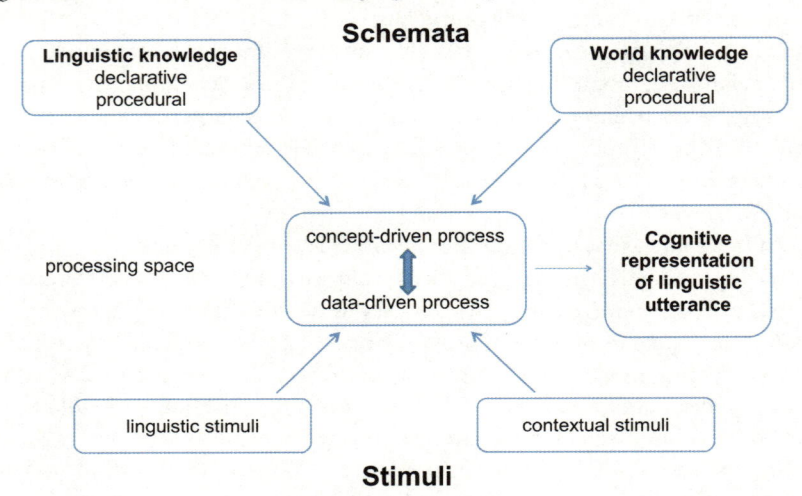

Figure 1: Authentic interactions and language learning

Schemata

- **Linguistic knowledge** — declarative, procedural
- **World knowledge** — declarative, procedural

processing space: concept-driven process ⇅ data-driven process → Cognitive representation of linguistic utterance

Stimuli: linguistic stimuli, contextual stimuli

3. The need for an elaboration of the Interaction Hypothesis – some issues

3.1 Reflective processes

Little keeps reminding us that communicative interaction as such will not suffice in institutional contexts. Without learners engaging in "metalinguistic and metacognitive processes of analysis and reflection" (Little 1996: 209), it is likely that the linguistic development of learners will fossilize at some stage. These reflective processes should preferably include all aspects of the teaching-learning undertaking. In other words, they will not only be directed towards formal aspects of the target language, but also aim at the evaluation of overall organizational processes, at the type of activities undertaken and, last but not least, at the learning results. Reflection leads to awareness-raising, which can be said to act as a "fermentation ingredient" for the learning process. At the same time, they introduce an element of authenticity into the classroom procedures.

3.2 Authenticity of interactions

Authenticity is said to be another prerequisite or basic requirement for the validity of the Interaction Hypothesis. However, given the complexity of the notion of authenticity in the foreign-language classroom, a brief clarification of what is to be understood by it in this context seems to be called for: communicative interactions are authentic if the learners are allowed 'to speak as themselves', that is, if they are not engaged in 'do-as-if activities' whose defining feature is 'a suspension of disbelief'. A more elaborate definition can be found in the writings of Leo van Lier (1996: 13): "An action is authentic when it realizes a free choice and is an expression of what a person genuinely feels and believes. An authentic action is *intrinsically motivated*". It is this latter definition that enables learners to "authenticate" any activity, even form-focused exercises which they might have chosen with the explicit intention of supporting their learning process.

3.3 The density of negotiation of meaning and deficient input

The Interaction Hypothesis makes sense for institutional settings if classroom procedures are not merely characterised by teacher-learner interactions, but if they are dominated by learner-learner interactions. This implies that classroom activities are by and large characterised by group and pair work. However, there are basically two types of frequently voiced counter-argument to a predominance of pair and group work, that is, learner-learner interactions in classrooms. First, several studies have come to the conclusion that the density or frequency of meaning negotiation and negotiations of forms in foreign-language classrooms is fairly disappointing (cf. Pica/Doughty 1985; Foster 1998). Van Branden, for example, observed more occurrences of negotiation of meaning –and thus acquisition-facilitating processes– in teacher-fronted interactions than in learner-learner interactions (1997: 628).

Secondly, it is claimed that the meaning-focus in the interactions prevents learners, for example, from negotiating inflectional morphology (cf. Sato 1986; Ellis 1999: 15). Moreover, Prabhu (1987: 81), in his seminal work on *Second Language Pedagogy*, claims that "sustained interaction between learners is likely to provide less opportunity for system-revision". And Guy Aston, echoing Brumfit (1984), evokes the danger of early fossilization "as learners will acquire from each other's interlanguage" (1986: 131). As the number of the above references makes obvious, it seems to be a widespread conviction in the research community that the verbal interactions of learners are not linguistically rich enough to support their linguistic development adequately. However, the data on which the critical assessments of learner-learner interactions are based seem to be suffering from one and the same basic flaw. More often than not, they derive from conventional mainstream classrooms that can be said to be by and large teacher-directed and which have not managed to engage learners in their own learning. These classrooms rarely involve them in reflective processes concerning the overall learning-teaching approach, and many activities rely on a 'suspension of disbelief'. In short, these studies are conducted in classrooms in which *authentic* communicative interactions in the sense outlined above are not the main constitutive feature of the activities.

4. The challenge for the Interaction Hypothesis – metalinguistic and metacognitive reflection in the classroom

The focus of the Interaction Hypothesis as formulated so far lies on the comprehensibility of input as well as on the selective attention that leads to gap-noticing and -awareness. However, the extent to which activities can be said to promote these metalinguistic and metacognitive processes –a prerequisite for overcoming the problem of fossilization, as indicated above– has not been sufficiently attended to. Swain's Output Hypothesis is an exception, though, since she points out that the learners' output also serves a metalinguistic function (1997: 119). At the same time, she deplores the fact that in "most of the research tasks used in the study of negotiation, this reflective process is not demanded" (*ibid*). And one has to add here that, as expected, this also has to do with the fact that these activities are largely absent from mainstream foreign-language classrooms. The challenge of learner-centred classroom approaches is to devise activities that engage the learners' reflective processes and bring learners to focus also on formal structures of the target language. It is here that a closer look at classroom procedures and various activity types is called for, and the following questions need to be responded to:

- What is the impact of the general classroom approach –and by implication activity types– on the quality of interaction?
- How do types of interaction relate to modes of learning, given the fact that language learning is a highly complex and multifaceted process?

These questions will be taken up in turn.

5. The impact of classroom approach and activity type on the quality of interaction

Several attempts have been made in the literature to distinguish various types of interaction in the classroom (cf. Seedhouse 2004). Leo van Lier's taxonomy, for example, distinguishes activity types according to whether there is a "differential emphasis on activity-orientation and on topic-orientation". The illustration of "more topic-orientation, less activity-orientation" includes "announcements, instructions, explanations, lectures" (1988: 155). This goes to show that there is a very wide concept underlying the notion of "communicative interaction". This also holds true of other taxonomies such as the ones presented by Ellis (1984) and Abbdesslem (1993). In the following discussion, the focus is much more restricted, that is, it is on the communicative interaction between learners and on how various interactive subtypes are determined by the activities learners engage in. Classroom approaches, no matter whether they are of the more traditional or of a strictly learner-centred type, often include an activity in which learners are encouraged to talk in pairs (or in small groups) about any topic they are interested in. Incidentally, this activity would qualify as "less topic-orientation, less activity-orientation" in Van Lier's system. The outcome and quality of these conversational interactions, however, might vary enormously, depending mainly on the type of learning-teaching approach the learners have been socialized with. In textbook-based courses, young learners tend to just reproduce phrases and topics also covered in their textbooks, whereas, say, in autonomous classrooms the interactions are much more authentic in the sense outlined above. The following two examples –derived from the LAALE project[1]– will illustrate this point. In both cases the learners were approximately 12 years old and had had English lessons for about 1,5 years. They were given exactly the same task instruction: "Talk about a topic of your own choice for about four to five minutes."

- **Conversational interactions about a freely chosen topic**

In the first example, learners, taught according to the principles of autonomous language learning (cf. Dam 1995), talk about a school trip to Poland:

(1) B: Have you been in Poland before?
    Mi: No. (.) Have you?
    B: No, never. Can you say any Polish words?
    Mi: Only one.
    B: What is it?
    Mi: Cieszyn [laughing][2]
    B: I have got erm a a Polish dictionary, or something like that, and I'm trying to learn to say 'I can't speak Polish'in Polish, of course.
    Mi: That must be/this must not be easy.

---

1   LAALE stands for *Language Acquisition in an Autonomous Learning Environment*. It was a longitudinal study over a period of four years. Identical data tests were carried out in German Gymnasium classes in order to facilitate the interpretation of the data (cf. Legenhausen 2001, 2003, 2009).
2   The town in Poland the class intended to visit.

> B: I don't think so. As their erm their letters is not the same way to say it like we do, so I ave to learn that before I can say all the words.

This exchange shows many features of ordinary, naturally occurring conversation, that is, features that could also be observed in interactions between native speakers –such as genuine information requests and responsivity. It contrasts markedly with the following example in (2).

- **Reproduction of *learning materials* (pseudo-communication)**

The exchange in example (2) shows hardly any features of an ordinary conversation. It was recorded in a textbook-based mainstream class that followed a communicative syllabus. The learners, having been classmates for at least 18 months, ask questions that can only be said to be mindless. What happens psycholinguistically in this interaction has little in common with the previous –more authentic– conversational exchange in (1).

(2) B: Where do you live?
R: I'm live in Mels, and you?
B: I live in Laven.
R: Eh, how old are you?
B: I'm twelve years old (.) Have you got a brother or a sister?
R: Yes, I have a sister. Sometimes he (.) she is ve (.), she is very silly.
B: What's her name?
R: His name is (.) her name is Monika.
B: Eh (…) live you, do you live in a house or a flat?

The learners obviously interpreted the task as a language-learning exercise or as a "didactic" task. They tried to cope with it by resorting to textbook phrases as "islands of reliability" (Dechert 1983), phrases which they had practised again and again. The interaction is characterised by a lack of responsivity and naked linkages. It is unlikely that any deep-processing occurs here and the relationship to learning processes must be of a completely different order. Some methodologists might still consider it "language use", though, which could possibly consolidate some kind of previous learning. Pseudo-communicative exchanges of this type, where no negotiation of meaning (or form) occurs, will not lead to much awareness-raising as is, in contrast, the case in the following type of interaction.

- **Conversational interactions with a task focus on *language* (metalanguage)**

When it comes to raising the learners' metalinguistic awareness, tasks or activities which focus on language as such seem to be the most obvious option. It is sometimes suggested in the literature on Task-Based Learning (TBL), however, that tasks focusing on language features belong to a form-focused pedagogy and cannot form part of a meaning-based approach. Some TBL educationists even go a step further. They claim that meaning-based tasks should have a real-world relationship, which implies for some of them that "an activity focused on language itself cannot be a task" (Skehan 1998: 268). This is no doubt a highly controversial statement. Is language not the main cognitive tool by which we come to grips with and make sense of the world? Contrary to the position taken by Skehan, it is claimed here that language as the focus and content of an activity should constitute an essential element of meaning-focused classroom approaches. The challenge, though, is to make it an attractive option for learners to engage in. The following example might serve as an illustration of a meaning-based activity focusing on language which learners found challenging and motivating. Two German classes were involved in an e-mail project together with four American and Canadian high-school classes (cf. Eck/Legenhausen/Wolff 1995: 142–144). These email projects tended to start with the exchange of 'hello and welcome messages'. It was thus possible to compile two corpora with identical text types –an L2 corpus of learner texts and a parallel L1 corpus of native-speaker texts. The task for the German learners was to compare the two text types with the help of a concordancing program. The learners became deeply involved in analysing their own texts against the foil of native-speaker texts. They, for example, noticed that the American high-school students quite often started their sentences with "because", which violated a rule that their English teacher had always insisted upon. Heated discussion evolved about "descriptive" and "prescriptive" rules of grammar, with the teacher being on the defensive.

The learners' own interlanguage was the content and focus of a meaningful activity. This is a convincing example of a language-focused, meaningful activity with a real-life relationship.

- **Conversational interactions with a task focus on a *language product***

If learners intend to write a text collaboratively, then the whole interaction consists of –or can even been defined as– negotiation of meaning and negotiation of form. Writing processes are characterised by phases of planning, composing, evaluating and revising, and all the suggestions made by individual learners will have to be evaluated, accepted, modified or rejected before a final version –ratified by all of them– is written down. In example (3), a group of four 14-year-old learners in grade 8, that is, after 3,5 years of learning English, had decided to write a story about "The Martian with the Magic Stick", and they agreed that the magic stick was to save the world from pollution. One of the girls (learner S) suggests that they should start with the phrase "once upon a time". The following interaction develops:

(3) S: Once upon a time.
    L: No.
    P: No.
    S: What, what-
    T: That's a fairy tale.
    S: Hm, but what, what if we say it in, in-
    P: another way.
    S: Hm. *Once upon a time*, not *once upon a time*, but *once in the future*.
    T: No.
    S: You can't say that.

The final written-down version of the corresponding text passage then reads: "One early morning a flying saucer landed on the top of the Statue of Liberty."

The first suggestion was "spaceship" and not "flying saucer", but learner P claimed they had "plates to fly on". Learner S then suggested "flying plates", which was rejected by learner L, who eventually, that is after some reflection, then came up with "flying saucer". This is an example of mutual scaffolding, that is, a pooling of knowledge resources. Writing a fictional story collaboratively necessitates intensive negotiations that imply metalinguistic reflections on form and meaning. The relationship to language-learning processes will again be different from the one in example (2), and possibly also different from that in example (1), since social aspects of learning come into play.

- **Computer-mediated interactions and the impact of reduced redundancy**

Synchronous text-based online interactions are more likely to lead to communicative trouble than face-to-face interactions. This has to do with the lack of an immediate situational context and with the lack of auditory or visual clues. Both aspects increase the vulnerability of the interactions, because there is a need to compensate for the lack of a situational context and the need, for example, to make paralinguistic features explicit. However, the reduced redundancy and ensuing vulnerability of the interactions seems to be a blessing from a language-acquisition point of view, since it provokes more negotiation of meaning and draws attention to certain conversational features that are taken for granted in face-to-face situations. The following illustration from an early MOO project[3] with students from Münster University, Germany, and Vassar College, Upstate New York, for

---

3   MOO is an acronym for *Multiple User Domain – Object Oriented*, and was used earlier on to construct virtual learning environments which were exclusively text-based. (cf. Legenhausen/Kötter 2005).

example, raises awareness about the importance of paralinguistic cues in face-to-face interactions:

(4) Jennifer says, Sollen wir jetzt auf Englisch sprechen? *[Shall we now speak English?]*
Rolf says, **Puh**, good idea, for a change.
Rolf says, **Oops**, 'puh' was, of course, still German.
Sirius says, "Is that similar to *Quatsch*? *[rubbish/nonsense]*
Rolf says, No, no, no, it's more the sound of relief you make after having done something difficult or strenuous.
Sirius says, I see.
Rolf says, What's English for that? I just can't remember now that I'm thinking about it.
Sirius says, I think we would say '**ahhhh**'.
Rolf [to Sirius], **AH**, yes, sure.

When claiming above that more powerful theoretical models are needed to explain the relationship between interaction and acquisition, this would imply that distinctions in the quality of interactions in examples (1) to (4) are taken into consideration and related to specific aspects of learning.

6. The interdependency of types of task, modes of interaction and modes of learning

The problem of trying to explain the interdependency of tasks, interactions and modes of learning has to do with the lack of a generally agreed-upon explicit model of language learning. In the absence of such a model, however, one could perhaps tentatively distinguish between:

- learning as a cognitive process, which would foreground the problem-solving aspect;
- learning as a social process as happens in the Zone of Proximal Development (cf. Vygotsky 1978);
- learning as a behavioural process in which consolidation of declarative and procedural knowledge occurs through practice.

This distinction will allow us to begin thinking in terms of which mode of conversational interaction might have a specific impact on which aspect of learning. The graphic representation in Figure 2 sums up the elements of the interdependencies.

Figure 2: Elements of interdependencies

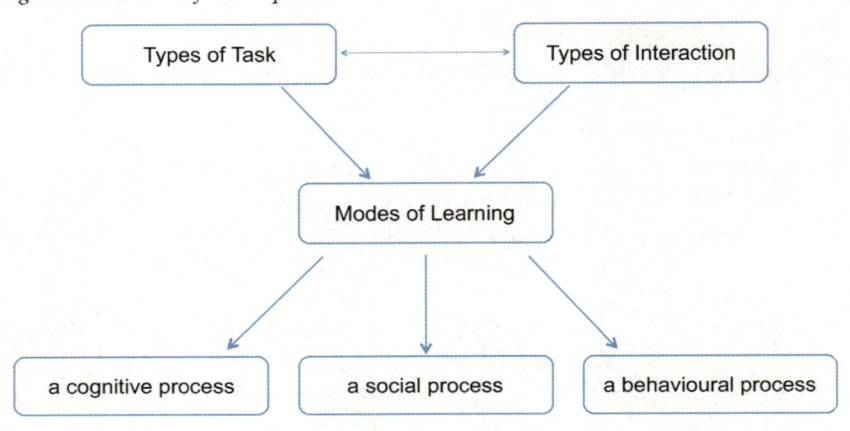

The following Figure 3 can be taken only as a first crude attempt at elaborating on specific interdependencies between types of interaction and modes of learning. Only the more relevant relationships are marked by an arrow.

Figure 3: Types of interaction

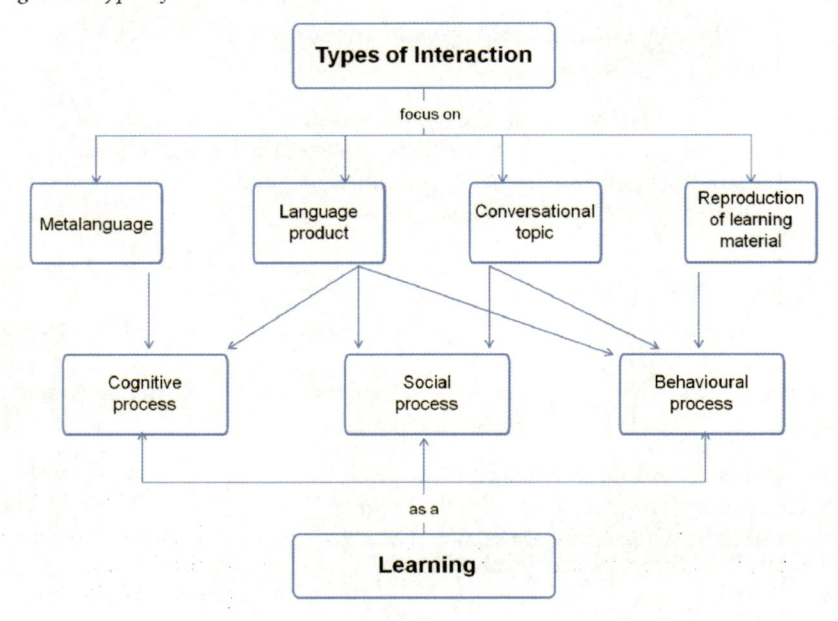

7. Concluding remarks

The Interaction Hypothesis has been around for quite some time now, and the beginnings might even date back as far as 1693, when John Locke (1989: 216) claimed that "[…] the right way of teaching that Language [French or Latin], […] is by talking it into Children in constant Conversation, and not by Grammatical Rules". The autonomy classroom might be said to have been informed by the Interaction Hypothesis, and it has provided convincing empirical evidence that authentic conversational interactions lead to impressive linguistic results (cf. Little/Dam/Legenhausen 2017). However, the "message" has not yet gained much ground in mainstream foreign-language classrooms. The reasons for this are manifold, the most important of which is that learners are not trusted to be able to work out the formal features of a foreign language by themselves. There is a deep-grained belief that grammatical rules can be acquired only via deliberate instructions. What is needed at this stage is to disseminate ideas about classroom activities that engage learners in metalinguistic and metacognitive reflective processes and which they at the same time find motivating and challenging.

Der Artikel geht kurz auf die Entwicklung von Longs Interaktionshypothese von 1980 ein, die seitdem eine Reihe von Modifikationen und Ergänzungen erfahren hat. Hier stehen Aspekte wie Reflexivität, Rückmeldungen, Aufmerksamkeitshinlenkung usw. im Vordergrund. Allerdings bleibt die Grundfrage weiterhin ungelöst, wie letztendlich zu erklären ist, dass Sprachverstehen bzw. kommunikative Interaktionen zum Sprachlernen führen. Hier fehlen allgemein akzeptierte, explizite Modelle zum einen zur Sprachverarbeitung und zum anderen zu Erwerbsprozessen, die die Ähnlichkeit der Abläufe bzw. Prozesse abbilden könnten. Die allgemeine Form, die diese Modelle annehmen könnten wird tentativ angedeutet. Das Hauptaugenmerk des Artikels liegt jedoch darauf, dass gezeigt wird, wie unterschiedliche Unterrichtsaktivitäten zu qualitativ unterschiedenen Interaktionsformen führen. Diese wiederum haben einen jeweils spezifischen Einfluss auf den Lernprozess. Es wird grob von einem Sprachlernen als einem kognitiven, einem sozialen und einem verhaltensbedingten Prozess unterschieden. Zu den jeweiligen Aktivitäts- bzw. Interaktionsformen werden illustrative Beispiele aus unterschiedlichen Unterrichtsprojekten gegeben.

Theresa Schenker & Fiona Heather Poorman
Yale University, United States
University of Education Karlsruhe, Germany

Students' Perceptions of Telecollaborative Communication Tools

Telecollaborative exchanges have become a popular tool for enhancing foreign language instruction and instructors have a variety of tools at their disposal for connecting students online with learners at other institutions or countries. Often a selection of one or two communication tools are used for these exchanges. While all communication tools have their distinct advantages and disadvantages, this study explores students' perceptions of the suitability of a variety of different electronic tools for communicating with native speakers online. L2 learners of German in the US participated in different kinds of communication tasks with native speakers in Germany and utilized a variety of formats including social networks, discussion forums, videoconferences, text- and voice-chat, and e-mails. After the nine-week electronic exchange, the American students evaluated the tools that were used in a post-survey. The results show that students generally enjoyed the synchronous communication modes more than the asynchronous ones. Based on the students' assessments, the article identifies strengths and weaknesses of the various tools used in the exchange and gives several recommendations for conduction telecollaborative exchanges in language courses.

1. Introduction

Telecollaborative projects which connect language learners at one institution with native speakers or language learners at another institution can offer a lot of benefits for students when planned carefully and implemented effectively. Telecollaboration can include communication via text-chat, voice-chat, email, discussion forums, videoconferencing, blogs, social networks, virtual worlds, and mobile applications. Research has suggested that telecollaboration can promote the development of intercultural competence (Jin/Erben 2007; Woodin 2001; Ware/Kramsch 2005; Tudini 2007; Schenker 2012; Belz 2007a) and that negotiation of intercultural meaning can take place between learners (Canto/Graaff/Jauregi 2014; Tudini 2007). Telecollaboration can also support second language learning (Kitade 2000; Kabata/Edasawa 2011), for example by helping students develop pragmatic competence (Chun 2011a; Belz 2007b), morpho-syntactic competence (Salaberry 2000), syntactic skills and vocabulary knowledge (Stockwell/Harrington 2003), reading skills (Taki/Ramazani 2011), and listening comprehension skills (Yanguas 2012). Other advantages of telecollaborative projects include: support of learner autonomy (Schwienhorst 2002), more equal student participation (Warschauer 1995; O'Dowd 2007), increased student motivation (O'Dowd 2006a), and more student interaction (Thorne 2006).

Even though most studies on telecollaborative projects report positive results and high student satisfaction (Lee/Markey 2014; Lee 2004) it is unclear which tools students prefer to use in the context of cross-cultural communication online. This study aims to fill this gap in previous literature by investigating students' perceptions of different communication tools used in telecollaboration as well as their enjoyment of these tools. In order to plan and conduct successful telecollaborative exchanges in the foreign language classroom it is important to take students' satisfaction with the proposed tools into consideration. The purpose of this study is to find out how students assess various online tools used to communicate with native speakers and what they perceive to be strengths and weaknesses of the tools so that instructors interested in planning a telecollaborative project can make an informed decision about the tools' effectiveness not only from an instructor's but also from a student's point of view.

2. Literature review

For a long time, the most popular tool for telecollaborative projects was email (Beatty 2010) which used to be described as the "best medium to bring language learners from all parts of the world together" (Brammerts 1996: 124). Even today, many projects include email as the primary communication tool because students are used to writing emails, the tool is easy to use, flexible (Rösler 2007) and well-suited even for shy students (Kötter 2002) and young language learners (Dodd 2001). Students who participated in email exchanges have usually given positive feedback (Vinagre 2005; Dodd 2001; Appel/Gilabert 2002; Schenker 2012; Chen and Yang 2014) and have also enjoyed the culture learning it has offered them (Stepp-Greany 2002). In spite of the predominantly positive feedback on email exchanges, one study (Stepp-Greany 2002), however, reported that only 38% of the participants indicated enjoying the authentic communication with native speakers through email. This finding confirms concerns by some researchers over the suitability of email for student-student interaction (Kötter 2003; Thorne 2003). In fact, not all studies confirm the general assumption that telecollaboration in language courses increases student motivation (Hauck/Lewis 2007) and some projects reported that students' motivation and participation in telecollaboration differed vastly (Chase/Alexander 2007).

Similarly to emails, the asynchronous nature of discussion forums and wikis make them popular tools among students as well. Students have reported especially enjoying the multitude of opinions and experiences in the forum (Evans 2009) and the language gains through use of wikis (Xing/Zou/Wang 2013). Asynchronous tools allow students more time to think and formulate elaborate messages (Bradley 2014).

Studies further revealed positive outcomes of chat-interaction in language classes. They displayed that students especially appreciated communication with students in different parts of the world (Xie 2002), instant feedback and the convenience of text-chatting (Jin/Erben 2007) and the positive learning environment (Kitade 2000). No difference was reported in the level of enjoyment of telecollaboration between students from different countries (USA, Japan, China, Korea). The vast majority of students enjoyed text-based chatting and thought it was a fun and informative project. Students communicating through audio-and videoconferencing with learners of the same language also considered these projects to be more fun than regular classroom instruction (Yanguas 2012). One study reported that text-chat was preferred over video-chat by ESL learners communicating on language learning social networking sites, especially when the communication partners were unknown to the students (Liu et al. 2013).

Some studies involving both asynchronous and synchronous communication tools revealed that students preferred the asynchronous tools (Hauck/Youngs 2008; Hauck/Lewis 2007) perhaps due to difficulties of scheduling across time differences (Hauck/Lewis 2007). However, one study involving both email and chat showed that half the students preferred the email and the other half the chat communication (Perez 2003). Other tools, such as blogs, Moodle, and Twitter, have also received positive feedback from students who used them in telecollaboration (Lee 2009; Lee/Markey 2014) and synchronous tools have been shown to make shy students feel more comfortable in participating (McBrien/Cheng/Jones 2009). Students' perceptions on the potential of use of Facebook for foreign language learning revealed mixed feelings (Terantino 2013).

Students also have positive attitudes about videoconferencing (Jauregi et al. 2011). Students participating in videoconferences as part of their language classes liked the quick pace of the communication and found it a more personal way to communicate than emails (O'Dowd 2006b). Students commented positively on the combination of tools in this telecollaborative project because of the distinct advantages of asynchronous (email) and synchronous tools (videoconference). One-on-one videoconferencing was also evaluated positively by students (Lee 2007), although another study indicated that students may perceive videoconferencing as a high-pressure situation (Kashiwagi *et al.* 2006). High school students who participated in a videoconferencing project reported very low enjoyment, partly because of lack of time for the videoconference (Yang/Chen 2007).

In spite of the fact that the majority of studies reported positive feedback from students participating in telecollaboration, there can always be shortcomings with different tools. In fact, synthesizing information from several articles, Lamy and Hampel (2007) suggest that learner experiences in computer-mediated communication projects are ambiguous and that for each positive finding a negative one also exists. This highlights the need for more systematic research into the experience and perception of telecollaboration by students. The importance of students' satisfaction with a communication tool is underlined by the findings of a study by Chun (2011) who revealed that student satisfaction with the selected tool meant increased participation in the chat activities. Most studies on telecollaboration analyze projects including one or two, rarely three, different means of communication and generally report positive student feedback. In order to better understand students' perceptions of different communication tools, the present study investigated students' enjoyment of a variety of tools used in cross-cultural communication.

3. Methodology

3.1 Research questions

1. Which tools do students prefer for communication within virtual exchanges?
2. What strengths and weaknesses do students perceive in the individual communication tools?

3.2 Instruments

To answer the research questions, a nine-week cross-cultural exchange between learners of German in the US and learners of English in Germany was established. Several commonly used tools in virtual exchanges were selected for the exchange project and assigned to be used for different exchange tasks. After the 9 weeks of the virtual exchange a post-survey was distributed and students rated their enjoyment of using the different tools and commented on perceived strengths and weaknesses. For the purpose of this article, only the American students' surveys were analyzed.

The post-survey included several sections, three of which were pertinent for this article. In section 1, students were asked to rate their enjoyment of the tools that were used in the exchange on a scale from 1–5 from *did not enjoy it at all* to *enjoyed it very much.* The second section asked students to list the tools they had used to communicate with their exchange partner for the text-and voice-chats. In the third section students were asked 6 open-ended questions about what they perceived to be strengths and weaknesses of the tools, what they liked best and least about each tool, which tool they liked best overall and which they would like to use in future virtual exchanges. Two multiple choice questions completed the survey. These two served to find out which tools students believed had contributed most and least to their learning of language and culture. The surveys were analyzed quantitatively to report descriptive statistics. The answers to the open-ended questions were hand-coded by both researchers and categorized to identify what students perceived to be strengths and weaknesses of the tools.

3.3 Participants

The participants in the virtual exchange were students at a small private university in the USA and students at a public university in Germany. Three sections of third-semester German at a US university, in all 36 students, participated in the 9-week project. Complete data was only available for 29 (15 female, 14 male) of the US students whose responses were used for data analysis. The majority of these students, 24 of the 29, were between 18 and 20 years old. Two students were between 21 and 23, and three were between 24 and 26. About half the students (48%) had spent time in a German-speaking country before the virtual exchange and 75% of the students had studied one or two other languages before or in addition to studying German. The students' majors included biology, engineering, math, psychology, art history, computer science, political science, philosophy, English, film studies, and others. No student enrolled in a third-semester German class had majored in German or any other foreign language. The majority of students (22) listed English as their native language, while two listed Italian, and the other five listed Chinese, Russian, Hindi, Japanese, and Vietnamese as their respective native languages.

The participants at the German university were enrolled in a teacher training program and were taking a course on using digital media in school. A total of 35 German students participated, of which 29 were female and 6 were male. Their ages ranged from 20 to 50 years of age, one student was 50 years, six students were between 27 and 33, and 28 students were between 20 and 26 years old. Several of these students had been on vacation to the United States before but none of them had spent any long-term period in an English-speaking country. All German students were teacher candidates for primary or secondary school; three were studying special-needs education and seven were studying to become English (EFL) teachers. All 35 participants listed German as their native language.

3.4 Description of project

The virtual exchange lasted 9 weeks and communication language was exclusively German. The project involved three 3rd semester German classes at a university in the US and one teacher-training class at a north eastern German university. Students in both classes communicated with each other through email, text-chat, voice-chat, discussion forums, and video-conferences.

There were different objectives for both countries participating in the exchange. For the US participants, the objectives were to a) provide students with an authentic opportunity to enhance their communicative competence in German by practicing the language with native speakers and b) to explore various tools for virtual exchanges to determine which ones are considered most suitable for language and cultural learning. For the German students who were enrolled in a teacher training program the overall aims were to c) present various possibilities of integrating new media tools in their future classrooms and d) to explore which tools are most suitable for communication within a virtual exchange.

The project concept was presented to the students at the beginning of the semester, at which time they were also informed of the requirements and goals, they were grouped for the discussion forum and matched with a tandem-partner for the chat activities.

3.5 Tools and tasks used in exchange

The virtual exchange employed email, text-chats, voice-chats, discussion forums, and videoconferences. Once students were matched with a partner from the other country, they used email to communicate with their tandem partner in order to set up their individual one-on-one text-and voice-chat meetings. Participants were required to conduct weekly text-and voice-chats in alternation on assigned topics with their tandem partner. The topics selected for the chats corresponded to the US curriculum and included, for example, discussions about present-day differences between former East and West Germany, current events, national identity, and cultural diversity. All tasks were open-ended topics about which students were expected to interact with each other in order to learn more about the target culture. Text-chats had a minimum time requirement of 30 minutes and voice-chats had to last for at least 15 minutes. Students were given a free choice of which program to use for the text-and voice-chat and were required to submit a weekly forum posting summarizing and reflecting on the chats as well as commenting on at least two of their group members' entries.

The purpose of the weekly discussion forums was to have students reflect on what they had learned in their individual conversations with their tandem partner and exchange more information and ideas with other participating students. In the discussion forum students were split into groups of 4–6 German and American students each in order not to overwhelm students with too many of the weekly required posts and comments. For this task the public discussion forum *ProBoards* was used as it is free of charge, user-friendly, and allows a well-arranged layout. Furthermore, it has several privacy settings, enabling only participants of the exchange to access the forum. Students were not restricted to length requirements for their posts, however, they were graded on a completion/non-completion basis as part of their homework grade.

The last tool used in the exchange was a videoconference which took place in the second-to-last week instead of the weekly voice chat. For this task, the US and German students were each split into three groups and each group spoke for approximately forty minutes with a sub-group of the partner class. Both universities' Tandberg videoconferencing equipment was used. Again, language for communication was exclusively German and all the sessions were moderated by the instructors. There were no pre-assigned topics for the videoconferences; instead, students were asked to contribute one question that they wanted to ask the partner class. As was the case for the text-and voice-chats, students subsequently reflected on the videoconference in their small groups in the discussion forum.

4. Results

4.1 Research question 1: Which tools do students prefer for communication within virtual exchanges?

While the video-conferences were conducted class-to-class with the video-conferencing software available at the institutions, students could choose different tools for text-chatting and voice-chatting with their exchange partner. On the post-survey students were asked which tools they had used for text-chatting and voice-chatting. The majority of students (27) used Skype for the voice-chat, with one student using the Facebook voice-chat function, and one student using the gmail voice-chatting option. Four different tools had been used for the text-chats: Skype was used by 21 students, Facebook was used by 14 students, and the gmail text-chat as well as the *ProBoards* (discussion forum) text-chat option were used by one student each.

The analysis of the post-survey responses of the students studying German in the US revealed that these students generally enjoyed using all of the communication tools used in this cross-cultural exchange. On the scale from 1–5 (5 = enjoyed it very much, 1 = did not enjoy at all), the averages of students' enjoyment were above 3 for all tools. Students enjoyed the text-chatting activities the most (M = 4.3, SD = 0.7, N = 29). In fact, not a single student indicated having disliked the text-chats. The second most favorite tool for students proved to be email (M = 3.96, SD = 0.69, N = 29), very closely followed by the videoconferences (M = 3.93, SD = 0.98, N = 29). Students rated their enjoyment of the voice-chat a little lower (M = 3.73, SD = 1.08, N = 29), but still overall enjoyed voice-chatting. The lowest enjoyment rating was reported for the discussion forum (M = 3.16, SD = 1.17, N = 29).

Figure 1: Enjoyment of Communication Tools

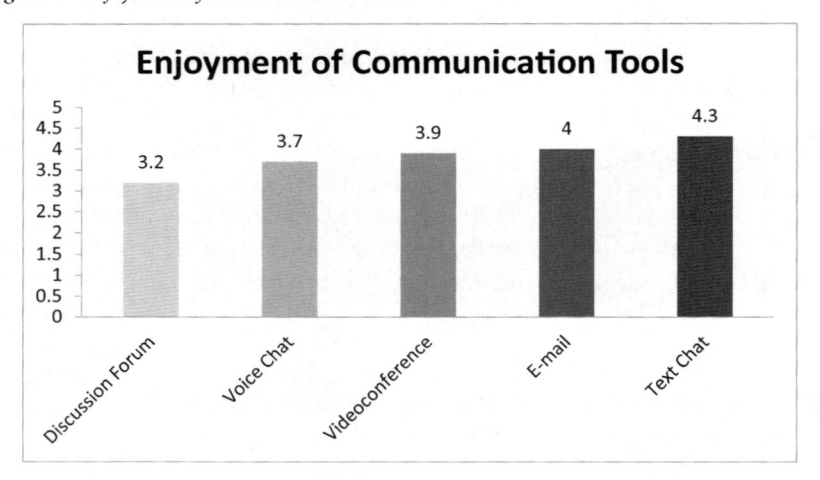

Enjoyment of Communication Tools

- Discussion Forum: 3.2
- Voice Chat: 3.7
- Videoconference: 3.9
- E-mail: 4
- Text Chat: 4.3

Additionally, students were asked which of the tools they judged to be of most use for their learning of German language and culture, and which tools they would prefer to use in a future virtual exchange. As can be seen in figure 2, the majority of students believed that text-chat had contributed most to their learning of German language and culture. The second most-useful tool for learning was the discussion forum, closely followed by the voice-chats. Only a few students considered the videoconferences and emails to be the most useful tool for learning a language and becoming acquainted with the target culture.

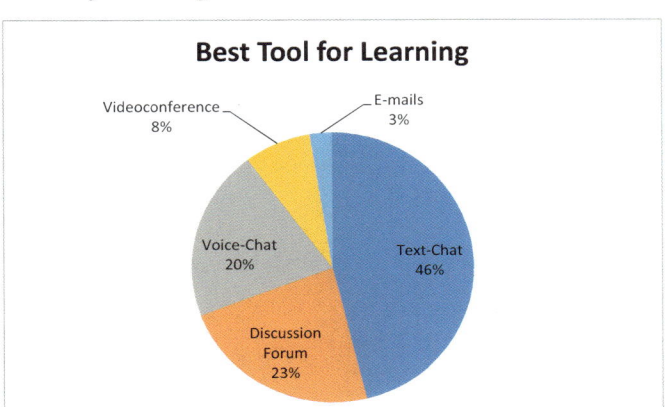

Figure 2: Best Tool for Learning

Best Tool for Learning
- Text-Chat 46%
- Discussion Forum 23%
- Voice-Chat 20%
- Videoconference 8%
- E-mails 3%

In line with these results, students' overall preferred tool for a virtual exchange was the text-chat. Voice-chat was also rated very highly and was the second most favorite tool. Several students wrote that Skype was their preferred tool. It was unclear if students referred to the voice-chats or the videoconferences here especially since the enjoyment factor for both of these two tools was almost the same. Interestingly, even though 23% of students had indicated that the discussion forum had contributed most to their learning, no one mentioned discussion forums as their preferred tool for a virtual exchange. Two students each reported emails and videoconferences as their preferred tool for a future cross-cultural exchange.

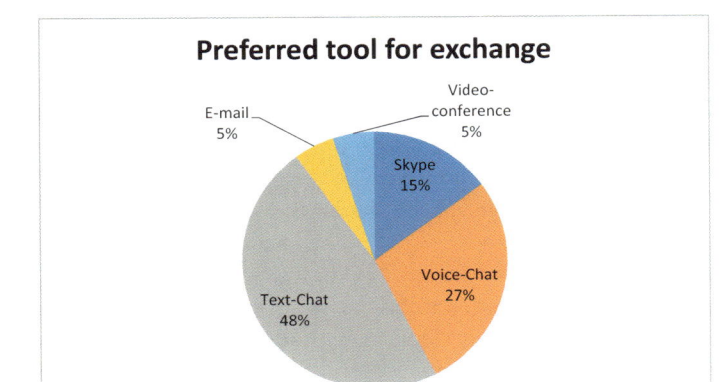

Figure 3: Preferred tool for exchange

Preferred tool for exchange
- Text-Chat 48%
- Voice-Chat 27%
- Skype 15%
- E-mail 5%
- Video-conference 5%

4.2 Research question 2: What strengths and weaknesses do students perceive in the individual communication tools?

The qualitative analysis of the students' responses to the open-ended questions on the post-survey revealed that students perceived several strengths and weaknesses when using the different communication tools. As email was a tool used mainly to negotiate times for the chats, students were not asked about advantages and disadvantages of that tool.

4.2.1 Strengths and weaknesses of discussion forums

Four strengths of discussion forums were identified in the survey responses of the US students. The main strength that students saw in the discussion forums was the flexibility due to its asynchronous nature. Students regarded this as especially beneficial because it gave them time to think, construct correct sentences, and make more substantive contributions. They also liked that it gave them regular writing practice through which they could learn new language constructions by using the German examples as a guide for their own compositions.

The second advantage that was reported was the simplicity of the tool. Students enjoyed that the discussion forum was so easy to use and that composing messages was quick and simple. Thirdly, the discussion forum allowed for community building to take place, which students saw as another great strength. They enjoyed learning about a lot of different opinions, discussing a variety of topics, and as a result, being "able to feel like part of a big group" (Student A29). Lastly, students saw different learning benefits in the use of discussion forums. These included the opportunity to learn more about the target culture, to practice writing in the target language, and to receive feedback on errors or questions.

The majority of students described only one weakness of the discussion forum tool: issues of participation. Students were unhappy about long waiting times in-between posts. They also felt that there were unequal contributions –some students posted a lot and frequently, while others were largely absent in the discussions. This sometimes led to a boring exchange that seemed a bit forced and sometimes even impersonal. A few students would have wished not to have been restricted to one small group for the discussions for the whole semester.

The second weakness that was mentioned had to do with the logistics of the discussion forum task. Students reported dissatisfaction with the discussion prompts which they perceived as too limited and narrow, as well as with the lack of formal feedback on their compositions. While many students had mentioned the formal writing practice as an advantage of the tool, a few students disliked the discussion forums for their resemblance to essay writing. Two students found the technology of the discussion forums tedious.

4.2.2 Strengths and weaknesses of text-chats

Three main advantages of text-chats were identified in the students' responses to the open-ended questions: the synchronous nature of the tool, the feedback, and the different learning benefits. Interacting synchronously with native speakers allowed students to practice speaking in real time and to develop a personal interaction through having real conversations. Additionally, students enjoyed the simple, convenient, relaxed, and casual atmosphere the text-chats afforded. The feedback –due to real-time conversation– was immediate and students saw an advantage in being able to ask questions and receive answers right away. This also helped students to learn about the German language.

A variety of learning benefits were also mentioned by students, such as the ability to practice informal language use. Students reported learning slang and colloquial German as a strength of the text-chats and they felt that they were able to learn how to speak freely and naturally. Additionally, the text-chats allowed students to learn more about the target culture. Other strengths of text chats that were mentioned in the students' responses include the absence of pressure or worry of making mistakes, and the ability to have good discussions in real-time while still having some time to think about responses.

The two main weaknesses identified in the responses include the time difference, which made scheduling the text-chats difficult, and the discussion topics. As with the discussion forum, some students found the pre-assigned topics too narrow and would have preferred a free conversation. Some students said it was easy to get off topic and talk about other matters of interest. The two other minor weaknesses of text-chats mentioned by the students were the length, which some found too long, and the inability to see the partners' reactions, due to which some students felt uncertain about how they came across to their partner.

4.2.3 Strengths and weaknesses of voice-chats

The students' perceived advantages of the voice-chats resembled those of the text-chats. The synchronous nature of the voice-chats was the main advantage again, as it allowed students to have a rapid exchange of ideas and get immediate feedback. Students enjoyed seeing their partners' facial expression and talking in real-time. Speaking face-to-face with a real person also made the interaction more personal, which was another benefit of this synchronous tool.

Similarly to the text chats, a variety of different learning benefits were experienced through the voice-chats. Students appreciated receiving help with pronunciation, learning to understand different accents, and practicing both their speaking and listening skills. Additionally, the voice-chats allowed students to build their vocabulary and learn colloquial expressions. Overall, students enjoyed getting to know their partners better through the voice-chats. They also thought the chats had a good length and were challenging in a good way.

Weaknesses connected to voice-chats were primarily the difficulty of scheduling the chats due to the time difference as well as technological problems with the audio or video software. Some students found it hard to hear or see their partner due to connection problems. Other weaknesses that students mentioned included a lack of sufficient German skills, which prevented them from understanding quickly spoken German and a sense of awkwardness and feeling overwhelmed.

4.2.4 Strengths and weaknesses of videoconferences

The main advantage students saw in the videoconferences was the class-to-class communication. Students thought it was fun to see the whole group and enjoyed the very collaborative exchange it enabled. Similarly to the voice-chats, being able to see all partners humanized the exchange for the students. Like the discussion forums, it provided students with insights into different views and opinions, students were able to ask many questions and talk a lot. In contrast to the voice-chats which were sometimes stressful for students, an advantage of the videoconference was that classmates were present for support.

As with the other tools, students also saw different learning benefits in the videoconferences. They enjoyed hearing many different accents in the partner group and receiving a lot of cultural information. Similarly to the voice-chats, students liked the combination of practicing speaking and listening. While some students had reported problems with their personal voice-chat technology, an advantage of the videoconference was seen in the stability of the technology. Overall, students thought that the videoconferences were a lot of fun.

Students perceived few weaknesses with the videoconferences. It was mentioned that it can be a bit overwhelming and hard to keep track of everything. The fact that only one student can speak at a time was also disliked. A few weaknesses were perceived regarding the technology. Although advanced videoconferencing equipment was used, some students found it hard to hear, and experienced the roaming camera as stressful.

5. Discussion

While previous studies generally used only one or two communication tools, this study aimed at exploring students' enjoyment of various tools in a cross-cultural virtual exchange, including text-and voice-chat, video-conference, email, and discussion forums. Even though concern has been expressed about the suitability of synchronous CMC between learners and native speakers of the language due to the potential of learner anxiety over communicating with native speakers (Satar/Özdener 2008; Lee 2004), students in this study saw many advantages in communicating synchronously with native speakers and preferred synchronous to asynchronous environments.

The results showed that students did not dislike any of the tools, but had a strong preference for text-chatting, which they not only enjoyed most in this exchange but from which they also felt they learned the most about German language and culture. Not surprisingly then, text-chat was also students' favorite tool for future virtual exchanges. Although the text-chat environment is not an easy one to master for language learners, especially because students can't use facial expressions or other non-verbal cues to help understand the message (Toyoda/Harrison 2002), the advantages of the tool outweighed the potential challenges for the students in the intermediate German class used for this study. In fact, the distance created by the absence of video and audio in the text-chats may have afforded students a sense of anonymity, which has been suggested to make communication less inhibited and support students in communicating more freely (Van der Zwaard/Bannink 2014). In other studies, students evaluated text-chatting in the foreign language classroom positively as well (Blake 2000; Sadler 2007) and enjoyed it more than other online language learning activities (Peters/Weinberg/Sarma 2009). One study showed that students' language learning anxiety decreased significantly after participation in text-chat activity, while this was not the case for participation in voice chats (Satar/Özdener 2008). The advantages students reported for text-chat are largely in line with what has already been reported as general advantages of synchronous CMC.

Voice-chatting and the use of Skype was students' second choice for tools to use in future virtual exchanges, in spite of the potential difficulties mentioned above. Students' responses in this project support recommendations made in other studies (Lee/Markey 2014) about using synchronous voice-chatting for establishing a good relationship with their exchange partner. The ability to practice listening and speaking, especially with regard to pronunciation, was regarded as advantageous here as well as in other studies (Bueno-Alastuey 2011). Dissatisfaction about technical issues has also been expressed by students participating in other voice-chat projects (*ibid.*) and should be addressed in future projects.

Although students enjoyed using email in this exchange, the tool was not preferred for future virtual exchanges and few students thought it was the best tool for their learning. Though in general email exchanges have received positive feedback from students (Vinagre 2005; Appel/Gilabert 2002), the delay in response and lack of real-time communication may make this tool less desirable for students in general. It has to be noted, that email was primarily used for scheduling chat times, so that the actual communication took place in other formats.

Delayed response times in the asynchronous discussion forums resulted in lower enjoyment of this tool. The discussion forum tool was the communication tool which students enjoyed the least, and even though 23% of students believed it had contributed most to their learning, no one chose it as a tool to use in future exchanges. Other studies have also shown that only a minority of students perceived learning benefits through participation in discussion forums (Stepp-Greany 2002) and that forum writing is enjoyed less than other online activities (Peters/Weinberg/Sarma 2009) or writing in other online formats, such as blogs, or wikis (Miyazoe/Anderson 2010). This may seem surprising especially in light of the advantages that students identified about the tool such as its flexibility and the increased writing practice it affords students. However, the flexibility and extra time to compose messages may be exactly what makes this tool unfavorable; students did not like having to wait many days for a response, and the participation and commitment to the forum differed greatly among students which resulted in unequal contributions.

One way to increase student participation and engagement with discussion forums may be to actively involve the instructor(s) in the discussions. A study by Tanyi et al. (2007) revealed that students participated more and saw more learning benefits in discussion forums which included instructor intervention. Another study suggested a video-based discussion forum using Facebook as the platform as a motivating alternative to traditional discussion forums (Huang/Hung 2013). This study suggested that students benefited from writing and speaking-practice at the same time and that they enjoyed establishing stronger peer relationships. However, some anxiety over the video-taping was also reported. The blogging format might also offer a more enjoyable alternative to the discussion forum and should be explored more.

6. Implications

The results of this study show that students enjoy text-chatting the most and prefer this tool over other synchronous as well as asynchronous tools for communicating with native speakers in a virtual exchange. Previous research has shown that text-chatting can allow students to participate in negotiation of meaning (Tudini 2003; Schenker 2015; Sotillo 2009) and has revealed positive effects of text-chat activities on various subsets of students' language skills (Rafieyan et al. 2014; Pellettieri 2000) as well as their language learning motivation (Freiermuth/Jarrell 2006). In line with these positive findings, the present study supports a stronger incorporation of text-chat activities with native speakers in foreign language classes.

In spite of the difficulties the immediacy of text-chatting and absence of facial cues may present for students (Toyoda/Harrison 2002), the challenges should be tackled as the learning benefits as well as student enjoyment of text chatting outweigh the potential drawbacks. Previous research has outlined suggestions on how to increase learning outcomes through text-chatting which should be taken into consideration when planning a virtual exchange. For example, the text-chat project should include tasks that promote negotiation of meaning (Blake 2000) and require complex structures or specific vocabulary (Sauro and Smith 2010). These could be video sequencing tasks (Sauro/Smith 2010), open ended tasks or two way tasks (Tudini 2003). The results of this study further suggest to include different kinds of tasks for virtual exchanges: a combination of specifically designed topics and activities that align with class objectives as well as opportunities for discussing topics of students' choice is advisable.

Additionally, the chat-logs should be saved and could be used for reflecting on inter-language (Toyoda/Harrison 2002) and for other in-class language activities (Jepson 2005). Making use of native speakers in authentic chatrooms is another suggestion for providing students with more opportunities for intercultural learning (Tudini 2007), although it may be overwhelming for novice language learners to participate in a chatroom where many people speak at once (Kitade 2000). Incorporating group chats, instead of one-on-one chats, with small group sizes can be another productive and collaborative chat activity (Freiermuth 2002).

Lastly, even though students' preferences for communication tools should be taken into consideration when planning virtual exchanges, it is important to keep in mind that the communication tool alone does not determine the success of an electronic cross-cultural project. As Dooly (2007) rightfully points out, regardless of a tool's potential for enhancing language learning, the specific application of the tool is as important. Results from this study highlight the following key factors impacting the success and enjoyment of a virtual exchange:

- Topic selection: students' overall enjoyment of a communication tool and virtual exchange is affected by their like and dislike of the assigned task and topic to be discussed; a combination of tasks may prove beneficial

- Participation: unequal or untimely student participation may lead to frustration and negatively impact a virtual exchange; equal student participation should be ensured
- Technology: technical problems may lead to frustration; support should be provided to students
- Tools: a combination of one-on-one and group communication tools can help students establish a relationship to their tandem partner while also benefiting from the opinions of many others by being part of a community of learners

7. Limitations and directions for further research

The relatively small sample size as well as short duration of the exchange need to be taken into consideration when deliberating the implications of this study's results. The results of this study provide only a snapshot of students' preferences for communication tools, because all participants were studying the same language at the same language level. It is possible that there might be differences in the preference of tools in virtual exchanges for learners of other languages and at other language levels. For example, learners of languages with non-Roman alphabets might prefer asynchronous environments as they need more time to compose a message. Future research should therefore investigate different language learners' perceptions of communication tools in virtual exchanges. Additionally, different preferences might exist for communicating with partners who are learners of the same L2. Thus, studies should look at students' perceptions of tools used for NNS-NNS CMC interaction as well.

While this study has shown that students prefer synchronous communication tools in virtual exchanges, especially text-chatting, future studies should also investigate other communication tools including blogs, Twitter, Facebook, and text messaging, to arrive at a comprehensive picture of students' perceptions of the suitability of different telecollaborative communication tools.

Telekollaborative Projekte, die Sprachlernende mit Muttersprachlern oder Sprachlernern einer anderen Institution mit der Intention eines kommunikativen Austausches verbinden, bieten vielfältige Möglichkeiten für den modernen Fremdsprachenunterricht. Hierbei kann eine Kollaboration über verschiedene Kommunikationskanäle stattfinden, beispielsweise im Text-Chat, Voice-Chat, in der Email-Kommunikation, in Online-Diskussionsforen, bei Videokonferenzen, über Soziale Netzwerke, Virtuelle Realitäten und durch Mobile Applikationen. Forschungsergebnisse zeigen, dass Telekollaboration interkulturelle Kompetenz fördern kann (vgl. Belz 2007a; Jin/Erben 2007; Schenker 2012; Tudini 2007; Ware/Kramsch 2005; Woodin 2001) und die Aushandlung interkultureller Bedeutungen ermöglicht (vgl. Canto/Graadd/Jauregi 2014; Tudini 2007). Des Weiteren wird durch

Telekollaboration im Allgemeinen der Zweitsprachenerwerb unterstützt und Lernerautonomie gefördert (vgl. Gläsman 2004; Schwienhorst 2002). Als weitere Vorteile gelten eine gleichberechtigtere Lernerbeteiligung (vgl. O'Dowd 2007; Warschauer 1996), erhöhte Lernermotivation (vgl. O'Dowd 2006a), und mehr Interaktion zwischen den Lernenden (vgl. Thorne 2006). Obwohl die Mehrheit der Forschungsergebnisse im Bereich telekollaborativer Projekte positive Auswirkungen für den Sprachlernprozess aufzeigen, ist oftmals unklar, welche Kommunikationsformen sich für eine interkulturelle Online-Kommunikation tatsächlich anbieten. Das Ziel der vorliegenden Studie war es, herauszufinden, welche Kommunikationsformen von Lernenden für diesen Zweck bevorzugt werden und welche Vor-und Nachteile jeweils festgestellt werden. Hierfür wurde ein 9-wöchiges Austauschprojekt zwischen Lehramtsstudierenden einer Universität in Deutschland und Deutsch als Fremdsprache Lernenden einer privaten Universität in den USA durchgeführt. Für die Untersuchung wurden diverse Kommunikationsformen wie Email, Text-Chat, Voice-Chat, Diskussionsforen und Videokonferenzen ausgewählt und eingesetzt. Am Ende des Austausches wurde eine Umfrage durchgeführt, in dem die Lernenden ihr Gefallen an den verschiedenen Tools bewerteten und erlebte Vor-und Nachteile erläuterten. Die Auswertung der Umfrage ergab, dass Lernende generell alle Kommunikationsformen gerne benutzt hatten, jedoch vorwiegend die synchrone Kommunikation im Text-Chat präferierten. Der Großteil der Befragten gab an, dass sie den Text-Chat am vorteilhaftesten für ihren Sprachlernprozess einschätzten. Obwohl die Text-Chat Kommunikation generell als Herausforderung für Sprachlerner gilt, da der Einsatz non-verbaler Kommunikationsstrategien wie Gestik und Mimik nicht möglich ist, überwogen in der Evaluation durch die Teilnehmenden die potentiellen Vorteile dieser Kommunikationsart. Die Ergebnisse dieser Untersuchung geben einen kleinen Einblick in die Vorlieben der Lernenden für Kommunikationstools, und können Lehrenden helfen, ein geeignetes Kommunikationsformat für einen virtuellen Austausch zu wählen.

Maria Eisenmann
Julius-Maximilians-University Würzburg, Germany

Differentiation and Individualisation through Digital Media

In terms of educational objectives, the use of digital media can affect the quality of teaching in a positive way, as it fosters self-directed and cooperative learning and supports the development of more open forms of teaching. Consequently, lessons are less teacher-centered and involve higher levels of student activity. Learning processes can be better individualised and differentiated through digital media not only because of the various ways of working alone, but also because of adaptable and adaptive software and Internet sources for example, through self-selected materials and students choosing their own learning approaches. Further advantages are gained by software that is both interactive and provides individual feedback on results or on learning status and/or proficiency. Digital media support learning processes in many ways. The following article will demonstrate how they can be used, e.g., for documentation, presentation, practice and repetition, finding, viewing, selecting and structuring, communication and cooperation, experimentation and simulation. In this respect, Web 2.0 not only offers interactive material on the Internet that can be very valuable, but due to its immanent error checking and its possibilities of direct feedback it also enhances autonomous learning. The contribution will show some of the many Web 2.0 tools and their benefits for the EFL classroom.

1. Introduction

Teachers today have to face an apparent contradiction: state standards, state assessment, time management in class, labelling of students and low budgets for materials on the one hand and buzz phrases in teacher training contexts such as individualisation, differentiation, cooperative learning and learner autonomy on the other hand. There seems to be a trend towards output orientation which can be measured in state assessments, but teachers often feel left alone when it comes to the question of input. Consequently, they have questions such as the following that need to be answered (Heacox 2012: 14–16):

- My curriculum is determined and influenced by the state standards. How can I differentiate when I'm required to teach specific content and skills and when I must prepare students for district or state assessments?
- With an already full school day, how can I find the planning time to differentiate instruction?

- How do I make differentiation 'invisible' to students so they don't feel that being assigned different tasks is unfair?
- How can I manage my classroom when students are doing different things at the same time?

One possible answer to these questions could be an increased use of digital media. They can affect the quality of teaching in a positive way, as they foster self-directed and cooperative learning and support the development of more open forms of teaching. The learning experiences that are made possible through new technologies and social software tools are active, process-based, anchored in and driven by learners' interests, therefore, they have the potential to cultivate self-regulated, independent learning. Thus, the increased use of digital media strengthens the ability of learners to prepare for their own learning, take the necessary steps to learn, manage and evaluate their learning and provide self-feedback and judgment, while simultaneously maintaining a high level of motivation. Recent reports (cf. e.g. Biebighäuser *et al.* 2012; Eisenmann/Ludwig 2014; Grünewald 2006; Heacox 2012) indicate that the integration of Web 2.0 tools into learning designs can make a qualitative difference by giving students a sense of ownership and control over their own learning. With a strong focus on differentiation and individualisation they also serve to integrate essential learning outcomes such as lifelong learning, informal learning and learner autonomy (Eisenmann/Ludwig 2014; Hamilton 2013).

2. The importance of differentiation and individualisation

According to Brügelmann (2002: 39), differentiated instruction can be subdivided into "differentiation from above" and "differentiation from below". While the first refers to a type of differentiation where the teacher is in charge of first diagnosing students and then providing them with appropriate tasks and material, as is the case in mainstream teacher-led classrooms, the latter shows parallels to the concept of learner autonomy and is present in more open and individualised teaching approaches. Differentiation from below refers to the students being in charge of choosing what they feel is appropriate for them with the teacher assuming the role of a moderator and guide. Possibilities of differentiation and individualisation can most commonly be found in the following fields: quantity and quality of learning contents (i.e., in the amount and depth of tasks and material), methods and participatory structures (i.e., working individually, in pairs or in groups). It is important to note that a class is not differentiated when assignments are the same for all learners and the adjustments consist of varying the level of difficulty of questions for certain students. It is not appropriate to have more advanced learners do extra work or be given extension assignments after completing their regular work. Asking students to do more of what they already know is ineffective, asking them to do "the regular work, plus" must inevitably feel punitive to them. But what does differentiation mean? Tomlinson (2014: 48) lists the following key principles of a differentiated classroom:

- The teacher is clear about what matters in the subject matter.
- The teacher understands, appreciates, and builds upon student differences.
- Assessment and instruction are inseparable.
- The teacher adjusts content, process, and product in response to student readiness, interests, and learning profile.
- All students participate in respectful work.
- Students and teachers are collaborators in learning.
- Goals of a differentiated classroom are maximum growth and individual success.
- Flexibility is the hallmark of a differentiated classroom.

These maxims lead to the conclusion that lessons can only be truly successful through individualised instruction in which all learners can find their appropriate learning requirements and learning environments. This means that wide-ranging learning opportunities, the opening of teaching and support for self-directed learning environments, i.e., the initiation of learner autonomy, are needed to help learners set their own personal/individual best learning conditions.

For this purpose, it is necessary for students to participate in the differentiating means in order to let them recognize their strengths and weaknesses autonomously, thus make them increasingly independent. If differentiation and individualisation are seen this way, personal responsibility and autonomy are eventually strengthened –an educational goal which is very closely connected to the educational goal of lifelong learning.

3. How digital media foster individualised instruction

In traditional EFL classrooms, collaborative learning has been recommended as an effective pedagogy that fosters skills of analysis and communication in a differentiated classroom. Web 2.0 tools have changed the way people communicate and network. As a consequence, the global learning landscape of the 21st century is being transformed and shaped by the uptake of digital communication tools and world-wide networked applications. How extensively have Web 2.0 tools affected education and foreign language learning? As online learning environments for today's learners make use of Internet sources with adaptable and adaptive software, the learning processes can be better individualised and differentiated. The concept of student-centered, self-directed and self-regulated learning has long been a pursuit of education and the integration of social software into learning designs seems to make a qualitative difference as it gives students a sense of ownership and control over their own learning and planning. Furthermore, there is also greater recognition of the potential of communication technologies to foster dialogue, networking and team skills among learners. The UK-based Committee of Inquiry into the Changing Learner Experience (CLEX 2009: 9) states that

> Web 2.0, the Social Web, has had a profound effect on behaviours, particularly those of young people whose medium and metier it is. They inhabit it with ease and it has led them to a strong sense of communities of interest linked in their own web spaces, and to a disposition to share and participate.

This indicates that digital native students want an active learning experience that is social, participatory and supported by digital media. Current research also points to a growing appreciation of the need to support and encourage learner control over the entire learning process (cf. Dron 2007; Eisenmann/Strohn 2012). As web-based multimedia production and distribution tools incorporating text (blogs, wikis, Twitter), audio (podcasting, Skype), photo (Flickr) and video (vodcasting, Internet videos) capabilities continue to grow, today's classrooms are faced with ever expanding opportunities to integrate social media and technologies into teaching and learning processes.

In the context of individualised instruction, but also learner autonomy, the following range of practical and pedagogical affordances and potential advantages have been mentioned in recent publications (cf. e.g. Blell/Kupetz 2005; Eisenmann/Ludwig 2014; Grünewald 2006; Reinders/Hubbard 2013; Reinfried/Volkmann 2012; Rösler 2007):

- **Independence from time and place**: technology facilitates learners easy access to various kinds of resources at any time
- **Flexibility**: contents can easily and quickly be altered and offer new types of activities
- **Storage and retrieval**: technology allows for easy storage and retrieval of learning and teaching materials
- **Recyclability**: contents can be taken over by other learning contexts and environments
- **Distributions**: easy distributions of contents and sharing with others
- **Authenticity of materials**: learners use real-world materials that are relevant to their individual interests

- **Interaction**: opportunity of language usage in settings outside formal education, e.g., through email, chat and social networking sites; allows all participants to change the parameters, thus influence the learning process
- **Situated learning**: focus on the relationship between learning and the social situation of the learner, which is enabled by the use of technology that allows access to real-world settings
- **Multimediality**: with regard to their learning styles, learners decide about the fashion of input resources, e.g., film, text, listening example, etc.
- **Non-linearity of information**: contents can be displayed dynamically
- **Hypertextuality**: updating, networking and linking up information online
- **Feedback**: possibility to get feedback fromthe teacher and to connect with other learners to obtain peer-feedback

Of course, the use of technology also entails possible pitfalls and constraints for both students and teachers that we need to be aware of (cf. Eisenmann/Ludwig 2014). Of crucial importance to attain the primary objective of student-centered learning is the need to acknowledge that learners' needs and preferences cannot be addressed as static constructs during the task procedure, as well as to provide suitable scaffolding to support the learning outcomes to be attained. Even more important to note is that it is not the computer that enhances learning progress, but the practice and context within which the computer is used (cf. Kern/Warschauer 2000: 2). In the centre is the pedagogical aim of the task, which in turn has design implications, as Hafner and Miller (2011: 82) suggest "language educators may draw upon the architecture of such spaces in order to design opportunities for autonomous learning in formal contexts".

Therefore, digital media can be used in a great variety of individualised learning processes, e.g., for documentation, presentation, practice and repetition, finding, viewing, selecting and structuring, communication and cooperation, experimentation and simulation. But teaching and learning in the virtual world has become more than simply using a different tool to transfer the same information as with traditional tools. Web 2.0 has created new genres and new identities, which means users also need new forms of literacy to interpret information. Therefore, as Warschauer (2004) points out, new teaching methods are required accordingly.

4. Examples of practice

In today's classrooms web-based language learning is most commonly used for practice purposes (e.g., online material), for information (e.g., web search, webquest), for communication (e.g., email exchange, chats, audio/video conferencing) and for presentation (e.g., homepage, weblog, Internet video). In the following, I will provide some practical examples of using digital media for dealing with mixed-ability classes by showing how computer-supported collaborative learning can be employed in order to promote differentiation and individualisation. In the context of concrete foreign language learning scenarios, some examples of internet-focussed and software-based implementation forms will be described.[1]

Research results (cf. e.g. Grünewald 2006) show that weak students learn better in a well-structured learning environment, while strong learners benefit from a less structured learning setting. This is especially true for hypertext applications such as the Internet, which provide learners with opportunities to determine and organise their learning paths themselves. While this is a great advantage for strong learners, weaker learners see themselves facing the enormous challenge of structuring the range of options and offers. With regard to Internet search a distinction is made between four different task types (Grünewald 2010: 44): (1) **The guided search** is the less individualised form of working with the Internet, in which the URLs are usually selected by the teacher in order to lead the students to a real sense of achievement as quickly as possible. (2) **The Internet rally** is a more complex search because it puts forward a question in terms of problem solving, which encourages the students to be creative and communicate as much as possible. Although students are also given clear and concrete task instructions, solving the tasks in different, individual ways is possible. (3) **The free search** is a very open form of integrating web-based instruction into the foreign language classroom, in which students search the Internet without a predetermined approach and without any given sources. Experiences show that this method has many drawbacks because learners have to handle the flow of information and their qualitative evaluation, which can easily demand too much of them. Moreover, learners can easily get lost in hyperspace and give up in frustration. (4) **The webquest**, which will be explained in more detail in the following.

Webquests are computer-based learning scenarios which foster autonomous, product-oriented and cooperative learning. At the same time, the use of different materials and media offers a considerable number of opportunities for differentiation and individualisation. They were first invented by Bernie Dodge and Tom March at the San Diego State University in 1995 in order to help their university

---

1   The Internet provides countless possibilities and options for teachers to use in the EFL classroom, e.g., websites such as http://www.lehrer-online.de/unterricht.php or https://learningapps.org. For a very good choice of edu-apps and webtools for "understanding, analyzing, applying, presenting, and creating" in the EFL classroom see Grimm and Hammer (2014: 6).

students work with the Internet. Dodge (1997: 1) calls them "an inquiry-oriented activity in which some or all of the information that learners interact with comes from resources on the Internet". Webquests offer different levels of difficulty and usually consist of six essential phases (cf. Dodge 1997; Moser 2008):

1) **Introduction** to topic and task or problem to be solved.
2) **Task**, which should be designed meaningfully. Creating the task is the most difficult and creative part of developing a webquest.
3) **Process**: the steps the students should take to accomplish the task such as group/pair work, time frame, etc.
4) **Resources**: online resources in particular, but also other materials such as books, pictures, films, etc.
5) **Presentation**, which can be done conventionally, e.g., with posters/handouts or again via new media and put online.
6) **Evaluation**: the way in which students' performances are evaluated; this can be done by the teacher or by the students themselves (self/peer evaluation).

Due to its currentness, topicality and authenticity, major benefits can be stated in the context of cultural studies and intercultural learning. Themes and topics can be developed autonomously and all results can be posted onto the Internet again. This can be of benefit for other learners and can thus enhance progressive learning. A great advantage for differentiated instruction is the fact that all students work on the tasks at their individual pace and in all different participatory structures (individual work, pair/group work). Simultaneously, learner autonomy is promoted according to materials and media that teachers provide their learners with. As well as the Internet, dictionaries, newspapers/magazines, coursebooks, etc. can also be employed. Students should be allowed a free choice of available materials and media. Thus, the focus of a webquest is clearly on individual research and information use rather than simple information gathering.

If teachers do not have or do not want to lose time or simply shy away from designing a webquest and are looking for something simple and easy to implement in their day-to-day school life, they could try an **email project**. Today, in fact, the implementation of email projects is widely used in the EFL classroom. They connect communication with speakers of the target language and contribute to the expansion of media literacy. The project can either take place with native speakers or with learners of the same target language, e.g., students of English in Denmark or Italy. In communicating with native speakers, it should be ensured that there is a benefit for both sides of the cooperation. Next to intercultural and interdisciplinary contacts, the students learn that English is used in authentic and real communication situations outside the classroom (→ see situated learning).

Another form of situated learning with easy access is the usage of a **chat**. This is a text-based synchronous form of communication with a focus on individualising the students' language learning processes because it allows not only two interlocutors but many users to interact at the same time. Pupils chat in their leisure time and are usually familiar with the technical procedures. Using a chat is a rewarding scenario, which can also function in order to accompany an email project with partners from any other country. For instance, if you work with a partner group at a joint project, it is possible to exchange via chatting, arranging appointments, making agreements, etc. This way the pupils learn about the specific characteristics of the chat language and the relationship between the network-specific communication conditions via chatting.

Another possibility for authentic communication can be found in **forums**. These are thematically organised electronic discussion platforms whose contributions are accessible to anyone using the Internet. There are thousands of different forums on all imaginable topics. In addition, most newspapers and magazines offer a forum that students can make use of. Authenticity is gained particularly by a language that differs strongly from standard English. Thus, students are being prepared to using the English language as a lingua franca, which allows them to express their own, unique thoughts and exchange ideas with speakers of other cultures.

More recent developments that have increasingly been used in foreign language learning are **podcasts** and **vodcasts** (videopods), media contributions that can be obtained via the Internet. Many podcasts and vodcast sites allow learners to generate questions about the content of the video and to get feedback on their answers. They can be very beneficial when used as a means of repetition of lesson contents or as an additional information source for topics discussed in class or by using their contents as teaching target (cf. O'Bryan/Hegelheimer 2007). Podcasts and vodcasts are particularly attractive for foreign language teaching, as they are for free and bring authentic, current audio material on any kind of subject into the classroom. They can serve as a basis for listening comprehension and enable individualised listening material because each student can listen to (a) different text(s). Podcasts help differentiated instruction by allowing different operating speeds and the chance to listen to passages several times. Another great advantage in terms of differentiated instruction is the possibility to collect these media files and listen anywhere and as often as students want to. Both thematically and with respect to the appropriate linguistic level, students' needs and interests can be responded to as a wide range of different content and levels can be transferred to the students' computers easily and without any problems of copyright.

In the last decade, in line with a policy change and reorientation, new ways to integrate users as interactively as possible were searched and found. Terms such as "community" describe new and contemporary design principles, which allow the users to participate significantly and to take part in the design of the Internet. Typical examples are wikis, weblogs and photo/video portals. According to Tomlinson and Ávila (2011: 144), "Web 2.0 generally allows for dynamic collaboration, but there is a device that stands out because of its potential for developing collaboration: the wiki". A **wiki** is an asynchronous interactive Web 2.0 hypertext system that allows users not only to read content but also to change it online. Wikis are text-based websites perfect for collaborative learning (cf. Moskaliuk 2010) and offer the opportunity to upload external content, such as pictures and files. The intelligent hypertext structure with internal and external links provides structure to wikis, which usually consist of separate pages connected with hyperlinks. "In sum, wikis have the advantage of being inexpensive, easy to set up, run, and monitor, while requiring only minimal technical experience on the part of teachers and students" (Grimm 2013: 234). Wiki projects can be carried out on various topics and in different approaches of learning and teaching. They are particularly useful in collaborative writing projects, e.g., creating wiki articles on topics that are treated in the classroom or creating your own dictionaries or grammar books. Additionally, wikis offer separate discussion spaces on each page created by users. These lend themselves perfectly to peer-review or student comments on the work of their classmates. It is a virtual cooperation in which you work on a common document and changes of individual users can be seen at any time. Unlike weblogs, wikis can be secured by providing authorized users with passwords in order to prevent unwanted guests or other disruptions.

An alternative to setting up a wiki is to create a **weblog (blog)**. While "wikis are meant to be more formal, inviting users to edit, revise, rewrite, and cite sources in order to create well-researched and polished content on topics of interest" (*ibid.*), weblogs usually feature rather personal, diary-style content. They consist of a series of entries arranged in reverse chronological order, are updated frequently with new information about particular topics and allow authors ("bloggers") to link to other web sites they find interesting or appropriate for the topic. In terms of individualised instruction in the EFL classroom, authentic and interactive blogs can be used, e.g., as online journals or learning diaries, as digital portfolios (e-portfolios) or as platforms for the exchange with teachers and/or other learners. E-portfolios seem more appropriate than traditional learning diaries to transform better ways of acquiring knowledge in a dynamic process of continuous presentation, testing and storage. They also promote the collective construction of knowledge and exploratory competences students need today (cf. Pugliese 2011: 196). Besides developing reading/writing skills and inter-/transcultural communicative competences, weblogs increase reflexive skills, and what is more, students benefit from personalising their individual learning process.

If a blog is designed by set video recordings rather than text-based messages it is called a **video blog**. Other sources for the EFL classroom are free video-sharing websites that let registered users upload and share video clips online. The most prominent one is most probably YouTube and its well-known slogan "Broadcast Yourself". But of course, there is a huge choice of other websites such as Clipfish, Dailymotion, Myspace, Myvideo, Travelistic, Videu, etc., and a variety of online video streams that are offered by most TV programmes. The overall aim of using a video blog or Internet videos is to enhance media literacy but also to facilitate students' self-employed proportion of their learning process and to help students to expand their own knowledge of foreign languages outside the classroom. Due to their cognitive and emotional proximity to the living environment and experiences of the learners, Internet videos are usually very motivating. We are surrounded by a visual culture and hybrid multi-modal media belong to the students' lives. Using them in the EFL classroom they learn about encoding and decoding procedures because text, images and sounds have to be "read" similar to linguistic signs. When creating tasks related to the work with Internet videos, it is important that the teacher provides tasks that allow the learners to deal with the foreign language in an authentic context that offers opportunities for interaction. The focus can be put on real-life tasks, which usually increase students' interest.

An important factor teachers today have to face is the students' immersion in and facility with digital technology, and in particular **social media**, which can be seen as a sub-category of computer technology: "instant messaging, Twitter, video games, Facebook, and a whole host of applications (apps) that run on a variety of mobile devices such as iPads and mobile phones. Such students are constantly 'on'" (Bates 2015: 28). Social media have a high impact on today's students, i.e., much of their lives revolve around such media. These may include the use of web conferencing tools such as Adobe Connect, the above mentioned streamed video or audio files, blogs, wikis, but also open learning management systems such as Moodle or Canvas. Mobile devices and services such as phones and tablets, Twitter, Skype or Facebook enable participants to continually share their contributions (cf. Bates 2015: 155). Kaplan and Haenlein (2010: 60) define social media as "a group of Internet-based applications that [...] allow the creation and exchange of user-generated content, based on interactions among people in which they create, share or exchange information and ideas in virtual communities and networks". What presumably distinguishes the digital age from other ages is the fast development of technology and our immersion in technology-based activities in our daily lives. Both students and teachers are still in the process of absorbing and applying the implications of Web 2.0 tools. Bates (2015: 194) describes the impact of the Internet on education as a "paradigm shift, at least in terms of educational technology". The basic question is how teachers can deal with this paradigm shift and how they can find a positive approach and a productive exposure to integrating social media in the EFL classroom.

Instead of fighting with students over them playing with their mobile phones during class, it is probably much better to encourage them to include meaningful English language communication and integrate social networking services (SNS) such as Facebook or Twitter into their classroom work. **Twitter** is a microblogging system that limits users to posts no more than 140 characters, which translates into one or at most three sentences, called "tweets". The great advantage of Twitter for EFL purposes and part of the system's appeal lies in its brevity, because users have to be as concise as possible. Students have to make their message short and focus on the essentials. But how can a teacher develop classes based around Twitter and mobile technology? How can Twitter enhance differentiated instruction and/or learner autonomy in language learning? High attraction lies in its real-time content that encourages people to befriend each other and interact with each other to a much higher degree than previous SNS models. In the EFL classroom it enhances self-organisation, i.e., Twitter functions as part of the digital personal learning environment and guarantees high student activation and student involvement because all pupils can participate simultaneously at their own pace. It can be used both synchronously and asynchronously, because everything written is documented and can be read and responded to later. Using Twitter is a great chance to promote discussion and debating competences and at the same time enhances media literacy, because only by working in class with social networks like Twitter you can show students how to use them wisely and safely. Students can then apply to other platforms what they have learned via Twitter, e.g., beneficial and profitable networking –one of the core competences students will need in their later lives. "The power of Twitter in the classroom lies in harnessing the instantaneous and ephemeral nature of the tool" (Kuropatwa 2007). As more concisely outlined by Nick Campbell (2009), Twitter use in education has the following four main advantages, most obviously for teachers: (1) Communicating class content, (2) sending out small, timely pieces of information, (3) encouraging collaboration and feedback, and (4) encouraging concise writing.

One of the many possible applications for using Twitter in the EFL classroom is an interactive, digital learning diary (e.g., www.twitario.com) or logbook, which, apart from allowing students to document their learning process, also enables them to enter in discussions with other students and/or the teacher if desired (cf. Eisenmann/Ludwig 2014). Furthermore, students can publish their Twitter diary on other social network spaces such as Facebook. If Twitter is used as a learning diary, it also offers opportunities to enter into transcultural encounters and target language discourse with native speakers of English. Twitter also allows students and teachers to share and comment on materials, students can tweet their own questions and observations about any topic. There is also the possibility of embedding products in the Twitter stream, e.g., videos, blog posts or photos.

In addition to basic communication, e.g., by direct tweets with classmates and teachers or announcements teachers can make, interesting and relevant websites can also be posted and shared by the whole class. One of the most obvious reasons to use Twitter in terms of individualised teaching is probably as a writing practice platform, i.e., for composition activities. Students can be asked to write a short story in under 140 characters. Such a writing project –either several micro-stories or a story in many parts– makes for a great EFL writing assignment. After following writers of short stories for some time or visiting and reading the creators' pages, students can be given a theme and encouraged to tweet their own stories. This can also be expanded into collaborative stories, where one person starts a story, which is continued by another one, etc. Both forms work very well on Twitter and are a beneficial way for EFL students to work on their writing. It is particularly invidualising because students can write a complete story collaboratively in large or small groups over several days or even months. This method can similarly be used for creating poetry, e.g., Haikus or Tankas, short poems with limited syllables and strict forms. John Hicks is an example of someone who writes Haikus in his posts on Twitter: http://twitter.com/blueheron. Teachers could have students follow one or two such people, choose a favorite poem, and explain their choice to classmates. The teacher can twitter a theme out to the class, and students have to come up with their own poem. As a follow-up activity students can use Twitter or a Twitter polling application to vote on the best ones. A similar way of using Twitter is in the context of twiction (a combination of "twitter" and "fiction"), which allows students to tell or summarise a story in one or more tweets (cf. https://twitter.com/twiction) (cf. Eisenmann/Ludwig 2014). While traditionally, students would use their logbooks to write a story, Twitter can be used instead. These ways of using twitter enable students to enter into meaningful and collaborative discourse in the target language with peers, the teacher and other users of twitter. Especially the discourse with other twitter users offers them the opportunity to come into contact with native speakers.

5. Conclusion

Digital media and their Web 2.0 tools support learning processes in many ways and enrich the EFL classroom today, particularly with regard to open forms of teaching and all cooperative ways of student-centered learning scenarios. Having an audience and being relatively public, online work connects tasks set in class to the real world outside the classroom. Users/students are individually responsible for the published. These developments, thus, offer significant potential not only for action-oriented foreign language teaching and learning processes, but also for differentiated instruction and individualisation in mixed-ability classes. The benefits of Web 2.0 tools are obvious: They are all collaborative and allow peer-to-peer-learning both inside and outside the classroom. Most of the applications are multimedial, multimodal and highly interactive. They can thus support diverse learner types and learning styles. While students embark into serious publications and real-life communication situations, tasks are usually focussed on the productive cooperation of the students and promote foreign language works in writing as well as in spoken form. Consequently, these qualities support social learning and both action-oriented and production-oriented ways of working effectively.

Lehrkräfte im modernen Fremdsprachenunterricht sehen sich immer mehr in einem Dilemma zwischen Kompetenzorientierung auf der einen Seite und der Forderung nach individueller Förderung auf der anderen Seite. Lernstandserhebungen, Vergleichsstudien und anderen Standardisierungstendenzen scheint die pädagogische Forderung nach Individualisierung, Differenzierung und Lernerautonomie im Fremdsprachenunterricht entgegenzustehen, bei der möglichst viele Lernertypen abhängig von ihren kognitiven, emotionalen und motivationalen Strukturen entsprechend ihren Voraussetzungen optimal gefördert werden können. In diesem Beitrag sollen Lösungen für diesen Konflikt aufgezeigt werden, indem durch den Einsatz digitaler Medien differenzierende Verfahren und Methoden für einen schüleraktivierenden und individualisierenden Fremdsprachenunterricht aller Schularten vorgestellt werden, die zeigen, dass sich eine Orientie-rung an Bildungsstandards und eine gleichzeitige Differenzierung und Individualisierung im Fremdsprachenunterricht nicht ausschließen. Nach Ausführungen zu den Grundsätzen von Differenzierung und Individualisierung folgen Erläuterungen dazu, wie das Web 2.0 als Ausdruck einer rasanten gesellschaftlichen Entwicklung das heutige Fremdsprachenlernen beeinflusst und wie es gleichzeitig gewinnbringend im Fremdsprachenunterricht eingesetzt werden kann. Der gezielte Einsatz der neueren Medien in individualisierenden und differenzierenden Lehr- und Lernkontexten ist nicht nur überaus motivierend, die verschiedenen Medien ermöglichen auch durch einen maßvollen, kritischen und individualisierten Zugang autonomes Lernen. Der Einsatz von digitalen Medien kann die Qualität des Unterrichts in positiver Weise beeinflussen, weil dadurch im Sinne offener Unterrichtsformen selbstgesteuertes und kooperatives Lernen gefördert wird. Lernerfahrungen, die durch neue Technologien und Social Software-Tools ermöglicht werden, sind in der Regel aktiv, prozess- und lernerorientiert –ein großes Potential zum selbstregulierten, unabhängigen Lernen. Die zahlreichen interaktiven und kollaborativen Elemente des Internets, die sogenannten Web 2.0-Tools, bieten Lernern hierbei die Möglichkeit, die Fremdsprache in authentischen Lernkontexten zu erfahren und in individuellen Lernprozessen zu nutzen. Anhand einiger konkreter Beispiele werden im vorliegenden Beitrag unterschiedliche technologische Tools im Hinblick auf Differenzierung und Individualisierung vorgestellt und ihr didaktischer Mehrwert diskutiert.

Saskia Kersten
University of Hertfordshire, UK

Email Communication in the EFL classroom

Emails are among the most routinely used means of communication in many people's lives, but both the content and the style between one email and the next can differ drastically depending on a number of factors, such as the relationship of the interactants, the level of synchronicity, the purpose of the email, the communicative situation, cultural background etc., making it a difficult genre to master. Using emails to communicate in English as a foreign language with both native speaker and non-native speaker peers offers the opportunity to foster the learners' genre and register awareness while engaging in authentic communication. This chapter outlines the features of email communication, highlighting the key findings of research in this area, including factors that influence, for example, the form of address and the style of emails and makes suggestions of how the use of emails can be integrated in the EFL classroom.

1. Introduction

Emails are one of the most important form of computer-mediated communication today and being able to compose an email in a foreign language (L2) is a skill that many language learners want to master, even if they already know how to write emails in their native language (L1), as conventions may differ significantly between different discourse communities. Learners may use other modes of communication (texting, chats etc.) more often than email in their day-to-day communication, but for example at university or in a corporate environment, email is still the prevalent mode of computer-mediated communicating (CMC). Thus, providing opportunities for collaborative learning using email communication both in- and outside an EFL classroom could be one way to teach new literacies and develop employability skills. In addition to that, emails also offer intercultural learning possibilities by coming into contact with other speakers of the target language and exchanging ideas and information as well as improving the language skills of the participants.

In his analysis of the language used in emails, Crystal (2006: 99–133) described the structure of emails as dictated by the technology, differentiating between obligatory and optional elements of email messages for the header and the main body of the message, respectively. The addresses of sender and recipient are obligatory (technical) elements, as these are necessary to be able to send an email at all. In addition, there is a subject line that provides a "brief description of the message" (*ibid.*: 102), which is in theory optional, but failure to fill this in often results in a prompt by the programme used as to whether the sender really wants to leave this field blank. Other header elements can be left blank, for example the cc (carbon copy), the bcc (blind carbon copy) and attachment fields and, consequently, "[t]here is very little scope for variation, within headers, because much of the information is dictated by the software" (*ibid.*: 101). The main body of an email, i.e. the part in which most of the message is conveyed, on the other hand, is shaped by other factors and may include many similarities with other form of communication: "apart from the technical aspect, it is doubtful whether one can consider email as something completely new" (Dürscheid/Frehner 2013: 42).

If an email shares features with other types of communication (in addition to letters, telegrams and memos show similar characteristics, see e.g. Dürscheid/Frehner 2013) and has been described as "a quiet phone call" (Crystal 2006: 130, quoting from a *The Simpsons* episode), it is surprising, at least at first glance, that this particular form of communication can at the same time also be challenging, as one would expect that language learners are already familiar with comparable genres both in their L1 and L2. This, however, may not always be the case, as there is evidence that writing contextually appropriate emails even in the L1 is not always easy (see section 3.2.). Although some of the more 'traditional' aspects of language competences, e.g. orthography, do play a role in composing an email, the main challenge for both L1 and L2 speakers of English lies in using the appropriate communicative strategies in the given communicative context. Which strategies are appropriate depends on a variety of contextual and social factors, as outlined in section 3. It is precisely the fluidity and the influence of many multi-facetted contextual, social and cultural factors that should also be considered when teaching email communication.

This chapter aims at providing an overview of the research into email as a form of computer-mediated communication (CMC), outlining the factors that shape the form, the function and, to a certain degree, the content of emails. It will then discuss studies on the challenges L2 learners of English face when writing emails in English.

Finally, it will make some suggestions how emails can be used not only as a topic in the English as a Foreign Language (EFL) classroom, but also as a medium for learning in general, creating an authentic means to communicate in an instructed language learning context and offering the possibility of fostering pragmatic awareness and new literacies.

2. CMC and collaborative language learning

One aim of incorporating CMC in EFL classrooms is to develop new literacies as well as (inter)cultural and pragmatic awareness in conjunction with what is sometimes termed linguistic L2 competences, that is, lexis, grammar, orthography and so forth. "The challenge with emails for many learners is not only a linguistic one, but can also be related to unfamiliarity with a target language's cultural norms or values" (Stanley/Thornbury 2013: 121). In addition, using email communication provides the opportunity to extend the language learning beyond the classroom by encouraging learners to interact in the target language outside the classroom with their tutors, their own classmates and other people, e.g. their peers, who speak the target language as a first or second language.

In the theoretical framework of Sociocultural Theory, first outlined by Vygotsky (1978), interaction is at the very heart of learning. Levy and Sttockwell (2006: 116) argue that the notion of language as a tool can be extended to include technological tools. Vygotsky's notion of the Zone of Proximal Development (ZPD), which posits that learning takes place while interacting, and thus collaborating, with peers who are more experienced and knowledgeable than the learner (or 'novice') while working on a task that is just slightly above the leaners' current level of competence (see e.g. Dunn/Lantolf 1998 for a more in-depth discussion and Ludwig/Van de Poel; Gabel/Schmidt and Rumlich/Ahlers, all this volume), can also be applied to learning how to communicate successfully using emails. In a classroom setting, such tasks can be instigated by the teacher or can arise from the communicative needs of the learners themselves. In order to ensure that leaners are working within their ZPD, tasks should be scaffolded, which means "helping the learner to overcome the gap between what they can do alone and what they can manage with the help of others (Levy/Stockwell 2006: 117). Email communication is one relatively easy way to incorporate CMC in the EFL classroom, not least because almost every learner already has an email address and is familiar with the technological affordances (Dudeney/Hockly 2007).

3. Email as a form of computer-mediated communication

Emails are by no means a new mode of communication, they are firmly established and routinely used by people all over the world. In some classifications of computer-mediated communication (CMC), and are described as belonging to CMC 1.0 (alongside forums and chats; see e.g. Chun 2011b: 665), as "email is considered an old mode" (Dürscheid/Frehner 2013: 35).

CMC in itself is not a unified genre and the various terms that have been put forward over the years to refer to communication via the internet and/or computer-based tools as a whole have been widely rejected by the research community as being too simplistic, for example the term *Netspeak* coined by Crystal (2006), for suggesting that there are at least some characteristics that are shared by all the modes of communication subsumed under this term. Many researchers have highlighted that, in the beginning, studies of CMC focused predominantly on trying to find defining features that describe CMC as a genre in its own right (for an in-depth discussion, see e.g. Dürscheid 2004; Dürscheid/Frehner 2013; Bieswanger 2013). After these attempts to define CMC as a whole, research then focused on the potentially emerging subgenres of CMC, investigating the language of chats, the language of newsrooms or the language of email, among others.

In terms of the medial dimension, "email is an example of asynchronous communication with one-way message transmission: Neither must the communication partners be logged in simultaneously, nor can they see how the other person is typing the message" (Dürscheid/Frehner 2013: 38). However, if email messages are exchanged in quick succession, they may become quasi-synchronous, which in turn affects the language used in them (see also section 3.1. below).

In her "faceted classification scheme for Computer-Mediated Discourse", Herring (2007) posits "two basic types of influence: medium (technological) and situation (social)" (*ibid*.: 10) on any kind of CMC. For each type of influence, a number of facets are outlined, which may apply to a varying degree to different modes of CMC (*ibid*.). She makes the point that the including technological factors (e.g. hardware needed, software used) "in this approach does not assume that the computer medium exercises a determining influence on communication in all cases […], although each factor has been observed to affect communication in at least some instances" (*ibid*.: 11). The inclusion of situational (social) factors, such as participant structure and participant characteristics, purpose, topic, norms etc. (see *ibid*.: 18–19) acknowledges that context is always a significant factor that shapes any form of communication.

With regard to email, various studies have shown that, again, there does not seem to be one single set of features that characterise the language of emails. Androutsopoulous (2006: 420) states that "[i]t is empirically questionable whether in fact anything like a 'language of e-mails' exists, simply because the vast diversity of settings and purposes of e-mail use outweigh any common linguistic features". This of course means that teaching how to write emails also cannot simply be accomplished by teaching learners a set of features that are supposedly typical for this mode of communication. Instead, learners should be enabled to develop an awareness of the different types of contexts and settings that shape email communication.

As Dürscheid and Frehner (2013: 46) point out, Koch and Oesterreicher's (1994) orality-literacy model may be a useful one when discussing CMC, including email communication. Rather than suggesting that there are dichotomies of formal vs informal, written vs spoken language, in this model, "there is a continuum within the conceptual dimension", the two poles of which are "'language of immediacy' (which is conceptually oral) and 'language of distance' (which is conceptually written)" (Dürscheid/Frehner 2013: 46). If email correspondents are well-known to each other (or have become more familiar with one another over the course of an email exchange), this may lead to the use of more conceptually oral language, including, for example, ellipses and other features associated with colloquial speech. If, one the other hand, the interactants are not known to each other, then the language in the email may be expected to be more conceptually written, that is, to be more formal. And as email communication is dependent on contextual factors, "Koch and Oesterreicher's model is a suitable approach to situate written interactions such as business and private email messages along the continuum of communicative immediacy and communicative distance" (*ibid.*: 47).

In the following section, some of the factors that shape email communication are illustrated in more detail using the example of salutations and closings in emails.

3.1 The influence of communicative context: greetings and closings

Shetzer and Warschauer (2000: 173) note that CMC "includes its own forms of salutations and greetings and, in some form, its own special use of abbreviations and symbols". There are, however, no hard and fast rules how and when these are employed. In addition, even the tentative conventions that may exist cannot always be transferred from one mode to the other and may even vary within the same mode depending on the communicative context, as how and when each of these features is used depends on a number of factors, for example familiarity, sender-recipient relationship, social status of the recipient and cultural and social norms, for example, of politeness.

Greetings may not always be used to start the main body of an email, as the header and general appearance of an email in an email programme may serve the function of a "virtual envelope", thus potentially making an additional greeting superfluous in the eyes of some senders (Biesenbach-Lucas 2005: 33; see also Danet 2001). In turn, "the absence or presence of a greeting formula and the type of greeting set the tone for the email conversation" (Waldvogel 2007: 456). One explanation that has been put forward why it may be acceptable not to include a greeting (of whichever format) is that, originally, emails were based on memoranda (see Kankaanranta 2005; Waldvogel 2007; Dürscheid/Frehner 2013), which typically do not open with a salutation. Users who are not familiar with this convention (or indeed with the text type memorandum itself), however, often employ, and expect, a greeting. Kankaanranta (2005; 2006), for instance, found that in English as a Lingua Franca email communication in company emails written by Swedes and Finns, many emails were framed by a greeting, a closing and a signature.

Apart from the communicative setting in which an email is written, the speed with which a recipient replies to an email may also determine whether and what form of salutation and closing is employed. "The tendency is that the greater the time span between two messages, the more information is required; the shorter the time span, the more information can be assumed to be available from the context of the interaction" (Dürscheid/Frehner 2013: 44), which means that if a reply is sent shortly after receiving an email, the more likely is it that greeting and/or closing formulas are omitted or shortened (for example by simply adding the initial at the end rather than the full name; see also Crystal 2006).

In addition to the swiftness of the reply, the type of message conveyed in the body of the email may also influence the presence or absence of a greeting. In her study, Kankaanranta (2005: 290) reports that, in her corpus of 282 emails, almost 80% of the messages contained a greeting, but there were still differences across message types, with the what she calls "Postman" and "Noticeboard" types (the former used to accompany attachments or forwarded information, the latter information on corporate issues for which no response is expected) exhibiting the least use of greetings (below 70%) and "Dialogue" messages, which represent the most frequent message type in the corpus, have the highest number of included greetings (nearly 90%). Consequently, the communicative function of the message may make it more permissible to omit a greeting, whereas in other communicative contexts, omitting a salutation may be perceived as impolite.

In another study, Waldvogel (2007) found that the use of greetings and closings in workplace emails differs in the two settings investigated. In one organisation, the majority of emails analysed contained no form of greeting, whereas in the other setting, the picture was reversed. These differences cannot be explained by the messages forming adjacency pairs (thereby making a greeting superfluous, see above) alone; instead these differences can, at least in part, be attributed to "organizational culture" (Waldvogel 2007: 465).

In addition to organisational culture, the underlying politeness norms of a discourse community may also play a role when writing emails. In a study of attitudes of both staff and students towards email communication, one international student expressed uncertainty as to what would be the most appropriate greeting and linked this uncertainty to intercultural differences (Lewin-Jones/Mason 2014: 81).

Chejnová (2014), who analysed 260 emails written by Czech students in their native language to academic staff, found that all emails contained a form of address and/or greeting and concludes that "students' e-mails to their teachers tend to have typical epistolary form" (*ibid*.: 181), but also observes that "there appears to be a difference in what teachers perceive as an appropriate form of address and what students perceive as appropriate" (*ibid*.: 186), particularly when it comes to the inclusion of honorific forms. Chen (2006) observed a similar dependency of formality of greeting on recipient status in her longitudinal case study of the emails send by one international student to peers and academic staff over the period of two and a half years. When writing to peers, the participant used informal greetings and closings from the beginning, while in her "early e-mails sent to professors", she "used a relatively formal style with epistolary conventions for the openings with formal address terms" (*ibid*.: 40). This, however, changed in emails to staff with whom she had been in contact with before, giving way to more informal forms of address (*ibid*.: 41).

The appropriate level of formality of email greetings can also vary depending on the diatopic variety of English used. Merrison *et al.* (2012: 1087) report a "much higher incidence of students using professional TITLES in the British corpus" in comparison with the Australian corpus they also analysed.

One conclusion that emerges from the literature is that whether a greeting and/or closing is included in an email and, if either or both are included, which form they take, does indeed depend on a number of contextual factors. The underlying 'rules' of what is considered to be appropriate depend on the Community of Practice (CoP) (Eckert/McConnell-Ginet 1992) in which the email communication takes place and whether an email initiates a communicative sequence or is part of a longer dialogue, as well as the speed with which messages are exchanged.

3.2 Doing politeness: Students' emails to academic staff

In this section, research on emails in a university setting, that is, mostly email communication between teaching staff and students[1], is discussed in more detail

---

1 Many of the studies on email communication focus on this communicative context, for an overview of studies on email communication see Dürscheid and Frehner (2013). For an extensive literature review on student-faculty email requests, see e.g. Economidou-Kogetsidis (2011).

and highlights some of the challenges both native and non-native speakers of English face when initiating an exchange. The first part outlines findings focussing on native speakers of English, while the second part discusses studies that either compare native and non-native language email communication or focus on the problems arising from the strategies employed by English as a Second Language (ESL) and/or English as a Foreign language (EFL) speakers. The majority of studies in this field analyses students' emails sent to staff, with most of them focussing on email requests, for example asking for a meeting or feedback. It highlights that there seem to be manifold underlying (social) norms and expectations that may influence the recipients' attitude towards the sender and the request and also illustrates that emails written by EFL learners may be perceived as being imposing and impolite.

3.2.1 Recipients' perceptions of native speaker email requests

Using "overly casual" language in emails, including abbreviations, when writing to university staff may have a negative impact on the student-instructor relationship (Stephens/Houser/Cowan 2009). In their experimental study investigating the attitudes of students and academic staff on email style at an American university, Stephens *et al.* (2009: 318) found that "overly casual email messages sent to instructors cause the instructor to like the student less, view them as less credible, have a lesser opinion of the message quality, and make them less willing to comply with students' simple email requests". 'Formal' emails in this study included a formal greeting and closing, standard punctuation and spelling, whereas the 'casual' emails contained neither a greeting nor a closing formula, exhibited many examples of non-standard spelling and punctuation, and also included examples of "shortcuts commonly found in text messaging" (*ibid.*: 309). In this study, the difference between the two email styles was very pronounced; it might be interesting to see how academic staff view emails that could be located somewhere less extreme on the cline between conceptual orality and literacy. In another widely cited experimental study (Jessmer/Andersson 2001), emails which were grammatically correct were viewed more positively than those that were what is termed "ungrammatical" in this study (e.g. typos, omitted punctuation marks, spelling mistakes and "fractured grammar", i.e. ellipses) (*ibid.*: 335).

Viewing these studies in the light of Koch and Oesterreicher's model of immediacy and distance, it could be concluded that the negative attitude towards emails that contain conceptually oral features, for example ellipses, stems from a mismatch in the perceived levels of communicative distance of the interlocutors. The recipients may interpret emails that contain conceptually oral language as being overly familiar and therefore inappropriate in a context in which they expect conceptually written communication associated with a greater degree of communicative distance.

Biesenbach-Lucas (2005: 41) advocates explicit instructions in how to compose emails and explicit practice of how to write email messages for university students in general. Furthermore, she makes the suggestion that "instructors at American universities could let [both international and American] students [...] know explicitly for what purposes they consider emails from students appropriate" (*ibid.*), thereby providing students with guidance on what is considered acceptable and what is not.

Merely knowing what is expected and how to meet these expectations following strict guidelines may, however, not be enough. Knupsky/Nagy-Bell (2011: 110) argue that "students' ability to appropriately modify email style could convey educational advantages"; in other words, being aware of the factors that shape email communication and being able to adapt to various context is a valuable skill for anyone composing an email.

3.2.2 ESL/EFL email communication in university settings

The effects of a potential clash between the communicative intentions of the sender and the expectations of the recipient as well as the need for some form of guidance or instruction are also apparent in studies that analyse email requests to university staff sent by ESL/EFL speakers.

Economidou-Kogetsidis (2011) identified what she calls "pragmatic failure" when non-speakers write to academic staff in English. Her study analysed emails written by Greek L2 speakers of English and asked British native speaker university lecturers to assess the appropriateness, more specifically politeness and abruptness, of these six authentic email messages using an online questionnaire (*ibid.*: 3199).

> The results revealed that the NNS [non-native speakers] students resorted largely to direct strategies (rather than conventional indirectness) both in the case of requests for action and for information, with the imperative ('please + imperative'), direct questions and want statements as the most preferred substrategies. (*ibid.*: 3206)

Some of the emails also contained dispreferred greetings, for example title and first name, which is "an acceptable construction in Greek" (*ibid.*: 3209), but not in English. In terms of the evaluation of the native English speakers, the omission of a salutation (classified as an avoidance strategy in this study) was perceived as abrupt and disrespectful by the assessors. The study concludes that the high degree of directness and lack of mitigation in conjunction with the omission of greetings and closings or use of inappropriate forms of address contribute to the email being perceived as "brusque, [...] which may sometimes verge on impoliteness" (*ibid.*). Focussing on the speech acts used in messages sent to academic staff, Biesenbach-Lucas (2005; 2007) analysed emails written in English by American and international students and identified several differences between the two groups. In "125 student-initiated email messages, sent by students enrolled in graduate level teacher training courses" (Biesenbach-Lucas 2005: 28), she found that the American students took greater initiative and "provided more potential response points" (*ibid.*: 40) than international students, concluding that "the sociopragmatic and pragmalinguistic resources of international students are more limited than those of native-speaking peers" (*ibid.*: 41).

What these two studies in conjunction with the others discussed above underline is that email writing is a highly culturally and contextually dependent act, which is of course not very surprising. It is also not surprising that politeness strategies are transferred from the L1 to the L2, regardless of whether they are appropriate in the L2 discourse community. This could be, at least partially, due to a general lack of pragmatic awareness in EFL learners (see e.g. Bardovi-Harlig/ Dörnyei 1998; Schauer 2006).

4. Email communication in the EFL classroom

In an environment where learning how to communicate via email in the L2 in only one of many topics in the language classroom and time is limited, lists of 'Dos & Don'ts' are often provided, often drawing on many different aspects of communication, ranging from 'check your spelling' to 'do not use an inappropriate email address'. There are many email etiquette guides available on the web, but these are often aimed at mainly a native speaker audience and may thus not be particularly helpful for L2 speakers of English. For example, the website http://www.101emailetiquettetips.com/states "Address your contact with the appropriate level of formality and make sure you spelled their name correctly." Although this is certainly useful advice, the appropriate level of formality depends on a variety of contextual factors and the degree of communicative distance between the interlocutors (see section 3), which may differ significantly from the learners' L1.

Economidou-Kogetsidis (2015) highlights another potential pitfall of overly simplistic instructions: recommending that L2 learners simply use more politeness strategies when composing emails in English may even be counterproductive, as an overuse of mitigation could result in the perception of the email as equally inappropriate and even insincere.

Translated to the EFL classroom, this could be interpreted as a call for more in-depth discussion of genres, text types, registers and politeness strategies, an area which is also addressed in the *Common European Framework of Reference for Languages* (CEFR) under *Sociolinguistic Competence and Sociolinguistic Appropriateness* (Council of Europe 2001: 118ff) and thus should play a part in EFL instruction (for a detailed discussion of research into foreign language writing, see Gabel/Schmidt, this volume).

Attempts to include emails in the EFL classroom, for example in coursebooks, are not new, but the discussion of the language used in them is often limited to what are commonly believed to be typical features of CMC as a whole, for example the use of emoticons and abbreviations, even though research has shown that CMC does not really have one defining set of such features (see above, section 3). Another piece of advice given is that an email is essentially the same as a letter. If more detailed information is provided, then a distinction is made between formal (or sometimes termed 'polite') emails and personal ones, pointing out that in the latter a more colloquial style is permissible. One coursebook, *English for Emails* (Turner 2013), however, is a notable exception. In this slim volume (described as a "short course") aimed at B1/B2 level learners of English, various different levels of formality, for example of salutations, are discussed (*ibid.*: 9) and many exercises call for the learners to rephrase a formal email in a more colloquial style and vice versa, thus raising the learners' awareness of differences in language use in a variety of contexts.

Instead of teaching a more or less explicitly prescribed way how to write emails, coursebooks and designated instruction manuals on how to compose emails could address the heterogeneity of email communication both in form and function. In addition to raising general language awareness, it is also a suitable topic to address cultural and intercultural differences and to discuss how contextual factors such as participant relationship and status may influence communication, thus giving rise to pragmatic knowledge as well as genre and text type awareness. In addition, using email communication in the EFL classroom can foster new literacies and provide ample opportunities for collaborative learning, as outlined below.

4.1 Fostering new literacies

Lotherington and Jenson (2011: 227) ask "why is it that the interactive screen-based media of the 21st century have taken a back seat in the classroom, where print literacies continue to predominate?". They then go on to argue that "[a]ssumptions about learners, language form and format, text types, and social discourses must all be re-examined" (*ibid.*).

Being able to use computer-mediated communication is one of the aspects of new, emerging literacies, sometimes referred to as "electronic literacies" (Shetzer/ Warschauer 2000) or "digital literacies" (González-Lloret 2014). Shetzer and Warschauer (2000: 172) describe literacy as "a shifting target" and electronic literacy specifically is described as consisting of many kinds of literacies, "depending on context, purpose, and medium".

González-Lloret (2014: 39f) lists computer literacy, informational literacy, critical literacy, multimedia literacy and computer-meditated literacy as all being part of digital literacy. Computer-mediated literacy in turn is defined as "the ability to communicate effectively with others through the Internet" (*ibid.*: 40). Most learners will most likely already use some form of CMC and therefore could be thought to possess a certain amount of computer literacy and computer-mediated literacy in their L1 and possibly also the L2.

However, as so many factors shape and influence what is deemed to be 'effective' and 'appropriate' communication, raising awareness of the different linguistic and paralinguistic choices used in different forms of communication certainly remains one of the aims of every language class. Here, collaborative learning in which groups of learners with varying degrees of competence in the respective areas work together and exchange their knowledge is one way of addressing this. Similarly, collaborative learning between members of different discourse communities (i.e. EFL learners and native English speakers or in English as a Lingua Franca settings) also provides authentic communication in which both sides can experience differences in style, register and communicative strategies (for a more in-depth discussion of authenticity in language learning, see e.g. Fourie, this volume).

4.2 Fostering pragmatic and intercultural awareness

"Computer-mediated Communication and learning environments provide unprecedented opportunities for learners from different cultures to interact and collaborate" (Zhang 2013: 1215). This collaborative learning can take place in a number of different ways: it can be teacher directed, meaning that the teacher initiates the learning and shapes the form of collaboration, for example by providing instructions on how and with whom to collaborate (Macaro 1997: 136). There is, however, also the possibility for learner directed and learner generated collaboration, for example when leaners work on a task and organise their own group work or even instigate the learning themselves (*ibid.*).

As CMC is likely to play a significant part in learners' lives already, it lends itself to being incorporated in activities that aim at raising the learners' awareness of differences in communication that are shaped by the participants and evolve as the relationship between interactants changes over time. "The learning of a language should recognise how language use identifies the individual as a participant to varying degrees in overlapping and differently structured discourse communities" (Corbett 2003: 93) and exchanging and analysing emails could be one way of providing learners with authentic examples of such language use. Alcón Soler (2008: 186) highlights using computer-mediated communication, and email communication in particular, in the classroom as one of the "potential environments in which pragmatic learning can occur". With regard to pragmatic learning, Limberg (2015: 280) states that

> Awareness of one's own and others' cultural norms, habits, and practices is a necessary condition for gaining pragmatic competence. In order to explore the differences that exist between native and target culture, it is first of all important to be aware of learners' communicative needs, social norms, and cultural practices.

These "cultural norms, habits, and practices" (*ibid*.) do not only apply to geographically distinct language communities or globalised discourse communities, but also to local organisational culture, for example in a business context (see e.g. Gimenez 2002).

4.3 Integrating emails in a collaborative language learning classroom

There are many ways in which to utilise email communication in an EFL classroom that go beyond coursebook exercises. These fall broadly into two categories: writing email messages as part of authentic writing tasks, for example as part of a task in a Task-Based Language Teaching (TBLT) context, or discussing email writing and examining emails that leaners have sent or received in the past to initiate a reflection on appropriateness and context of language use.

4.3.1 Email for out-of-class communication

Bloch (2002: 131f) argues that communicating with the teacher outside the classroom setting allows learners to experience a form of communication not normally present in a traditional classroom:

> The students in this study seemed to intuitively understand that email is more than just language; the ability to send and receive messages provides a writing context where relationships can be negotiated through written language. Thus, to be successful email users

requires more than simple fluency; it always requires the ability to both express oneself using a variety of language forms and rhetorical strategies as well as to know when it is appropriate to use these different forms.

Apart from communicating with classmates and tutors outside the classroom, another scenario that is widely advocated is that of establishing email links with other learners, ideally matching native and target language in a tandem or so-called keypal projects (the electronic equivalent of penpal schemes; see e.g. Dudeney/Hockly 2007, chapter 5; see also Eisenmann, this volume; for a more detailed discussion of learner preferences for different online tools, see Schenker/Poorman, this volume). These would allow them not only to engage in authentic communication, but also provides an opportunity to exchange information about a number of topics. When learners engage in keypal projects and the correspondence is maintained for any length of time, then they also may have the opportunity to witness how they develop their own Community of Practice and may thus be able to reflect on how the email communication evolves over time and is shaped by, among other things, by communicative immediacy or distance. In order to raise pragmatic awareness, keypal schemes should not solely be relegated to out-of-classroom activities, but need to be appropriately integrated and scaffolded during class time (see below, section 4.3.2. and also Legenhausen, this volume).

Dudeney/Hockly (2007: 65) add that email can also be used as a collaborative writing tool outside the classroom: "For example, in groups, learners are asked to produce a story based on a painting, with Learner 1 starting the story, which is then forwarded to Learner 2, who adds to the story […], and so on".

4.3.2 Reflecting on appropriateness

Discussing authentic emails during class and thus scaffolding the potential out-of-class communication, is another option. Younger EFL learners may already be well versed in communicating using social networking sites or other means of communicating online and may transfer the strategies used in these contexts to email messages. This, however, may be perceived as impolite, as outlined above, particularly in a context where there is a perceived difference in status between sender and recipient or a high degree of communicative distance.

Students could also exchange emails with their classmates and then exchange their perception of these messages to facilitate a classroom discussion on the difference between intended meaning and perceived meaning of these messages, highlighting that emails lack some of the cues available in face-to-face communication. The different strategies that are employed to overcome this could then be discussed, for example including the many different functions emoticons can have in CMC (see e.g. Skovholt *et al.* 2014). In this context, the use of guides on how to write emails could also be used, for example to initiate a discussion on what constitutes an appropriate greeting in different contexts, comparing differences in cultural preference where applicable and the context-dependence of any kind of communication (see also Bloch 2001), regardless of whether it is CMC of not.

Economidou-Kogetsidis (2015) suggests the use of examples of appropriate and inappropriate emails by both NS and NNS speakers which are compared, evaluated and discussed. She (*ibid.*) also advocates discussing different politeness norms depending on recipient status and cultural norms in the L1 and L2 culture, leading to a discussion about language, sometimes referred to as *languaging*: "Languaging about language is one of the ways to gain new knowledge about a language or consolidate existing L2 knowledge" (Storch 2011: 284).

For more advanced learners, for example in a tertiary education context, Koch and Oesterreicher's model (see above, section 3) can be used to explain and discuss the cline of conceptually oral and conceptually written language, leading to heightened register awareness.

4.3.3 *Email tasks*

In a Task-Based Language Teaching (TBLT) context, email communication can be included to create tasks that necessitate the use of the L2. González-Lloret and Ortega (2014b: 5) in their introduction to a volume on technology-mediated TBLT stress that tasks should be chosen "so that new technologies can be chosen and yoked with real 'tasks', rather than being chosen as mere translations or extensions of exercises and activities of various kinds into computer platforms". They go on to argue that "technology in itself has created a whole set of real-world target tasks" (*ibid.*: 6) and list corresponding by email among these.

For example, emails can be used to communicate with other people (either from the target language culture or with other participants using English as a lingua franca) to learn more about the respective cultures of the participants. Here, the main focus of the task is not on the language itself, but rather the content. Investigating different email messaging conventions in different countries and comparing these with the learners' own practices is another potential task that could be incorporated in a TBLT classroom.

5. Conclusion

Email communication is multi-facetted and ubiquitous, but also not without challenges for both inexperienced L1 and L2 users of English. Because of the array of factors that influence the language used in emails, effective and context-appropriate email communication skills have to be fostered, either by explicit instruction or exposure to authentic email communication in a variety of settings or a combination of both.

Discussing email communication in the EFL classroom is a way of addressing several goals of communicative language teaching, among them engaging in authentic communication, providing learners with language in a variety of different contexts and raising pragmatic awareness. By incorporating this authentic form of communication both inside and outside the classroom, discussions about language, adding to the learners' knowledge of register and appropriateness, can be initiated. By engaging in keypal projects that allow learners to communicate with their peers in the L2, their sensitivity to the difference of language used in different Communities of Practice can be enhanced and they are given a first-hand opportunity to observe how communication evolves over time. And in general, composing emails as part of larger tasks, whether in a TBLT setting or not, is an authentic writing task that hones many different skills, one of them being writing in the L2.

6. Acknowledgements

I would like to thank the anonymous reviewers, the series editors and my colleague Tim Parke for valuable comments on drafts of this chapter.

Dieses Kapitel gibt einen Überblick über die Möglichkeiten des Einsatzes von Emails als eine Form der computervermittelten Kommunikation im fremdsprachlichen Englischunterricht. Da es sich bei Emails nicht um eine einheitliche Textsorte handelt, stellen sie für Fremdsprachenlernende eine Herausforderung dar. Um erfolgreich zu kommunizieren, benötigen die Lernenden nicht nur fremdsprachliches Wissen, sondern auch Wissen über die Gepflogenheiten der Emailkommunikation in den jeweiligen Sprachgemeinschaften. Diese hängen wiederum stark vom Kontext und der Beziehung der Interaktionspartner untereinander ab. Dieses Wissen können Fremdsprachenlernende durch kollaboratives Lernen und authentische Interaktion erwerben, in dem sie selbst an Emailkommunikation in der Fremdsprache teilnehmen und/oder über sie reflektieren und dies ggf. durch weitere Unterrichtsaktivitäten ergänzt werden.

Veronica dal Bianco & Lawrie Moore-Walter
University of Applied Sciences Burgenland, Austria

Tools and Collaborative Tasks for Enabling Language Learning in a Blended Learning Environment

This chapter describes how technology can effectively be used to facilitate collaboration among students and teachers on blended learning language courses. More specifically, it focuses on

- *how collaboration encourages students to construct meaning together and take responsibility for their learning*
- *practical examples of collaborative tasks for pairs of students, small groups, and the whole class, where the teacher is more, less or not at all involved*
- *the tools that we have employed to enable these tasks to be done on our blended language courses.*

1. Introduction and context

1.1 Context

The teaching context is one in which students are doing a 2-year, blended learning, part-time Master's degree in Knowledge Management at a university of applied sciences in Austria. During these two years, the students must take one 50-hour Professional English course per semester. All courses are hosted on a virtual learning environment (VLE). By encouraging collaboration with the help of technology during the online phases of the blended learning language courses, the overall aim is to provide students with meaningful opportunities to develop their language skills and collaboratively build their knowledge base.

1.2 Advantages and disadvantages of blended learning

From the student's perspective, blended learning offers a clear advantage in that students are more able to determine when and where learning takes place. Nearly all of our students work full-time in addition to pursuing their master's degree. Additionally, many of them travel distances of up to 100km to reach the university; as such, the blended learning component of the course allows them to reduce by half the number of times they commute to the university.

A further advantage of blended learning is that it embodies mobile learning, i.e. learning inside and outside of the classroom using various devices (Hockly 2013: 80). We have found that use of mobile devices for language learning can also emerge without advice or assistance from the educator; in fact, learners are often the main initiators of technology in the classroom. We find it is the role of the teacher not only to encourage the use of technology and mobile learning, but also to actively hand to students the ownership of technology inside and outside of the classroom. Doing so heightens self-direction, which in turn increases motivation. Feedback (Dal-Bianco 2012) has shown that the majority of our students are highly motivated, often spending more time working on their English than required.

A potential drawback to blended learning is that students might feel that tasks conducted during online learning phases are disconnected from face-to-face tasks. Students show a clear preference (84%) for tasks to be integrated through a flipped classroom model whereby online tasks either prepare students for future face-to-face tasks or where the online tasks reflect on and build upon the content of a previous face-to-face session (Moore-Walter/Dal-Bianco 2015).

1.3 Role of collaboration in blended learning

Collaboration encourages students to construct meaning together and take responsibility for their own learning as well as for that of their peers (Dooly 2008: 21). By collaborating on tasks and conducting them together using English, students communicate resourcefully and negotiate meaning. Illes (2012: 510) writes:

> In order for learners to practise meaning making and the concomitant problem solving by activating their capacity, teachers have to create conditions that force students to go beyond conformity and actively participate in interpretative procedures. Language learning tasks should therefore present challenges that lead learners to make the extra effort to crack the code and find solutions that do not necessarily offer themselves in everyday interactions.

Blended learning is such a solution as an element of creativity is required to do tasks in an online environment as opposed to the traditional classroom, where gestures and facial expressions can help to convey meaning. We have, therefore, found that students need to be more exact in negotiating meaning due to this as well as to the asynchrony of some tasks. This necessary specificity in language expression results in increased creativity, detail and accuracy when communicating online.

When collaborating on blended learning tasks, students support and scaffold one another, providing input and creating content with each other. Instead of relying only on the teacher to set learning outcomes, students can also create their own sub-goals within the framework of the task and can work together to achieve these goals. In addition, we find that collaboration in blended learning settings requires even more learner autonomy as the teacher is not physically present to oversee and direct learning. Thus, it is especially important that students find the tasks engaging and perceive collaboration as beneficial/a win-win situation. In our experience, students working alone are more likely to neglect tasks or assignments, but students working collaboratively are reluctant to let their peers down.

1.4 Role of technology in supporting collaboration

Technology-supported learning includes using apps, blogs, wikis, social media tools, websites etc. to facilitate learning in and outside of the classroom. The content is typically user-generated, its creation involving a high degree of interactivity and user feedback, characteristics that are commonly associated with collaborative learning (Dooly 2008: 22). Consequently, technology can play an important role in supporting collaboration, especially in the online phases of a blended learning course. However, pedagogy must be the driver: "As with any technology, it is not the technology itself that enhances teaching or learning, but rather the use to which it is put" (Hockly 2013: 82). Further aspects that should not be overlooked are accessibility, inclusivity and technical skills, i.e. Do all students have the hardware/software to access these sites/tools? Is broadband internet access available? Do learners have the skills and expertise to use the technology effectively? The latter will be addressed in more detail in "The Role of the Teacher". Nevertheless, we have found that technology, successfully employed, can be highly motivating, but it has to work. If this is not the case, e.g. the tool is not user-friendly or internet access is unreliable, then collaboration and task completion take longer, which 25% of our students mentioned as a drawback of technology and thus demotivating (Moore-Walter/Dal-Bianco 2015).

1.5 Role of the teacher in online collaborative language learning

It is generally agreed that teacher role depends on the learning context and that there has been a steady shift to it becoming more facilitative (Dal-Bianco/Mac-Sween 2008: 3682). In addition, teachers should be doing their utmost to develop learners' critical thinking skills, which can be achieved by actively engaging students in the learning process and encouraging them to take responsibility for their learning (Dooly 2008: 21). It follows, therefore, that the teacher is no longer the sole knowledge/content imparter, i.e. "the sage on the stage", but rather the "guide on the side", i.e. a facilitator of learning. In our teaching context and experience, there are three main areas where support/facilitation/scaffolding by the teacher is paramount to ensure that collaboration is successful so that learning can take place. These are described below, and are also mentioned in "Description of practice" in connection with the corresponding collaborative task and tool.

Prior to using technology, teachers need to make informed decisions about which tools can be used to promote collaborative learning, always bearing in mind the desired learning outcomes. In addition, teachers must acquire the expertise and digital skills so that they can guide students to use these tools and to convince them of their benefit. During collaborative tasks, the teacher's role is then to monitor and to troubleshoot if technological problems hinder students' from doing tasks. In our experience, setting up a Help forum where students can report problems like this (as well as problems with task) enables support to be provided quickly either by the teacher or by classmates.

The second area concerns forum contributions. To ensure that communication is effective, students need to be made aware of what constitutes a quality forum post before doing collaborative tasks. We have found that giving students explicit tips and providing language starters to be helpful, e.g. "When responding, try to go beyond a "yes" or "no" or "I agree". Give advice, ask questions to clarify something you're unsure about, suggest alternatives, extend on an idea, offer a resource link for more information, or otherwise engage with one another's comments. Useful starters that you can use are: I was intrigued by…; When you mentioned …; it made me wonder….; Have you thought of…; What about…?" Students also need to be told how many postings are required, whether their postings will be assessed, and if yes, what will be assessed – collaboration, content and/or language. Last but not least, they need to know how their contributions effect their overall grade. Hence, the teacher's role initially is to inform and guide students; during tasks, it shifts to monitoring, facilitating and providing appropriate assistance and feedback.

The last area deals with training students on how to provide quality peer feedback, e.g. on each other's written assignments, presentations etc. According to Morgan (2005: 29), this includes explaining why and how peer reviewing can benefit students, and then giving students several opportunities to review each other's work. Since this is a time-consuming task, we have found that giving students credit for their reviews improves the quality, which is why we also provide models of sample reviews for a specific activity (e.g. of students' thesis abstracts) that would receive full points, partial points and no points. In addition, students can be given a rubric that clearly outlines which aspects they should focus on in the feedback. Once again, the teacher's role is to guide, scaffold and to provide timely feedback.

1.6 Drawbacks of collaboration

Although we are convinced that collaborative tasks can enhance learning and benefit all involved learners, we do occasionally encounter learners who resist collaborating with their classmates. This can be for a variety of reasons, but our students cite the fact that it takes longer to do tasks or because some group members shirk duties as key demotivating factors when collaborating (Moore-Walter/Dal-Bianco 2015). There are several ways to counteract this, the first being to clearly communicate the goals and learning outcomes of collaborative tasks. If students know why they are conducting a task, they will be more motivated (Egbert 2015) While achieving a higher grade is sometimes a motivating factor for students, only 3.3% of our students mentioned that it is the main reason why they collaborate to increase their grade (Moore-Walter/Dal-Bianco 2015). In addition to grades assigned by the tutor, students can be responsible for allocating participation points to each other. For example, each student has 5 points to divide up among the members of his or her group, with only the teacher knowing how the points are distributed. The points a learner receives constitute part of that learner's overall mark for the assignment.

Another drawback to setting collaborative tasks during online phases of blended learning courses, this time from a language learning perspective, is that it is difficult to ensure that learners are working and communicating in English. It is possible to have students record themselves as proof that they speak English when collaborating, but we find this inconsistent with self-directed learning and learner autonomy. We can, therefore, only remind students to take advantage of this language learning opportunity and encourage them to use English rather than L1 –at least for the majority of their communication. We have mature learners who are mostly highly-motivated learners; however, it could be problematic to guarantee that younger, less-motivated learners speak English during collaboration.

2. Description of practice

The following section outlines a variety of collaborative tasks and tools that we have included in the face-to-face and online phases of our blended learning language courses. See table 1 for an overview of the tools described in this section. As mentioned in the Introduction, our students are doing a Master's in Knowledge Management, which is why our ESP courses utilize materials and focuses on skills relating to this field. Our descriptions of practice are, therefore, embedded in this learning context. At the end of each task, we have also included suggestions for how it can be adapted. The section starts by looking at tasks where students collaboratively engage with course content, and then moves on to tasks with more of a language & skills (productive & receptive) focus. However, since activities sometimes have more than one aim, there can be a certain degree of overlap. The section ends with tasks where collaboration is between teacher and student.

Table 1: Overview of tools

Tool	Task
Flipped classroom	
Skype, forum, chat, online lesson, iVocalize	Students prepare as a group for face-to-face activities
Skype, forum, wiki	Students reflect on activities and content from a recent face-to-face session
Peer feedback	
Moodle workshop, forum, Vocaroo, MailVu	Peer review of assignments
Content creation	
Padlet, Pinterest	Collaborative documentation of resources
WeVideo, YouTube, PodOmatic, audioBoom, Vocaroo	Creating a videoed news broadcast
wiki plugin for VLE	Creating a Wiki
Vocabulary acquisition	
Quizlet, VLE glossary	Documenting vocabulary collaboratively
Kahoot, Open Broadcaster	Interactive quizzes
Wordle, forum	Creating word clouds
Pronunciation training	
Dragon Dictation app	Dialogue dictation
Speaking tasks	
Skype; forum; VLE	Online meetings
Ah Counter app	Uhms and Ahs
Collaborative writing	
Google Docs, Lucidpress	Collaborative report writing
Edublogs, Blogger, blog plugin on VLE	Collaborative blog writing
Developing listening skills	
Lyrics Training	Competitive Lyrics training
Vocaroo or audioBoom; blog; wiki; VLE	Collaborative dictogloss
TED website; Skype; Quizlet; Wordle; VLE	Collaborative listening
Developing reading skills	
Forum; VLE	Jigsaw reading
Forum; VLE	"Save the last word for me"
Forum; VLE	Academic reading circles (ARC)
Teacher-student collaboration	
Jing, Vocaroo, audio recorders, mobile phones	Teacher-student feedback

2.1 The flipped classroom

We approach the flipped classroom model either as a preparation for an upcoming face-to-face lesson or as a follow-up to a previous face-to-face lesson. In a survey of our students, a clear preference (72%) for tasks which follow-up on the previous face-to-face session was indicated (Moore-Walter/Dal-Bianco 2015). However, during informal feedback with students, several expressed a desire to be better prepared for in class content, especially when that content was new to them. This could be done through assigning tasks that allow students to acquaint themselves with a new topic before the face-to-face session.

Table 2: Task: Students prepare as a group for face-to-face activities

Task: Students prepare as a group for face-to-face activities	
Aim	To free up classroom time in order to create opportunity for fluency practice; to promote team learning; to familiarise students with course content
Tool	Skype, forum, chat, online lesson, iVocalize
Example	Content which needs to fulfil curriculum requirements, e.g. change management or information systems, might not be familiar to students. The teacher uploads input material to the VLE; students read through the material and make notes for discussion. Student-student interaction –see "Developing Reading Skills" for examples of collaborative tasks– can take place via Skype (in pre-determined small groups), in a forum or through a chat function (whole class), or live in the ensuing face-to-face session.
Adaptations	Instead of the content being teacher-generated, the students can do research into the topic in order to gather their thoughts. Students can divide the topic into subareas, with each group doing research on the subarea. Students introduce their research on a forum or in an online meeting room such as iVocalize. Alternatively, groups can present their findings during the face-to-face session as an information gap exercise.

Table 3: Task: Students reflect on activities and content from a recent face-to-face session

Task: Students reflect on activities and content from a recent face-to-face session	
Aim	To promote reflective learning, to follow-up on content
Tool	Skype, forum, wiki
Example	Face-to-face content is related to a specific topic from the curriculum, e.g. leadership and motivation. In class, students discuss their thoughts about the topic and generate a definition with best practice examples from their experience and/or knowledge. During the subsequent online phase, students work in pairs or small groups to do further research into the topic, expanding on or adapting best practice examples and supporting their findings with academic sources. Coordination for research is done via Skype. Students then post their findings on a forum, including relevant implications for their classmates. Subsequently, students are required to respond to other postings with questions about those postings. As previously mentioned in "Role of the teacher", we outline early on in the programme what constitutes a quality forum post to avoid superficial postings, such as "I agree". Finally, students receive a mark based on their original research and post as well as on how thought-provoking and relevant their responses to other postings are.
Adaptations	This task can also be used for business skills such as emailing or for language work such as rules of tenses. For emailing, students would bring in emails they have written and received and discuss in class how successful or unsuccessful these were. Together, students generate a check list of what makes an effective email. Online, students do further research into the topic and post their findings in a wiki. Thus, the class as a whole develops a list of key phrases and content guidelines for emailing. For language work, students are given in class examples of e.g. the present perfect in a text and need to work out the rules. They research online and find further examples of the present perfect in authentic sources. These are posted in a forum, and students are encouraged to create quizzes on the VLE, e.g. Moodle quiz, for each other to do.

2.2 Peer feedback

In our experience, many students find peer feedback (on task, skills and/or language) a highly beneficial, collaborative activity. 63% of our learners think that their peers can provide good ideas, with many learners commenting that they appreciate a different point of view, especially one that is not tied to a teacher-assigned grade. However, 12% of our students feel that they do not always receive good quality feedback or that their classmates do not have useful ideas to contribute (Moore-Walter/Dal-Bianco 2015). As mentioned in "Role of the teacher", this makes it essential to explain the rationale for incorporating peer review and to train students to do this.

Table 4: Task: Peer review of assignments

Task: Peer review of assignments	
Aim	To encourage students to learn from one another, to reduce tutor marking time
Tool	Moodle workshop, forum, Vocaroo, MailVu
Example	Students individually create a written assignment, for example a letter of motivation. They upload the first draft of their letter to e.g. a forum or a Moodle workshop, where it is viewable by their reviewer. The reviewer, following a rubric/marking scheme, provides comments and suggestions for improvement. The original writer can accept these ideas, but is not forced to or can write back to their reviewer to clarify unclear points. However, for peer review to run smoothly, the teacher needs to be involved in coordination. It is useful to create a deadline for the first draft of the assignment so that all students have a text when the peer review phase starts, avoiding a situation where one partner is ready to review and be reviewed, but the other is not. Furthermore, as already mentioned, the teacher needs to provide guidance on quality peer reviews and/or oversee students in creating their own expectations of quality reviews. While a good deal of supervision by the teacher is initially required, students quickly become comfortable with the process; we start with a low-stakes peer review on a task such as this letter of motivation and lead up to the high-stakes task of having students review a classmate's master thesis abstract. Peer review is especially effective for abstract writing, as students are often able to review the content of classmates' abstracts better than the teacher can, because the students are all equally engrossed in the research and can provide insightful suggestions.
Adaptations	Peer review also works well for oral tasks, e.g. a recorded presentation posted on a forum. In this case, students can give oral or written feedback, following a marking scheme as mentioned above. Students record their presentations and reviews using MailVu, a video recording tool, or Vocaroo, a voice recording tool. We encourage students to take notes on what they will include in their feedback, but not to script it and then read it aloud, which reduces fluency.

2.3 Content creation

Content creation in this context entails collaboration with the goal of conducting a task and producing content; English is the medium of communication but not the focus. Our students are motivated to conduct tasks together because they allow authentic communication and give students a chance to build confidence in speaking English (Moore-Walter/Dal-Bianco 2015).

Table 5: Task: Collaborative documentation of resources

Task: Collaborative documentation of resources	
Aim	To encourage peer teaching, to encourage learners to take responsibility for their learning
Tool	Padlet, Pinterest
Example	Groups of 3–4 students are assigned the task of leading an in-class discussion on a topic of their choice. After deciding on the topic, students conduct research and then document sources and ideas on a shared Padlet wall or Pinterest board. Each group member can add, delete and organise content; the result is a visual outline of the discussion that they will lead in class. After the discussion, the groups can share their Padlet/Pinterest sites with the rest of the class, further supporting peer-teaching.
Adaptations	Padlet and Pinterest can also be used to create a list of favourite language learning websites, articles, or videos, e.g. TED talks. The teacher or an assigned student creates a Padlet wall or Pinterest board where all students can post. Students choose a relevant TED Talk that they think will benefit their classmates. They post a link to the talk, including a short list of benefits of the talk. As a follow-up assignment, students watch a few of the talks on the list and vote for the video they find most useful. Another use of Padlet is for collaboratively documenting ideas students come up with when brainstorming for e.g. a group project or presentation.

Table 6: Task: Creating a videoed news broadcast

Task: Creating a videoed news broadcast	
Aim	To reflect upon past learning, to provide practice of vocabulary and functional language; to provide fluency practice
Tool	WeVideo, YouTube, PodOmatic, audioBoom, Vocaroo
Example	In the final semester of the programme, our students create a news broadcast in which they highlight their learning experiences over the previous four semesters. Their goal is to create a video for incoming students on knowledge management related topics and as well as tips and tricks for succeeding in the programme. Before class/online, groups brainstorm ideas e.g. using Padlet, on what they would like to include in the broadcast; they are allowed time in the face-to-face sessions to collaboratively discuss their ideas, prepare their contributions and video each other and the university. During the following online session, they edit their videos and prepare the final version to show on the last face-to-face session of the programme. WeVideo has powerful collaboration tools, but these are only available with the premium version. Our students often publish on a private channel YouTube.

| Adaptations | Instead of a video, students can create a podcast using tools such as PodOmatic, audioBoom or Vocaroo. They can combine different audio files to create one final podcast featuring different learner perspectives on the programme. |

Table 7: Task: Creating a Wiki

Task: Creating a Wiki	
Aim	To create a knowledge base
Tool	Wiki plugin for VLE
Example	Early in the programme, students are assigned the task of creating a collaborative knowledge base about a topic related to the study programme, in our case knowledge management. Groups can choose an area to research, e.g. communities of practice, intellectual capital or information theory. The groups research their areas, selecting key information and relevant links to compile on a wiki page. The contents are viewable and editable by all members of the class and a peer review process throughout the study program encourages learners to edit content as the students become more familiar with the material. Our students find the wiki a valuable resource, referring back to it as the programme progresses.
Adaptations	A wiki can be used to document language learning, with a separate page for each of the skills and language (vocabulary, grammar, pronunciation). For example, each time students learn a grammar rule, it can be added to the wiki as a type of online filing system. A group of students takes responsibility for an area, e.g. reading, and that group makes sure that the wiki page is updated each time reading is discussed in class or students learn about a reading subskill. To ensure that students do not become specialists in just one area of English, groups can swap which wiki page they maintain each semester.

2.4 Vocabulary acquisition

Since the 1970s, there has been a gradual transition in language instruction from a strong emphasis on grammar to an increasingly important role of lexis in communicative competency (Thornbury 2002: 14). In informal feedback and needs analysis with our learners, a common complaint from students is that they consider their lexical range to be inadequate. The following tasks address this issue.

Table 8: Task: Documenting vocabulary collaboratively

Task: Documenting vocabulary collaboratively	
Aim	To expand students' lexical range
Tool	Quizlet, VLE glossary
Example	Students can document vocabulary from face-to-face and online sessions in a class Quizlet set. Terms can be uploaded, copied and pasted or manually entered. A definition or a translation can be provided or chosen from a list based on previous users' entries. We assign a student or group of students to be responsible for entering that session's vocabulary terms. Games and quizzes can be created from the terms, which are then viewable to the public or to a select group of users, e.g. a class; vocabulary can be revised on desktop computers or on mobile devices with the Quizlet app. With the paid teacher's version, the tutor can view class progress, including which terms are problematic and how often each individual class member has practiced the terms. This can be used as a basis for class participation points during online phases.
Adaptations	A VLE glossary plug-in, e.g. Moodle glossary activity, can be used to collect relevant vocabulary terms gleaned from an extended reading task. Students read a longer text and add useful terms to the glossary, including a definition or context example. The glossary can be expanded throughout the study programme to create a content-specific online glossary, which can be exported and given to students upon graduation.

Table 9: Task: Interactive quizzes

Task: Interactive quizzes	
Aim	To revise vocabulary, to challenge students
Tool	Kahoot, Open Broadcaster
Example	Kahoot is an interactive tool for creating quizzes which can be integrated into face-to-face instruction; with a few tweaks, Kahoot can also be used during online session. A student, pairs/groups of students or the teacher creates an initial set of multiple choice questions and projects the quiz onto the wall so that it can be seen by the class. Using mobile devices or desktop computers (e.g. in a computer lab), students (individually or in pairs/groups) enter the unique ID of the quiz (there is no need to register) and include their names so that it is clear who is ready for the quiz to begin. The questions and answers for the quiz are then projected for the whole class to see; on mobile devices, the students can choose the correct answer and submit their choices. For each question, a time limit is set and students who answer quickly get more points than slower responders. There is a leader board to see who has the overall highest points.

Tools and Collaborative Tasks for Enabling Language Learning 115

Adaptations	Kahoot is designed to be played in face-to-face settings; mobile devices do not show the quiz questions or answers, but rather a colour-coded button for selecting an answer. This design feature is meant to make the quiz more interactive; however, it makes using Kahoot in online settings less straight-forward. Using a live screencasting tool such as Open Broadcaster allows the quiz creator to capture the contents of his/her screen and stream it to a group of viewers, in this case the rest of the class. The students view the questions and answers to the quiz on their desktop devices and choose their answers with their mobile device; alternatively two browser windows can be opened so that the users can view the questions in one window and choose their answers in a second window. This is a synchronous tool, so a time must be arranged with learners to do the activity.

Table 10: Task: Creating word clouds

Task: Creating word clouds	
Aim	To document vocabulary, to introduce oneself, grammar practice, as a lead-in to a text
Tool	Wordle, forum
Example	Individually, each student writes a short text introducing themselves. This is copied and pasted into Wordle, which displays the most frequently used words (limit can be chosen) in a graphically appealing form. A link to this word cloud is posted on a forum for the rest of the class to read and who then reply (individually), formulating statements (or questions, depending on the aim of the activity) about this student, e.g. Scotland, golf are two words in the Wordle; student statement (question) –You learnt to play golf in Scotland. (or: Did you learn to play golf in Scotland?). However, students must first read each other's posts to avoid unnecessary repetition. After a specified time, the student who created the Wordle posts their original text, revealing the true facts about him or herself. One word of caution: since Wordles are stored in the cloud/on the Wordle server, students should be reminded not to include their real name or other personal information in too much detail in their Wordles.
Adaptations	Wordles can be used as a lead-in to a text or to pre-teach vocabulary. For example, the teacher creates a word cloud from a content-related text that students will be reading, and posts the URL on a forum. Individually, students clarify unknown words and post educated guesses about what the text is about. As above, they must first read each other's posts to avoid repetition. The teacher could also ask a student to document vocabulary from a lesson or text in a Wordle for the rest of the class to access online.

2.5 Pronunciation training

Although most English language learners learn English in order to communicate with other non-native speakers, and although the goal of eliminating L1 accent and achieving a native-level pronunciation has not been considered crucial for some time (Jenkins 1998: 119) our students regularly express the desire to subjectively improve their pronunciation in order to be better understood by colleagues and peers.

Table 11: Task: Dialogue dictation

Task: Dialogue dictation	
Aim	To raise awareness to pronunciation errors, to give students speaking practice
Tool	Dragon Dictation app
Example	In pairs, students write a short (approximately 2 minute) dialogue. The topic can be of their choosing with no restrictions placed by the teacher, or the teacher can assign a set of phrases around which the dialogue should be written. Using the Dragon Dictation app, the students record their dialogue. The app transcribes the dialogue into written form. The students compare the app's version of the written dialogue with their own version and highlight where the app did not understand their pronunciation. They can repeat the dialogue, altering pronunciation until the app transcribes their dialogue accurately.
Adaptations	This tool can also be used to transcribe a short negotiation or interview between two students. In this case, the speech is spontaneous and students can then read the transcript to see what was not correctly understood by the app, or look through the transcript to see if certain key phrases were included. They can also check to see which fillers they tend to use and how often –see "Uhms and Ahs" task below.

2.6 Speaking tasks

Oral discussions are a great way to develop students' speaking and listening skills and can be scheduled for the online phases of courses e.g. via Skype. Since participating in webinars is something students have to do more and more at work, online discussion is an authentic and relevant task that can incorporate speaking, listening, personalisation, content creation/review and language practice. The topics to be discussed depend obviously on the course content. The discussion itself can be in preparation for a group project or presentation. It can also be after input on, for instance, how to conduct a successful meeting (face-to-face and online) and revising/learning functional language for chairing and participating

Tools and Collaborative Tasks for Enabling Language Learning 117

in a meeting. Below is a concrete example from our blended learning courses, followed by a collaborative activity done in pairs that raises students' awareness to their use of fillers when speaking.

Table 12: Task: Online meetings

Task: Online meetings	
Aim	To encourage learners to speak and listen to each other
Tool	Skype; forum; VLE
Example	Students read an article (in class) on a course-related topic, e.g. about organisational structure and knowledge sharing, and learn some relevant word partnerships. The follow-up online task is to have a 45-minute meeting with 2 classmates (date, time, tool, persons are agreed in class) to explain how their own organisations are structured, what kind of knowledge work each person does and to discuss whether the organisation's structure lends itself to effective and efficient knowledge sharing. Students then talk about the pros and cons of having online meetings in a foreign language. During the meeting, they take notes collaboratively (Google Docs), which are edited and posted on the VLE for the other groups to read and for grading by the teacher.
Adaptations	Students record their online meeting and transcribe part collaboratively. Together, they then underline language that is good, i.e. helps to convey the message, as well as parts that caused confusion. The latter is analysed as to what went wrong and subsequently improvements are suggested.

Table 13: Task: Uhms and Ahs

Task: Uhms and Ahs	
Aim	To raise awareness to words and sounds used as fillers when speaking
Tool	Ah Counter app
Example	Students download the app to their mobile phones and individually prepare a short talk on a topic of their choice. In pairs, one person gives their talk while the other listens attentively tapping the ah button (for sounds such as ah, um or er), interjection button (for inappropriate use of words such as and, well, so, but, like, you know) or repetition button (for unnecessary repetition of e.g. I…, I…, I…, or this means…, this means… etc.). The resulting score is emailed to the student, who should try to improve his/her score by repeating the activity a few more times. Students then swop roles.
Adaptations	The Dragon Dictation app could also be used to raise awareness to fillers used/overused when speaking –see "Pronunciation training".

2.7 Collaborative writing

Storch distinguishes between cooperative writing and collaborative writing. In cooperative writing, students divide tasks and roles for a written task and each student completes his or her own section, editing together at the end. In contrast to this, collaborative writing encourages learners to actively write together and negotiate at all stages of the writing process (Storch 2013: 2–3). Hence, meaning is actively created together and transposed to the written form.

Table 14: Task: Collaborative report writing

Task: Collaborative report writing	
Aim	To encourage truly collaborative writing
Tool	Google Docs, Lucidpress
Example	In our experience, students' first reaction to group report writing is to divide up tasks. In order to discourage this, we allow time in class for students to write their reports together instead of assigning the report writing for homework as is often the case. This enables the teacher to monitor writing and ensure collaboration. Students verbally compose their text before creating the written version. During the following online session, students edit the report using Google Docs' collaborative, synchronous editing function.
Adaptations	Rather than a report, groups can write articles and create an online newsletter using Lucidpress. The articles are written in class, posted online, then peer edited by a different group.

Table 15: Task: Collaborative blog writing

Task: Collaborative blog writing	
Aim	To develop writing skills
Tool	Edublogs, Blogger, blog plugin on VLE
Example	A class blog is created with Edublogs or Blogger. Students think of interview questions that they would like to ask each other. For a get-to-know-each-other activity the questions can be personal, e.g. "What did you do last weekend?", while for a reflective activity, the questions can be more academic, e.g. "What is the most valuable lesson you learned from the guest lecturer in the Knowledge Management Strategies course?" The first student online posts his/her question; the next student online must respond to the first question, then post their own question, creating response-question chain.

Adaptations	Instead of questions and answers, students can write the first half of a sentence which is to be completed by the next person to visit the blog. An example is Student A: "Your favourite leisure activity is…" Student B "reading novels. The best movie you've ever seen is…" Student C: "Casablanca. The place you want to go on holiday is…" and so on.

2.8 Developing listening skills

Our learners often listen to songs or watch TV shows in English. While this is certainly enjoyable, it does not always lead to active learning. In order to support learning, tasks need to be not only enjoyable, but must also encourage learners to focus on understanding and gaining knowledge (Nation/Newton 2009: 3–4). The following task helps learners to concentrate on more thorough understanding.

Table 16: Task: Competitive Lyrics training

Task: Competitive Lyrics training	
Aim	To encourage learners to listen for detail
Tool	Lyrics Training
Example	Lyrics Training is a website where students can listen to songs and type in missing lyrics in a gapfill-like task. Our students have turned this into a collaborative task by creating Lyrics Training parties during online phases of the course, i.e. they get together and take turns typing in lyrics. Points are given to students who complete the lyrics of a song accurately.
Adaptations	Teams of students can practice songs on the website during online phases and take part in an in-class competition wherein teams of students complete the lyrics, with one student typing and the others giving answers to the missing lyrics.

Table 17: Task: Collaborative dictogloss

Task: Collaborative dictogloss	
Aim	To encourage learners to listen for detail; to introduce language; to practise language
Tool	Vocaroo or audioBoom; blog, wiki, VLE

Example	Dictogloss is normally a classroom activity in which the teacher reads out a short text that the learners (individually; then in pairs/groups) try to reconstruct. Hence, it combines listening, collaboration and writing. On blended learning courses, this can be done in the online phase, either in preparation for or as a follow-up to a specific language focus (grammar, vocabulary, functional language). The teacher makes a voice recording of the text, e.g. using Vocaroo or audioBoom, and posts the link to the listening on the VLE. Individually, students listen and reconstruct the text. After a pre-determined number of listening attempts, a learner (first come, first served) posts her/his version on a blog or wiki on the VLE. Using their reconstructed texts, the other students edit and supplement till collaboratively they have reconstructed the text. Finally, the teacher posts the tape script for comparison, and clarifies (online or in the following face-to-face session) language that was problematic.
Adaptations	Rather than the teacher recording a text, a relevant listening from the class course book or the internet can be used.

Table 18: Task: Collaborative listening

Task: Collaborative listening	
Aim	To encourage learners to listen for gist & detail
Tool	TED website, Skype, Quizlet, Wordle, VLE
Example	Our students very much enjoy listening to TED talks. So, how can listening to the talks on this website (or any other listening source, for that matter) be done collaboratively? One way is to initially select/agree upon a specific talk (can be done by the teacher, a student, or a pair/small group of students). While listening (individually), the learners take notes listing the main points as well as useful vocabulary and phrases, which are expanded after a second listening. Students (3–4) then have a Skype meeting at a pre-determined time to share what they understood, as well as to discuss how they coped with the listening, e.g. what helped or hindered them. As a follow-up and to consolidate learning, students write a short summary, compile a vocabulary glossary (e.g. Quizlet) or one student makes a word cloud (e.g. Wordle) of useful terms. These are posted on a forum, blog or wiki on the VLE for the other groups to view.
Adaptations	After listening, students can consult the tape script, highlight what they noted down, and then discuss and compare in a Skype meeting how much they really were able to comprehend. Another adaptation involves students noting down e.g. three things they learnt and found particularly interesting/one thing they did not understand and want to. Sharing, comparing and clarifying these aspects is then the focus of the online discussion.

2.9 Developing reading skills

Our academic students are often unfamiliar with a top-down approach to reading wherein a general overview of the text is attained before delving into more detail about the text content. Students often want to understand every word; Silberstein stresses the need for learners to be able to "sustain ambiguity" when confronted with an unfamiliar term. The first task helps students to become more comfortable with understanding the gist of a text rather than specific content. The other tasks encourage a more detailed analysis and interpretation of a text.

Table 19: Task: Jigsaw reading

Task: Jigsaw reading	
Aim	To encourage students to use a top-down approach to reading; to facilitate peer-teaching
Tool	Forum, VLE
Example	Jigsaw reading is a well-known activity in which a longer text is divided up amongst a group of students. Students read and summarize their section of the text, presenting their summary to the group. In this way, students get an overview of the text without needing to read it in its entirety. We choose enough subject-specific texts so that there is one text for each group of 5 students. Each text is then divided into 5 parts; one part for each member of each group. Hence, with a class of 20 students, there would be four articles being read. The students have a week to read their section and to write a short summary to post in a forum created for their article. After all summaries have been posted, the groups compile the summaries into a longer document, proofreading to eliminate any discrepancies or repetition of information. The final summaries of the four articles are made available on the VLE to the whole class. We encourage the learners to reflect on the key information extrapolated from each of the articles so that they realise they can learn even if they do not understand or even have access to all of a text.
Adaptations	Instead of reading, students listen to different audio files or videos or to different parts of the same (longer) listening.

Table 20: Task: "Save the last word for me"

Task: "Save the last word for me"	
Aim	To encourage learners to engage with complex reading texts and with each other
Tool	Forum, VLE
Example	This task was designed by McDonald *et al.* (2012) to facilitate group interpretation of a complex text, and adapted by deNoyelles, Zydney, and Seo (2014) for an online learning environment. After reading the same text, half of the class (6–7 people) is asked to post (individually) a short excerpt from the text that he/she thinks is important or complex on a discussion forum, without explaining why. The remaining students read the posts and respond saying why they think the student chose this part of the text and what it could mean. At the end of the activity (dates have to be set for each part of the activity), the learner who initially selected the excerpt explains their interest in it and summarises what they have learnt from reading their peers' interpretations, hereby having the "Last word". Students reverse roles the next time the activity is done.
Adaptations	Interpretation of a text passage (by half the class) could be done as a lead-in to students reading the article, and vice versa.

Table 21: Task: Academic reading circles (ARC)

Task: Academic reading circles (ARC)	
Aim	To enable students to gain a deeper understanding of a text by collaborating
Tool	Forum, VLE

Example	ARC is an approach to reading based on the premise that students can achieve a deeper understanding of a text by working on it collaboratively rather than individually (Seburn 2015: 42). It has been piloted successfully at Toronto University on reading and writing foundation courses for undergraduates. There are three parts to ARC: 1) a common, course-related text which all students in the group (5 persons) read but depending on their 2) assigned role, from a different perspective. There are 5 roles: the leader situates the text for the group, i.e. purpose, audience, gist and bibliographic information, and incorporates the other students in their roles in the ensuing discussion; the contextualiser identifies people, places, events and does further research on these as well as on any quotes mentioned in the text; the visualizer finds information that is graphically represented, such as charts, graphs, images etc.; the connector makes connections to similar events, studies or personal experiences and explains these; and finally, the highlighter focuses on lexical items. Thus, each person adds to the understanding of the text. The third part is the follow-up group discussion, which is normally done in class and where students report back on what they discovered. Finally, each group then presents their findings to the rest of the class. The latter activities can easily be adapted for a blended learning course, whereby students first report back to their group and discuss their findings on Skype. The outcome is then documented collaboratively in a blog for the rest of the class to see.
Adaptations	The above procedure can also be used with a listening text or video.

2.10 Teacher-student collaboration

One of the disadvantages of blended and online learning is that students can feel isolated at times, which leads to higher drop-out rates (Simpson 2000: 9). We find that an occasional email or instant message to students, especially non-participators, can greatly increase motivation. Our students cited socializing and getting in touch with their peers as a benefit of online collaboration. Furthermore, positive reinforcement by the tutor was mentioned as a motivating factor for collaboration (Moore-Walter/Dal-Bianco 2015).

Table 22: Task: Teacher-student feedback

Task: Teacher-student feedback	
Aim	To motivate students, to give students feedback on task and language
Tool	Jing, Vocaroo, audio recorders, mobile phones

Example	Students (as groups or individuals) submit an assignment electronically or complete an online task for the teacher to assess. Rather than providing written feedback, the teacher gives oral feedback using voice recording software/tools or via screencasting. The latter can be done with Jing, a free screencasting tool that captures any movement on the screen and simultaneously records audio. Language errors are highlighted with the cursor while the teacher comments on the error and/or suggests improvements. The file is saved in the cloud and a link can be posted on the VLE or emailed to students. Audio feedback is highly appreciated by students, as it tends to be more detailed as well as more personal than written feedback. In a survey conducted in 2010, 75% of our students (n=44) found audio feedback to be an excellent/very helpful way of providing feedback (Dal-Bianco/MacSween 2010: 31). Screencasting, which simulates what the teacher would normally do in a face-to-face situation, but which has the added value of students being able to watch/listen to the feedback more than one time, makes it an even more effective form of giving feedback, as the following student quote exemplifies: "I think this way of giving feedback is very helpful and leading to the desired results, because it catches your ears AND eyes" (*ibid.*: 32).
Adaptations	For pure audio feedback without screencasting, Vocaroo offers free online voice recording. Feedback on task achievement can be recorded and posted on the VLE or emailed to students.

3. Discussion

A key reason why the tasks in this chapter work well is because they are meaningful and relevant to our students' needs. Nevertheless, the fact that there is grade pressure should not be underestimated from a motivational perspective. Hence, if students do not collaborate, they get a lower grade or no grade at all. The tasks we have included do not only need to take place in a blended learning context; in fact, we also use some of them in our other university courses, which are 100% face-to-face. In this case, they are assigned as homework or during self-study components of courses. We simply scale down the number of tasks assigned to students and make sure that a choice of which tasks to conduct is given. Because learner response to doing collaborative tasks on our courses has been overwhelmingly positive (87% of our learners), we have also been able to convince colleagues to try out collaborative tasks in their courses as well.

In our experience, getting in-company or language school course participants to collaborate in English outside of class time is more difficult. These learners often associate tasks on their computers with work. By setting tasks that can be done with apps on mobile phones and tablets, e.g. documenting and learning vocabulary on Quizlet, this can be circumvented. These are then often perceived as games and, as a result, participants are more likely to do them. A further idea to encourage collaboration among language course participants is to start the task during class but to stop when learners are beginning to find the activity fun. We find participants are eager to pick up where we left off in class, just to find out what happens next.

To thrive in a blended learning context, students need time to develop as self-directed and reflective learners (Macdonald 2008: 115). Therefore, we advise students to conduct a mini-SWOT analysis each time they do a task, i.e. they analyse what they found easy and what they found difficult when completing the task and why. Over the course of time, self-assessment becomes ingrained and students almost subconsciously reflect on what they do. If students keep a reflection log, they can look back on the tasks they completed over the previous semester and see their progress tracked from task to task. Reflection is something our students do not find easy to do at first, but often comment that the act of reflection was one of the most useful and thought-provoking aspects of their English instruction. The following is an example of a reflection on a listening task students conducted in the first semester of their study programme:

> In our music selection of this week, we decided for one song of Bon Jovi and one more song of Coldplay. It is a challenging exercise in the level "intermediate" with song texts in the category medium or hard. To be honest, I do not pass an exercise by the first try but it makes still fun to go on with the lyric-trainer website and I hear and read new terms and phrases.

The tutor's response to the reflection was to ask follow-up questions about why the student thinks she was not successful first time round. We find that self-assessment needs to develop over time, with later assessments becoming more perceptive.

Even though blended learning requires the teacher's physical presence for only part of the course, there is still significant hands-on involvement required by the tutor. Many of our students are participating in a blended learning context for the first time and enter the programme with the assumption that they will have 50% less work because the class is 50% online. The teacher needs to be a motivating factor, especially early in the programme when students are still adjusting to course requirements. In our experience, models of useful forum posts, regular emails to students, clearly defined tasks and deadlines as well as clear and structured assessment of tasks help to convince students of the usefulness of blended learning tasks. Without this framework, students tend to become lost and motivation falls.

As the programme proceeds, students become comfortable with their responsibilities and learner autonomy increases. We find that our course evaluations improve significantly in the second semester, with students making comments such as "best class at the university", "Thank you. I can't believe I enjoy English lessons."

4. Conclusion

Collaborative tasks utilizing technology to facilitate the learning process can enhance language learning in a blended environment, but only as long as tasks are effectively designed, implemented and scaffolded by the teacher. Paramount is, however, the importance of considering pedagogy before technology. Students value technology but only when it adds to their learning, not when it is used with no apparent benefit. Likewise, collaboration –it is not a means to an end but should add to the learning experience. As previously mentioned, some of the tasks and/or tools we have described are inspired by our students, which leads to higher motivation and engagement (Martinez 2008: 117; Dörnyei/Csizér 1998: 217). However, we have found that while students often have ideas as to which tasks and sources they would like to use, they are not always aware of how to use them collaboratively without guidance by the teacher.

When we asked our students about what motivates them to work collaboratively for English, 75% chose the answer, I can learn from classmates, 50% that it reduces workload and 52% that it improves their English (Moore-Walter/Dal-Bianco 2015). In addition, 92% of the students felt that collaborative tasks are more effective if there is time in class to work on the task, something that can easily be organized in a blended learning course. However, although this implies a generally positive student attitude towards working together, teachers should not forget to explicitly state their rationale for and emphasize the benefits of doing collaborative tasks. To sum up, if tasks are relevant and meaningful and tools wisely selected, then constructing meaning together and taking responsibility for one's learning can be an engaging and rewarding learning experience for students and teachers alike.

Blended-Learning bezeichnet eine Lernform, in der Präsenzlernzeiten durch Elemente des E-Learning ergänzt oder ersetzt werden. Hierbei kommen verstärkt auch Techniken des Mobilen Lernens (M-Learning) zum Einsatz, die es Lernern ermöglichen, durch portable Medien, wie Smartphones und Tablets, überall und zu jeder Zeit zu lernen und durch entsprechende Aufgabenstellungen die Kommunikation innerhalb einer bestimmten Lerngruppe unterstützen können. Erfahrungen aus unserer eigenen Unterrichtspraxis an einer österreichischen Fachhochschule haben gezeigt, dass die Integration technologiegestützter

Lernszenarien in den Fremdsprachenunterricht im Sinne des Blended-Learning-Ansatzes motivierend auf Lerner wirken und zu einer Steigerung echter Lernzeit führen kann. Die Nutzung neuer Technologien bietet Lernern hierbei vor allem die Möglichkeit, selbstgesteuertes und gemeinsames Lernen miteinander zu verbinden, Lernergebnisse-und Produkte zu diskutieren und anderen zur Verfügung zu stellen. Kollaborative Lernprozesse regen Lerner dazu an, neues Wissen gemeinsam zu konstruieren und einzuüben und dabei Verantwortung nicht nur für ihr eigenes Lernen, sondern auch das für ihrer Co-Lerner, zu übernehmen (vgl. Dooly 2008: 21). Hinzu kommt, dass das gemeinsame Bearbeiten von Aufgaben Lernern Gelegenheiten bietet, die zu erlernende Fremdsprache aktiv in authentischen Kontexten zu nutzen. Vor diesem Hintergrund beschäftigt sich dieser Beitrag mit der Frage, wie der Einsatz neuer Medien kollaborative Lernprozesse in Blended-Learning Sprachkursen fördern kann. Hierbei wird besonders der Frage nachgegangen, wie kollaborative Lernszenarien Lerner dazu anregen, Wissen gemeinsam zu konstruieren und so auch Verantwortung für ihr eigenes Lernen zu übernehmen. Eine gemeinsame Aufgabenbearbeitung in Online-Lernumgebungen stellt Lerner hierbei vor besondere Herausforderungen. So sind sie unter anderem gezwungen, kreativ mit den Besonderheiten oft asynchroner Interaktionsmöglichkeiten umzugehen, welche sich klar von synchroner Face-to-Face-Interaktion unterscheiden. Die in diesem Beitrag vorgestellten Tools und Unterrichtsbeispiele zeigen, wie Lerner dazu angeregt werden können, Inhalte eigenständig erarbeiten, sich gegenseitig dabei unterstützen, selbst gesteckte Lernziele zu erreichen und ihr eigenes Lernen zu evaluieren. Der Fokus liegt hierbei nicht nur auf der gemeinsamen Erarbeitung von Unterrichtsinhalten, sondern auch auf der Steigerung produktiver und rezeptiver sprachlicher Fähigkeiten. Der Lehrkraft kommt hierbei eine besondere Rolle zu, die weit über die der traditionellen Wissensvermittlung hinausgeht.

Thorsten Merse & Fiona Heather Poorman
Ludwig-Maximilians-University, Germany
University of Education Karlsruhe, Germany

Voices from the University Classroom: Using Social Media for Collaborative Learning in Language Teacher Education

This article provides an insight into the use of Social Media for collaborative learning in higher education at university level. It describes several online collaboration scenarios that took place between university classrooms in the German universities of Karlsruhe and Muenster consisting exclusively of pre-service foreign language teachers within their teacher education programs. In this specific context, the students were given the opportunity to discover, experience and reflect on the collaboration and learning processes facilitated by social media, and to develop an understanding of how such media could be implemented in their own future practice as foreign language teachers. This article sets out to explain the link between Web 2.0 technologies and collaborative learning and describes the theoretical foundations of this course that formed the pedagogic rationale of the project considering concepts of digital literacy, collaborative learning and communicative language learning. The central part of this article illustrates in detail how the collaboration was put into practice in three distinct online scenarios: using a wiki to collect professional knowledge, creating a reading diary using a blog, and discussing the pedagogic challenges of online media within a social network environment. The description of each scenario is complemented by an evaluation of the individual working processes and the students' perceptions of the online collaboration. This article concludes with a reflection on the potential of implementing online collaboration using social media in the context of foreign language teacher education and the value of the project for enhancing pre-service teachers' professional knowledge.

1. Introduction

Over the past two decades, Social Media have become one of the most frequently used means for connecting people globally and for sharing and gathering information. More recently, this has also influenced the way new technologies have been used for and in educational contexts. These changes are strongly connected to the transformation of the Web from a uni-directional environment, also known as Web 1.0, to a collaborative workspace. O'Reilly (2005) describes the development of the internet from Web 1.0 to Web 2.0 in the change of platform-based programs and applications as well as the possibilities of active participation and the compilation of collaborative knowledge. The Web 2.0 is based on a constructivist idea, which encourages learners to participate in collaborative work and to express themselves independently and self-determinedly. Millions of users upload photos, audio-files, videos and other creative products on an hourly basis, hyperlink them, and share them with other users. As the number of people with fast internet access and high-capacity devices is simultaneously increasing, this trend will continue to grow exponentially and the internet will establish itself as a space of social networking and active contribution to societal, political and other processes. This calls for educational institutions worldwide to equip students with digital literacies needed to navigate these "new discourse practices" (Elsner/Viebrock 2013: 22).

The stories and messages presented by the entertainment and knowledge sectors are becoming increasingly multimedial. To be able to interpret and critically evaluate them, one needs to have an understanding of the creative and technical processes of their production, the authors and origin of the information as well as of their linguistic characteristics and interlinkings. Furthermore, one ought to possess intercultural competences to understand and negotiate meaning conveyed through multimedial messages emerging from diverse cultural contexts. These qualifications reflect the target objectives of modern foreign language teaching and at the heart of these skills lies "an ability to engage with digital technologies which requires a command of the digital literacies necessary to use these technologies effectively to locate resources, communicate ideas, and build collaborations across personal, social, economic, political and cultural boundaries" (Dudeney/Hockly/Pegrum 2013: 2). Foreign language teaching is strongly affected by the before mentioned changes as language and literacy are closely linked and all literacies are inevitably connected to the communication of meaning (cf. Dudeney/Hockly/Pegrum 2013), the recognized overall goal of communicative language teaching.

Nowadays, most students, prospective teachers and qualified instructors regularly use social media for communicative purposes and social interchange with friends and acquaintances, be they near or far. More and more frequently in higher education, educators are integrating social media such as e-learning platforms, wikis, and forums when preparing, planning and teaching courses, e.g. to distribute assignments. The question is, however, if collaborative online work with social media is also thoroughly implemented within these courses and if educators recognize that collaboration is important in the language classroom as it encourages both social skills and thinking skills and mirrors the way in which learners may have to work in an academic setting and definitely once they leave it (cf. Beatty 2010). With a view to implementing collaborative online work via social media in tertiary education and thus putting the potential of collaboration described by Beatty into practice, a cross-university project was set up by the authors of this article to use social media for collaborative learning in university classrooms.

2. The context of this course: opening up the university classroom

During the summer terms of 2014 and 2015, the University of Muenster and the University of Education Karlsruhe endeavored to merge two language teacher education courses in a collaborative e-learning environment. One collaborative scenario took place in the summer term of 2014 between one course at the University of Muenster and one course at the University of Education Karlsruhe. The second collaboration scenario was implemented in the summer term of 2015, again between two courses of the same institutions. All students participating in these courses are training to become foreign language teachers and have chosen the courses due to their particular focus on online media and technology in the foreign language classroom. During the online collaboration, students used social media and Web 2.0 applications such as a classroom wiki, blogs, and social networks for a virtual exchange project that enabled interaction of students from remote places who would otherwise have no possibility to meet in order to negotiate ideas and work together on assignments. The fact that the students from Muenster and Karlsruhe could not meet in person necessitated the use of social media for the exchange that unfolded while both university classrooms opened up virtually. Before the online collaboration began, the first weeks of the courses were used to introduce students to relevant theory and pedagogical concepts (see below in the discussion of the pedagogic rationale) so as to establish a common ground between the courses from which the exchange could develop. In the subsequent weeks, the online collaboration was prepared and reflected on during regular course time, whereas the actual collaborative online work took place outside the classrooms in e-learning phases.

Previous to the first online exchange in the summer term of 2014, the students from both institutions were asked to participate in an anonymous pre-survey that was administered by using the online tool *Survey Monkey*. With this survey, we wanted to challenge the common belief or myth that younger learners are technologically savvy (cf. Dudeney/Hockly/Pegrum 2013), which is reflected in the frequently found term "digital natives" (Prensky 2005) that suggests the idea of a homogenous, digitally knowledgeable generation. Instead, we wanted to arrive at a more nuanced understanding of the students' experience with online media. Therefore, the survey served to elicit the students' prerequisites regarding their use of social media and Web 2.0 technologies, e.g. whether they were familiar with certain media, for what purposes they used these media in their private lives, or whether they use online media rather to consume or also to create content. A total of 24 students participated in the anonymous online survey (13 from Muenster, 11 from Karlsruhe), yielding the following results for their experience with blogs, wikis and social networking sites.

Wikis: Almost all students were familiar with using wikis receptively. According to their answers, all students (with one exception) used wikis to search for information. While the majority of students used wikis several times a week, two students indicated that they used it once a day and three students used it several times daily. One student used wikis several times a month, another student several times a year. As regards the productive use of Wikis, 20 students indicated that they had never used a wiki to contribute or alter information, two students used a wiki to contribute information several times a year and one student indicated a contribution of information several times a week.

Blogs: When it comes to using blogs receptively, most of the students were familiar with blogs as such and only three students had never followed a blog at all. One student read blogs several times daily, two students read blogs once a day and three students read them several times a week. The majority of students (9) indicated that they read blogs several times a month and five students read them several times a year. With regard to using blogs productively, the majority of students (16) had never written anything on a blog or created their own blog. Seven students, however indicated that they wrote on blogs several times a year via the commenting function.

Social Networking Sites: The survey also inquired into students' use of a specific social networking site, namely Facebook. All students were active users of Facebook, the majority of students (14) used the site several times a day, seven students used it once daily and two students indicated that they used it several times a week. In contrast to blogs and wikis that were used –if at all– more receptively to consume content, Facebook appears to be an online environment that is used more actively and productively by the participants.

Based on the discussion of the survey results in class, the students emphasized that they would like to work with blogs and wikis in the online exchange project. For one, the students wanted to familiarize themselves with online media they were less familiar with, rather than focusing on the well-known social networking site *Facebook*. Secondly, the survey results stimulated the students' interest in discovering the more productive and creative facets of online media, which also informed the way the instructors designed and implemented the subsequent collaboration tasks and refined the pedagogic approach to this online exchange.

The overall objective was to provide pre-service teachers with a rich environment in which they would be able to 'experiment' with online media in meaningful ways and then reflect on their experience in an educational setting. Simultaneously, the objective was to give students the opportunity to critically discuss the potential of online media for their future practice as foreign language teachers and the possibilities of incorporating social media and computer-mediated communication (CMC) tools in the classroom. This article aims at offering in-depth insights into the pedagogic rationale underlying this cross-institutional course and outlining the key concepts of digital literacies, collaborative learning and communicative language teaching which were central to this rationale. Moreover, this article will describe and evaluate the practical procedures of engaging the course participants in meaningful collaborative work using social media, including the students' reflections and opinions after task completion. Using these practical examples, this article will further discuss the potential of social media for collaborative learning scenarios in higher education, especially in the context of foreign language teacher education.

3. Pedagogic rationale

The emergence of Web 2.0 technologies and the fall in the price of obtaining information and communication technologies have enabled all manner of educational institutions to equip classrooms with computers, laptops and tablets, and the increasing availability of new online tools such as Wikis, blogs, discussion forums and social networking sites provides teachers with free possibilities of engaging their students in online interaction and collaborative work without the need of detailed technical knowledge or ability (cf. O'Dowd 2010). Hence, the importance of adequate teacher training programs for using these technologies is on the increase and as Guichon and Hauck (2011) point out, this necessity is enhanced by the fact that teachers not only require the ability and technical knowledge to assess the affordances of any given tool but also require the competency to use the technology according to the learners' needs, to task demands and to desired learning outcomes. To avoid using digital media for the mere purpose of doing so, one of the main aims of the online collaborative project was to present participants with meaningful ways of using Web 2.0 technologies for language learning purposes and to remind them that "[w]hen considering implementing CMC tools in the language classroom one has to make sure that the pedagogy and not the technology drives the activity" (Görtler 2009: 75). To enhance the students' knowledge and awareness of the pedagogy behind using online media, an understanding of three main pedagogic guiding concepts was developed in class, namely *Digital*

Literacy, Communicative Language Learning and *Collaborative Work*. These concepts provided the theoretical foundation of the project.

3.1 Digital literacy

The interest in digital literacy can be located within the large-scale pedagogic aim of developing multiliteracies. In suggesting that developing literacies must go beyond mastering the ability to read and write written text, the New London Group (1996) put forward their influential concept of a *Pedagogy of Multiliteracies* in which the teaching and learning of literacy is re-conceptualized in a much broader manner. They highlight that the changing realities of social and globalized environments require new types of literacy. These changes are marked by two aspects: "the multiplicity of communication channels and media, and the increasing saliency of cultural and linguistic diversity" (The New London Group 1996: 63). Both aspects produce a multiplicity of discourses and a plurality of text types that learners must be empowered to understand and negotiate to participate in the various spheres of modern-day life (*ibid.*: 61). The New London Group also stresses that the "modes of meaning-making" (*ibid.*: 64) which become evident in the various discourses and texts clearly exceed textual components, and include other modes such as visual or audio. This becomes particularly important in a world of mass media, multimedia and new technological communication channels that rely on diverse modes and semiotic resources to make meaning, which learners must master competently in order to understand, participate in and critically reflect on the discourses they encounter. The immediate call for foreign language education is to support learners in developing the multiliteracies considered crucial for the 21st century (cf. Elsner/Viebrock 2013). Given the omnipresence of online media in today's world, digital literacy has become a crucial component of the set of multiliteracies that learners need to develop. Hence, it was a guiding aim of both university courses to convey to the students the theoretical concept of digital literacy and its various dimensions, and also foster a practical and critical understanding of this concept. The closely related concept of media literacy (e.g. Volkmann 2010: 219–221), which usually revolves around various types of media and is not exclusive to online media, was also embraced, yet narrowed down to the particular interest in social media. The following section provides an overview of the digital literacy dimensions that were central to the courses (cf. *ibid.* for a similar categorisation).

Even though the mastery of technical skills is not considered the most crucial aspect of media or digital literacy (cf. Elsner/Viebrock 2013: 28), it can be argued that knowledge of the ways in which online media function is a necessary starting point in order to engage with media in the first place. This holds true for consuming media (e.g. knowing how a blog is structured when following its content), but is probably even more crucial for the productive and creative possibilities of using media (e.g. setting up a thematic blog and knowing how to publish information). For both aspects, it is important to know how to operate an online medium adequately, and to understand how an online medium is structured, also in comparison to other media (cf. Volkmann 2010). Even though younger learners and students might be considered digital natives operating all online media with ease, one might be advised to call to greater caution here and stress that students might also require a careful introduction into the technical aspects of an online medium. The findings from the survey conducted within the project underline this assumption. Therefore, the classroom should offer ample time to students to learn how collaboration can technically work, e.g. on a wiki platform. This ensures that students are at the same level when initiating projects with online media.

In addition to the technical skills, it is important that students are empowered to choose a medium according to their needs and purposes with a view to achieving specific goals, and to develop strategies and skills to process and produce media-based content in order to meet these purposes and goals. This requires that learners have procedural knowledge (cf. *ibid.*) when using and producing media, which is a key supplement to the more declarative knowledge of the technology of a medium as such. This emphasis on both consuming *and* creating content is emblematic of the New London Group's pedagogy of multiliteracies that sees learners as active agents and designers of their social futures, and it also encapsulates the participative potential of Web 2.0 applications that break down clear-cut dichotomies of users and creators (cf. Elsner/Viebrock 2013; Merse/Schmidt 2014). One example of this purpose-oriented dimension of digital literacy would be to use media for researching and evaluating information, then synthesize such information to solve a problem or generate new ideas, and finally disseminate new information online, e.g. by publishing it in a wiki.

With the changing potential in the utilization of online media in the Web 2.0, Elsner and Viebrock point out that today's *produsers* –a term they borrow from Bruns (2008) to describe how consumers gradually become producers of web content– "not only need functional literacy skills but also a good command of critical literacy" (2013: 24) to reflect on the way they use online media. This critical and reflective dimension of media literacy is also foregrounded by Volkmann (2010: 220), who stresses that learners must be critical towards the messages conveyed by media (and, by extension, towards the messages they themselves send out through media). Elsner and Viebrock (2013: 29) also demand a critical reflection on the limits and opportunities of using online media –which requires that each medium is evaluated individually rather than generalizing online media per se. They also challenge an all-too optimistic view on media and emphasize that "[t]his critical perspective is even more demanded against the backdrop of the non-committal attitudes to be observed in much of the web-based interaction" (*ibid.*: 24). Hence, the call is for using online media not just because they are available and easy to use, but to utilize online media critically, reflectively and meaningfully with genuine purposes for communication and interaction, and then to be reflective about whether the use of media has been carried out purposefully.

3.2 Collaborative learning

The role of social interaction has often been claimed to be a crucial prerequisite for language learning. This sociocultural perspective derives from Vygotsky's concepts of social interaction, which emphasize the role of interaction for learning (cf. Vygotsky 1962; 1978). CMC tasks and activities lend themselves to interaction between learners by the mere nature of their technology. However, it is important to point out that participant interaction is not necessarily equivalent to collaborative learning, and considering the recent inflation in the use of the term "collaboration" in the field of language learning and social media, it is important to define the concept behind this term for the following discussion of the described project.

Henri and Rigault (1996) outline collaborative learning by differentiating it from cooperative learning, these two terms often being used interchangeably. Cooperative tasks are those for which learners can divide the work between one another and then complete it individually. In contrast, collaboration is "a coordinated synchronous activity that is the result of continued attempt to construct and maintain a shared concept of a problem" (Roschelle/Teasley 1995: 70). The aspect of simultaneity might have been crucial at a time when amendments and additions to products could only be implemented by individuals after having shared the updated version as is the case with many forms of traditional media. However, the advancement of the Web has made synchronous and asynchronous work by several authors on one document possible and feasible. Online multi-authorship offers individuals the possibility to work on one product asynchronously while enabling them to immediately observe and comprehend any additions or changes having been executed by the co-collaborators. It is preferable for individuals to use their skills in a complementary manner to solve a problem which they could not solve by themselves, and therefore the collaboration creates a shared basis on the meaning and workings of a process or product (cf. Schrage 1990). For students to collaborate effectively in groups, a common goal, an incentive to collaborate plus independency from the instructor is required (cf. Hathorn/Ingram 2002). According to

Paulus (2005) this criterion can be fulfilled through the instructional design of the task given to the group. In CMC contexts, where learners are often geographically separated, collaboratively designed tasks might be interpreted as cooperative projects, as students divide parts of the tasks up, work on them individually and then conflate their efforts to a final project (cf. Paulus 2005). To target this regularly occurring phenomenon, one needs to carefully choose Web 2.0 technologies which by their very nature encourage collaborative methods, this being the reason why a course wiki was used in the project, as students were able to work on the assigned topics simultaneously from several individual devices while communicating by way of a chat function at the same time. Moreover, it was considered important to address the methodological idea behind the concept of collaboration in class before assigning the tasks. Besides the general suitability of collaborative activities for learning purposes, collaborative working methods offer chances specifically for language learning as they help learners reflect on their language production. This is because constant communication is needed and participants attempt to create meaning when communicating with co-collaborators (cf. Swain 1995).

3.3 Communicative language learning

Collaborative Web 2.0 technologies offer rich possibilities for communicative language teaching as they allow for easy integration into all kinds of communicative activities (cf. Görtler 2009). Most of these technologies such as chats and social networking sites belong to the category of computer-mediated communication applications. The definition, however, has been used in a broader sense to include blogs, wikis and other tools that can be used synchronously and asynchronously for collaborative work (cf. Görtler, 2009).

A substantial amount of current research in the pedagogy of foreign language teaching and learning explores the benefits and challenges of CMC. Using technology creates opportunities for the use of language in authentic contexts, which also encourages students to strive for autonomous use of the target language (cf. Kessler, 2009). Previous research has also supported the fact that CMC is a socially rich environment (cf. Arnold *et al.* 2005) and helps learners build a classroom community, fosters interaction and gives students the opportunity to provide each other with support (cf. McDonald/Gibson 1998; McKenzie/Murphy 2000; Sengupta 2001). Additional benefits include the development of intercultural competence (cf. Müller-Hartmann 2006; O'Dowd 2003; O'Dowd 2007), the general improvement of communication skills (cf. Lee 2002), and the increase in learner motivation (cf. Godwin-Jones 2003), to name but a few. Besides the many advantages CMC offers for language learning purposes, research has, however, also indicated several shortcomings such as technical problems (cf. Belz 2002), tensions and miscommunication between participants (cf. Belz 2002; O'Dowd/Ritter 2006; Ware 2005), as well as the fact that there are still many poorly educated teachers (cf. Müller-Hartmann 2006; O'Dowd/Ritter 2006). It has been widely acknowledged that the role of teachers in internet-mediated teaching is crucial (cf. Belz 2003; O'Dowd 2007) and therefore language teachers need to learn how to incorporate social media and CMC tools into the classroom by experiential learning supported by model teaching (cf. Müller-Hartmann 2006).

Besides exploring and reflecting on the potential of social media for collaborative language learning processes, and with an aim to increase students' digital literacies, this joint project carried out a learning-by-doing and an experience-based approach to utilizing social media for learning purposes in the university classroom. The goal was to engage students in meaningful collaborative work and communication using social media, and offer tasks that allow students to plan, design and create their own social media products. The remaining part of this article will demonstrate how this pedagogic rationale was put into practice in three different projects during the online collaboration between Karlsruhe and Muenster students.

4. The wiki project: collecting professional knowledge

During the summer term of 2014, the students jointly learned how to use a class wiki for collaborative writing by producing their own wiki entries. A wiki is a very suitable tool for such purposes as it is a collection of webpages that are linked together and reflect the collaborative work of many authors. Unlike blogs, wiki pages are not chronologically organized but linked in different ways, for example, according to topics or through hyperlinked headwords (cf. Beldarrain 2006). Wikis are considered to be highly collaborative (cf. Beldarrain 2006) as edits are recorded and logged when students work on a project collaboratively and changes are finalized once the co-collaborators approve. Apart from the possibility for collaborative work, using wikis in the classroom offers many learning opportunities for the development of digital literacy skills, especially for information literacy.

The constant retention of each iteration of posts in wikis presents users with the opportunity to understand the evolution of a wiki page, and if considered appropriate, users can even replace the current version with a previous iteration (cf. Kessler 2009). This is the distinguishing difference between wikis and other CMC tools, as a contribution is neither a comment nor a response but rather an alteration of a previous contribution. Kessler (2009: 79) describes a wiki-based text as "a constant state of potential collaborative change". The fact that wikis are readily accessible and extensively open to anyone contributing often results in the opinion that information is altered too easily as to be considered reliable. However, this openness to collaboration can also lead to the correction of erroneous information (cf. Kessler 2009). Therefore the system of a wiki can only work positively with users who are serious about working collaboratively and who follow the group conventions and practices (cf. Godwin-Jones 2003). Only by using and authoring wikis, learners are able to understand the potential of this technology. There are several wiki providers offering different features and structures, a fact which needs to be considered when creating wikis in educational contexts. Depending on the learner group, Schwartz *et al.* (2004) recommend defining a set of criteria for evaluating these options and suggest considering cost, complexity, control possibilities, clarity and desired features before choosing a provider.

In this particular wiki project, *Wikispaces* was used, a provider offering educational wikis that are free of charge. After the registration process, teachers in their role of organizers can set up a new wiki with little effort and use the dashboard surface to micro-manage all procedures: inviting students as members to the wiki space, using the newsfeed of the dashboard to make announcements, and creating individual projects within the wiki. Other options include an events-section with a calendar for time management and setting deadlines, and also an assessment function in which teachers can retrace the activities of the students while they are working on a predetermined project. *Wikispaces* offers a clear structure for a classroom wiki, with easily recognizable icons representing certain functions and activities. Yet it might still take a while, both for teachers and students new to this system, to fully understand the layout and the functions of this wiki, and most importantly, to learn how to collaborate in an assigned project and negotiate and edit the emerging wiki entries.

For the wiki collaboration, a project was created in which students were to explore and describe in detail how exactly a certain online medium, website or media tool could contribute to a learner's development of a particular language skill (e.g. listening or writing). To this end, the students had to research potentially suitable tools and evaluate their potential for the chosen targeted skill, and then transform and synthesize the information they gathered into a wiki entry. In smaller groups of up to four members, students worked together in sub-pages, with each sub-page providing the environment for collaboration in this project: a surface for viewing the existing text, an editing function to alter the text (e.g. one student starting with the presentation of a website for listening and evaluating benefits, with-at a later point in time-another student adding their opinion to the previously written text), a revision section to return to previous savings, and a discussion thread (e.g. in order to make suggestions for changes or further additions). The objective was to create a well-reflected and researched collaborative wiki entry representing the shared efforts and negotiations of the whole group. This required that students actually built on and supplemented each other's text additions by contributing their own information and opinions to those which fellow group members had already produced. In line with a wiki's common function as a resource and information medium, the idea was also to develop valuable teaching knowledge available for sharing with other teachers, and to use a wiki as a give-and-take support network to search for, and present to others, best-practice examples and professional knowledge.

After two weeks of independent work outside the university classroom, with the instructors withdrawing and helping out solely when technical problems occurred (e.g. registration process, loss of membership data), the students presented their wiki entries in class and reflected on the shared results and collaboration processes. In general, students maintained that they enjoyed using the wiki as a new social medium and experienced the sharing of ideas with other students as enriching. The types of wiki entries that were actually developed, however, differed to quite some extent. One group's result clearly represented a shared product in which the members co-constructed the text by adding and changing information in the editing process and by negotiating changes in the discussion feed. Said group reported that this was an elaborate and time-consuming process, as the information posted by one member had to be checked by other members, too, so that they had the basis to be able to form an objective opinion and arrive at an educated judgment on the suitability of a medium to foster a certain language skill. The same students also said, and this was confirmed by the other groups, that they were unsure as to who should start by posting an idea, as the first person to write might become the subject of immediate criticism or judgment. During the process, however, it turned out that –if the shared mission's goal was to work towards a fruitful entry– constructive criticism was felt to be helpful and it was insightful and rewarding to learn from other students' expertise. This indicates that collaborating on a wiki requires a community of trust and respect as a basis for disclosing to others one's own ideas, and that it also takes time –especially in collaborations where students do not know each other in advance, or work from remote places– to develop mutual trust.

Interestingly, the other groups bypassed the construction of a shared wiki entry with collaborative editing and revision. Rather, individual group members would begin with posting an idea on how a certain online medium could be used for competence development, and then other members would post their ideas on a different medium without engaging with what group members had previously posted. This shows that there is not necessarily an in-depth processing of the information others contribute, and that the final outcome could also result in an unconnected list of various teaching ideas. Surprisingly, two groups did not use the text surface of their sub-page at all, but posted their ideas right into the discussion feed –again in an unconnected way without referring to or commenting on previous discussion points. In their reflections, the students who produced these types of outcome stressed that still they had produced a list of teaching advice that might *potentially* be useful, but remarked that this list was not necessarily reliable because the knowledge it represented was not double-checked or critically edited. The same students also recognized, especially in comparison to the first group described, that they had not fully exploited the potential that a wiki holds in store and that they had engaged with the collaboration task rather superficially. To improve their work, some students suggested that an even more careful introduction to the purposes and processes of the wiki might be necessary and that face-to-face classroom sessions could also have been used for interventions and reflections to show other paths of use of a wiki –rather than making the wiki collaboration an independent project with little or no guidance during the process. Other students added that *precisely* because they had not collaborated in an ideal way they were now more aware of what is actually important when creating a shared outcome on a wiki.

5. The blog project: creating reading diaries

The term 'blog' is a coinage of the words Web and log. Blogs were originally created to link several webpages which the creator of a blog considered important or interesting. Next to the collection of links, these early forms of blogs consisted of comments and description of contents of the linked sites. This way people with similar interests or those working on specific topics were able to conflate information, intertwine and exchange it (cf. Raith 2009). In the course of the development of the internet, blogs were extended to the use of audio and video files as well as to other forms of media which authors considered relevant for their blogging interests. Often the textual and multimedia content of blogs revolves around a particular topic, hence there are food blogs, tourist blogs or educational blogs, to name but a few. Solomon and Schrum (2010: 18) point out that "blogs are extremely popular because they give a voice, platform, and audience to anyone who has an idea and wants to express it". This potential of blogs is noteworthy for foreign language education as it gives learners the opportunity to express themselves and publish on a topic they find meaningful. Since the introduction of blog-hosters in 1999, blogs are easy to access and create with little or no command of programming languages. This development has caused the amount of blogs to grow exponentially with the result that the Meriam-Webster Publisher elected "Weblog" to be the word of the year 2004 (cf. Richardson 2010).

To put blogs to productive and collaborative use across the two university classrooms, the idea of keeping a reading diary, an established method for teaching literature in foreign language classrooms, was transferred to a participative Web 2.0 context for students to create their own reading diary as a blog. In this scenario, two aspects that are typical of reading diaries were altered: normally, reading diaries are kept as an individual reflection on the experience of reading a literary text and they are usually private texts not intended to be shared with a larger audience. Instead of being an individual result, the reading diary blog was now designed to be a collaborative product by several authors, all with access to the same blog, and all with the right to publish on it. Even though each entry was published by an individual student, it was the sum of all these individual entries that made the whole reading diary blog a shared piece of work, turning the reading diary into a multi-voiced, yet highly personal record in which diverse opinions on and experiences of the same literary text conjoined. Secondly, all groups decided to keep their blogs public, thus opening up their personal reflections to a wider audience and other classroom peers. With this openness of the reading diary blog, further discussions were able to unfold: followers could comment on the entries and engage with the authors to confirm or challenge the content of their entries, turning the reading diary blog into an interactive and dialogic platform.

The student groups were able to choose freely which literary text they wanted to read and turn into a blog diary, provided that they had never read that particular text before. Similarly, they could decide on which blog provider they wanted to use to set up and maintain their blog, a choice which required some research on the suitability of available blog providers (e.g. free of cost, allowing for multiple authorship). The students had four weeks to agree on a literary text, set up the blog, and bring it to life with entries on their reading experience. They were further encouraged to comment on each other's entries and share their blog to create an audience for their product. In addition, the students were introduced to the concept of a reading diary in class and studied pedagogical publications on reading diaries and weblogs (e.g. Raith 2006; Klemm 2008) so that they had a range of ideas on text contents and what to publish in the entries (e.g. an individual response to the text, filling the gaps of the text, re-writing a situation from a different perspective, presenting songs associated with the text, creating visual collages etc.).

Figure 1: Example of students' reading diary blog

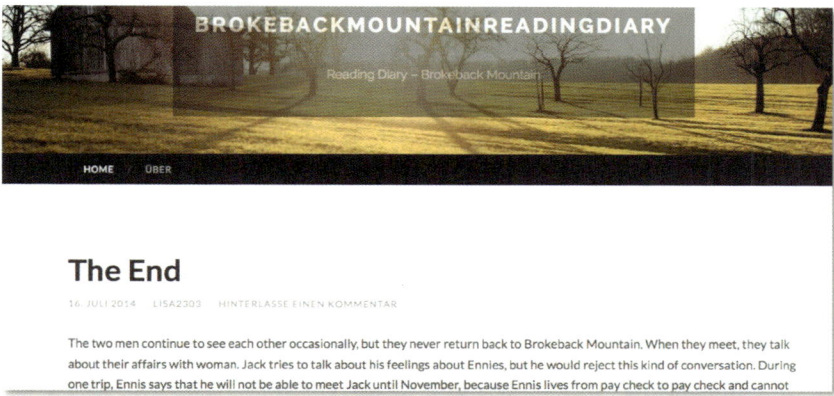

After four weeks, the students presented their results in class and reflected on their experience of creating a collaborative reading diary blog. Among the literary texts chosen for the blog were Annie Proulx' *Brokeback Mountain* (cf. Figure 1 for the result of this reading diary), Jonathan Safran Foer's *Everything is Illuminated,* Lois Lowry's *Number the Stars* and Sherman Alexie's *The Absolutely True Diary of a Part-Time Indian*. Each blog was in itself a unique collection of entry types, some with a more analytical or interpretative approach, some with a more creative focus. While all entries contained written text, many students also embedded images, songs and audio files, excerpts from videos or added hyperlinks to other sources in their entries making the blogs a multimodal and multimedia experience. In some cases, students also added other literary texts such as poems or they chose information in the wider socio-cultural context related to the literary text they had read. Students unanimously agreed that they enjoyed the freedom of choice regarding the content of the entries ('what to write about') and that they could follow up ideas they found interesting, meaning that all students were committed to their individual entries because they were felt to be personally meaningful. In reflecting on the collaboration, some students pointed out that the reading diary blog, in contrast to the wiki, allowed greater independence from the other group members, but still there was a sense of collaborative achievement in the end because the blog could only come to life with all contributions merged, and the blog as a whole was more than the sum of its parts, i.e. its individual entries. In the course of reading other entries with their unique contributions and reflections, several students found the experience enriching as it added new dimensions to the perceptions of the literary text they had hitherto held.

While the students certainly enjoyed their in-depth engagement with the literary texts and found working on the reading diary blog enriching due to the possibility of expressing their own opinions, several students remarked critically that their hopes of having an audience which actually followed the blog had been dashed. Although none of the students minded the fact that the blogs were public *per se* –quite the contrary, this lead many students to put more effort into the quality and the language of the entries– the sense of a missing audience caused many students to wonder about whom they were actually writing for, and what sense their writing had if nobody but the group members actually followed the blog entries. As blogs do not only rely on the voices expressed on this platform, but also on an audience that engages with these voices, some students called into question the purpose of creating a blog at all. If used in their own future classrooms, the students agreed that strategies would be necessary to find and increase the audience for a blog, e.g. by sharing it on social networking sites, advertising it to friends, or encouraging other classes (e.g. by using the project eTwinning) to follow their example. This would be facilitated if the time-span were longer, i.e. over the course of a school term.

At the end of term and after completion and presentation of the collaborative products (the classroom wiki and reading diary blogs), students were asked to complete an online survey once more using the survey tool *SurveyMonkey*. They were asked to evaluate the social media they had used and give their opinion on the suitability of incorporating social media in the classroom for language learning purposes. A total of 21 students completed the survey (11 from Muenster, 10 from Karlsruhe). The participants evaluated the use of wikis both as suitable (16) and as very suitable (4 students), and only one student was of the opinion that wikis were not a suitable tool for language learning purposes. Similar results showed for the use of blogs: 18 students evaluated these as very suitable while 3 students rated them as suitable. This shows that the teacher candidates of these university courses are generally open-minded towards using these social media in their future classrooms. Having experienced the use of these media themselves in the context of this teacher education course, while simultaneously critically reflecting on that use, might be seen as an important step in the professionalisation of future teachers when it comes to implementing online media in learning scenarios.

6. Social networking sites: discussing pedagogic challenges

In the summer term of 2015, the second virtual exchange between Karlsruhe and Muenster students moved social networking sites into focus (in particular Facebook). While the students in the courses of 2014 initially said they would prefer not to use *Facebook* during the exchange but rather be introduced to other less well-known online media, in the end they remarked that it would have been worthwhile to explore the educational potential of *Facebook* precisely because it is such a wide-spread medium and it would be good to know what *Facebook* might hold in store for collaboration and learning languages. Therefore, the instructors chose to work with *Facebook*, while holding on to the pedagogic rationale underlying the teacher education courses of the previous term.

In general, a social networking site (SNS) provides users with a profile, a friend list, chat options and the capability to send private or public messages, to create events and to post and receive feedback (cf. Ekoç 2014). SNS offer new opportunities for students to connect with their classmates, peer learners and their teachers on a level that is more personal and motivating in many aspects than in past times (cf. Blattner/Lomicka 2012). There is a large variety of SNS available, and most providers share many of the key features. One very prominent example is the SNS Facebook with approximately 1,49 billion active users in June 2015 (cf. Facebook Newsroom Statistics 2015). Active users are those individuals who have logged on to their *Facebook* accounts at least once within 30 days.

Facebook combines a variety of CMC-tools such as a messenger function, the possibility for one-on-one and many-to-many text-and voice-chat options, the possibility to create private groups and to publish various hypermedia such as text, picture, sound and video, as well as the opportunity to comment on postings (cf. Solomon/Schrum 2007). Research on the potential of SNSs for language learning purposes is increasing, and in recent years Facebook has been explored as a new social medium for collaborative language learning (cf. Lantz-Andersson/Vigmo/Bowen 2013) with results demonstrating that it can foster the development of intercultural competence (cf. Jin 2015), increase socio-pragmatic competence (cf. Blattner/Fiori 2011), and promote learner autonomy as well as help teacher candidates develop and improve their learning and teaching skills (cf. Rubrico/Hashim 2014).

To showcase one possibility of implementing a SNS in the classroom, *Facebook* was used as the platform for a virtual exchange between the students of Muenster and Karlsruhe. For the exchange, a closed group was created, thus access to the group was available only to students participating in the exchange who had been selected by one of the instructors. A total of 28 students participated in the exchange, of which 18 were students enrolled in Karlsruhe and 10 at the University of Muenster. The students were further divided into cross-institutional groups of three or four students, and in these small groups they had to work on two assignments (cf. Figure 2). In group chats, they were asked, for example, to talk about media literacy, compare their learning outcomes and then evaluate how the theoretical concept of media literacy might affect their future foreign language lessons. In another group chat, students had to transfer their knowledge of media literacy to the idea of using *Facebook* in the classroom, thus evaluating its possible advantages and disadvantages. After each discussion, students were asked to write a summary of their chat, post this summary to the group wall, and then discuss their results by posting comments.

Figure 2: Example of two assignments within the Facebook exchange

Topic	Activity
What have you learned about the concept of media literacy so far? What do you think are important aspects? How do they affect your future language teaching?	1. Text-Chat with your exchange group and discuss the topic (at least 30 mins). 2. Write a summary of your discussion on the group wall. 3. Read at least two other summaries and comment on them.
How does using *Facebook* correspond to your concept of media literacy? What are the advantages / disadvantages? Do you think it could be used in the EFL classroom?	1. Text-Chat with your exchange group and discuss the topic (at least 30 mins). 2. Write a summary of your discussion on the group wall. 3. Read at least two other summaries and comment on them.

In the end-of-term evaluation, students were asked to share their opinions directly on the group wall and comment on the benefits and challenges encountered in the exchange and to evaluate the potential a Facebook exchange could hold for language learning purposes. The responses were mostly homogeneous: the participants enjoyed the opportunity to exchange ideas with students from other institutions and assessed the chat communication as beneficial for their own language learning, mainly because it enhances their competences for written communication. Several students criticized the obligation to post a chat summary on the group-wall as that invariably led to repetitions which were considered as boring to read. Other challenges and critical remarks included difficulties in finding a suitable and convenient time for the synchronous group-chat, and using a social media tool such as *Facebook* for educational purposes when actually students felt this to be an invasion into their private use of digital media. Several other students who were studying to become primary school teachers stated that they saw hardly any possibility of transferring their social media experiences to their future pedagogic work and would not use Facebook in primary education settings. The overall opinion, however, was that the exchange and use of a SNS in an educational context could support students in their reflection on the general use of this technology and sharpen their awareness of the potential and drawbacks of using Facebook. To conclude with, students also said that the *Facebook* exchange showed them how collaboration can lead to a nuanced discussion of important educational topics.

7. Conclusion

The online exchange projects between the University of Education in Karlsruhe and the University of Muenster described in this article represent a twin focus. For one, a context for collaborative work on assignments in a higher education setting was provided using social media tools with the overall goal of exploring and critically reflecting on used tools and the practical implementation of these. The second, equally important focus of the exchange mirrored the fact that all participating students are pre-service foreign language teachers. Therefore, the online-based scenarios were intended to provide an experiential environment in which students could learn how to use media purposefully, with the objective for them to discover ways of integrating online media meaningfully in the context of foreign language learning.

Collaboration via social media such as wikis, blogs or social networking sites is one way of using the productive, creative and participative potential of Web 2.0 applications and supporting students in the exchange of ideas and working towards a negotiated task outcome. For course instructors, it is essential to scrutinize the social media tools available and to identify how the structural make-up and the functional logic of each medium can facilitate or engender collaboration. Instructors and teachers need to develop complex tasks with relevant themes for collaboration that encourage each student to contribute individual content and opinions to the shared final outcome. For the participants of this exchange –as the pre-survey results indicated– it was essential to move from a more receptive use to a productive and collaborative use of media, which required that students had to learn how to use online media such as wikis and blogs in a Web 2.0-oriented way. The students' reflection of the collaborative processes, as well as the analysis of the resulting media products, showed that in general the social media used *can* provide a suitable environment for solving tasks, working together and presenting a final product. It must be said, however, that the 'high hopes' frequently connected with the use of social media in educational settings might not always be met, and that their alleged potential does not *per se* play out productively in the classroom, e.g. when students bypass the collaborative potential of a wiki or when the interactive potential of blog comments to negotiate meaning is not always fulfilled due to lack of an actual audience, as the examples have shown. Therefore, collaborative learning environments using social media require strategies that allow students to embrace the full potential of the social media used. Further research is needed to investigate the detailed micro-processes that occur during the collaborative processes in order to understand why some collaborative settings work well and others can be prone to failure.

When it comes to the focus on teacher education pursued in the courses and in the online exchange, the described approach aimed at enhancing students' digital literacies and give them a 'taste' of how online media could be incorporated meaningfully in language learning. To achieve this, the use of social media and the collaboration was designed so that students would have to deal with the various dimensions of digital literacy theoretically and practically: e.g. knowing how a medium is operated technically, understanding the potential of a medium to achieve certain learning goals and actually putting a medium into practice, and then reflecting critically on learning outcomes (cf. Guichon/Hauck 2011). All of these steps seem to be necessary for teacher candidates to be prepared for planning, conducting and evaluating learning scenarios that make ready use of social media. Indeed, the online exchange between the courses provided a protective environment to try out, and then reflect on the actual use of media, while at the same time freeing the students from the general assumption that they would be treated as omniscient digital natives. The outcome of the cross-institutional exchange indicates that after using social media tools themselves, teacher candidates develop a high capacity to critically reflect on the suitability and potential of using such tools in the language classroom and to evaluate their respective advantages and disadvantages. It would be interesting to investigate in how far the participants of this teacher education course would perceive of the knowledge they were able to acquire throughout the course projects as helpful for their actual profession as soon as they have begun their teaching practice. Such insights could then be fed back into higher education to update and improve the concepts employed in media-oriented courses for teacher education.

Heutzutage werden Soziale Medien fast selbstverständlich zum kommunikativen und sozialen Austausch genutzt. Auch im universitären Bereich erhalten diese Formen zunehmend Einzug, beispielsweise durch E-Learning Plattformen mit Chat-Funktionen oder den Einsatz von Wikis und Foren. Dabei stellt sich jedoch die Frage, ob und wie die neuen medialen Kanäle in Seminaren kollaborative Arbeitsformen unterstützen können, um Studierende sprachlich und medienpädagogisch auf ihre Tätigkeit als zukünftige Fremdsprachenlehrende vorzubereiten.

Der vorliegende Artikel bietet einen Einblick in den Einsatz Sozialer Medien für kollaborative Lernzwecke auf universitärem Level. Es werden neben den zugrunde liegenden theoretischen Grundkonzepten der digitalen Medienbildung, Kollaboration und des kommunikativen Fremdsprachenunterrichts auch diverse kollaborative Projekte beschrieben, die im Sommersemester 2014 und 2015 zwischen Lehrerbildungsseminaren in der Fremdsprachenwissenschaft an der Universität Münster und der Pädagogischen Hochschule Karlsruhe durchgeführt wurden. Die Studierenden erhielten durch die Kooperation die Möglichkeit, verschiedene Soziale Medien für kollaborative Lernzwecke kennenzulernen, einzusetzen und über ihre Vor-und Nachteile zur Fremdsprachenförderung zu reflektieren.

Dabei werden im Artikel der Einsatz von Wikis zur Sammlung und Archivierung von Lernergebnissen, das kollaborative Erstellen eines Lesejournals durch die Verwendung eines Blogs und ein virtueller Austausch innerhalb eines Sozialen Netzwerkes detailliert beschrieben und diskutiert, sowie durch die Ergebnisse der Teilnehmerevaluation komplementiert. Am Ende des Beitrages steht eine allgemeine Reflexion des Potentials von Sozialen Medien für kollaborative Zwecke in der universitären Lehrerbildung sowie für die Förderung digitaler Medienkompetenz bei zukünftigen Lehrkräften.

Christine Fourie
University of Antwerp, Belgium/Stellenbosch University, South Africa

Facing (and Facebooking) Authentic Tasks in a Blended Learning Environment: Metacognitive Awareness Demonstrated by Medical Students

In the ongoing quest for authenticity and authentic tasks in the language learning environment, the emphasis is shifting towards the role of the learner to ensure an authentic learning experience. Within the medical communication training context this shift is especially significant as students will be responsible for the healthcare of patients during consultations after completing their medical studies. In multilingual South Africa an ethnographic study was performed at the University of Stellenbosch where blended learning, which included a closed Facebook group, was introduced to first year medical communication training students. Data was analysed according to the principles of grounded theory and the results included an outline of the metacognitive awareness about the nature of tasks that these first year students displayed and reported upon. The main elements from this outline, namely interactive, relevant and personalised learning are, according to existing research, also the essential parts for an authentic learning experience. However, the data shows that these elements are best realised during collaboration amongst students themselves, as well as between students and the teacher. Therefore the outline intends to be a guideline for teachers on how to collaborate with students in a blended learning environment in order to raise metacognitive awareness and to work towards an authentic communication training experience.

1. Introduction

As an increasing number of people are crossing borders between countries, the ability to communicate in more than one language becomes an urgent need. The urgency to cross these linguistic barriers is significant in the professional medical context where the well-being of the patient can be directly related to the communication between doctor and patient (Buller/Buller 1987; Stewart 1995). Linguistic borders are also encountered in a pre-professional phase as more and more foreign students enrol at universities. Furthermore, medical students will be involved in health care as soon as they qualify and this responsibility suggests the need for authenticity and authentic tasks in the communication training context. That is why the content for responsibly designed communication training courses aimed at medical professionals rely on the communicative functions typical used in the professional context (Pretorius 2015; Weideman 2013). As this context for learning is nowadays almost inevitably a blended context (Graham 2006) teachers need guidelines on how to utilize tasks in blended learning in order to address students' learning needs for authenticity (Pinner 2014; Laursen/Frederiksen 2015).

In multilingual South Africa medical students took part in a communication course where the structure and content of the course reflect the communicative functions typically used in the medical consultation timeline (Van de Poel 2013). A closed Facebook group and an autonomous online module provided two additional learning platforms next to face-to-face teaching in class. Data were analysed to determine students' metacognitive awareness about the nature of tasks in order to address the following research questions: What metacognitive awareness about tasks do medical communication students demonstrate? Furthermore, how can this awareness inform their learning experience?

2. Literature review

2.1 Authenticity in language learning

The adjective *authentic* is used in everyday language to describe an object or concept that is made or done the same way as an original, that is trustworthy, not false or an imitation and true to one's own personality, spirit, or character (Merriam-Webster). However, in the language learning environment, *authenticity* is often narrowed down to one meaning, which refers to the teacher that is providing the student with a learning experience that is taken from or very closely resembles life outside the classroom –or the environment where the target language will be used (made or done in the same way as the original). This learning experience would make use of material taken from the student's 'real' life experience in the target language, such as magazine articles, video clips of advertisements, songs and recorded conversations in the target language. From this point of view, the focus is on recreating the language modeled by native users (Pinner 2014).

Though, in more recent years, the emphasis has shifted beyond recreating the real life outside the classroom with learning material and tasks, to include a more comprehensive meaning of authenticity by focusing on the student's learning experience and linking authenticity to awareness about learning and learner autonomy (Van Lier 1996), as it is "the learner who chooses whether to bring authenticity to their learning" (Ashton 2010: 3). Holliday (2013) further explores this personalised dimension of authenticity by explaining that it is not a distinctive phenomenon that is presented as such, but that authenticity is experienced when learning and learning materials are meaningful or significant from a personal point of view to students, so that, as Van Lier (1996) explains, motivation for learning becomes intrinsic.

Apart from learning being personalised, Danish authors Laursen and Frederiksen (2015) focus on the necessity for students to believe that the language learning tasks are relevant to their future careers, before they can experience the authenticity of the learning activity. By implication the authentic nature of a task will be the student's subjective point of view. In a medical training context the relevance and authenticity of the learning experience and learning material gain special importance, as after their training period, these young professionals become directly responsible for the health and well-being of their patients. However, the authentic experience is not the sole responsibility of the student. According to Rystedt and Sjöblom (2012: 785) authenticity is "an interactive achievement, i.e. something that participants create in moment-to-moment interactions". This coincides with the notion that authenticity is dynamic by nature and that "authenticity in any given context always depends on the interplay between the language learners, the teacher, and the tasks and material embedded in the social situation of the classroom" (Laursen/Frederiksen 2015: 64).

Based on these existing research principles and for article Therefore, next to personalised and relevant, the interactive nature of tasks is the third element that characterizes authentic learning experiences.

2.2 Interaction and learning communities

In everyday life interaction refers to two or more people or things influencing each other by allowing a two-way flow of information (Hornby 1974). Focusing only on people, there is general consensus that meaning is produced through the interactions of individuals and that interaction is a natural attribute of face-to-face communication (Rafaeli 1988; Blake 2000; Wang 2004). Furthermore, as language is often the medium of interaction and communication, it is taken for granted nowadays that interaction should be an integral part of the language learning process and that "interaction is both a means and a goal in language learning" (Wang, 2004: 374). This is why learning communities can be of value, as membership encourages learners to engage in their own learning, which in turn can facilitate interaction with peers and the teacher as they collaborate to achieve a shared goal (Pike/Kuh/McCormick 2010). Furthermore, desired educational outcomes such as students' persistence and graduation have been to linked to engagement in the process of learning (Inkelas/Weisman 2003; Pike/Kuh/McCormick 2010).

When interaction between individuals is focusing on a specific objective, they are collaborating. Collaboration is in general a recursive process where people are working together with others to achieve shared goals (Merriam-Webster). Collaborative learning is an active process and refers to learning that incorporates group work and interaction between students as well as between students and the teacher (Dooly 2008).

In the online era collaboration and communication is continuously spreading towards mediated interaction, beyond face-to-face interaction. In the educational environment this tendency manifests itself as blended learning where there are increasing shifts towards person-to-person mediated interaction and person-to-software mediated interaction. Within this context it is important to define the adjective interactive, which is used here to describe a situation or system that involves a response or exchange of information. Three broad levels of interactivity, that rely on the nature of the exchange, can be defined: Firstly, where there is no interaction and where a response is not related to a previous message; secondly, where the response is reactive and directly related to a previous message and thirdly where there is interaction as one response is related to a number of previous responses and where there is a relationship between these responses, such as with face-to-face interaction (Rafaeli 1988).

This third level of interaction that relies on the relationship between responses can also be enabled by social networking sites, such as Facebook. Facebook makes it possible for people to write or post a message, but also for two or more people to have an on-going written conversation in response to each other and this process can encourage collaborative language learning strategies (Peeters 2015). However, existing research shows that it is necessary to facilitate the Facebook learning community appropriately by taking care that learners establish their online social presence before they utilise the online platform for learning (Peeters/Ludwig 2017).

In a medical consultation setting face-to-face interaction between doctors and patients becomes more important as Western medicine becomes more patient centred with increasing emphasis on the consultation and conversations with patients (Van De Poel *et al.* 2013). The importance of effective medical communication has been supported by research that shows a corresponding relationship between improved doctor-patient communication and improved patient health results (Stewart 1995). Patients relate their satisfaction with the doctors' mode of communication with their evaluation of the medical care (Buller/Buller 1987). Furthermore, cultural misconceptions can result in humiliation and doctors being marginalized by colleagues (Gasiorek/Van de Poel 2012) thus reinforcing the need for medical communication training.

2.3 Metacognition and tasks

It is generally accepted that, from an educational point of view, the concept *metacognition* refers to the learners' awareness about their own knowledge and the regulation of this knowledge (Schraw 1998; Veenman/Van Hout-Wouters/Afilerbach 2006). According to research there is enough evidence to suggest that metacognition is not directly related to intellectual ability, but that metacognition can improve achievement on top of intellectual ability (Veenman/Van Hout-Wouters/Afilerbach 2006). From this point of view it will be beneficial to all learners if they can improve their metacognition. Metacognition mainly develops through the experience of problem solving (Schraw 1998). For the purposes of this research, metacognition will be defined and divided into declarative (knowledge and awareness about the person, the task and the strategy) and procedural knowledge that refers to the learners' abilities to regulate their own learning activities and problem solving processes. (Flavell 1979; Schraw 1998; Tarricone 2011; Veenman/Van Hout-Wouters/Afilerbach, 2006). In order to narrow down the focus of this article, it is significant to note that knowledge about the task includes amongst others awareness of the context of the task, awareness of task demands and an awareness of the nature or inherent and distinguishing characteristics of the tasks (Tarricone 2011).

Research done by Shea et al. (2014: 186) claim that a group with a collective goal can share metacognition within that group in order to coordinate a shared task and to improve the outcome of collective task performance. By implication the metacognition of the individual group members will also be boosted during this process.

3. Background

3.1 Meeting the needs of the rainbow nation

South Africa, the rainbow nation, has eleven official languages with corresponding cultures. Though a vibrant society, this multilingual country is understandably also characterised by communication challenges. English is widely regarded as the lingua franca and is the language used by the government and business sector, even though this status is not official. Results from the 2011 census show that South Africa's two largest linguistic groups are isiZulu and isiXhosa speakers. Afrikaans is the third largest home language and English the forth (South African Government 2014).

In order to address this demanding communication context, which can have a significant impact on patient health outcomes (Buller/Buller 1987; Stewart 1995) and to deal with the limited time available for medical communication training, the Faculty of Medicine and Health Sciences and the Language Center at the University of Stellenbosch, together with the European *Medics on the Move* (*MoM*) redesigned the existing Afrikaans second language medical communication programme for first year medical students. The online *MoM* programme, originally developed in 2006 and based on communicative functions typically used in the medical context, has since been translated to six European languages at beginners and advanced level with translation support for six other languages (www.comforpro.com). In 2012–2013 this programme was adapted and adopted to suit the South African context and the result was a medical communication training module in Afrikaans –*MoM-SA*.

MoM-SA uses a blended learning approach that involves face-to-face teaching in class that is combined and extended with an online module. The pedagogical foundation for the course is task-based learning with activities that reflect the medical context (*Medics on the Move* 2014). The book and the online module follow a similar structure. Both consist of ten units that follow the consultation timeline approximately. Each unit consists of medical scenarios and for the online module (that makes use of audio files throughout) this is followed by pronunciation, vocabulary, grammar and communication support and training exercises applicable to that unit. These exercises are corrected after each attempt and the correct answer with support is given. An online library with comprehensive pronunciation, grammar, meaning and communication training resources also exists. The course book, which contains similar training exercises in vocabulary, grammar and communication, is accompanied by a grammar book that provides and overview of the Afrikaans grammar with examples from the medical context (Van De Poel/Fourie 2013).

3.2 Introducing a closed Facebook group

Based on the evaluation of the pilot of the course in 2013 (Van de Poel/Fourie 2013) the anticipation was that the online module would be a challenge to the 2014-students. As the course was planned for the beginning of the academic year, the students would be new to academic culture and possibly lacking computer skills. Therefore a closed Facebook group was created with the initial purpose of creating an online learning community with a focus on medical communication training in Afrikaans, but also to lower the threshold for online learning (Fourie 2015). Students were invited to post general questions (either in English or Afrikaans) about the course and two tasks had to be answered on Facebook. For the first task, which was compulsory, students had to create a medical word list that complemented work done in class. The second task was optional and students could post short medical anecdotes in the target language. The teacher was a member of and active within this Facebook community. Therefore the Facebook group was an online extension of the classroom context, other than the online module that was meant for autonomous learning. As students new to Afrikaans would find posting in Afrikaans challenging, they were allowed to write posts in English which was in agreement with the objective to lower the threshold for online learning.

3.3   Examples of tasks that integrated the three learning platforms

The tasks students had to complete, integrated the three learning platforms –classroom, online module and Facebook group. For example, Unit 5 of the course book and online module is focusing on presenting a medical report. Both course book and online module begins with a scenario where medical colleagues are discussing patient Bulelwa. Students were advised to follow the online module's scenario and to note words with difficult pronunciation and those with unfamiliar meanings before the start of the class. Furthermore, the second scenario of the Unit is focusing on questions to elicit explanations and students had to prepare three questions which they, as doctors, would ask a fellow student during the next class –within an informal role-play context. During this lesson words with difficult pronunciation and meanings were discussed and the scenarios were read together in class. Towards the end of the lesson 20 minutes were allocated for a role-play activity. Another task in the course book-chapter contains three images of patients each with five prompts (symptoms, associated symptoms, medical history, family history and social history). Each student had to choose a patient and present the patient to a peer. During this exercise the lecturer was available for support, which mainly consisted of vocabulary and grammar related questions. Homework for the following lesson was to prepare a two-minute presentation (assessed task) about any imaginary patient. For the next lesson the class was divided in two groups with a co-teacher taking one group. Each student (doctor) had to present a patient to the whole group and the group (colleagues) could ask the doctor questions about the imaginary patient. As part of their preparation, students were advised to go through the online module's scenarios from units one to five and to choose their own relevant material. Students were also given the optional task to post a real life anecdote about a patient on the Facebook group in the target language. Examples were given in class and students had two weeks to participate in this task. During the final session students also completed a written test covering basic vocabulary, grammar and communication-related skills. For the duration of these lessons mentioned above, students posted alongside the given tasks also voluntary comments on Facebook about the logistics of sessions, acknowledging others' contributions, apprehension about compulsory tasks, as well as comments regarding technical issues with the online module.

4. Methodology

4.1 Approach

By changing the existing medical communication training programme to blended learning, as well as by including the closed Facebook community, a new approach to medical communication training in the Western Cape context of South Africa was introduced.

From the initial phases of the development and implementation of the *MoM-SA* program onwards, a team of researchers was involved and a mixed method approach was used to collect data. By using quantitative as well as qualitative data, the purpose was to gain information about the group as well as about the individual student. For the purposes of this research a mainly qualitative approach was used. Furthermore, during both the 2013 and 2014 courses, the researcher for this study was a participant-observer as well as the practitioner studying her own practice. Her purpose was to understand the teaching and learning environment as fully as possible (Waters-Adams 2006). Some of the known advantages where research is conducted by teachers themselves are that the teacher-researcher gains a better knowledge of the teaching and learning environment, which in turn supports the facilitation of change (Dörnyei 2007).

As the general purpose was to understand the impact of a new approach, this research can be seen as ethnographic research (Dörnyei 2007). Ethnographic research is putting increasingly more emphasis on studying processes and to gain understanding of these processes and experiences in the same way as its members do (Chamaz 2014) and it is especially valuable at the beginning of new projects where it is important to delineate real needs and constraints in an unknown context (Government of United Kingdom 2014). Furthermore, the ethnographic approach takes into account participants' understanding of their own behavior and culture. The approach also relies on the researcher's engagement in the target community over a longer period of time, thus resulting in the emergent nature of the research (Dörnyei 2007). Therefor, to accommodate the flexibility associated with ethnographic research, an emergent research design was chosen. "Emergent design refers to the fact that data collection and analysis can develop and be transformed as a consequence of what is learned during the earlier phases of the research" (Morgan 2008: 761).

4.2 Participants

The participants (N = 35) were first year medical students, enrolled for a compulsory 16 hour (eight sessions) communication course in Afrikaans for medical purposes at the University of Stellenbosch, one of the three universities in the Western Cape province. The three dominant languages in the Western Cape are English, Afrikaans and Xhosa. English was the home language of 31% of the 2014-intake of students, while the home languages of the remainder of the students were Tsonga, North-Sotho, Zulu, South Sotho, Xhosa, Pedi and Tswana.

As mentioned above, the researcher was a participant-observer and the practitioner studying her own practice. She is South African, a native speaker of Afrikaans and fluent in English. Her involvement with medical communication training started in 2012 during the material development process when the original *MoM*-material was adapted and adopted for the South African context and she was the lecturer (as an employee of the University of Stellenbosch) during the piloting of the material in 2013 (Van De Poel/Fourie 2013). In March 2014 she taught the second group of first year students.

5. Data

5.1 Collection instruments

A significant aspect of ethnographical research is to make use of multiple data sets (Dörnyei 2007) in order to incorporate various viewpoints and a variety of data sets have been collected for the *MoM-SA* project. For the purpose of this study specific data relevant to the question (What metacognitive awareness about tasks do medical communication students demonstrate?) have been selected, including the following:

1. Pre-course questionnaire with Likert scale and open questions on the languages students speak, how confident they feel using these as well as the frequency hereof and what they think would be the best way to learn a new language
2. Usability study following a Logic Framework (Van De Poel/Fourie 2013) apart from answering a set of matrix questions, students also had the opportunity to provide structured narrative comments on their learning experiences
3. Post-course questionnaire that included an open question that required 2014-students to evaluate the use of Facebook as part of the course
4. Recorded and transcribed post course focus group discussion on students' transition from school to university; whether they think it is necessary to speak

a language other than English in a professional medical environment and how they think a new language should be learned (2014-students)
5. Entries/posts on closed Facebook group (2014-students)
6. Pre-course questionnaire on availability of and access to computers and internet (2014-students)

5.2 Data collection

The questionnaires were completed individually on paper during the first and final lesson, as well as during an evaluation session that took place after the final lesson. The focus group interviews were also conducted and recorded during this final evaluation session. The text (all posts) of the online Facebook group was copied and saved.

5.3 Data handling procedure

All the data collected as text were analysed according to the principles of grounded theory. The strategies grounded theorists use include amongst others the viewpoint that data collection and data analysis can occur simultaneously and influence each other, which puts the focus on the analysis of actions and processes rather than on pre-conceived themes and structure to support theory construction. The systematic analysis of narrative data is therefore important in the process of developing new conceptual categories as well as inductive abstract categories (Charmaz 2014).

In general, three phases of coding can be distinguished (Dörnyei 2007). Through the process of several readings the text is first broken into chunks (open coding). This initial coding process is descriptive and relates strongly to the data and not on preconceived hypotheses (Charmaz 2014). Then more abstract connections are made to resemble concepts and subcategories (theoretical coding) and finally a core category (or categories) are identified that becomes a/the focal point of the research (selective coding). By using this process grounded theorists aim to code the meaning suggested by the data (Charmaz 2014).

The data directly related to and focusing on the closed Facebook was also analysed according to grounded theory at an earlier stage and reported upon (Fourie 2015). The outcome of this analysis was also taken into account as an integral constituent of the current research (see Appendix 1).

5.4 Data handling

The answers to the questionnaires were submitted to Survey Monkey Gold (www.surveymonkey.net) as separate sets of data. The focus group interviews were transcribed and submitted to Survey Monkey Gold as another set of data.

In Survey Monkey Gold the following open questions with students' comments were selected and exported to Excel:

7. What I liked about the method (structure and content of the course)
8. What I would like to see changed about the method
9. What I liked about the lessons
10. What I would like to see changed about the lessons
11. What I liked about the approach (the teaching, the books and online materials)
12. What I especially liked about the grammar book
13. What I especially liked about the general course book
14. What I liked about MoM online
15. I will/won't recommend MoM for Medical Students to other medical students, because
16. I will/won't use MoM online again, because
17. How do you think one learns a new language
18. General comments
19. My recommendations for this course
20. Have their been instances where you did not understand what the other person was saying here on campus or where someone did not understand what you were saying?

Through a process of several readings, these comments were tagged according to general task features valued in students' communication learning process. Repeated keywords, opinions and experiences that referred to the same idea were used as labels to tag the data. Documenting these carefully, the data were exported to Microsoft Word and were grouped together under sub-concepts, according to abstract connections. After more readings and also by organizing the information in tables, several core categories regarding students' awareness about tasks were identified.

These subcategories were again organized to reflect core categories such as *structure, well-being of students, types of activities, linguistic content of tasks, timing and pace of learning* as well as *the nature (inherent characteristics) of tasks*. For the purposes of this research, the nature of the tasks as a category was explored in more detailed as this category provides the guiding characteristics or principles underlying the other categories.

6. Results

According to the data, the nature of tasks consists of three elements or essential qualities, which are the interactive, relevant and personalised nature of tasks. An analysis of these three elements resulted in a framework that demonstrates students' metacognitive awareness about the nature of tasks that supports medical communication training in a blended learning environment. See Tables 1, 2 and 3 for this framework of the interactive, relevant and personalised nature of tasks. For a more detailed analysis, see examples in Appendix 2.

Table 1: *A summary of students' awareness of the **interactive nature of tasks** supporting medical communication training within a blended environment*

Components	Classroom descriptors	Facebook group descriptors	Online module descriptors
Regularly using spoken language with lecturer & peers	Accommodating atmosphere needed Rehearsed & spontaneous responses take place		
Integrating spoken language with theory/grammar in flexible way	On-demand & spontaneous learning with lecturer		On-demand learning with guidance of lecturer
Receiving support & assistance	From lecturer & peer Support via course & grammar book	From lecturer & peer	Support manuals in library of online platform
Giving support	To peer	To peer	
Getting involved with activities	Individual willingness to make mistakes Individual & group responsibilities allocated Participation: optional and compulsory	Individual willingness to make mistakes Individual & group responsibilities allocated Participation: optional and compulsory	Exercises & quizzes
Receiving feedback	From peer & lecturer Engage in own learning process	From peer & lecturer Engage in own learning process	Audio with pronunciation & correct answer

Components	Classroom descriptors	Facebook group descriptors	Online module descriptors
Providing feedback	To peer Engage in collaborative learning	To peer Engage in collaborative learning	
Gathering supportive information	More on content (meaning, vocabulary, grammar, pronunciation) More on instructions	More on content (meaning, vocabulary, grammar, pronunciation) More on instructions	Library has more information on content (meaning, vocabulary, grammar, pronunciation)
Verifying content & contributions	With lecturer & peer	Facebook provides open access for group-members & constant overview	Repeating exercises with auto correct
Integrating all learning platforms	Dynamic nature of lessons	Dynamic nature of collaborative learning	Dynamic nature of learning (preparation and reinforcement)

Table 2: A summary of students' awareness about the **relevant nature of tasks** supporting medical communication training within a blended environment

Components	Classroom descriptors	Facebook group descriptors	Online module descriptors
Learning medical communication skills relevant to future career	Content of resources and activities based on medical context	Tasks related to medical context	Content based on medical context Potential use of module in future
Learning communication skills relevant to everyday conversations	Social conversations in class Possible to apply content on medical context to everyday contexts	Social interaction	Possible to apply content on medical context to everyday contexts
Voicing personal, academic & pre-professional experiences	Accommodated by teacher and peer	Share positive experiences and challenges on a daily (hourly) basis	

Components	Classroom descriptors	Facebook group descriptors	Online module descriptors
Self-evaluating	Determine own needs based on progress	Ability to express own needs and read similar needs of peers	Repeat exercises based on needs (teacher guidance needed)

Table 3: A summary of students' awareness about the **personalised nature of tasks** supporting medical communication training within a blended environment

Components	Classroom descriptors	Facebook group descriptors	Online module descriptors
Experiencing individual feedback	Feedback from teacher & peers	Feedback from peers (& teacher)	
Experiencing personal convenience		Personalised timing and place	Personalised timing and place
Accommodating different learning styles	Awareness raised in class		
Accommodating different educational backgrounds	Awareness raised in class		
Accommodating different abilities & needs	Personal needs addressed	Express individual needs	Use according to own needs

6.1 The interactive nature of tasks

Medical students value the interactive nature of tasks in communication training. When referring to the interactive nature of language learning they apply the meaning of the word to all three main levels of interaction (Rafaeli 1988). The most readily understood of these is the third level where one response can be related to all the previous responses and where there is a relationship between the agents making the responses. Although written language can also fit into this category, students specifically refer to the use of spoken language in class, which is also the mode they will mostly use with patients. The learning and tasks performed via the online module fall in both the first and the second level of interactivity. For the first level, there is no response and students can, for example, simply read and listen to a scenario and then randomly choose another scenario to read. The second level is obtained where the response is reactive and directly related to a previous message (Rafaeli 1988). Examples would be automated corrections for answered exercises or being redirected to the online library as support in determining the reasoning behind a specific answer.

The posts on the Facebook group (see Table 1) were level three interaction where there is a continuing relationship between responses and the people writing the responses. However, if group members are not responding to a post, this could be seen as second level interaction. The most noticeable difference between the third level posts on the Facebook group and face-to-face communication, is the real-time verbal communication in face-to-face contexts.

Students' awareness about the interactive nature of tasks performed in class (see Table 1) highlights the regular use of spoken language in the target language with the lecturer. However, these (rehearsed and spontaneous) conversations relied on the accommodating attitude of the lecturer and a stress-free atmosphere in which students could gain confidence. In a similar way, the regular use of spoken language with peers was also valued, both in compulsory group work and spontaneous conversations. In these conversations with the lecturer and peers, grammar, vocabulary or pronunciation related explanations about a specific language feature could either be spontaneously raised by the students or pointed out by the teacher in a flexible way. Apart from these explanations, students also wanted to experience verbal support from the lecturer as well as from peers in their preferred language of communication and not always in the target language. The support could include pronunciation support, translation support as well as guidance on how to use the printed and online resources. According to the students, learning took place when they got involved with activities which required individual as well as group responsibilities and alongside this they valued both optional and compulsory participation. They claim that personal involvement with activities generated learning that had its own energy, but that a willingness to make mistakes was necessary for this degree of involvement. They also report that the dynamic energy of the lessons was facilitated by the fact that the tasks performed on the three different learning platforms were integrated with each other in that sense the three platforms were interacting with each other.

According to the data, the interactive environment of the Facebook community of practice was also significant. For a previously done analysis of this data, see Appendix 1 (Fourie 2015). As with the classroom, student involvement with activities is also a necessary component for the sustainable energy of the Facebook learning environment. Furthermore, the interactive nature of accomplishing tasks was characterized by four more metacognitive components, the first referring to Facebook functioning as a channel through which students can gather additional information such as content and instructions for tasks. The second component refers to the open access of Facebook that enabled students to have continuous access to peers' contributions in order to verify their own. A further result of this continuous access was that students had constant opportunity to receive feedback on their progress made, as well as opportunities to provide feedback and in that sense engaged not only in their own learning, but also in the learning of others. A similar component was the opportunity to receive and provide assistance and support with problem solving.

The interactive nature of the autonomous online component is based on the quizzes and exercises that show the number of correct answers and the corrections for wrong answers and allows for repeated practice. When giving the correct answers, the exercises also provide feedback and links to resources, such as the relevant section from a grammar manual. Students also appreciated the interaction between different learning platforms as some class activities needed preparation, which was done by completing exercises on the online module or reading and listening to scenarios. However, students claimed that they needed the teacher's guidance in order to do so.

6.2 The relevant nature of tasks

The relevance of tasks is the second element about the nature of tasks and related to the context of students' future careers in the medical profession. The data about tasks done in class, show that students appreciated learning communication skills relevant to consultations with patients and discussions with other medical professionals. The course book, grammar book and class activities supported learning of medical communication skills as medical terminology, medical scenarios and examples from medical contexts were used. Students also claimed that communication skills based on activities in class can also be applied to everyday contexts, for instance communication skills that involve greeting a patient can also be applied to greeting friends.

The use of Facebook became relevant to students as they had the ability to voice personal experiences while working on tasks and received appropriate feedback and support.

As with the content of the tasks done in class, students also appreciated the fact that the online module's scenarios and exercises were based on the medical context.

Furthermore, the practical application of this module also added to its relevance as students claimed that the online module as a smart phone application could be useful during future medical rounds when communication with patients and colleagues will be necessary.

6.3 The personalised nature of tasks

The third element that students report upon in the data about tasks, refers to the personalised nature of tasks (Table 3). The course book used in class regularly created opportunities for students to reflect on their personal progress so that students could determine and formulate their changing linguistic needs on a continuing basis. Different learning styles of students were accommodated by discussing various learning preferences and by explaining different ways on how to approach different tasks. Apart from various learning styles, different educational backgrounds were accommodated as students were for instance made aware of different experiences in terms of literacy and computer literacy backgrounds.

Learning via the closed Facebook group was personalised as students could voice individual needs, not only about academic challenges associated with tasks, but also about their well-being and they could receive (or give) personal feedback. This process was further encouraged by the convenience of learner control over the timing and place of the process. The open access feature of closed groups on Facebook also made it possible for students to take part in self-evaluation as individual progress could intuitively and constantly be compared against the posts of others (Fourie 2015).

Though the content and activities of the online programme are structured with gradual increase of grammatical complexity, it allowed for personalised learning, because students have free choice to access the online module according to their own needs. However, students needed teacher guidance in order to understand how to address their needs with the online module. Furthermore, the convenience of choosing a time and place to utilize the programme made it possible to adjust learning to personal needs. Apart from this, individuals could choose how many times they wanted to do a specific exercise.

7. Discussion

Experiences generated by tasks are significant in a medical communication training setting as students will, towards the end of their studies, rely on what they gained through these experiences, when they are at the same time directly responsible for patients' health. By implication authentic language learning via authentic tasks becomes significant in training.

This research explored students' metacognitive awareness associated with the nature of language learning tasks, which showed that students valued three main elements, namely the interactive, relevant and personalised or meaningful nature of tasks. Previous research has shown that the combination of these three elements can create an authentic learning experience, but students need to be made aware of these elements in order to work towards authenticity (Rysteldt/Sjöblom 2012; Van Lier 1996). This coincides with Stockwell's (2012) viewpoint that students learning a new language in a blended environment will need teacher guidance in order to understand how to use online tasks so that individual learning needs can be met. That is for example the reason why students reported that they appreciated the compulsory tasks, because in spite of initial apprehension, they could not only engage in learning, but also raise their metacognition about the process of solving language learning problems.

Taking into account that meaning is produced through the interactions of individuals and that interaction is a natural attribute of face-to-face communication (Rafaeli 1988; Blake 2000; Wang 2004) it is understandable why students value conversations with the teacher and peers as an integral part of communication training and why, accordingly, tasks should generate conversations. Although written language can also fit this category of third level interaction, students specifically refer to the use of spoken language in class, which is also the mode they will mostly use with patients in a doctor-patient setting. Even though the online module does not allow for interaction between people, it is valued for its second level interactive nature where online tasks allowed for reactive responses so that students could engage in learning. The interactive written posts on Facebook could move beyond the classroom restrictions in terms of limited space and timing. Furthermore, as the students spontaneously referred to the online module in their Facebook posts, the Facebook group complemented the online platform by providing the appropriate online third level (or human) interaction that the online module lacks (see example of activity under 3. Background).

The course was relevant as the content of resources and tasks performed in class and via the online module were directly based on professional medical consultations. Accordingly, any task that included a grammar focus, can be related to a sentence spoken in a scenario that is part of a medical consultation. The relevant nature of the Facebook platform was not only due to the fact that Facebook functioned as a learning community for medical pre-professionals, but also due to the fact that students could share and therefore acknowledge personal experiences and challenges alongside task-related posts (Peeters/Ludwig 2017). Students therefore voiced their awareness about the relevant nature of tasks from a general and professional as well as a personal point of view.

Learning became personalised not only when various educational backgrounds and learning styles were acknowledged and choices about tasks (especially via the online platform) could be made, but also when students could express linguistic as well as personal needs and receive individualized feedback (and the Facebook platform is especially functional in this regard). Paradoxically, the individual experience and challenge became more meaningful when shared. This paradox is significant as it points towards collaboration. According to existing research a learning community, such as the closed Facebook group, can optimize learner engagement which can improve educational outcomes (Pike/Kuh/McCormick 2010).

Therefore, even though students are responsible for their own learning and to complete tasks in a blended environment (Ashton 2010), other research (Stockwell 2012; Dooly 2008; Rysteldt/Sjöblom 2012) as well as the above data have shown that students need the teacher's guidance as well as input and support of peers (from within a learning community) to take this responsibility on. As metacognitive awareness about tasks is raised through experience and involvement with tasks (Schraw 1998) and can be shared (Shea *et al.* 2014) the claim can be made that raising metacognition is a collaborative effort with an authentic learning experience as a positive outcome. This points to the notion that the teacher has to take responsibility to facilitate this dynamic process, which "depends on the interplay between the language learners, the teacher, and the tasks and material embedded in the social situation of the classroom" (Laursen/Frederiksen 2015: 64). In a blended learning environment the same principles apply, but the interplay between teacher, students and tasks becomes more complex as it extends beyond the classroom to an online module and social networking site.

8. Conclusion

This ethnographic study was performed in South Africa as part of a larger research project where blended learning, which included a social networking site alongside the classroom and online module, was introduced to first year medical communication training students. Based on a data analysis, the result was an outline of the metacognitive awareness about the nature of tasks that these first year students displayed and reported upon within a blended learning context. The main elements from this outline are interactive, relevant and personalised learning. According to recent research that broadens the notion of *authenticity* in education, the essential parts for an authentic learning experience are in fact interactive, relevant and personalised learning (Ashton 2010; Holliday 2013; Rysteldt/Sjöblom 2012; Van Lier 1996). From this point of view authentic learning is a dynamic process and not the sole responsibility of the teacher, but also relies on student involvement with learning and on collaboration between students themselves, as well as between students and the teacher.

Therefore the outline (see Tables 1, 2 and 3) intends to be a guideline for teachers on how to collaborate with students in a blended learning environment in order to raise metacognitive awareness and to work towards an authentic communication training experience. The reality and responsibility of a doctor-patient consultation awaits in the future of these students, but by raising awareness about the nature of tasks, students can take a step towards authentic communication training and gaining the skills required for consultations.

Recommendations are for research to delineate the individual components of the elements associated with authenticity in more detail and to reconcile this with existing research. Following on this study, research will explore the metacognitive strategies and procedural knowledge of students employed in the process of problem solving within a blended communication training context.

Appendix 1: Facebook related data analysed for previous research

Table A: Overview of how using Facebook raised students' metacognitive awareness in the process of learning a language for medical purposes: students progressed towards three targets by developing the metacognitive components that are described.

			Metacognitive awareness raising
Targets	**Components**	**Descriptors**	**Facebook related narrative data**
	Gaining knowledge and skills about oneself as a (language) learner or communicator		
Identity	Gaining motivation	Enjoyment	Experiencing communication and tasks as fun and enjoyable
		Interest	Experiencing communication and tasks as interesting
		Involvement	Engaging with tasks, peers and lecturer
	Gaining confidence	Comfort	Closing close the gap between the 'abstract' academic world and real life social situations
		Overview and perspective	Gaining perspective by having an overview of peers' contributions Verifying own experiences
		Non-threatening atmosphere	Experiencing communication as informal and therefore less threatening, compared to a more formal academic environment
	Building community	Shared experiences	Sharing positive/negative experiences with peers
		Inclusivity	Experiencing a positive sense of community, openness and inclusiveness
		Peer support	Receiving and providing peer support
	Gaining knowledge about task – learning to medically communicate		
Effectiveness	Gathering information	Instructions	Confirming instructions for online and classroom tasks
		Content	Instructions
	Verifying content & contributions	Open access	Content
	Gaining knowledge about (language) learning strategies		
Efficiency	Receiving & providing feedback	Feedback on progress	Requesting peer/lecturer feedback for reassurance Providing feedback
	Managing time	Time saving	Experiencing communication (almost) in real time (but social activities may interfere) Just-in-time learning
		Individualised schedule	Accessing communication and learning at any time (own time, own space)
		Limitless opportunities to communicate	Communicating as often and as long as needed
	Experiencing convenience	User-friendliness	Experiencing tool as easy to access (low threshold) Learners access tool regularly for social reasons
	Receiving assistance	Assistance with problem solving	Possibility to receive peer/lecturer assistance with a task
		Technical assistance	Possibility to receive technical assistance (with *MoM*-online)
	Interactive learning	Student–student	Potential to interact with peers on learning tasks
		Student–lecturer	Potential to interact with lecturer beyond classroom
		Student–learning	Potential as a dynamic platform on which learning takes place

Appendix 2: Data analysis with examples

Table A: Students' awareness about the interactive nature of tasks that supports communication training.

	Components	Descriptors	Examples
In class	Regularly using spoken language with lecturer	Accommodating attitude of lecturer Stress-free atmosphere to ask questions Rehearsed and spontaneous responses Confidence gain	Conversations initiated in class as big group or in small groups Presentations Role play Games (board games in small groups) Songs Lecturer flexible to respond to questions and needs as they become relevant in specific situations Guidance on how to use printed and online resources Feedback in groups on tasks done in coursebook Feedback in class on tasks done on online platform and Facebook
	Regularly using spoken language with peers	Rehearsed and spontaneous responses Confidence gain	
	Integrating spoken language with theory/grammar (flexible)	Just-in-time learning	
	Receiving support	Lecturer and peer support Course book and grammar book support	
	Getting involved with activities	Energy Individual and group responsibilities Willingness to make mistakes Participation: optional to compulsory	
	Integrating all learning platforms	Dynamic nature of lessons Integrating classroom tasks with those on Facebook and online platform Online platform and course book with similar structure (familiar)	

Closed Facebook group (community of practice)	Getting involved with activities	Energy Individual and group responsibilities Willingness to make mistakes Participation ranging from optional to compulsory	Contributing (posting vocabulary) towards a wordlist-task that is an extension of work done in class Posting anecdotes
	Gathering information	Content instruction	Posts with administrative detail
	Verifying content & contributions	Open access	Viewing all posts made by all other students Spontaneous posts with comments and feedback within hours Supporting peers, e.g. with translation support Assistance with online programme, e.g. technical issues
	Receiving & providing feedback	Feedback on progress Engaging in learning process on individual and group level	
	Receiving support/assistance	Assistance with problem solving Technical support	
	Integrating all learning platforms	Dynamic nature of learning Integrating Facebook tasks with those done in class and online platform	Posts on Facebook regarding instructions of class and online tasks Feedback in class on Facebook task
Online	Gathering information	Scenario's, exercises/quizzes on meaning, sound and grammar	Questions can be repeated to practice Audio with correct answer
	Receiving feedback and support	Variety of resources (library)	Links to systematic explanations of grammar, word maps and translation support Online and course book with similar structure (familiarity of content and structure) Addressing technical issues on Facebook Grammar issued from conversations can be resolved at a later stage online (with teacher guidance)
	Integrating all learning platforms	Dynamic nature of learning	

Table B: *Students' awareness about the relevant nature of tasks that supports communication training.*

	Components	Descriptors	Examples
In class	Learning communication skills relevant to consultations with patients	Content of resources and activities based on medical contexts	Medical terminology Medical scenario's Examples from medical context Communication skills regarding greeting a patient can also be applied to greeting friends etc.
	Learning communication skills relevant to discussions with colleagues		
	Learning communication skills relevant to everyday conversations	Application of medical contexts to everyday contexts	
On Facebook	Voicing personal experiences	Posting and sharing positive experiences and challenges on a daily (hourly) basis	Posting support with upcoming assessments Posting and voicing frustration due to technical issues with online module and receiving immediate feedback
	Voicing study/ pre-professional experiences	Posting and sharing academic experiences on a daily (hourly) basis	
Online module	Learning and reinforcing communication skills relevant to discussions with colleagues	Content of online module based on medical context	Scenario's, exercises and grammar support based on medical context Claiming the online module will be useful while doing medical rounds
	Learning and reinforcing communication skills relevant to consultations with patients		
	Using the online module in future	Potential use of module in future and after course completion	

Table C: *Students' awareness about the personalised nature of tasks that supports communication training.*

	Components	Descriptors	Examples
In class	Self-evaluating	Students determine own needs based on progress	Personal advice Describing different learning styles Explaining different ways on how to approach a specific topic Students made aware of various literacy and computer literacy experiences before coming to university. Advice given Differentiated work in course book and online Opportunities to reflect progress in class activity in course-book
	Accommodating different learning styles	Awareness raised	
	Accommodating different educational backgrounds	Awareness raised	
	Accommodating different abilities and needs	Personal needs addressed	

	Components	Descriptors	Examples
On Facebook	Giving and receiving personalized feedback	Students voice individual needs	Students respond spontaneously to posts made by others
	Experiencing convenience	Personalised timing of activities Personalised assistance	Students can access Facebook in their own time and place.
Online	Meeting individual needs	As much practice as needed Use according to own needs	Though content and activities are structured with gradual increase of complexity, students have free choice to access platform according to own needs. Exercises can be repeated.
	Experiencing convenience	Personalised timing of activities Personalised assistance	

Die zunehmende Globalisierung führt nicht nur zu einer gesteigerten Mobilität in der Arbeitswelt, sondern auch zu einem sich wandelnden Kommunikationsverhalten, das vor allem durch eine zunehmende Mehrsprachigkeit gekennzeichnet ist. Kommunikation und Interaktion finden zunehmend über geografische, sprachliche und kulturelle Grenzen hinweg statt. In Arzt-Patienten Gesprächen kommt erfolgreicher Kommunikation eine besondere Bedeutung zu, da das Wohl des Patienten in direktem Zusammenhang zu der Kommunikation zwischen Patient und Arzt steht (vgl. Buller/Buller 1987; Stewart 1995) und eine mangelhafte Kommunikation nicht nur die Therapietreue negativ beeinflussen kann, sondern auch das Risiko von Fehldiagnosen und falschen Behandlungen erhöht. Da angehende Mediziner oft direkt nach Abschluss ihres Studiums mit der Kommunikation mit Patienten konfrontiert werden, sollte diesem Bereich, nicht zuletzt in Hinblick auf eine immer stärker zunehmende Mehrsprachigkeit, bereits im Studium eine besondere Bedeutung zukommen. Die Integration authentischer Materialien und Aufgaben sowie das Durchlaufen authentischer Kommunikationssituationen in mehrsprachigen Kontexten ermöglicht es Lernern, sich auf ihren späteren Berufsalltag besser vorzubereiten. Da universitäre Lehre zunehmend Elemente des Blended-Learning Ansatzes integriert (vgl. Graham 2006), ist es wichtig, Lehrenden Guidelines an die Hand zu geben, wie sich Aufgaben zur Förderung authentischer Kommunikation in Blended-Learning Umgebungen lernerorientiert integrieren lassen, um dem Ziel "to address students' learning needs for authenticity" (Pinner 2014; Laursen/Frederiksen 2015: 64) näher zu kommen. In Hinblick auf das veränderte Rollenverhalten in Onlinelernumgebungen kommt Lernern selbst hierbei eine zentrale Rolle zu.

Dieser Beitrag berichtet über die Ergebnisse einer ethnografischen Studie, durchgeführt an der Universität Stellenbosch, Südafrika, welche unter Bezugnahme auf die Grounded Theory ausgewertet wurden. Studierende im ersten Fachsemester nahmen an einem Kommunikationskurs im Blended-Learning Format teil. Die Präsensveranstaltungen wurden durch die Teilnahme an einer geschlossenen Facebook-Gruppe und einem unabhängigen Onlinemodul ergänzt, welche Studierenden die Möglichkeit boten, auch außerhalb der formalen Interaktion im Seminar, miteinander zu kommunizieren. Im Fokus der Analyse stand das Bewusstsein der Teilnehmer bezüglich der Aufgabennatur, die mehrheitlich als interaktiv, relevant und personalisiert beschrieben wurde und somit denen authentischer Lernerfahrungen ähnelt. Des Weiteren hat die Datenanalyse gezeigt, dass sich diese Elemente am besten in kollaborativen Lernumgebungen realisieren lassen. Daher ist dieser Beitrag vor allem als Handlungsanweisung für Lehrende zu verstehen und soll Wege aufzeigen, das metakognitive Bewusstsein von Lernern zu steigern.

Kris Van de Poel & Jessica Gasiorek
University of Antwerp, Belgium
University of Hawai'i at Mānoa, Honolulu, HI, USA

Collaborative Academic Acculturation Processes in a Blended-Learning Approach

Students entering university find it challenging to academically acculturate (Darlaston-Jones et al. 2003; Leki 2006; Brinkworth et al. 2009). This is even more so for language learners. This paper will report on the efforts undertaken to make an academic writing course for first-and second-year English majors more effective through the inclusion of a collaborative, online component. By blending online and face-to-face components in the course of the twelve-week programme, students actively engaged with peers in preparing writing assignments. Moreover, they were stimulated to collaboratively define the applicability and use of the materials, thus functioning as 'peer-teachers'. Learners thus collaborated across the boundaries of the traditional classroom, engaging with new media in a bottom-up approach, while enlarging their traditional working space to encompass the virtual world. Our data show that overall, students responded positively to the inclusion of this component of the course, but that they found different approaches and collaboration structures most effective for different course content.

1. General introduction

Several studies have shown that students entering higher education (HE) find it challenging to learn and adapt to the norms and practices of a HE environment– in other words, they find it challenging to *academically acculturate* (Darlaston-Jones *et al.* 2003; Leki 2006; Brinkworth *et al.* 2009). Research indicates that first-year students often have an easier time with social acculturation than academic acculturation: following the transition to a HE environment, their social well-being is often higher than their academic well-being (De Geest 2012; Van de Poel/Gasiorek 2012b). Additionally, academic proficiency test results and targeted questionnaire data indicate that first-year language majors overestimate their academic capacities and preparedness (cf. Van Dyk/Van de Poel/Van der Slik 2013 for a South-African perspective; Van Dyk/Van de Poel/Van der Slik in prep. for a Flemish perspective). In order to help first-year students both be successful in their courses and acculturate to HE settings, it is important to help them improve their awareness of the standards and norms of HE, as well as improve their academic (reading and writing; listening and speaking) skills.

To become a successful member of the academic community, students must be or become academically literate –that is, they must develop the skills to communicate and function with ease in an academic environment (cf. Boughey 2000: 281; Hyland 2006, 2009: ix). Becoming academically literate is a cumulative process in which reading, writing, critical thinking and self-management, among other skills, need to be gradually learned and repetitively practiced. Academic writing, in particular, plays a critical role in attaining and demonstrating academic literacy, and is an area where students frequently struggle, with a high risk for failure (e.g., Johns 1997; Howes 1999; Street 1999; Snow 2005; Hyland 2006).

Even though academic literacy is 'foreign' for all young students (Van de Poel/Van Dyk 2015), it is even more so for second or foreign language (L2) learners. These students face not only a new kind of discourse, i.e. academic discourse, but also have to approach it in a language they are still in the process of learning. As the HE student population becomes increasingly diverse, HE classrooms are increasingly filled with individuals at different stages of academic language proficiency, and with different learning preferences, paths, routes and routines. In this situation, we suggest, an autonomous approach to language learning may be the most effective and efficient for students. In other words, we suggest that learners can and should be encouraged to take control of planning, monitoring and evaluating the learning process and outcome and show willingness and motivation to initiate and regulate their learning (Little 2004; Nguyen/Gu 2013; Murray 2014).

However, because (L2) learners in HE are not always ready to take up the responsibility for their own learning –in other words, they are not fully autonomous and often wish to hear the 'authoritative' voice of a tutor or lecturer– it is important to provide support systems for them that facilitate taking ownership of their learning (cf. Stracke 2007). More specifically, we may need to make them aware of the impact they can have on their own learning by showing them a range of ways toward becoming-at a minimum-co-owners of that process.

To this end, for L2 students, foreign language interaction can be regarded as an opportunity to collaborate in solving their language-related problems, scaffold each other, and co-construct new language knowledge (cf. Donato 1994; Ohta/Foster 2005; Swain 2000; Luzzatto/Di Marco 2010). If students are to develop this knowledge and skill set with respect to academic language norms and use, these opportunities should be embedded in an academic context. Collaboration, then, has the potential to play an important role in academic acculturation (although see Colpaert/Gijsen (this volume) for a critical review of collaborative learning). In this article we will focus specifically on peer collaboration, and how it can lower the (perceived) threshold for students' engagement with the requirements of the academic setting. In this, we extend work by Dobao (2014: 498), which examined the opportunities that pair and small-group task-based interaction offer for peer collaboration and L2 vocabulary learning, to academic literacy more broadly (i.e., both reading and writing). In doing so, we argue that in HE settings, learners can and should be active participants in their own learning, as well as their peers' (cf. Barkley 2014: 4).

Given the limited contact hours in university courses, it is not always possible to provide students with extensive opportunities for peer collaboration along with teaching required curriculum content in the classroom alone. Rather, new routes have to be found. This article will report on the efforts undertaken to make an academic writing course for first-and second-year English majors (L2) more effective through the use of a *blended learning approach,* combining online and face-to-face interaction in which students were explicitly guided to work collaboratively.

A blended learning approach can be a compelling option when course programmes suffer from being overloaded, student numbers are high, staff hours are being reduced, or the student population is highly heterogeneous and there is a need to cater to a diverse set of learning needs. A blended approach "combine[s] face-to-face instruction with computer-mediated instruction" (Graham 2006: 5). In this, students experience a combination of lecturer-directed classroom interaction and self-guided online learning and (in our case, peer) interaction. To the extent that students decide on their own learning route and content while engaging with the online component, this approach is generally regarded as having a positive impact on the learners' autonomy (Little 1991). Provided that the computer-mediated component is not just a mirror copy of or 'data dump' of in-class content, the approach can turn learners into co-owners of the teaching and learning process in a true constructivist spirit (Van de Poel/Fourie 2013). Since the blended context provides an opportunity for interaction and collaboration which class sizes may not cater for, blended learning has the potential to allow more intense social and academic networking than might otherwise be possible. Ideally, this should give participants opportunities to co-construct more mature cohesive reasoning patterns (cf. Reuven *et al.* 2003) through which they are able to reach "a high level of critical thinking" (Laat *et al.* 2007: 90).

In what follows, we discuss how collaboration in an online environment was integrated into first-and second-year academic writing courses at the University of Antwerp (Belgium). The initiative was aimed at giving the learners the opportunity to exchange ideas with fellow students preparatory to and as an integral part of a number of writing assignments and to reflect on the course content as well as to inform their personal learning trajectory through peer collaboration and peer review. We will first discuss how instructors incorporated the assignments and instructions into the existing courses and created an informed blend. We will then present and discuss data on students' reactions to this collaborative aspect of both courses, highlighting their implications for collaborative language course design and how it can support students' academic acculturation.

2. Case study: blended learning in academic writing courses

During the 2013–2014 and 2014–2015 academic years, use of a collaborative learning space, hosted on the online social network Facebook, was integrated into two academic writing courses at the University of Antwerp (Belgium). These courses, which were each four months in duration (one term), were a required component of the curriculum for first-year and second-year majors studying English literature and linguistics, as part of the language and literature BA degree program (BA *taal-en letterkunde*). The students who participated in the project were independent users of the language with (upper) intermediate language proficiency in English (Language test report 2013). Their native language was Dutch. There are no entrance requirements for language studies at Flemish universities, so students can enter university with a variety of scholastic backgrounds. In practice, the first year is a selection year with just over half of students typically passing their first-year examinations (e.g., 51.4% passed in the 2013–2014 year).

Most students who enrol in this degree program study two languages, and start their HE studies with general introductory courses on literature and linguistics. As part of their curriculum for English, students take different courses on English language and literature as well as English Proficiency. In the first year English Proficiency course, writing instruction focuses on writing in an academic context and represents two out of 20 credits for English (of a total of 60 credits for the first year). The main focus of the first year writing component is foundational academic acculturation and initial introduction of related writing skills (writing-through-reading). In the second year English Proficiency course, students have another two credits addressing academic writing. In this second, more advanced course, the focus is on genre-specific features of academic writing.

Before they were offered as blended, both the first-and second-year academic writing courses had weekly contact sessions supported by online language awareness raising activities and reflection exercises with theoretical summaries provided in a book. The materials used in these courses are the result of an extensive needs and error analysis and have been evaluated on an ongoing basis (Van de Poel/Gasiorek 2007, 2009a+b, 2010, 2012a+b). From 2013–2014 onwards, both courses were supplemented with a closed Facebook group to foster reflection and self-regulation through guided online activities (or e-tivities) that were designed to keep learners engaged, motivated, and participating (Salmon *et al.* 2015). The courses' Facebook groups, which constituted online collaborative learning spaces, are the focus of the discussion that follows.

In the first-year course, all students contributed to one large forum. The students were asked to confer with their peers about three monthly writing assignments on a closed Facebook group. The assignments revolved around linguistic topics about which the students had to form an opinion and formulate supportive argumentation, which they then wrote up in short individual essays. Students were instructed to incorporate the most helpful feedback on their writing from their peers before handing in their writing assignments. The instructions for each task were designed to encourage collaboration and offer specific guidance for effective collaboration strategies. The following is an example of instructions for the first-year course:

- Post (at least) one question in the Facebook group concerning your assignment. You can also ask your fellow students for tips and tricks concerning particular aspects academic writing.
- Before you upload your assignment, pick the Facebook answer you think was most helpful and write it down below.
- Reply to (at least) one question and try to link it to your own text.
- Upload your assignment.

The texts were individually corrected by a writing consultant, after which the students received feedback and tips for improvement, and were required to hand in and upload an edited version.

In the first year course, no tutor was present online, as it was thought that the threshold for peer-to-peer communication would be lowered without 'surveillance' from those who were formally evaluating them. The intention was that this lowered threshold would lead to a more extensive and genuine language output (Lloyd 2012) and an increase in social engagement between fellow learners (Dam 2008). The aim of the project was to engage students in online peer collaboration and negotiation and raise their awareness with respect to the quality of their own writing assignments.

The second year course takes writing-through-reading as a starting point and focuses on specific topics and issues in academic discourse, with an emphasis on awareness raising. Here, peer collaboration was structured such that students first worked on their assignments (four in total) in small groups of approximately six students each, before sharing their findings in the 'Scriboratory learning community', a closed Facebook group that included all students in the course.

This following is an example of instructions for the second-year course, about academic lexicon:
The following paragraph, adapted from a first-year student essay entitled *To 'Know' a Language?* is not written academically.

Procedure:
- Rewrite the paragraph as an academic text, with special attention to register, vocabulary and grammar, adding comments about what you are changing and why.
- Make use of the Scribende scale for chapters 5, 6, 7 when writing and peer reviewing each other's text. Remember, you are allowed to differ in opinion from your peer. After all, it is your text.
- Provide a good title and a two-sentence summary of the text as well.
- Exchange your summaries in your little groups.
- On the Scriboratory, upload what you think is the most annoying error in this text. All of you should vote for the worst error (any argument welcome).
- Add the top 3 of errors at the bottom of your text.

Because the writing assignments are academic in nature (and require more follow-up and support than the first year students' assignments) and there are fewer concerns about threshold-lowering for second-year students, a group of four junior researchers, called 'Scribenders', supervised the Scriboratory group, but did so with a light hand. Students were told:

> Take part in discussions and let your voice be heard. Remember that the Scribenders are only there to foster communication and to add food for thought once every two weeks. The purpose of the forum is to establish peer-assessment and peer-to-peer communication through sharing ideas, annotating, editing and commenting the assignments.

In what follows, we present students' evaluations of the online components of these writing courses.

2.1 Method

In the first year, $N = 112$ students participated in the Facebook group and completed a usable end-of-course evaluation questionnaire. In the second year, $N = 68$ students participated in the combination of small groups and course-wide Facebook group, and completed a usable end-of-course evaluation questionnaire.

The questionnaires consisted of several closed-format questions using a five-point Likert-type scale (1 = strongly agree, 5 = strongly disagree). Respondents were invited to provide additional comments to questions in comment sections after these closed format questions. Identifying information was collected as part of these questionnaires, which allowed us to match students' responses to these questions with their academic performance (i.e., marks) in the courses.

Eight questions assessed students' evaluation of the peer collaboration opportunities in each course (i.e., the Facebook forum in the first year course, and both small groups and the Scriboratory forum in the second year course). These questions asked students how much they read other posts, felt the discussions helped them better understand what writing in an academic context is, believed they became more skilled due to active participation, liked using the peer collaboration opportunity, gained confidence discussing language topics, and gained confidence in academic writing, as well as how comfortable they felt discussing things in these forums, and how comfortable they felt writing after working in these collaborative groups. These items formed a reliable scale (α = .85 for the first-year Facebook forum; α = .84 for small groups in the second year; and α = .85 for the Scriboratory in the second year), and were thus averaged for each of these collaboration contexts to create a single *engagement* composite.

Students were also asked for their impression of the collaborative forums (including whether they thought it was for *academic* or *social* purposes; two items), how appropriate it was for a tutor or instructor to be present in these online spaces, and what consequences a tutor's presence had or would have. Second year students were also asked to assess their level of activity in each of the two collaborative spaces (i.e., small groups and the Scriboratory). Finally, all students were asked to evaluate the viability of Facebook as an educational tool for foreign language learning.

2.2 Results

2.2.1 First year course

Overall, students appeared to evaluate the Facebook group positively: evaluation scores, $M = 2.69$, $SD = 0.69$, were significantly more positive than the scale midpoint, $t(111) = -4.80$, $p < .001$.

Interestingly, first year students' evaluations were negatively correlated with students' in-class assignment scores ($r = .21$, $p = .026$): in other words, the more students reported being engaged (via these eight questions), the *lower* their average in class assignment scores. One possible explanation for this is that students who were struggling (i.e., scoring lower on assignments) may have been more likely to feel that they needed help, and to see the forum as a useful resource than students who were doing well in the course and thus did not feel like they needed additional support. In the comments following the evaluation questions, there were a range of opinions expressed regarding the utility of the forum; some thought it was helpful, while others did not. Class assignment scores were the only outcome that was associated with evaluation scores; the evaluation composite was not related to students' course performance (e.g., final course mark) in any other way (all p's > .17).

Generally, students thought the Facebook forum was for educational purposes ($M = 1.72$, $SD = 0.56$); they did not think it was more for social purposes ($M = 3.89$, $SD = 0.89$) than for academic purposes. They generally did not think that it was appropriate for a tutor or instructor to be on Facebook ($M = 3.18$, $SD = 1.04$), and did think that the presence of a tutor would have influenced participation ($M = 2.74$, $SD = 1.05$). With no tutor present, students reported that they did not feel monitored on the forum ($M = 3.57$, $SD = .93$).

After taking the course, students were generally supportive of the idea that Facebook can be useful for foreign language learning ($M = 2.17$, $SD = 0.75$), can be a tool for education ($M = 2.13$, $SD = 0.76$), and that educational institutions should support resources on Facebook for peer-to-peer learning ($M = 2.42$, $SD = 0.82$).

2.2.2 Second year course

In the second year, students also appeared to be engaged with the peer collaboration opportunities made available to them, albeit to different degrees. Student evaluations of their small group experiences ($M = 2.37$, $SD = 0.61$) was significantly more positive than the scale midpoint, $t(67) = -8.50$, $p < .001$. However, students' evaluation of their experiences with Scriboratory ($M = 3.09$, $SD = 0.65$) was lower than for small groups, $t(67) = -7.57$, $p < .001$, and not significantly different from the scale midpoint, $t(67) = 1.18$, $p = .24$.

Evaluation scores in each context were positively correlated with active participation in small groups ($r = .43$, $p < .001$) and in the Scriboratory ($r = .53$, $p < .001$). Self-reported active participation in small groups was correlated with higher assignment ($r = .33$, $p = .006$), practical online component ($r = .25$, $p = .038$), and final course marks ($r = .34$, $p = .004$). However, self-reports of active participation in the Scriboratory were not significantly related to marks in Scribende (though the relationship with final grades was only marginally non-significant: $r = .23$, $p = .063$). Evaluation scores were not related to students' course performance (for either small groups or Scriboratory: all p's > .32).

Generally, students did not feel the Facebook group was more for social purposes than for academic purposes ($M = 3.94$, $SD = .81$); they generally thought it was for educational purposes ($M = 1.92$, $SD = .78$). They did not think that the presence of Scribendors influenced participation ($M = 3.31$, $SD = 1.07$) and did not feel monitored on the forum ($M = 3.78$, $SD = .94$).

Following the course, second year students were generally supportive of the idea that Facebook can be useful for foreign language learning ($M = 2.09$,

$SD = 0.81$), can be a tool for education ($M = 1.95$, $SD = 0.87$), and that educational institutions should support resources on Facebook for peer-to-peer learning ($M = 2.62$, $SD = 0.90$).

2.3 Discussion and recommendations

Overall, students' evaluations indicated that they were positively disposed toward online, collaborative experiences that supplemented more traditional in-class instruction. This is consistent with recent work by Salmon *et al.* (2015), who found that benefits of using social media within a MOOC included enhancing learning through the social and informal interaction with peers.

A number of studies have reported on HE students' inadequate preparedness levels, mediocre academic performance, and significant drop out rate, particularly during the first year of study (cf., for instance, Brinkworth *et al.* 2009; Darlaston-Jones *et al.* 2003; Hellekjær 2009; Hyland 2009; Leki 2006; Van de Poel/Gasiorek 2012a; Van Dyk/Van de Poel/Van der Slik 2013). Clearly, these are issues that need addressing. Given both limited resources and heterogeneity of the student population, it is important to look for new routes to support academic acculturation. One way to facilitate students' academic acculturation is supporting their academic literacy development through relevant assignments. Raising students' awareness of academic literacy is critical for their academic success. Therefore, academic literacy support should foster students' efficient and critical reading, support their reading and writing integration, and raise their metacognitive awareness –know what and know how– to help them better self-reflect and self-direct.

With these issues in mind, the results of this case study are encouraging, as they suggest that a blended learning approach, and specifically one involving online peer collaboration opportunities, may be a fruitful means to help students become more academically literate. However, students' responses –and most notably, their different responses to different collaborative formats in the second year course– indicate that there is not a 'one-size-fits-all' model or solution to online collaboration. Rather, different types and structures of online collaboration were preferred for accomplishing different goals.

In the first year course, the primary aims were to introduce writing in an academic context and help socialize students into the norms and expectations of a HE environment. Here, the focus was on acculturation, and on laying foundations for improving students' academic literacy. In this context, students responded positively to an inclusive and unsupervised collaborative space where they could 'safely' ask their peers questions as they built basic, foundational knowledge and skills. Their responses indicated that they liked the forum as it was formatted, and that they did not want additional supervision or direction (e.g., by a tutor) in this kind of environment. Although we did not see an immediate or clear association between forum evaluation and students' marks, we contend that if the goal of the course is socialisation and general familiarity with the academic genre, students may still experience benefits beyond those measured in course performance.

In the second year course, in contrast, the primary aim was to build genre-specific academic writing skills. Here, the focus was on developing working knowledge of discrete components of academic writing (such as argumentation, features of academic discourse, academic grammar and lexicon, the use of sources). In this context, students seemed to like collaboration in small groups better than collaboration involving the entire class, presumably because it was a better fit for completing more specific, focused activities. Active participation in these small groups was also more tightly linked to course performance than was collaboration in the Scriboratory (i.e., forum involving the entire class). The findings thus highlight that it is important to line up the configuration and use of blended and online tools with the different goals and needs, since students seem to respond better to formats that are more clearly aligned with the course goals. This finding indeed suggests that we cannot just say 'it's collaborative, so it's great!', but need to in fact be more thoughtful about the developing curriculum and syllabus (as discussed in Colpaert/Gijsen (this volume)).

Because of the way in which the assignments were structured, students not only actively engaged in internalising the materials they were also stimulated to collaboratively define their applicability and use, thus functioning as 'peer-teachers' in interaction with each other. Moreover, they also engaged in peer review in the closed Facebook group, where the tasks required collaboration. Thus, learners collaborated across the boundaries of the traditional classroom engaging with new media in a bottom-up approach enlarging their traditional working space to encompass the virtual world.

There are, of course, limitations to both online collaboration and blended learning approaches more generally that should be acknowledged. First, there is a skill-based threshold for engagement: both lecturers and learners have to be (or become) proficient and comfortable working in an online environment for them to be able to take advantage of the opportunities these course components offer. Second, students need to learn and adapt to an additional set of norms and practices –those of relating to and learning from each other through social media (which is often more informal than a traditional classroom). Finally, and critically, students have to be willing to engage with each other. In the second year student group, for instance, learners felt somewhat more reluctant towards engaging in a large group as opposed to smaller and more focused groups.

A key question to consider as we look ahead is how students are perceived and treated by HE. Traditionally, learners have been treated as passive recipients of knowledge that is curated and delivered by an 'expert' instructor. Blended (and autonomous) learning approaches alter this treatment, as they invite, and ultimately require, students to take charge of their own learning process. This study suggests that students are responding positively to this change. In this way, the approach seems to have succeeded in creating an environment suitable for and encouraging collaborative learning in a strong community. Moreover, students claim to have reached their self-defined learning goals, thus coming closer to being academically acculturated.

In sum, this case study highlights the positive potential for a blended learning approach in fostering students' skills and knowledge related to academic literacy. However, it also cautions that as course designers we need to be thoughtful and specific about the nature of what we design. Collaborative online learning is not perfect in itself and some design will fulfil particular needs better than others and thus will better contribute to solving particular challenges. In the end, thoughtful and informed design will support students in becoming autonomous lifelong learners and identify their own academic, social, vocational and personal challenges.

Junge Menschen, die ein Studium aufnehmen, empfinden den Anpassungsprozess an universitäre Lern-und Kommunikationsprozesse (*academic acculturation*) oft als Herausforderung (Darlaston-Jones *et al.* 2003; Leki 2006; Brinkworth *et al.* 2009). Diese Erfahrung wird von Studierenden einer Fremdsprache als besonders herausfordernd wahrgenommen, da von ihnen eine weitestgehende Kommunikation in der Fremdsprache verlangt wird. Die Ergebnisse universitärer Eignungsprüfungen sowie die Daten gezielter Fragebogen haben gezeigt, dass Hauptfachstudierende einer Fremdsprache im ersten Semester sich bezüglich ihrer akademischen Fähigkeiten und Bereitschaft überschätzen (vgl. Van Dyk/Van de Poel/Van der Slik 2013 für den südafrikanischen Kontext; Van Dyk/Van de Poel/Van der Slik i. Vorb. für Flandern).

Das Problem scheint vor allem auf ein Kommunikationsdefizit und eine nicht ausreichende Information der Studierenden bezüglich der Anforderungen zurück zu führen zu sein (vgl. De Geest 2012; Van de Poel/Gasiorek 2012).

Dem konstruktivistischen Lernansatz zufolge sind Lerner aktiv an der Ausgestaltung ihrer eigenen Lernprozesse beteiligt, wozu sie jedoch nicht immer von Beginn an bereit sind. Um Lerner in der Übernahme von Verantwortung für ihr eigenes Lernen zu unterstützen, ist eine kontinuierliche Bewusstmachung ihres Einflusses auf ihre eigenen Lernprozesse erforderlich. Vor diesem Hintergrund bietet die Interaktion in der Zweit- und/oder Fremdsprache, sowohl online als auch persönlich, Lernern die Möglichkeit,

Sprachprobleme in Zusammenarbeit mit anderen zu lösen, sich gegenseitig in ihren individuellen Lernprozessen zu unterstützen und neues Wissen zu schaffen (vgl. Donato 1994; Ohta/Foster 2005; Swain, 2000).

Dieser Beitrag beschreibt, wie Erst-und Zweitsemesterstudierende mit Englisch als Hauptfach in einem zwölf-wöchigen Seminar zum wissenschaftlichen Schreiben durch gemeinschaftlich zu bearbeitende Online-Aufgaben dazu angeregt wurden, sich mit dem spezifischen akademischen Diskurs ihres Fachs auseinanderzusetzen. Durch die Kombination von Präsens-und Online-Elementen hatten Lerner die Gelegenheit, Schreibaufgaben gemeinsam zu bearbeiten. Zusätzlich wurde von ihnen verlangt, die Anwendbarkeit von Materialien zu definieren und fungierten so als *peer-teachers*. Durch Einbeziehung von virtuellen Lernorten fand Lernen somit auch außerhalb des Klassenzimmers statt.

Die erhobenen Daten zeigen, dass Studierende dies im Allgemeinen als positiv empfanden, aber auch, dass sie, je nach Inhalt und Aufgabenstellung, unterschiedliche Ansätze und Formen des kollaborativen Lernens bevorzugten. Des Weiteren wurde das gemeinsame Lernen von den Studierenden als authentisch empfunden. Dies und ihr Empfinden, den Leistungsanforderungen gerecht zu werden, trug zu einem besseren Empfinden bezüglich ihres Akkulturationsprozesses (*academic acculturation*) bei.

Stephan Gabel & Jochen Schmidt
University of Münster, Germany

Collaborative Writing with Writing Pads in the Foreign Language Classroom – Chances and Limitations

Past research has shown convincingly that the enormous difficulties that second language learners face when writing texts in the L2 can at least partially be overcome if the texts are produced by learners in small groups rather than individually. By collaborating, it has been argued, learners experience a reduction of the complexity of the writing process, so that such activities provide 'procedural facilitation', especially if they use word processors. Similar claims have been made regarding computer-mediated communication in the writing process, where past research has concentrated on evaluating the educational application of tools like email, tandems, MOOs, wikis and blogs. With the advent of writing pads such as TitanPad, which make it possible to produce texts both synchronously and asynchronously via a computer network, the repertoire for the foreign language teacher has been enriched in this respect beyond doubt. This study investigates the potential of this new tool to foster the writing skills of foreign language learners and presents some practical proposals for utilizing pads in the classroom and beyond.

1. Introduction

Even though nobody earnestly doubts the value of writing skills in foreign languages, writing has received surprisingly little attention in the foreign language classroom (cf. Wolff 1991: 34; Brookes/Grundy 1998: 10; Bloom 2008: 103; Matz 2014: 33). This may partially be due to the fact that many practitioners have regarded it as not essential for achieving intercultural communicative competence, a "handmaiden of the other skills" (Rivers 1968: 241) that needs no special attention as it develops naturally from writing skills in the mother tongue and oral communicative competences in the foreign language, it was believed. Still, there have always been others who view it as very valuable since it promotes foreign language learners' overall L2 competences, so that writing is seen as a foreign language 'learning activity' (cf. Weissberg 2000: 52; Harklau 2002: 345; Harmer 2004: 31; Thaler 2012: 198) that must not be neglected. Despite current trends from a discrete to a more holistic treatment of the traditional language skills in the foreign language classroom, so that teaching focusses on 'comprehension' (listening, reading and viewing), 'conversation' (listening and speaking) and 'composition' (reading and writing) (cf. Lynch 2012: 73f), writing still has a special status: it has become widely accepted that writing is a 'taught' skill that is not likely to develop automatically without intervention through practice, and consequently writing needs special attention in the classroom (cf. Melouk 2013: 219).

Another major change in the attitude towards writing has occurred regarding its special communicative role. Writing had been perceived as the skill that is most suited for individual practice ever since the language laboratory fell into disgrace. While oral skills and attempts at developing them required the presence of others in the end, written text production was meant to be a solitary activity for the student to further develop that skill. The only form of collaboration would occur after the text had been written, when the students received feedback from their instructors or, more recently, their peers. Research into writing processes of foreign language learners has, however, revealed that collaboration in the stage of production can indeed be very helpful for foreign language learners (cf. Wolff 2000: 111). This and the fact that writing and the nature of written texts have changed since the dawn of the Digital Age and, especially, the advent of web 2.0, has given rise to methods that make the writing of texts a truly collaborative act. Modern media provide not only a platform of communication and collaboration between learners, they also allow for the production of digital documents that often take the form of hypertexts or multimodal artefacts (cf. Evans 2012: 218).

This paper will investigate how and under which conditions such collaboration can be promoted by means of electronic writing tools. Here, the main focus will be placed on the use of writing pads, a relatively new type of software that allows users to produce texts asynchronously. In order to assess their potential in promoting foreign language students' writing skills a survey of previous research into foreign language writing will be presented. Against this backdrop the utility of writing pads will be discussed and contrasted with other electronic tools that have already gained popularity among teachers, namely word processors, blogs and wikis.

2. Research into foreign language writing

Research into foreign language writing has identified some of the reasons why learners often feel overwhelmed when prompted to produce written texts. First and foremost, this has to do with the enormous complexity of the writing process itself. Even in L1 writing is a very complex cognitive activity as the analysis of 'think-aloud' protocols during the composition process has shown (Flower/Hayes 1981: 367ff). Among other things it involves decisions about the overall intended message to be conveyed by the text, thinking about possible readers and their needs, deciding on the general organization of the text as well as on paragraphing and possible sub-headings, choosing a title, reflecting on the form of the language (finding appropriate expressions, checking spelling and syntax), constantly reviewing passages already written, deleting, adding to, modifying or reorganizing the text, providing examples to illustrate points, adding stimuli that might catch the reader's interest, referring to the ideas of others, proofreading, and many other such sub-processes (cf. Brookes/Grundy 1998: 7f). What is more, these processes do not occur in a linear order when mature writers produce written texts, but in a quite chaotic sequence that cannot be predicted.

Flower and Hayes (1981: 369ff) have summarized the cognitive processes that experienced writers employ in their model of the writing process, in which they distinguish processes of planning (goal setting, organizing and generating), translating (turning ideas into visible language), reviewing (evaluating and revising) and monitoring (deciding what to do next). These composition processes are further complicated by the need to consider the task environment (the topic, the intended audience, the writer's own goals and the part of the texts already produced) and to retrieve factual, strategic and linguistic information from long-term memory.

According to Scardamalia and Bereiter (1986: 783–91), expert writers are able to handle these processes because they use problem-solving and goal-oriented recursive strategies. They …

- create an organizing structure for a composition, for which they use their well-developed knowledge of discourse schemata.
- generate far more content than they will use in their compositions because they can search their memory effectively for the availability of information (metamemorial search) and retrieve it from it (heuristic search).
- can deal with 'higher-level tasks' and easily switch between 'higher' and 'lower-level tasks' (*ibid*.: 787) because spelling and punctuation are largely automatized procedures to them.
- plan purposefully by breaking up the overall goals into sub-goals and react flexibly to problems by revising their goals during the composition process.
- continually reprocess the text already produced, so that there is constant 'internal' (to further develop contents) and 'external' revision (to gear it towards the intended audience) (*ibid*.: 790).

In contrast, inexperienced writers lack all these skills. They do not know the necessary discourse schemata, cannot search their memory efficiently when generating content, struggle with the mechanics of writing, do not develop global plans, but draft their texts right from the start Scardamalia and Bereiter (*ibid*.: 789) call this 'rehearsal"– and proof-read their texts, but do not reprocess them more deeply. To compensate for these deficits learners need procedural support (cf. below).

These general tendencies from L1-related writing research have also been identified in L2, where most research suggests that the composing processes in L1 and L2 are quite similar. Unskilled writers in L2 face more or less the same problems as unskilled writers in L1, while expert writers go about composition tasks in very similar ways, no matter whether they write in the medium of L1 or L2 (Rowe Krapels 1990: 49). What distinguishes text production in a foreign language from writing in the mother tongue are limitations of the learners' linguistic and sociocultural knowledge. Krings (1989: 427) regards these as the main reason for his observation that second language learners do not 'plan' their L2 texts in the same way as their L1 texts. Similary, Wolff (1992: 120) stresses second language learners' unfamiliarity with the writing conventions in the target culture, so that they find it difficult to apply the writing-related strategic competence they developed in their L1. Even if they have extensive procedural writing skills in L1, this is not sufficient for them to become good L2 writers because they lack the necessary declarative knowledge in L2 (Wolff 2000: 109).

Despite these differences, the model by Flower and Hayes is believed to form a useful basis for research into second language writing as well, and there indeed seems to be 'a core of similarities between L1 and L2 writing' (Brookes/Grundy 1998: 8). Yet, it had to be adapted to account for the additional observations. As L2-related writing research has shown, second language learners often resort to their mother tongue during their planning, for instance, which requires a transition of the plans into L2. Therefore, activating and applying their knowledge of L2 are viewed as additional sub-processes in second language writing (Börner 1992: 299). Similarly, reduction or even avoidance strategies play a role in L2 if the linguistic means do not allow for the adequate realization of the plans in the medium of the target language. To account for these additional difficulties that second language writers face, Börner (1989: 355 and 1992: 301), Krings (1992: 70) and Zimmermann (2000: 85f) have extended the model, so that it includes planning and generating processes in L1, formulating and translating procedures, L2-related linguistic problems and strategies for dealing with them.

It needs to be stressed that the perspective chosen in this paper is based primarily on the process approach to writing, which is just one way of modelling and teaching writing. It has been criticized on grounds of its being focussed largely on cognitive processes, while ignoring the interactive, sociocultural and textual dimensions of writing (Gordon 2008: 244ff; Oxford 2010: 249f). Moreover, some of the practical proposals for the teaching of writing that were derived from this were denounced because they were misguided like the assumption that when learners know and understand what expert writers do, they will be able to use recursive processes on their own (Roen 1989: 199). Hyland, for example, maintains that 'learning to become an expert writer does not involve mimicking a set of heuristics' (2002: 61). The model in its original form does not, however, claim that it can reveal how expert writers' skills have evolved. Trying to teach the underlying skills in any more or less direct way would indeed be doomed to failure (cf. the discussion in section 3). Despite its weaknesses, the writing-as-process approach has its merits in that it provided important insights exploited in the practice of ELT. Among other things it encouraged

> self-discovery and authorial 'voice'; meaningful writing on topics of importance […] to the writer; invention and pre-writing tasks, and multiple drafting […]; a variety of feedback options from real audiences; […] the idea that writing is multiply recursive rather than linear […]; and students' awareness of the writing process (Grabe/Kaplan 1996: 87),

so that it forms the basis of many methods used in the teaching of writing. The view taken here is that for the teaching of foreign language other perspectives on writing like the 'genre' and the 'functional approach' (cf. Gordon 2008: 244ff; Oxford 2010: 249f) can be seen as an enrichment of process writing rather than a replacement, or, as Gordon puts it, they can be used "in conjunction with the process approach" (2008: 245).

3. Teaching writing as a process – Collaborative writing

When writing was seen as merely a "support skill" (Gordon 2008: 245), teaching it in the foreign language classroom was limited to teacher feedback on the final product. All too often the emphasis was then placed on accuracy whereas content and appropriacy played only minor roles (Hudelson 1988: 213). There was also the danger of either overwhelming the student by over-correction, which "discourages substantative revision" (Barkaoui 2007: 40), or responding in a manner too sketchy to trigger more than surface modifications of the text (cf. *ibid*.). 'Responding' to content and making suggestions is considered more helpful to the learner (cf. Harmer 2007: 121), but can still be detrimental to further developing writing skills if the feedback only leads to a revision of drafts in response to the teacher's reaction, thus strengthening student dependency (Gordon: 245).

Process approaches to teaching writing have changed this view and lead to the insight that learning to write entails a major transition from a language production system dependent at every level on inputs from a conversational partner to a system capable of functioning autonomously. […] The oral language production system [...] must in some way be reconstructed to function autonomously instead of interactively (Bereiter/Scardamalia 1987: 1).

For this transition it is necessary to provide assistance to the learner, which can, for instance, either take the form of "substantive facilitation", i.e. specific help given to the learner in the composing process (e.g. teacher feedback on a text), or of "procedural facilitation" (Scardamalia/Bereiter 1986: 796). The latter is of a more unspecific kind, so that it enables students "to carry out more sophisticated composing processes by themselves" (*ibid.*).

One way of achieving procedural facilitation is by breaking up the highly complex process of writing into sub-processes or 'stages' like pre-writing, planning, drafting, pausing, reading, revising, editing and publishing (cf. Williams 2003: 106f), so that these can be focussed and worked on in isolation. Wolff (1991: 38 and 1992: 125-131), for instance, suggests activities that are meant to foster content generation, textual planning, audience orientation, critical evaluation of contents and form and revision by means of brainstorming, organizational charts, reading-writing loops, and textual analyses. Most of the available sets of classroom materials for teaching writing are also based on this idea. The volume on *Process Writing* by White and Arndt, for instance, wants to "nurture the skills with which writers work out their own solutions" (1991: 5) by offering practice activities concentrating on the generation of content, on developing a focus, on structuring the ideas, and on drafting, evaluating and reviewing the text. Brookes and Grundy (1998) also cover the exercises for developing the mechanics of writing and confidence building activities. According to Silva, the teacher's role in such approaches is to help students develop viable strategies for getting started (finding topics, generating ideas and information, focusing, and planning structure and procedure), for drafting (encouraging multiple drafts), for revising (adding, deleting, modifying, and rearranging ideas) and for editing (attending to vocabulary, sentence structure, grammar and mechanics) (1990: 15).

Alternatively, group arrangements have been suggested to achieve the same effect. Williams (2003: 131), for instance, stresses the fact that most writing meant to be read by others is the result of collaborative efforts (even if this collaboration is limited to the reading of drafts or final proofreading), so that the writing classroom ought to be transformed into a writing workshop where groups of learners cooperate over a longer period of time: "Groups provide the students with frequent opportunities to interact with one another through writing and talking about their writing" (*ibid.*: 140), which means that they receive feedback on their work in progress and revise their texts on that basis. For this purpose

Gebhard suggests using writing conferences and peer review sheets with checklists of possible problems that students can use for their responses (cf. 1996: 242).

Often, however, the cooperation ends when it comes to the composing process itself as students still produce their texts individually. Students are given "ample time", yet write their texts individually "with [...] minimal interference" (Silva 1990: 15). This can also be seen in Hyland's proposals for developing control of genres, which comprises cooperation in the analysis of genres, in first rehearsals for text production, in which the students and the teacher jointly construct a first model text, and in the revision stage, but not in the construction of the text, which is viewed as an independent student activity (cf. 2003: 21). In contrast to that other researchers and practitioners have suggested group arrangements for the actual writing process and have stressed that here division of labour facilitates the task for each individual because the sub-processes of writing become the shared responsibility of the whole group (cf. Donath 1991: 167; Wolff 1992: 124; Legenhausen 1996: 86).

Collaborative writing "reduces the complexity of the writing process" (Legenhausen/Wolff 1990: 327), which is partly due to the fact that some specialization is likely to occur, so that the individual students take on different roles like that of a keyboard operator, grammarian, speller, technician, etc. (cf. Groundwater-Smith 1993: 18). Typically one student will take over the role of the scribe or secretary, who is in charge of the mechanics of writing and records the text. As a result the other group members can "concentrate on the language, think about what is being written, and evaluate it in a more objective way [...] than they judge their own individual efforts." (Harmer 2004: 77). Especially if the group uses resources such as dictionaries, more such specialization is likely to occur; so some students might focus primarily on the linguistic accuracy and appropriacy of the text produced, while other students' main responsibility would be the generation of content for the text.

As process-oriented research (e.g. Dam/Legenhausen/Wolff 1990; Legenhausen/Wolff 1991; Legenhausen 1996; Zeni 1994) has convincingly shown, text production in small groups is extremely beneficial to learners. The collaboration forces the learners to verbalize their ideas, which are subsequently evaluated by their peers, so that instant feedback is provided (cf. Legenhausen 1996: 87). What's more, any such contribution may trigger counter-proposals that are further negotiated by the group, so that the learners must support them by arguments and thus lay open their own evaluation criteria (cf. Dam/Legenhausen/Wolff 1990: 327). Similarly, they have to activate and explicate their text-linguistic knowledge when it comes to assessing the text's coherence, the appropriacy of phrases or more general questions of style and the text's overall organization. In very much the same way the collaborative planning of the text makes it necessary for the learners to explicitly state their plans (cf. Legenhausen/Wolff 1991: 350). What normally happens within the individual writer's mind therefore becomes subject of a negotiation process. Discussion and decision-making raises the awareness of both evaluation criteria and planning strategies and makes them more available to the learners. In other words, what happens in such groups is constant peer reviewing, which is extremely helpful to them because it indirectly also develops their ability to edit and revise their own texts when writing individually. According to Bonk and King, research indicates that learners "internalize the scaffolding of more capable peers when writing collaboratively" (1995: 22).

Another side effect of the conversational work learners often transfer means for structuring their written discourse from their oral interaction. When content is being discussed, the learners will often adapt a speech-into-writing approach. During the discussion they use discourse-structuring devices to secure comprehension by their peers, which will then be adapted to the written medium, thus also enhancing comprehension on the part of potential readers. Quite naturally they will reflect on their audience because the group members act as "'test-readers' for the developing text" (Dam/Legenhausen/Wolff 1990: 329). This need for taking the reader into account is something that inexperienced L2 writers normally face great difficulties with (cf. Brookes/Grundy 1990: 19).

Finally, the threat-to-face is reduced for the individual learner. Especially in a classroom context, writing is perceived as a very 'risky' activity by many learners because of the permanence of the final product, its relationship to the identity of the writer and the role it plays in assessment. Writing texts in groups lets learners share responsibility for the product (cf. Harmer 2004: 73), so that such tasks are less threatening; collaborative writing thus "lowers the anxiety associated with completing tasks alone and raise students' self-confidence" (Mulligan/Garofaro 2011: 5).

Most importantly, however, such collaborative writing triggers social processes between learners that make them work "in their 'zone of proximal development' […], reaching beyond the level they could reach on their own" (Zeni 1994: 224). In other words, by collaborating inexperienced writers can in fact develop more sophisticated writing skills (Mulligan/Garofaro 2011: 9), so that they do not necessarily need individual feedback from instructors or tutors to push forward their boundaries. Therefore, collaboration is, perhaps, the most natural route to individual competence in writing (*ibid.*: 216). Moreover, learners' general language competence also improves through the active participation in the text construction process as verbalizing learning and writing strategies plays a crucial role in the construction of new linguistic knowledge (Swain 2000: 109 and 113). Similar effects can be expected with regard to their world knowledge and their social skills (Keller 2013: 244f).[1]

4. Computers as tools in the writing process

That computers can be very helpful in promoting writing skills has long been acknowledged (e.g. Börner 1992: 297; Stubbs 1992: 207f, Pennington 1996: 31). Having second language learners work with word processors facilitates the drafting process (Hyland 2003: 144f), for instance, and also improves their editing and revision behaviour, so that their writing strategies are positively influenced (Dam/Legenhausen/Wolff 1990: 331ff). Learners tend to revise their texts more intensely and the texts so produced become more accurate and more coherent (Hyland 2003: 147). Moreover, word processing encourages non-linear writing processes, and there is increased experimentation with means of expression and organization (*ibid.*: 146), which also contributes to improving the quality of the final products. In short, it fosters higher-level writing skills (cf. Bereiter/Scardamalia 1987: 797).

Still, the research regarding the use of word processors has not been as conclusive as initially hoped for, which is partially due to variation in research design and contextual factors. When producing texts individually, most L2 students do not fully exploit their word processors' capabilities for revision and editing, for example. They may be 'computer savvy', yet not have developed advanced keyboarding skills and still be unfamiliar with text block moves, deletion and restoring procedures, split screen functions, etc., which would allow for more global rather than just local editing of their texts (Hyland 2003: 148). All these skills need to be developed before the full potential of word processors can be exploited (O'Brien 2004: 16). The same is true with the orthographical, lexical

---

[1] It is important to note that collaboration represents a challenge that further complicates the writing process because multiple authors are involved and, consequently multiple points of view, which need to be coordinated (Lowry/Curtis/Lowry 2004: 70). The authors must deal with conflict and establish consensus when they negotiate the agenda, identify tasks and divide labour and responsibility. For expert writers this can be detrimental because such negotiation costs time, so that their commitment often decreases if the cooperation takes places over extended periods (cf. *ibid.*). For second language learners who collaborate on less complex tasks for a limited period of time, however, the opposite is true.

and grammatical support that word processors offer (spelling, grammar and style checkers, thesauri). These can be problematic because they provide de-contextualized and therefore fallible advice only, so that students can be misled if they overrely on such features of the software (Hyland 2003: 148; O'Brien 2004: 17). As a consequence, full familiarization with the software is a prerequisite for exploiting the potential of word processors.

In order to further support second language learners Börner (1992: 302ff) suggests implementing additional functions in word processors, many of which have become widely available in the meantime, such as visual planning tools that allow for generating mindmaps on the computer (Berger/Trexler 2010: 13). Other proposals have been made regarding the integration of heuristics that 'steer' students through a revision of their texts by means of teacher-generated prompts (Hyland 2003: 149). Since modern word processors now include annotation and editing tools that make it possible to review the whole composing process by tracking comments, contributions and revisions, not only by individual writers, but also by multiple others, the chances for providing such assistance have been greatly enhanced. This aspect will be investigated in more detail in the context of online writing tools that enable the asynchronous collaborative production of texts.

It needs to be stressed, however, that if the word processor is used by individual students rather than groups of learners, a rather decreased writer collaboration in the classroom results. There seems to be less initial planning of the text when working with a word processor than working with pen and paper. This planning is rather sequential than conceptual (Haas 1989: 201f). Another aspect that some studies have noted is an increased focus on surface phenomena and a preoccupation with physical appearance (Hyland 2003: 147). Students can become absorbed by the computer when they produce texts in relative isolation, concentrate on their own texts rather than exchanging ideas about them with their peers or instructors, through which they might gain a deeper understanding of texts and audiences (*ibid*.: 151). Such effects may, however, have been partially caused by a lack of experience with word processing, especially learners' unfamiliarity with the editing functions, which will only manifest after some time, so that they are indiscernible in short term studies (O'Brien 2004: 17).

These problems can also be alleviated if students are properly aided in word processing by providing them with opportunities for peer support and collaboration (Hyland 2003: 148) as is the case with text production in groups. When small groups of learners produce texts synchronously with paper and pencil, for example, the writing process is hampered because the text produced so far is rarely fully visible to all group members, which limits the possibilities for its in-depth analysis and the negotiation of alternatives. It is the computer screen that makes the text become more accessible (Dam 1989: 85; Legenhausen/Wolff 1991: 353), thus facilitating writing-reading loops and furthering the collaboration and interaction within the group. This may be the reason why quite a number of studies register a greater improvement in student writing if the texts are written with computers rather than with traditional pen-and-paper methods (e.g. Lin et al. 2014: 422).

A discussion of the roles computers can play in students' written text production cannot be complete without at least briefly considering its potential for analysing genres and investigating content matter in preparation of the composition. Alerting students to the features of target language genres, for instance, would traditionally take the form of a guided discovery. The students would be asked to analyse texts representative of a particular genre and aided by means of teaching materials or scaffolding (Hyland 2002: 82). Such analyses are meant to provide them with clear criteria for the revision of their own texts, so that they are enabled to detect typical stylistic and linguistic problems. By using concordance software and corpora, on the other hand, students can investigate more or less independently genres and familiarize themselves with the conventions governing the type of text they are meant to produce. The computer would then be used as a 'research tool' (Hyland 2003: 170). Moreover, students can employ the software as a 'reference tool' (*ibid.*) on an *ad hoc* basis to explore patterns in the target language whenever they face linguistic problems, patterns that they can imitate in their written texts. Using concordancing software has the clear advantage that the students gain direct access to linguistic data themselves, so that no 'middleman' (Johns 1994: 297) is necessary, who guides them through their investigation of grammar, vocabulary and genres. Working with such software has become increasingly feasible for students as there are now tools available that can be used as an add-on to the word process where students simply have to double click on words to obtain frequency and contextual information about words or phrases (Hyland/Hyland 2006: 95). Finally, needless to say, the Internet is of great help to learners since they can use it to obtain content for their projects in the planning and drafting stages, but also to 'publish' their work in the end (Hyland 2003: 158).

5. Computer-mediated communications and the writing process

While word processors are still closely linked to the production of printed matter, most written communication in the 21st century is entirely electronic, which already implies a dramatic change in the perception of writing. This is because "an electronic text only exists in the act of reading" (Bolter 1992: 20). Furthermore, texts produced electronically are not necessarily permanent any more. Unlike texts made available in print, they can still be modified when reader responses alert the writer to problems, so that at no point they are definitely finalized. As a result, at least some forms of electronic communication such as text-messaging and computer-mediated chats share some of the qualities of spoken communications in that they are immediate forms of interaction, are quite spontaneous and transient, and involve the frequent swapping of the roles of the sender and the recipient of the information (cf. Harmer 2004: 7f).

This causes changes in writers' attitudes towards their respective texts. They plan them less carefully and are often more flippant in the choice of expressions because they are less binding (cf. Eck/Legenhausen/Wolff 1995: 32f). Therefore it comes as no surprise that such genres like email also share quite a number of linguistic features with spoken texts. While written texts are normally very "explicit, self-contained and highly structured" (McCarthy 1991: 149) because the message expressed must be complete and unambiguous to function with no recipient present, computer-mediated acts of communication often lack these characteristics. They can be considered (textual) utterances located "half-way between traditional written production and oral exchange" (Paramskas 1993: 127), so that electronic genres like email and chatrooms blur the distinction between oral and written discourse (cf. Hyland 2003: 144). Among other things, these written texts contain more colloquialisms and more interjections. Moreover, they are lexically less dense than written discourse and employ discourse-structuring devices like 'you know' that are emblematic of spoken discourse. In addition to that, computer-mediated communications have given rise to new conventions that replace the paralinguistic features of spoken discourse such as typographical conventions (the use of capital letters for 'shouting') and emoticons (to express emotions, to convey a message 'between the lines' or to signal 'sarcasm' or 'irony'), which help the reader to disambiguate potentially unclear messages (cf. Palme 1995: 181).

These features result primarily from the more interactive nature of writing in computer-mediated communication. Email messages, for instance, "are in some respects no less interactive than speech" (Uhlírová 1994: 280) because they are embedded in a communicative exchange in which responses from a partner are expected and can, again, be reacted to in case misunderstandings occur: The communication can be more context-dependent than 'normal' writing. As a result, writers go about the task of producing messages in computer conferences in a different way than in less interactive contexts, they write more spontaneously and do not edit their texts as carefully as they normally do (*ibid*.: 277). This and the above-stated textual characteristics can be very helpful for beginners' first steps in written L2 text production. While writing their messages, they can adopt a speech-into-writing approach and will develop the procedural skills that will facilitate subsequent text production in more detached contexts. At the same time the exchange raises learners' awareness of their audience, which Hyland regards as essential for effective writing instruction (cf. 2002: 83).

No matter whether such 'computer conferences' (Hyland/Hyland 2006: 93) take place 'synchronously' (students communicate in real time via discussion software) or 'asynchronously' (responses to one writer's contributions are delayed) (e.g. Evans 2012: 221), they have the advantage that they integrate reading and writing and encourage extensive practice of these skills. Moreover, they can promote "collaboration and interaction both within and beyond the classroom." (Hyland 2003: 143) Email projects, for example, may turn the classroom into a workshop, in which cooperation in the planning, drafting, composing and reviewing stages and division of labour occurs almost automatically (Eck/Legenhausen/Wolff 1994: 47). Since learners are writing their texts for a real audience, thus developing authentic communicative needs, they go about the writing with great enthusiasm and thoroughness (Donath 1991: 8), an increase in motivation which must be considered to be beneficial to developing this skill.

Similar claims have been made concerning synchronous exchanges in 'tandems' (computer-mediated collaboration between pairs of learners who do not share an L1 and are studying the L1 of their partners; cf. Hockly 2015: 81) and 'MOOs' (a text-based 'Multi-user, Object Oriented' group site on the Internet, which allows for the creation of virtual classrooms; cf. Hyland 2003: 154). Kötter, for example, who investigated tandem interactions in a MOO, sees reasons to believe that participating in such exchanges improves learners' written skills (cf. 2001: 303). Whether or not all this also improves writing quality in the end remains unclear though (cf. Hyland 2003: 154). The rapid flow of messages in a MOO or other forms of Internet Relay Chat is often disjointed and incoherent, which can be too challenging for weaker students, thus discouraging them. Moreover, learners' own contributions may be so simple and malformed that they hardly assist the acquisition of higher-level writing skills.

This discussion shows that it is hard to assess the extent to which such 'early forms of telecollaboration' (Hockly 2015: 83) contribute to the development of second language writing. Much here depends on the project or task in which the exchange is embedded because this determines the kinds of responses that each learner will receive. Feedback by peers, for one, can be extremely valuable to second language learners if it alerts them to formal or conceptual problems in their texts: Such comments motivate revision and revisions are made on that basis

(Hudelson 1988: 214). Although it has often been observed that peer responses tend to focus rather on meaning than on form (e.g. Kessler 2009: 84), they still foster greater grammatical accuracy and overall quality of writing (*ibid*.: 80). Research has also shown that previous peer response training increases the effectiveness of the reviewing (cf. Hyland 2003: 203). Even then, however, success is not guaranteed. Liang (2010), for example, reports on a college writing course, in which sophomores shared their essays with peers and received online feedback from these (the peers had been trained for that purpose). Still, this setting seldom triggered revision-related discourse, but rather content discussion and social talk, so that the outcomes were less satisfying than had been initially hoped for (*ibid*.: 57).

Effective peer feedback, to our minds, requires a situation where the participants in the exchange want to reflect on the linguistic qualities of the contributions and are or become interested in polishing them up. In other words, the activity of writing and revising must have a joint purpose for the learners for the collaboration to bear fruit. Simply imposing individual writing tasks on them and asking peers to assist them is not sufficient. The situation must be authentic to the partners, a condition that is, for example, fulfilled when the whole text production process is a collaborative effort for which all group members feel responsible.

6. Online writing tools – writing pads

With the dawn of ever more increasing possibilities in a Web 2.0 world, new forms of computerized technologies keep pushing technical boundaries to offer unlimited connectivity to data, their production and publication alike, which includes unlimited access to texts as well as tools for writing and editing them. In a teaching and learning context, these new means greatly enhance collaborative L2 writing as they give rise to new methodological ideas, thus enriching L2 writing instruction. With these innovative tools, the disadvantages of asynchronous writing collaboration can be overcome. It is no longer necessary for students to save documents and send them to their co-authors, who would edit them and send them back: Today's electronic tools rather "allow collaborators to work in a synchronous environment on a single document; groups of students can create, share and edit them online" (Berger/Trexler 2010: 5f).

Two such tools that have already been researched quite extensively are blogs and wikis. 'Blogs'[2], for example, have been used both individually and collaboratively

---

2 A 'blog' (abbreviated from 'web-log') is a website that resembles a diary in that it consists of various 'posts', which originally were written by a single author. Other than

to keep a learning diary (Klemm 2008: 37). Studies focussing on the effectiveness of blogs in writing instruction indicate that blogging may achieve greater improvement in writing skills than pen-and-paper diaries if the learners "want improved writing skills" (Lin *et al.* 2014: 430). So, whether this is the case depends on the nature of the writing task or its authenticity to the learners. Moreover, the act of writing is still an individual one and the learners receive only delayed responses to 'posts', which do not necessarily lead to a revision of text by the original author. As regards 'wikis'[3] there is likewise much evidence that supports an optimistic view on their capacity to improve writing skills. The research is, however, quite inconclusive regarding what skills exactly are promoted. Some studies maintain that wikis encourage a stronger focus on content, i.e. the structure and organization of the information they contain (Elola/Oskoz 2010: 53), so that as long as the form of the language does not interfere with the message, learners are quite "unconcerned with the accuracy of their partner's writing" (*ibid.*: 62). Similar observations have been made by e.g. Kessler (2009: 84). On the other hand, there are studies which suggest that peer collaboration and scaffolding may also foster "attention to form for the improvement of language accuracy" (Lee 2010: 271). Still, wikis seem to make students generally more susceptible to feedback because they share responsibility for the writing activity (*ibid.*: 261). They can also change the writing behaviour of the students collaborating. If these have the chance to also 'chat' about their text in the early stages of text production, they will tend to agree on the structure of their texts earlier in the writing process than individual writers, who do that throughout the composition process (Elola/Oskoz 2010: 62f), which indicates that they plan their texts more thoroughly right from the start. Regarding lower-level operations like polishing the texts grammatically and lexically, the opposite seems to be true: individual writers seem to be doing that towards the end of the writing process, whereas in collaborative writing this happens all the time (*ibid.*: 62). These partially contradictory findings may have to do with the fact that wikis are essentially asynchronous writing environments that do not integrate the instant feedback available in face-to-face writing conferences

---

written diaries they are, however, organized in anti-chronological order (so that the most recent entry is shown first). More recently, blogs have been used by multiple authors for various purposes such as sharing views on certain topics.

3   'Wikis' are content-based Web 2.0 platforms that allow for the modification of the information they contain by multiple writers, so that their structure will emerge from the interests of the authors. Wikis are more interactive than blogs because they provide authors with the opportunity to transform and erase their contributions when they receive feedback.

like those discussed in section 3. As Scrimshaw maintains (with regard to word processing), it is only real-time collaboration that leads to the investigation of alternatives among learners.

Some of these disadvantages can be overcome if learners are given the chance to respond to other learners' contributions with very short delay or even (more or less) simultaneously as is the case with modern writing pads, most of which descend from 'EtherPad', an open-source piece of software that allows for the real-time editing of texts on the Internet (without the delays that other platforms would incur).

Figure 1: Introductory page of the pad environment TitanPad

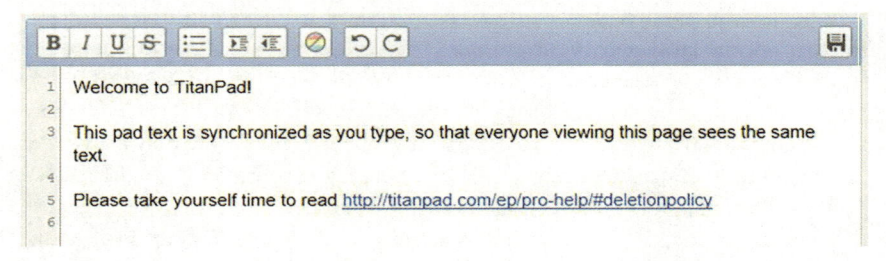

```
1  Welcome to TitanPad!
2
3  This pad text is synchronized as you type, so that everyone viewing this page sees the same
   text.
4
5  Please take yourself time to read http://titanpad.com/ep/pro-help/#deletionpolicy
6
```

Such writing pads invite users to work on one textual document simultaneously in a secure online environment in true real-time. The following section will be devoted to a discussion of the features of TitanPad,[4] one such program that, in our opinion, has great potential for writing instruction in and outside the (computerized) classroom and which is currently gaining ground among teachers (cf. also Merse/Schmidt 2014: 166ff).

TitanPad provides potential writers with an online workspace that resembles the layout and function of a simplified or reduced writing program. Key to the platform is the note section, in which the text as such can be typed in by all group members, the so-called 'pad members'. The layout functions of this note pad are rather rudimentary. Pad members can only produce text in one given, standardized font and cannot change the font-size. However, they can choose from a small selection of tools to use bold type, italicize, underline or cross utterances. As regards other formatting features, writers can insert bullet points as well as

---

4   EtherPad has been taken over by Google, so that many idealists have issued their own real-time editors for collaborative writing. TitanPad, for instance, was set up by a non-profit association of IT professionals based in Austria. [cf. https://titanpad.com/ep/about/about; retrieved October 15, 17:11.]

indented lists or paragraphing. Other, more advanced forms of layout and textual structuring are not available. In other words, textual production in the pad environment is reduced to a bare minimum in comparison with more professional writing software. Still, written utterances can be deleted or corrected at any time in the note section as in any other writing software. Changes to the text can also be undone at any time by any pad member. The focus of the pad lies primarily in the process of textual production and thus keeps matters simple for the writers.

Added to the note section, the pad features a time-stamped chat function, in which questions can be asked, comments be added or extra content be provided, as well as an activity box, which indicates who is currently online and working in the pad. Consequently, writers can not only collaborate in the production of text, be it simultaneously or asynchronously, but also give additional feedback to each other or exchange their views on the text, which enables them, as exemplified below, to lay open their planning and revision strategies.

Figure 2: Collaborative text production

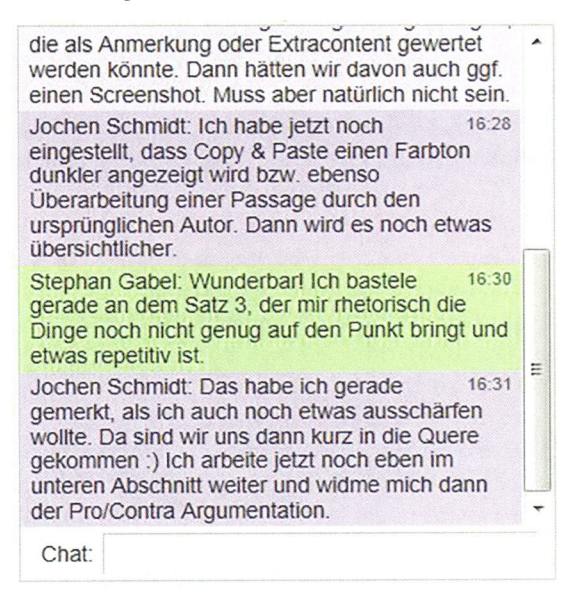

> die als Anmerkung oder Extracontent gewertet werden könnte. Dann hätten wir davon auch ggf. einen Screenshot. Muss aber natürlich nicht sein.
>
> Jochen Schmidt: Ich habe jetzt noch eingestellt, dass Copy & Paste einen Farbton dunkler angezeigt wird bzw. ebenso Überarbeitung einer Passage durch den ursprünglichen Autor. Dann wird es noch etwas übersichtlicher.   16:28
>
> Stephan Gabel: Wunderbar! Ich bastele gerade an dem Satz 3, der mir rhetorisch die Dinge noch nicht genug auf den Punkt bringt und etwas repetitiv ist.   16:30
>
> Jochen Schmidt: Das habe ich gerade gemerkt, als ich auch noch etwas ausschärfen wollte. Da sind wir uns dann kurz in die Quere gekommen :) Ich arbeite jetzt noch eben im unteren Abschnitt weiter und widme mich dann der Pro/Contra Argumentation.   16:31
>
> Chat:

Setting up such a pad is quite straightforward. One group member will create his or her own private space on the platform and invite others, e.g. via email. Upon registration, the authors select their own particular colours. Afterwards each individual keystroke is highlighted in the writer's respective colour, so that their textual contributions to the pad as well as the online chat can be differentiated between and monitored accordingly. The pad, that is the note section as well as the chat, can be saved any time. Also, an automated saving function secures the textual input at regular intervals. Each pad member can return to these saving points to review the writing process or retrieve 'lost' data or changed fragments of the text. Additionally, the note pad can be exported to any writing software for further work, e.g. spell-checking, word-count, formatting, etc. Export to and connection with online resources, e.g. websites, is possible as well. In case the pad members, for instance, collectively wrote a film review, the final product can eventually be published online.

The most interesting tool of a writing pad, particularly in a learning and teaching context, is the so-called 'time slider' function. As indicated above, the whole writing process, each contribution to the note section as well as the chat function, be it the minutest detail, is monitored and saved by the pad. With the time-slider function, pad members have the possibility to review the complete writing process from its beginning to its end. When launched, the time-slider replays the writing process in real time. Viewers can stop, rewind, move forward or end the 'tape' at any moment. The revision of both, the collaborative writing process as well as the individual contributions and writing strategies of each pad member, are greatly facilitated by this feature. The time-slider can be accessed and launched at any point in the collaborative writing process. It can also be stored for later revision or research.

As regards the potential of a writing pad as a learning environment to train textual production, a closer analysis of the process of collaborative writing in a pad environment is needed. Here we will consider only real time collaboration, which is the feature that distinguishes writing pads from other online writing tools. Once the task for a collaborative writing process has been assigned, prompted either by the teacher or the learners themselves, learners will soon realize that, because of the character of a collective effort, the writing process needs to be structured and planned lest the process result in utter chaos. While beginners might need the actual experience of the unproductive, yet exhilarating hullabaloo that emerges when three or four pad members start writing and deleting words, sentences or full paragraphs simultaneously, they will, out of frustration, soon resort to the chat function in order to coordinate their writing process. A first idea on how the textual production in a pad unfolds might be gathered from the following screenshot, which depicts an earlier step of the writing of this very article.

Figure 3: Text production in a pad

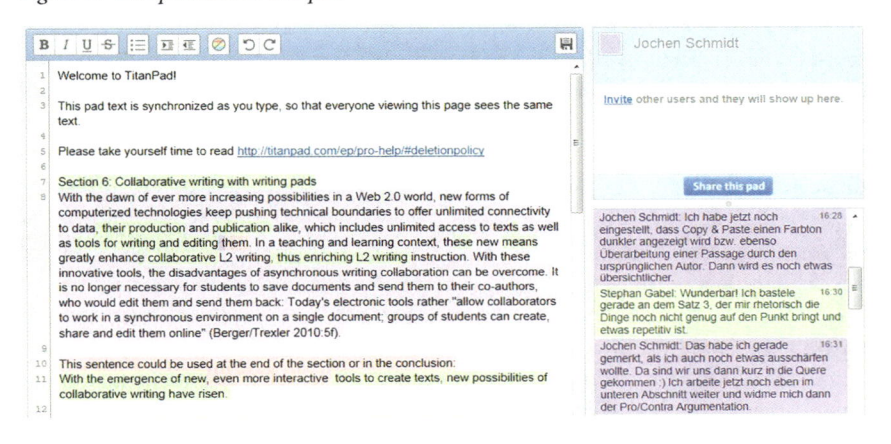

[screenshot of TitanPad interface showing collaborative text editing with chat sidebar]

Learners, beginners as well as more advanced ones, would engage in writing as a truly communicative effort, in which they meet with an authentic obstacle that can only be overcome by meta-communicating about the writing, without a need for the teacher to interfere.[5] In this respect, the planning and actual writing of texts has from the very beginning the potential of a highly interactive process with a remarkable sociocultural dimension. Discussion and decision-making are thus vital incipatory steps before the task itself can be approached. In this particular form of collaboration, learners are forced to express their ideas regarding content, explain their strategies and weigh out the pros and cons of their respective suggestions, which in turn are immediately confronted with feedback from their pad members, thus inviting more thorough explanation, re-evaluation, a more careful line of reasoning or, if necessary, additional counter-proposals.

Quite necessarily, initial planning needs to be re-negotiated and revised when new challenges or obstacles are noticed by the group members. Thus, the process of textual production as well as its underlying plan is in constant flux, and so are the roles of the learners who work on the text. While some pad member can focus on generating or revising content (in order to avoid repetitions, redundancies or argumentative gaps and pitfalls), others can concentrate on stylistic questions or linguistic problems that may occur, consulting (online) dictionaries, checking spelling, punctuation, morphology and syntax, or, as will inevitably happen with L2 students, translating suggestions made in L1 into the L2. The process

---

5   Otherwise, the instructor might consider some short initial training with the software or some awareness-raising regarding the writing process.

of revision, including the addition, deletion or alteration of phrases as well as complex utterances or full paragraphs, is thus carried out synchronously under constant supervision by the other pad members. It is the immediacy of this truly synchronous collaboration that provides rich opportunities for peer support and collaboration as well as it facilitates constant interaction within the group.

This processual approach to writing a text collaboratively will almost certainly decrease the learners' dependence on the teacher. The self-teaching by immediate observation, the authentic need to assess contributions by others as well as by oneself, result in a very high level of learner activation because of the task's immediacy and the high degree of personal involvement. Because none of their contributions will necessarily be permanent, the learners will tend to experiment more in their writing than in classical classroom scenarios. In the absence of a threat-to-face and the resulting reduction of pressure or anxieties, collaborative writing in a pad environment can be a highly motivating enterprise, so that the classroom is converted into a writing workshop that renders itself extremely useful for autonomous language learning. The learners are invited to work in a peer setting, in which less advanced students can benefit via scaffolding from the strategies used by more mature peers. Moreover, the strategies themselves are likely to be negotiated (via the chat function), which raises their awareness of the writing process and, indirectly, also enhances their language learning awareness.

While learners can work rather independently, guidance by the teacher is possible at any time since the pads allow for inviting 'guests'. This way, the teacher can be enabled to monitor the group processes, provide impulses or other forms of assistance to the whole group as well as give individual feedback by tracing back a specific learner's contributions (making use of the colour-coding). This need not be limited to highlighting linguistic problems, but can also refer to more general textual characteristics such as the line of reasoning, the text's persuasiveness, etc. Finally, teachers could use the time slider to track the writer's collaborative processes, examine what changes were made, by whom, how often and at what stage. Thus, the writing pad offers additional support for internal differentiation, in that it does not require a differentiated set of open or closed tasks to facilitate the writing process of all students[6]. Since the content of the time-slider function can be saved for later review(s), the possibilities for reflection are endless. The whole process of

---

6   For additional support teachers could still consider supplying a word bank, for instance, links to websites that the students could use to explore the content matter of their texts, examples of the textual genre that learners could investigate, or recommendations for writing.

text production can, for example be eventually reviewed and discussed, either with the group or the whole class so as to further promote learners' awareness of writing.

With all these possible benefits to training writing skills via writing pads, certain challenges must be considered. First of all, although most pads are free of charge and registration, the right infrastructure-a computer or smartphone-is a prerequisite for successful participation. Second, proper training that familiarizes learners with the platform and its functions may be necessary for them to use this tool effectively and to prevent the above-mentioned initial frustrations. Third, motivation is key for the independent, autonomous ways of collaborative work outlined here. Writing pads are most productive when learners are interested in or even enthusiastic about the task, so that they are no passive bystanders with a consumerist attitude, which would hinder collaboration if not halt it. Whether or not this is the case will depend on the way the writing activity has been methodologically embedded. Finally, the time-slider function, and its potential for detailed analysis, feedback and criticism comes at the price of being very time-consuming. Even though the results are worth the occasional extra effort, future generations of the software might include tools for increasing the speed with which the text production is being replayed.

7. Conclusion

As the above reflections indicate, the emergence of new, more interactive online tools for text processing has given rise to new possibilities of writer collaboration. Particularly the potential of synchronous collaborative writing with writing pads augurs well for improving L2 writing skills in an autonomous learning environment. While gaining in popularity in the classroom, pad work still awaits conclusive research, so that further classroom application is needed as well as testing in the primary, secondary and tertiary institutions. Currently, we are investigating the potential of online writing pads with L2 beginners in secondary school as well as college students. Although our work has only just begun, one observation can surely be made. Like with all software, programs can never be evaluated independent of the methodological context. In other words, it is the pedagogy behind their use that can make the difference, or, as one CALL pioneer maintained "it's not so much the program, more what you do with it" (Jones 1986: 171).

Obwohl auch fremdsprachliche Kompetenzen im „Schreiben" in jeder Altersstufe von großer Bedeutung sind, hat die Erforschung des fremdsprachlichen Schreibens und methodisch-didaktischer Maßnahmen zu seiner systematischen Förderung während der letzten Jahre verhältnismäßig geringes akademisches Interesse auf sich gezogen. Dieses galt in der jüngeren Vergangenheit insbesondere der Entwicklung „interkultureller (kommunikativer) Kompetenzen", wobei der Schreibkompetenz, trotz eines grundsätzlich holistisch angelegten Kompetenzaufbaus aller sprachlichen Fertigkeiten, in einem stark auf verbale Kommunikation ausgelegten modernen Fremdsprachenunterricht eine eher dienende Funktion zukam, was zu deren Vernachlässigung führte. Dennoch ist die Entwicklung des fremdsprachlichen Schreibens von besonderer Relevanz, denn das fremdsprachliche Schreiben ist keine Fertigkeit, die sich beim Vorliegen anderer funktionaler Kompetenzen in der Zielsprache durch einfache Übertragung automatisch aus der Muttersprache entwickeln lässt, sondern systematisch erlernt und erweitert werden muss. Sie bedarf daher besonderer Aufmerksamkeit (vgl. Weissberg 2000; Harklau 2002; Harmer 2004; Thaler 2012; Melouk 2013).

Die enormen Schwierigkeiten, mit denen sich Fremdsprachenlernende beim Schreiben von Texten unterschiedlicher Gattungen in der Zielsprache konfrontiert sehen, werden, wie die diesbezügliche Forschung schlüssig dargelegt hat, vor allem durch die Komplexität und Mehrdimensionalität des Schreibprozesses verursacht. Es wird daher gefordert, das Schreiben durch geeignete unterrichtliche Maßnahmen prozedural zu entlasten (vgl. z.B. Scardamalia/Bereiter 1986; Wolff 2000). Eine besonders vielversprechende Maßnahme ist in diesem Zusammenhang, Schüler die Texte kollaborativ verfassen zu lassen, z.B. in Kleingruppenarbeit, so dass die Lernenden während des Schreibprozesses nicht auf sich allein gestellt sind. Gerade weil die Schüler bei der Planung und Ausgestaltung der Texte ihre mentalen Prozesse verbalisieren müssen, auf ihre Vorschläge sofortiges Feedback von anderen Gruppenmitgliedern erhalten und mit alternativen Planungen und Formulierungen konfrontiert werden, wird der Erstellungsprozess für den einzelnen Schreiber vereinfacht (vgl. Dam/Legenhausen/Wolff 1990; Legenhausen 1996; Zeni 1994).

Das gilt umso mehr, wenn die Textproduktion in der Zielsprache durch den Einsatz von Computern und entsprechender Textverarbeitungsprogramme unterstützt wird, weil dies zu verbesserten Planungs-, Erstellungs-und Revisionsprozessen führt. Die Lernenden werden experimentierfreudiger und die sprachliche Qualität der erstellten Texte dadurch letztendlich besser (vgl. Börner 1992; Pennington 1996; Hyland 2003). Für das gemeinsame Schreiben in Kleingruppen ergibt sich darüber hinaus der Vorteil, dass der bereits erstellte Text für jedes Gruppenmitglied leichter zugänglich ist als bei der handschriftlichen Textproduktion, was die Interaktion über ihn erleichtert (vgl. Dam 1989; Legenhausen/ Wolff 1991).

Während diese „klassischen" Formen der computergestützten Textverarbeitung bereits intensiv auf ihren Nutzen für den Fremdsprachenunterricht hin untersucht worden sind, sind die neueren Formen der Telekollaboration noch weitgehend unerforscht. Hier gilt das Interesse derzeit vor allem asynchronen Formen des kollaborativen Schreibens, wie es sich z.B. im Rahmen von Email-Projekten, dem Tandemlernen, der Kooperation in MOOs oder dem Erstellen von Wikis und Blogs vollzieht (vgl. Eck/Legenhausen/Wolff 1994; Kötter 2001; Hyland/Hyland 2006; Kessler 2009; Berger/Trexler 2010; Elola/Oskoz 2010; Hockly 2015). Allerdings haben alle diese Formen der Telekollaboration den Nachteil, dass das eigentliche Schreiben weiterhin individuell erfolgt, so dass der Schreiber erst mit einer gewissen Verzögerung jene Rückmeldungen auf seine Beiträge erhält, die die Schreibprozessforschung als vorteilhaft identifiziert hat.

Das jüngste Aufkommen von sogenannten 'writing pads', virtuellen Schreibplattformen, die es Benutzern ermöglichen, gemeinsam von verschiedenen Rechnern aus an einem geteilten Textdokument zu arbeiten –sowohl synchron als auch asynchron–, kann diesen Mangel beheben. Angelegt sind diese Pads als multimodale Lernplattformen, die neben einer von mehreren Computern (oder anderen elektronischen Hilfsmitteln) aus gleichzeitig bedienbaren Textverarbeitung eine Chat-Funktion zum kommunikativen Austausch über den entstehenden Text sowie viele weitere nützliche Funktionen enthalten (vgl. Merse/Schmidt 2014). Dadurch laden diese „Schreibwerkzeuge" zu einem im hohen Maße eigenständigen Lernen ein, in dem durch die Kollaboration und das folgliche Miteinander-und Voneinander-Lernen der beteiligten *Padmembers* im Idealfall ein kollektiver Schreibprozess entsteht, in dem die Koautoren in ständigem Kontakt stehen. Dies bereichert zweifelsohne die methodisch-didaktischen Möglichkeiten für die Schulung des fremdsprachlichen Schreibens. Der vorliegende Artikel untersucht diese Möglichkeiten und gibt praktische Hinweise für dessen Implementierung.

Judith Buendgens-Kosten
Goethe-University Frankfurt am Main, Germany

Writing for a 'Real Audience'? The Role of Audience in Computer-Assisted Language Learning

CALL – computer-assisted language learning –often emphasizes micropublishing: sharing learner-created texts and other work online through means such as blogs, video repositories (YouTube), or social networks. One of the advantages of micropublishing, as opposed to traditional ways of sharing texts with the teacher or within the classroom, is the presumed existence of a 'real' audience. At the same time, few learner blogs are successful in attracting large numbers of readers outside the immediate social circle of the learners. This contribution argues that a distinction between the actual, physical audience, as attested by user statistics, comments, trackbacks, and the symbolic audience, that is the learners' and teachers' conceptualizations of the audience, is key to understanding audience in CALL. Using the example of blogging –both in class and in the context of self-directed language learning– it outlines how important audience design is for didactic design, and how audience conceptualizations interact with other elements of the didactic design, such as form-focus vs meaning-focus.

1. Introduction

Traditionally, publishing was a strongly gate-kept activity. In the early internet, some of these gates were removed –such as editorial control– but a high degree of technical competency was needed to e.g. create one's own website. On the web 2.0 (O'Reilly 2005), micropublishing has become so easy that e.g. sharing news on Facebook may not even be perceived as a form of publishing anymore.

In this paper, I will look at social media in CALL (computer-assisted language learning) from the perspective of micropublishing, with a focus on the audience of micropublishing and on the audience conceptualizations held by micropublishers and their teachers. In other words, this paper focuses on how writers *think about audience* in online contexts, and how this impacts their writing in the foreign language.

As an example throughout this paper, I will use blogging, a form of technology that may be viewed as a precursor to many web 2.0 tools (blogging predates the onset of the web 2.0 as defined by O'Reilly by a few years, cf. Rosenberg 2009). Traditionally (e.g. cf. Herring *et al.* 2004), blogs were understood as websites with reverse chronologically ordered texts (blog posts) that consist of elements such as texts, titles, images/multimedia, hyperlinks and metadata, and to which readers can react by writing comments. Today, reverse chronological order is not a determining factor anymore, as many blogging tools allow for alternative arrangements of texts at the start screen of the blog. Blogs may be easier to define through family resemblance/prototypical examples, than through an exhaustive list of features (cf. Geest/Gorp 1999). Blogging practices are changing, too, as blogging develops new niches and loses old niches to other tools (e.g. edublogging remains important, though teenage 'journal style' blogging has lost popularity, as social networks are more frequently used within this age group). Blogging is the web 2.0 tool that has received most attention in empirical CALL research (Wang/Vásquez 2012: 417), reflecting its major importance in educational settings when compared to other web 2.0 tools.

Blogs can be used in many educational scenarios. In principle, one can write a blog to which no reader ever gains access. Some scenarios focus on a very specific audience (fellow students, the school community), and may only give these groups access to the blog. These are legitimate use cases, and they can be highly relevant whenever there are concerns about privacy.

Yet, the discourse about blogging as educational tools seems not to focus so much on blogs as parts of closed school-wide learning management systems, or password protected group blogs accessible only to a small number of people; instead, discussions of blogging often *preassume the publicness* of the blog.

The focus of this paper will be on notions of audience in blogging-based CALL, and *claims* and *assumptions* connected with audience. This means that the paper does not attempt to quantify positive or negative effects of audience, when seen as *an actual group of readers* that interact with learners, on learners. Instead it aims to raise awareness of the *symbolic functions* of audience and the impact of how we think about audience (audience conceptualizations).

This paper consists of three main parts. Firstly, I will suggest a distinction based on Ong's understanding of audience that may support discussions of audience in CALL contexts more generally, and blogging for language learning specifically. Secondly, building on existing research on non-educational and educational non-CALL blogging, I will discuss what we know about audience and audience conceptualizations in blogging, and how CALL design reflects or could at least reflect this. Thirdly, I will address two aspects of audience and audience conceptualizations that are specific to CALL settings: native vs. non-native speaker audience and meaning vs. form focus.

1.1 Two perspectives on audience

Unlike in face-to-face contexts, where an audience is fairly easy to identify (though see Goffman (1981) for some of the complexities), the audience of written documents is usually less clear. As Ong (1975: 17) argued:

> [...] *the writer's audience is always a fiction. The historian, the scholar or scientist, and the simple letter writer all fictionalize their audiences, casting them in a made-up role and calling on them to play the role assigned.*

What applies to letters, books, and school essays also holds true in asynchronous CMC (computer-mediated communication). Of course, there is what may be referred to as 'readership', or Audience 1: individuals who access a specific online text. When doing so, they leave traces –visitor numbers, trackbacks, and/or comments– that allow a writer to learn more about his or her readership post-factum. They are, in a way, the 'physical audience'; the genuine individuals constituting the audience.

But this readership, or Audience 1, is not what guides the writer –and cannot be what guides the writer, as he or she has no direct access to them. He or she may use sources of information as outlined above to inform his or her writing, but only insofar as those pieces of information may inform the writer's *model* of the audience; his or her *audience conceptualization*. This model may be referred to as Audience 2, or as symbolic audience.

The symbolic audience is twofold: on the one hand, there are assumptions about the demographic of the readership; on the other hand, there are assumptions about the function of the readers. Do millions read this blog, or just a few people? Are they friends and family, or strangers? Do they seek information or entertainment? Do they learn from the blog, or do they evaluate it? Even when the demographic is perfectly known, we engage in fictionalizing the audience (cf. Ong's example of a student writing an essay with the teacher as audience 'demographic' in need of being fictionalized). When blogging in a non-password protected blog, however, even the 'demographic' of the readership is unknown. I disagree with Raith's assertion that "[t]he audience for weblog writers is obvious and the blogging community a real, existing community" (Raith 2009: 278). Of course, there are tightly-knit blogging communities, especially in the edublogging scene. Yet, even the blogosphere– or one's slice of the blogosphere– needs to be actively conceptualized by learners (on the level of Audience 2), and cannot always be easily tapped into (on the level of Audience 1). Lampa states that while "small, tightly knit bundles of blogs" possess "a kernel of real interactive community", for most bloggers, "the blogosphere's wider community must be imagined in the mind of the individual" (Lampa 2004).

An important observation that supports the distinction between Audience 1 and Audience 2 is that of Brake, who states: "the interviewed bloggers often appeared to envision their readerships as they would like them to be, rather than attempting to discern exactly who they might be or what attitudes they might have" (Brake 2012: 1062). In other words, Audience 2 is not a reflection of Audience 1; in fact, data about Audience 1, even if it is available (usually in the form of 'demographic' characteristics, such as number of visitors, country, browser-choice) is often not used as a basis for conceptualizing one's audience.

In much of the literature on blogs, audience is used as a unitary notion: a distinction between symbolic audience and readership is not usually considered, or at least not made explicit, in discussions on the effect of publicness of blog texts on the learning process. The focus in many didactic designs seems to lie on the *potential* audience: it is stressed that blog posts can –potentially– be read by everyone. The specific characteristics of this potential audience are less frequently addressed: the potentially global audience (of individuals interested in middle school science reports or elementary school art projects) remains vague, the focus seems to be on a general 'opening' of the classroom, rather than on reaching a specific kind of reader. The potential audience is, as a concept, a mix between Audience 1 and Audience 2; it is not the actual readership, but the readership that a text might have.

2. Readership vs symbolic audience in practice

In this section, I will discuss both Audience 1 and Audience 2 'in action', that is (a) what we know about what audience conceptualizations and actual audience look like in different blogging settings, and (b) how these are actively designed and purposely created in CALL.

Often, work on CALL can profit if it takes non-CALL contexts into consideration. For example, observations on how a new medium or a new technology is used in non-education, or in education but in non-CALL contexts, can inform CALL designs. In this section, I will regularly refer to two types of non-CALL blogging: (1) free-range blogging and (2) educational blogging. 'Free range' blog is a playful label for private blogs that are not created for educational settings; what Alm (2009: 207) refers to as "[b]logging practices in the real world". Educational blogs –edublogs– are blogs created in educational contexts, though the label is both used to refer to learners', as well as to teachers' blogs, i.e. to blogs written by educators to reflect on their teaching practice. In this context, only the first type of educational blogs, blogs by learners, will be considered.

2.1 A limited readership is the norm

For 'free range' blogs, the readership may not necessarily be large, nor do bloggers need to assume that it is. Blood's classic observation summarizes this nicely:

> Just as email has made us all writers, weblogs have made all of us publishers. And weblogs are publications, designed to be read by someone, whether it be a large global audience or (as is more commonly the case) a micro-audience of hundreds-or only a handful-of people. (Blood 2002: x)

While some blogs –often referred to as *A-list blogs*– have massive global readerships, the majority of blogs reach fairly small numbers of readers, and may, to point to only one indicator for readership (Audience 1), receive no or only very infrequent reader comments. Lampa (2004) calls this the "abject obscurity" of most bloggers.

2.2 Designing for Audience 1

In non-educational blogging, a wide range of strategies are used to attract readership, as numbers of Audience 1 are related to financial rewards for blogging. Strategic choice of content, careful community management or paid advertising are among the many options for creating and increasing an Audience 1. In educational blogging, these strategies are not usually feasible. In fact, efforts at reaching an Audience 1 beyond the classroom itself (which does constitute an audience, yet none that could not be reached through many other forms of writing or speaking within the classroom setting itself) are rarely described in the literature.

We know that some teachers actively recruit an audience, using a practice that might be called "audience management" (as opposed to audience conceptualization, which takes place on the level of Audience 2). This behavior is rarely discussed in the literature - Ellison and Yuehua Wu (2008: 116) mention it in passing – but it is clearly attested by actual teacher behavior[1]. Teachers act in a way to guarantee the existence of an Audience 1, which, though, might differ significantly from the kind of audience envisioned by learners (Audience 2), as the Audience 1 created through such practices can be expected to closely reflect a teacher's pre-existing network. Here, the potentially worldwide audience of individuals interested in the subject matter of the blog might be realized as fellow teachers interested in educational blogging.

---

1 A popular place for this seems to be Twitter, where many teachers who blog with classes share their students' work, see e.g. @DeputyMitchell.

The literature includes one example (Campbell 2004) known to the author of teachers explicitly instructing learners in building an audience for their blogs beyond the classroom by actively building a network. Interestingly, this one example used the blogging community LiveJournal (http://www.livejournal.com/), where individual bloggers are connected through "friends" and "interests", not unlike modern SNSs (Social Networking Service) such as Facebook, making it fairly easy to recruit readers from within the larger LiveJournal community.

A very specific way to engineer an Audience 1 is posed by telecollaboration set-ups, in which multiple groups are combined into one blogging project to serve as each other's audiences (cf. Ducate/Lomicka 2005; quadblogging.com). In language learning settings, the composition of groups is usually of such a type to intentionally bring together native speakers and learners of a language (see discussion below). Instead of using students' or teachers' pre-existing networks, a network is specifically created for the purpose of the blogging activity. The question of content quality is replaced by the question of social ties, and interest in the texts can be superseded by interest in developing social ties. Such set-ups are reminiscent of blogging communities like lang-8 (lang-8.com, cf. Buendgens-Kosten 2011), which are based on reciprocity systems – 'I read your text, so that somebody reads my text'.

Within an internet filled with high-quality content, a student-created blog has to 'compete' against Wikipedia entries, journalistic venues, etc. Who, is the question, would read a learner's explanation when there are expert blogs available on the same topic? This is not meant to imply that student blogs cannot be highly successful in attracting audiences. Examples for this are, i.e., Tavi Gevinson's "The Style Rookie" (thestylerookie.com), or, more contemporary, Martha Payne's "NeverSeconds" (neverseconds.blogspot.com). Nonetheless, unless the topic of a blog is very specific, a niche, most readers will not peruse these blog posts for interest in their content, but rather for social reasons, as discussed above. The potential global audiences are realized as personal social networks – those of the teacher (fellow teachers), those of the students (friend, family), or those of the class/exchange group. This leads to a certain mismatch between the potential often associated with the publicness of blogging ('world-wide audience'), and the actual Audience 1.

Within a limited-time class project, developing helpful audience conceptualizations (Audience 2) may be easier than developing the skills and network to practice effective audience management on a scale that transcends one's immediate social network (even though the ability to manage audiences is a valuable skill on its own). This is what the next section will focus on: what we already know about audience conceptualizations, and how they can be influenced.

2.3 Audience conceptualizations of bloggers

What is known of the audience conceptualizations of bloggers? The best data is available for 'free range' bloggers. Brake delineates, based on interviews with bloggers, five different types of audience conceptualizations: Narrowcast & Dialogic bloggers write for a group of known individuals ("friends"), while Broadcast & Telelogic bloggers understand their audience as an indefinite group of strangers. Among these, Narrowcast and Broadcast bloggers do not expect reactions from their audience, while Dialogic and Telelogic bloggers do. A fifth category falls outside of this one-way/two-way –the friends/strangers grid: self-directed bloggers practice "blogging as an end in itself" and do not see themselves as writing primarily for an audience (Brake 2012: 1062). These five conceptualizations should not be interpreted as fixed characteristics of bloggers: "It is important to note, however, that some of the interviewed bloggers expressed varied (and sometimes contradictory) framings of their practices and attitudes toward their readers at different points both in their interviews and in the evolution of their blogging practices" (Brake 2012: 1062).

Scheidt (2006) has applied Langellier & Peterson's (2004) audience typology to blogs, specifically to those of adolescent bloggers. She found, based on a content analysis of 102 blogposts from 12 different blogs, that "audience as witness to the experience" (50.6%) and "cultural theorist assessing the contestation of meanings, values, and identities in the performance" (25,8%) made up the audience conceptualizations of most blog posts, with "therapist unconditionally supporting emotions" (12.4%), "narrative analyst examining genre, truth, or strategy" (7.9%) and "critic appraising the display of performance knowledge and skill" (3,4%) being rare (Scheidt 2006: 205f).

This shows how differently audiences can be conceptualized, and suggests that in those cases where the didactic design or the teachers does not strongly stress one conceptualization over another, audience conceptualizations can be expected to vary within a group –and, as Blake (2012) has argued, even within a person over time.

When looking at learners directly, rather than at teachers, Brake's observation concerning the limited interest in Audience 1 is supported. In interviews with university students blogging during an instructional-design seminar, Buendgens-Kosten and Brombach (2013) found that while students were quite enthusiastic about the *potential* for comments (high importance of Audience 2), the only comments they had observed were in the form of feedback from their teacher. They did not notice the comment made by a subject expert who had commented on their blog (low importance of Audience 1).

In a study conducted by Ellison and Yuehua Wu (2008), which was also situated in a (non-language learning) university setting, the relationship between Audience 1 and Audience 2 panned out slightly differently. Here, students maintained individual blogs, but commenting on each other's blogs was a required activity, stressing the classroom-as-audience. Some learners responded very positively when fellow students commented on their blogs, making the Audience 1 visible (Ellison/Yuehua Wu 2008: 112). When one student had gotten a comment from an outside-of-class author he had mentioned in his post, this was perceived positively by all students. However, individual students who did not receive any comments expressed frustration. Apparently, "knowledge of the size of the potential audience for one's blog posts made a lack of attention more distressing" (Ellison/Yuehua Wu 2008: 113).

2.4 Designing for Audience 2

As stated above, few teachers seem to specifically teach audience management. On the other hand, teachers will usually refer to audience conceptualizations in some way (see, for example, Buendgens-Kosten (2016a) on how teachers introduce blogs to learners without blogging experience). Support for audience conceptualization happens –for example, when teachers warn students that they have to follow copyright laws when blogging, as their blogs are 'public', or when they suggest how thrilling it is to blog, as anybody in the world might read their texts. This, though, is not always viewed explicitly as a way to shape the audience conceptualizations of learners.

3. Specifics of audience in CALL/BALL

Above, we discussed audience and audience conceptualizations in different blogging scenarios –free range blogging, educational blogging in general, and blogging for language learning specifically. It will not be necessary to outline in detail in how far these different contexts differ. Instead, we will point out two dimensions that are specific to discussions of audience in BALL (blogging-assisted language learning): (1) the role of speaker status of audience members, that is how (physical or symbolic) audiences of native or non-native speakers are viewed, (2) the important distinction between form-focused and meaning-focused learning activities, and how this distinction impacts BALL.

3.1 Types of audiences in BALL – the role of speaker status

One important difference between BALL and blogging in non-language learning educational settings is the relevance of the NS/NNS distinction. Being read by a 'real audience' (cf. e.g. Johnston 1999) makes the blogging experience more 'authentic', and the native speaker audience is perceived as the 'most real' audience of all (cf. cultural authenticity, Buendgens-Kosten 2013).

Regarding CALL-communities, we know that "[t]heir designs reflect assumptions about what a native speaker is, and about the functions native speakers have in language learning. Each language status-related design decision shapes not only the underlying software structure, but also has an effect on user behaviour, and may impact the learning experience and learning outcomes" (Buendgens-Kosten 2014: 34). In BALL-contexts, we can expect a similar effect: assumptions about the role of native speakers for the language learning process –often based on assumptions about authenticity in language learning– will influence audience conceptualizations, specifically the role of native speakers-as-audience.

Generally, it is assumed that language learning bloggers want native speaker readers. Lang-8, a language learning blogging community, advertises with slogans such as "Let our community of native speakers support your language learning" and "A new language learning platform where native speakers correct what you write." (lang-8.com, 23/02/2015). Bloggers at Lang-8 regularly comment on the relevance of native speaker readers, specifically requesting more feedback, and expressing their high hopes for comments and corrections from native speakers.

The following student quote from Alm (2009), who discusses a language learning blogging project within a university-level intermediate German language course, also illustrates this preference for native speakers: "If a native speaker had read my blog it would have been interesting to read any comments they left" (Alm 2009: 212). At the same time, finding a native speaker audience is perceived as being difficult –in Alm's study, the only learner who succeeded in building a native speaker audience had his or her former exchange partner as a reader (Alm 2009: 211f). Contradicting these assumptions about the desirability of a native speaker audience, Alm also documents indications for a resistance to an audience of native speakers:

> Others were not prepared to share their work with their peers or expose it to native speakers, possibly out of fear of criticism from 'strangers reading and commenting on my attempts to write in German.' A private blog was perceived as a safer learning environment where 'others cannot see what you have written.' They were not interested in feedback from foreigners; 'it was also good just to get feedback from people you knew.' Some also felt that their blogs would not be interesting to the public.

It is not absolutely clear, though, if this resistance was against native speakers or "foreigners", respectively, rather than against individuals without close ties (non-peers, strangers) reading one's texts. When native speakers are in short supply in one's immediate social environment, as many foreign language learners (unlike many second language learners) experience, native speakers are often identical to total strangers ("B" sector in Table 1). In other words, these statements can be read as concerns on the y-axis (Do I want native speakers to read my texts?) or as concerns on the x-axis (Do I want people without pre-existing ties to read my texts?).[2]

Table 1: Four audience types

	Pre-existing ties	No pre-existing ties
Native speaker audience	A: Exchange group (native speakers)	B: Interested public (international audience)
Non-native speaker audience	C: Friends, family, exchange group (fellow learners)	D: Interested public

Writing in the target language can be justified within the logic of the classroom as a classroom (Breen 1985) without reference to specific audiences. Yet, when the existence of an outside-the-classroom audience is brought forward as a key element of the blogging and learning process, language choice needs to be appropriate for the audience envisioned. The audience envisioned does not, automatically, have to be a native speaker audience –blogs written in a language of wider communication may as well aim at a lingua franca-using group or a group of fellow learners. However, any language choice is both reflective of the envisioned audience, and constitutive of that audience. This also applies to code-alternation and avoidance of code-alternation as part of code choice (Bell 1984; Buendgens-Kosten 2016). When the role of audience is stressed, audience conceptualization and language choice need to be aligned.

---

2   Accordingly, it is not surprising that the public nature of blogging sometimes faces opposition, including in non-CALL contexts. In the study by Raith (2009), for example, 25% of students chose a paper-based assignment instead of blogging: "They did not want anybody to read their texts; therefore, they didn't use weblogs themselves. Although most of them did not specify reasons for that fear, they would feel uncomfortable with an online audience in mind" (Raith 2009: 286). From a didactic point of view, the presence of a (potential) audience can challenge the idea of classrooms as protected spaces.

3.2 Focus on form versus focus on meaning and audience conceptualizations

The distinction between focus on form and focus on meaning is one of the key distinctions in SLA today. Do we discuss holiday plans to practice the *going to* future, or to create a list of favorite holiday activities? Blogging can be done either with a stronger focus on form or with a stronger focus on meaning, although usually elements of both will be present.[3] In writing contexts, this is also framed as a distinction between accuracy –correct use of forms– and fluency or expressivity –using language to express ideas quickly and lively.

These foci –a form-stressing accuracy focus and a meaning-stressing fluency/expressivity focus– are closely intertwined with audience conceptualizations. The argument for using blogs to foster accuracy is implicitly one about audience expectations. If blogging encourages learners to produce more target-language-like texts, this is because bloggers assume that this is expected from their readers. On the other hand, if they are encouraged to express themselves freely, to show their views on different matters in creative ways, then this assumes that the audience, above all else, values a specific kind of content or style of writing. These two are viewed as opposing points on a continuum rather than as contradictory poles –as some blogging projects aim to increase both accuracy and fluency/expressivity.

In a questionnaire distributed to ten German secondary school students of English who had used blogging, Raith found that –asked about the influence of the online audience– 90% responded within the category "Writing personally", defined as "Some mentioned that this was meant to express attitudes, others wrote that they wanted to tell their opinion". The category "Making it interesting and understandable", understood as both "write accurately, so that others will be able to understand their texts" and "make the texts interesting", however, was indicated by only ten percent of the bloggers; hence, by one person (Raith 2009: 284f). What is remarkable here is not so much that this or that type dominated, but that, even within one group of learners, there were clear differences in how they understood their FL blogging activities.

In language learning contexts, a third perspective is possible: viewing the audience as an entity which values neither correct prose nor creative expression, but which constitutes something akin to virtual teachers. This can be observed well in the language learning blogging community Lang-8: "Some texts, most conspicuously those that contain grammar drills, but also, to a lesser degree, those that

---

3   The exception proves the rule, e.g. a language learning blogger quoted in Buendgens-Kosten (2016b) blogged grammar drills.

contain school-essay type texts, may be written for an audience viewed primarily as a teacher (**reader-as-teacher**), while those that set out to teach content matter, language and culture, or that try to establish rapport through diary-type entries, may not be written for such a reader-as-teacher audience. This, of course, is not a clear-cut distinction, and bloggers' understanding of their audience may change over time" (Buendgens-Kosten 2016). Important here is that, if audience is stressed in a CALL setting, then didactic focus and audience conceptualizations should ideally align.

4 Conclusion

This paper looked at notions of audience in CALL blogging. It discussed how BALL, as a micropublishing activity, is closely tied to notions of audience.

It is based on the assumption that audience has two aspects: The Audience 1 (physical audience/readership), and the Audience 2 (conceptualized audience/symbolic audience). It argues that this distinction is relevant to understand blogging in CALL contexts, even though, more often than not, it is not made sufficiently explicit in the literature.

Currently, we generally have a basic understanding of Audience 2 in blogging, but very little knowledge about Audience 2, specifically in language learning blogging contexts, although we know that speaker status and focus on form/focus on meaning are important categories.

From a practical perspective, the key idea is that designing tasks for social media-based CALL involves designing an audience. Learners may require support in their development of audience conceptualizations, as well as in their development of Audience 1 management strategies (unless the focus is on symbolic audience only).

Important desiderata for research would serve to better understand the audience conceptualization held by learners in BALL contexts. We need more research on conceptualizations actually held by students, and on how these relate to the audience management strategies/information available about Audience 1, and the audience conceptualization support provided by the teacher.

Moreover, it should be considered if learning outcomes/learner satisfaction with a blogging project are related to audience conceptualization. Are some types more helpful than others for specific learning goals? In addition, what role does audience conceptualization play for language choice, presence/absence of code-alternation, and focus on accuracy vs focus on meaning?

A comparison between the role audience conceptualization for different micropublishing tools, as well as between micropublishing and sharing oriented tools, might prove interesting as well.

CALL – *computer-assisted language learning*, also das computervermittelte Sprachenlernen – betont oft *micropublishing*, die Online-Publikation von Lerner-produzierten Texten und anderen Lernerarbeiten auf Blogs, Videorepositorien (wie YouTube) oder in den sozialen Netzwerken. Einer der Vorteile von *micropublishing*, verglichen mit der traditionellen Vorgehensweise, bei der Texte nur mit dem Lehrer/der Lehrerin oder innerhalb des Klassenzimmers geteilt werden, ist die angenommene Existenz eines ‚realen' Publikums für diese Produkte. Gleichzeit lässt sich aber beobachten, dass z.B. nur sehr wenige Schülerblogs signifikante Leserzahlen erreichen. Dieser Beitrag stellt dar, wie wichtig die Unterscheidung zwischen einem tatsächlichen, ‚physischen' Publikum (belegt durch Nutzerstatistiken, Blogkommentare, Trackbacks) und einem symbolischen Publikum (Lerner- und Lehrerkonzepte der intendierten Leserschaft) für das Verständnis von *Publikum* und *Öffentlichkeit* in CALL allgemein ist. Anhand des Beispiels von Blogging – schulischem Bloggen und außerschulischem Bloggen – will der Beitrag aufzeigen, dass *audience design* ein wichtiger Bestandteil des didaktischen Designs ist, und dass *Audience*-Konzepte mit anderen Aspekten des didaktischen Design interagieren können (z.B. Formfokussierung vs. Inhaltsfokussierung).

Simon Falk
Philipps University of Marburg, Germany

"Let's Work Together" – How Mobile-Assisted Language Learning Can Contribute to More Collaboration and Interaction among Students

Mobile learning indicates a type of learning that is ubiquitous. Although learning can happen everywhere and at any time, mobile learning depends on various factors such as the learner's self-determination and self-management. Virtual learning spaces open up a myriad of possibilities for exchange and collaboration between users. This inevitably leads to the question as to how this collaboration can be fostered. In this article, I focus on the aspects of learning space and its importance for collaboration with mobile (digital) media. I will first prepare the theoretical background and then look at results from a study conducted with students from a German university.

1. Collaboration in the 21st century

> *"Unity is strength… when there is teamwork and collaboration, wonderful things can be achieved."*
> (Mattie Stepanek 1990–2004)

It is quite needless to say that there are benefits of working together if two or more persons aim to achieve a common goal. This can be seen from the example of scientists using their cumulative knowledge to find a cure for a disease instead of working on their own. They might get positive results in a shorter period of time by working together. Of course, there are examples of collaborative acts in various other situations that require certain problem-solving strategies. Social changes, such as rapid technological developments, influence the forms and means of collaboration. One such change concerns the ways in which information is gathered. Smartphones, tablets, or other mobile devices are being used more and more by young people when it comes to communicating and interacting with each other. Different areas such as family, friends, learning, knowledge, and working are much more intertwined in terms of spatial and temporal access than they would have been without technological support. Students speak in favor of partnerships in the context of the so-called 21st century skills, including communication and collaboration skills, as they prepare to carve out their career in an increasingly complex work environment in modern times. In case of a partnership, some of these skills precisely describe the terms that contribute to collaboration with others. Along with shared responsibility for work and appreciation for individual contributions, flexibility and willingness to help should be exercised to make necessary compromises to accomplish a common goal (Gerstein 2013: 271–272).

The focus of this article lies on fostering collaborative acts in educational contexts by using digital mobile devices. For this reason, I will first describe the collaborative principles in multimedia learning and then depict the role of traditional and modern forms of learning spaces. Within this context, the roles of the teacher and the student are being examined with regard to their awareness of learning spaces. After taking a closer look at possible assessment forms of collaborative work, I will discuss the research conducted with the participants in a media-focused didactic seminar at the Philipps University of Marburg. The main research question was: How to raise awareness about new forms of learning spaces by using mobile devices?

1.1 Collaborative principles in multimedia learning

Multimedia learning seems rather a fuzzy concept, at least one that can have various connotations depending on the individual using it. On the denotative side, it means "a lot of media" deriving from *multi-*"many, a lot, much" and *media* "media (plural of medium)". However, multimedia can have different meanings in different situations. For example, if you watch a clip on YouTube while texting someone, you would already be considered to be in a multimedia situation. This does not have to be an explicit learning situation, though it can become one, as we will see in a later section. In this article, I will refer to Mayer's definition of multimedia (Mayer 2014: 2–3), which includes the presentation of both words in spoken or written language and pictures, such as illustrations, photos, or videos, that are often considered to be texts in varying forms. Another term that represents a similar idea relating to the use of different sensory channels for transmission of information is *multimodality* or *multiple coding*. I deliberately refrain from using this term because it does not fully incorporate the actual medium that is used for learning.

Thus, multimedia learning refers to the learner's individual construction of knowledge based on the information they get from words and pictures as well as the interaction with the medium –eg., TV, tablet, or smartphone– itself.

Along with the feedback or the working memory principle, the collaborative principle is rated among the category of advanced principles of multimedia learning (Mayer 2014: 9). Its main idea depends on the structure of the learning task that needs to be processed as well as on the learning environment; it can be subdivided into three related principles that determine when and under which conditions collaboration will positively affect learning in a multimedia environment (Kirschner/Kirschner/Janssen 2014: 548)

1. The learning task should be cognitively demanding enough to require collaboration, thus prompting the effective use of a collective working memory
2. Cognitive processes and information necessary for learning are effectively and efficiently shared among group members
3. Multimedia environment provides the necessary tools for effective and efficient communication about the task content as well as the coordination and regulation of the process involved in carrying out the tasks in order to minimize transactional activities

In higher education, learning platforms such as Moodle or Blackboard are widely used by teachers and students. Learning materials and tasks can be shared, which means sharing the knowledge to solve such tasks. In this case, it seems to be a question of designing the right task in order to meet the above-mentioned needs. If the task being carried out offers only low-threshold complexity, it is likely to be solved individually and not collaboratively. The same example can be applied to the second sub-principle, thereby affecting the necessity to share cognitive processes with others. Looking at the third sub-principle, which describes the multimedia environment, it can be stated that the number of tools being offered for effective and efficient communication does not significantly change the outcome of a task as long it has low-threshold complexity. Hence, an adequate number of possible tools should be highlighted.

1.2 Learning space as collaborative space

The question of what defines a learning space cannot easily be answered without taking a closer look at relevant research areas. In Germany, progressive educational approaches (*reformpädagogische Ansätze*) had a certain influence on neighboring educational fields by promoting inclusion of extracurricular activities, such as field trips or explorations, in the concept of extracurricular learning spaces (Königs 2015: 90). On the other hand, projects such as the Airport project by Michael Legutke (cf. Legutke/Thiel 1983) and his contributions to the role of the classroom for foreign language learning have changed the perspectives of the constitution of learning spaces. However, the term learning space is still ambiguous. Kurtz (2015: 108–111) rightly points out that there is a relationship between (learning) places and (learning) spaces. Compared to learning places, learning spaces cannot be easily located due to their non-existent physical boundaries –in fact, virtual spaces or those mentally constructed are infinite in most cases. The

Internet and Web 2.0 serve as a good example of unlimited space in which content is constantly generated and modified by its users. Kurtz (2015: 109–111) identifies 12 closely related dimensions of learning places/spaces. I will focus on two of these dimensions, namely *novelty space* (*Novität*) and *affectivity/quality of experience* (*Affektivität/Erlebnisqualität*). Both these dimensions deal with the subjective perception of places and spaces by the learner. Novelty space describes the tension between familiarity and novelty being influenced by various location-specific parameters. These parameters may be symbolic, social, physical, material etc. In this dimension, the aspect of novelty can be beneficial with regard to the use mobile devices in foreign language learning by triggering the learner's curiosity while being in a familiar place. Affectivity or quality of experience also emphasizes sensuous experiences gathered within a (learning) space, where the learner self-assesses the quality of the respective location (whether physical or virtual) and then decides if it is relevant enough for their learning.

There is a myriad of factors in both dimensional concepts that can hardly be predicted owing to the high level of subjectivity. It seems rather difficult to say exactly why a learner chooses a certain place for their learning. Does familiarity weigh more than novelty or is it the other way around? Because of this difficult situation, we have to prioritize a crucial point with regard to (foreign) language learning: raising awareness of the new role of learning spaces. It has already been shown with empirical data that the use of digital media can have positive effects on the self-awareness of students' linguistic performance – for example, on their speaking skills (cf. Pontes/Shimazumi 2015) – or also on their self-awareness in an intergenerational sense (cf. Arich-Gerz 2008).[1] This, in turn, leads to the following question: Who is responsible for raising awareness about new collaborative learning spaces – the teacher, the student, or the respective device?

Even though many mobile devices, such as smartphones or tablets, are of a highly complex nature, they are not likely to be able to perform this task. Collecting data might help the device to gain insights about its user and make valid predictions about user behavior. However, this will take a lot of time and raise many ethical questions. Therefore, in the following two paragraphs, the focus will lie on the role of the student as well as on the role of the teacher.

---

1   Pihkala-Posti (2015) gives another example of collaborative activities in virtual space by referring to a game-based approach with Minecraft.

1.2.1 The role of the student

The role of the student is essential for a positive learning outcome in collaborative mobile-assisted language learning scenarios. Laal, Laal, and Khattami-Kermanshahi (2012: 1698) state that "collaboration is a philosophy of interaction and personal lifestyle where individuals are responsible for their actions, including learning and respect the abilities and contributions of their peers." This brings out the strong interplay between individual and collective activities. The success of one learner could help others to be successful. This results from the fact that collaborative learning groups try to attain a common goal. Socio-cognitive views on learning emphasize learning as an active social process in which collaborative interactions are viewed as a key determinant of the content of learning activities (Lee/Ryu 2013: 197). In virtual spaces, the circumstance that there is no face-to-face collaboration might even strengthen mutual confidence and assistance. One unique benefit of mobile-assisted (language) learning is that it depends on the learner's self-determination and self-management. They, on an individual basis, decide when and how to work on a task, depending on variables such as intrinsic motivation, curiosity, attention focus, or control. These factors are relevant when it comes to the so-called flow of activities (*ibid.*). The term "flow" goes back to Csíkszentmihályi, who described this phenomenon as a holistically controlled feeling under which one acts with total involvement or engagement with a particular activity, with a narrowing of the attention focus (cf. Lee/Ryu 2013: 198). The height of individual flow experience is determined by one's skills (high or low) and one's challenge (high or low): Flow only occurs when the ratio between these two is adjusted. For example, if the challenge (of the task) is very high and the learners' skills are very low, the learners are likely to be anxious. If their skills, on the other hand, are higher than the requirement, they are likely to be bored. Thus, a balanced ratio is needed in order to enhance a flow. In collaborative activities, social flow might replace individual flow. The main thought behind this idea is that every individual has to evaluate the advantages and disadvantages of working together with others to resolve a problem. In many cases, the benefits of collaboration can only be achieved at an extra cost to the individual – e.g., they might require more effort and time to complete the task and can even be hindered by the phenomenon of "social loafing" which describes a collaborative situation in which people make less effort to achieve a common goal compared to an individual work situation (Lee/Ryu 2013: 201). Hence, development of collaborative activities does not only involve presenting new forms of learning spaces in which the interaction can take place, but also requires raising the students' awareness of possible new learning opportunities and related flaws (cf. Mansor 2007: n.p.).

1.2.2 The role of the teacher

It is a fallacy to believe that new forms of learning spaces, as well as advanced technology combined with higher learner autonomy, automatically lead to a diminished role of the (foreign) language teacher. Instead, professional changes can be observed, creating new roles as learning facilitators, consultants, or also learning coaches (cf. Falk/Gerlach 2016: 26–27). Legutke and Rösler (2005: 175) mention that enhancing collaborative work by integrating digital media in the education of the foreign language teacher is associated with new challenges for both teachers and learners. According to Legutke and Rösler, these challenges are implicitly named in five dimensions of change, some of which I have already dealt with in the previous two paragraphs: *Encounters beyond the classroom walls, enhanced access to a great variety of resources, learning formats, learner roles,* and *teacher roles.* In the following, I want to highlight three key areas that are essential to the role of the teacher. First, media literacy can be seen as a fundamental requirement for the teacher to create, implement, and evaluate tasks on the basis of digital (mobile) media. The controversial concept of students as so-called *digital natives* has often led to the assumption that any support on part of the teacher becomes redundant. It could, however, be disproved that students growing up with use of digital devices have an immanent media literacy (cf. Falk/Gerlach 2016). The second key area is the promotion of autonomous learning.[2] Closely related to the topic of media literacy, teachers should not fully give away the control of what has to be learnt but still foster the ways to learn and resolve tasks on their own. In this case, digital media can be useful and work as supportive tools for multimedia language learning, which allows a great amount of autonomy on part of the learner. However, some kind of control must be ensured up to a certain degree through the teacher. Collaborative learning, which is central in this article, is clearly a shift from the typical teacher-centered setting toward a collaborative state in which other processes based on students' discussion and active work with the course material take place (Laal *et al.* 2013: 1428). Following the previous aspect of autonomy, the third area covers the learning content. Owing to curricular standards, the teacher needs to carefully choose how much time they must spend on certain content-related matters. The selection of appropriate learning material, for example, is hampered by a great variety of resources that can be found online. Therefore, it is rather time-consuming to pick adequate materials.

---

2   In this case, autonomous learning should not be seen as the opposite of collaborative learning. Every form of collaborative learning includes a certain degree of autonomous learning.

1.3 Forms of assessment

In previous paragraphs, we have already seen assessing mobile device-based activities depend on the outcome that needs to be assessed. In the following section, tests or exams that have been taken with smartphones, laptops, or tablets are not taken into consideration, for the aspects of learning spaces and self-determination/self-management are of little relevance in these cases of assessment. I will rather focus on self-and peer assessment as well as on collaborative assessment. Self-and peer assessment can be helpful for students to monitor their own learning. As part of a larger group, learners can estimate their own work and that of others. This might be rather subjective, however, that the teacher could get a holistic view of all the group members. Recent empirical studies furnish clear evidence that students show increased motivation and improve achievements and positive acceptance in mobile assessment systems for self-and peer-based classroom assessment (Chen, "Mobile assessment" 2010: 229–236; de-Marcos *et al.*, "Auto-assessment" 2010: 1069–1079). Similarly, collaborative assessments can be performed via mobile devices that function as support tools facilitating the complex task of assessing group work. The role played by learning spaces for learning outcome can also be considered if the respective system is context-aware and can extract, interpret, and use context information and also adapt its functionality to the current context of use (Nikou/Economides 2013: 349).

2. Research context

I will now present findings from a small empirical study conducted in a foreign language didactics seminar that took place in the summer term of 2015. Data was collected via questionnaires at the first and last sessions of the seminar. The analysis is compiled in a qualitative way, with the inclusion of certain quantitative parts.

2.1 Research questions

This study aims to find out the concept of learning spaces for future teachers and explores to what extent this concept changes in the course of the seminar, with its focus on the development and implementation of tasks with digital (mobile) devices. The idea behind this is to see if it is possible to raise awareness about the payoffs and pitfalls of new forms of learning spaces.

Therefore, the first questionnaire contained eight questions and socio-demographic data (gender, age, and fields of study). The first three questions dealt with the individual use behavior of mobile devices. The fourth question explored which digital devices had been used by teachers during their time as students. Fifth, sixth, and seventh questions dealt with the personal understanding and definition of a learning place/space and a learning situation, as well as the benefits relating to the implementation of mobile devices in the field of education. Finally, the eighth question asked the participants to state whether they would use mobile devices for learning purposes in their future job as a teacher.

The second questionnaire contained exactly the same questions as fifth to eighth questions. The intention was to compare the answers and see if there had been any changes in the thought process. Additionally, the first four questions of the second questionnaire dealt with the individual use behavior of digital (mobile) devices during the three-month period of the seminar.

2.2 Methodology

All subjects involved in the study were undergraduate student-teachers[3] (*Lehramtsstudierende*). The seminar consisted of 14 face-to-face sessions in which several basic principles and methods for the development and implementation of tasks with digital (mobile) devices were covered. In addition, content and work assignments were delivered through an online learning platform. In order to be assessed, the students had to develop and present a small project that could be implemented in the classroom. In total, 20 students were enrolled in the course, which took place on a weekly basis from April 2015 to July 2015. Eighteen students (five male, 13 female) participated in the first questionnaire, and their average age was 23 years. In the second questionnaire, only 11 students participated (four male, seven female), and their average age at the second assessment was 22 years.

3. Research findings

Using a five-point Likert scale (1 = *fully disagree* to 5 = *fully agree*/1 = *not good at all* to 5 = *very good*), the respondents rated their use behavior of digital (mobile) devices. This quantitative approach facilitates improved comparability. In the following, I will number the respective questions (Appendix I) and mark them with a subscript indicating the survey period (e.g., $Q3_{t1}$ = Question 3, first survey period). Answers from open questions were summarized into categories according to their meanings. Data interpretation and a discussion of the results can be found in the fourth paragraph. The scope of this article only allows me to sketch selected findings.

---

3   Since there is no equivalent expression for *Lehramtstudierende* in the English language, I refer to them as student-teachers.

Q1₁₁: *Do you use mobile communication devices such as smartphones, tablets etc.? If so, what are they exactly?*

Figure 1: Use of mobile communication devices

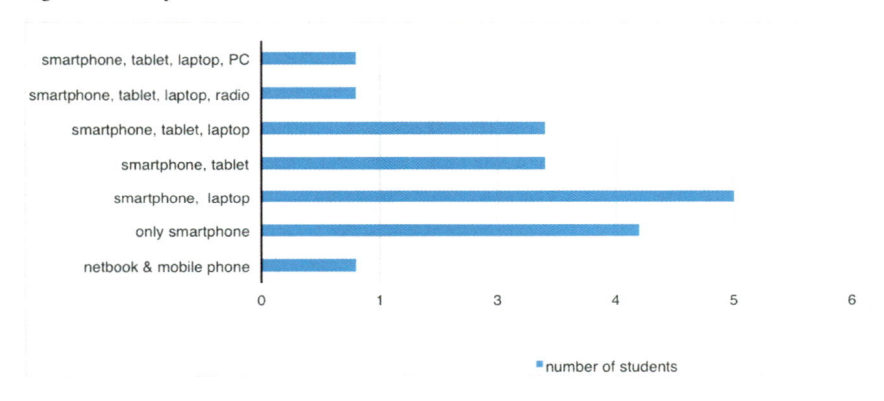

Device combination	Number of students
smartphone, tablet, laptop, PC	~1
smartphone, tablet, laptop, radio	~1
smartphone, tablet, laptop	~3
smartphone, tablet	~3
smartphone, laptop	5
only smartphone	~4
netbook & mobile phone	~1

■ number of students

Q5: *What do you understand by the term "learning place?"*
Q6: *What do you understand by the term "learning situation?"*
Q7: *What benefits do you see by the use of mobile devices in the educational sector?*

Table 1: Categories from questionnaires 1 and 2

Q5₁₁ Learning place	Q5₁₂ Learning place

• Affective elements
  o place of retreat
  o privacy
  o positive atmosphere
• Physical space
• Virtual space
Example: *"[…] is a place where I can work completely undisturbed."*
	• Physical space
	• Virtual space
	  o collaboration with other users
	• Media use
	Example: *"Learning can happen everywhere if a mobile device is available."* *"Especially, virtual learning spaces allow higher collaboration among learners.*

Q6₁₁ Learning situation	Q6₁₂ Learning situation

• Environment/conditions
  o interaction with others
• thematic relevance
• media use
Example: *"A learning situation occurs at school or at home."* *"A learning situation depends on what the group has to learn."*
	• Conditions
	  o location-independence
	  o conscious vs. unconscious
	• didactic relevance
	Example: *"A learning situation can occur anywhere and anytime."* *"[…] every situation that is induced consciously or unconsciously."*

Q7$_{t1}$ Possible benefits	Q7$_{t2}$ Possible benefits
• Reduced workload • Higher motivation • Individualization • Creativity Example: "[…] *younger generations grow up with it and they will be more motivated to use it for it reduces the work.*"	• Reduced workload • Autonomous learning • Compensation for deficits on part of the students • Creativity • New tasks Example: "[…] *for the use in the classroom if the devices lead to an augmentation, modification, or redefinition of tasks.*"

Both columns show the most frequent answers paraphrased and finally categorized for an improved level of comparability. Particular aspects, which are highlighted, will be discussed in the fourth paragraph.

Figure 2: Future use of mobile devices

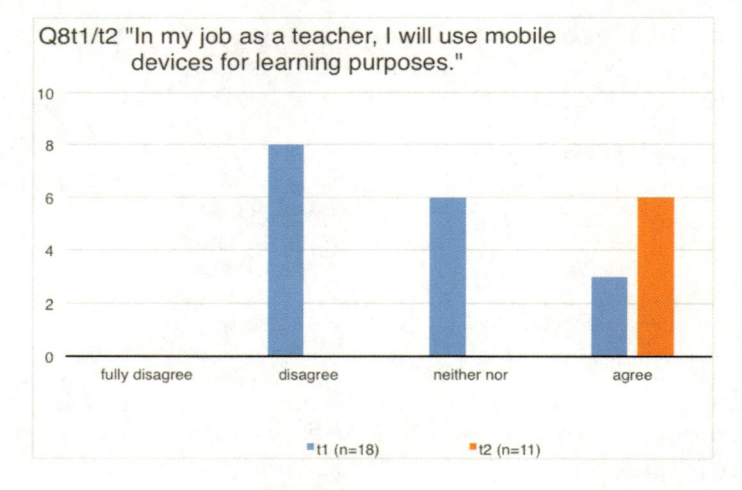

Q8t1/t2 "In my job as a teacher, I will use mobile devices for learning purposes."

t1 (n=18)   t2 (n=11)

4. Interpretation of the findings

The first figure shows that every participant actively used mobile communication devices at the beginning of the course. Most of the students even used two or more mobile devices (n=13). When they were asked to assess their own skills in dealing with the respective devices, the majority chose the items "good" or "very good". However, a summary of the answers to the question about how they use the devices unveils that they are mainly used to contact friends or organize their lives. Only a small number of students declared that they use mobile apps for learning purposes.

Table 1 shows the categories that were formed from both questionnaires. The fact that the data has been made anonymous does not allow us to directly find a connection between the answers of one and the same person. Another restriction to this study was the high fluctuation and the drop-out rate of some of the participants. Answers and categories can, therefore, only give an indication of the cognitive developments of those students regarding concepts of learning spaces. Taking a closer look at Question Number Five, we can see that in the first session the understanding of the term "learning place" had already been quite differentiated. Several answers show a distinction between physical and virtual learning places/spaces; these answers also emphasize the significance of affective elements. Some respondents clearly pointed out that virtual space represents an important place of retreat and offers privacy. Others also indicated that this place of retreat offers them the chance to work for themselves without being disturbed by others. This could be interpreted as a preference for individual flow. This view, however, slightly changed toward a more collaborative sense after the three-month seminar. Here some of the participants revealed that they see virtual space as space for collaboration with other users. They named less affective elements and showed a more open attitude toward media use. Dealing with topics, such as virtual collaborative activities, in the seminar, the students might have re-evaluated their objections against working with others.

Question Number Six revealed at the beginning of the seminar that some of the students had already established a link between learning situations and interaction with other learners. This aspect, however, does no longer come up in the answers to the same question at the end of the seminar. Yet, a shift can be observed in the understanding of the term "learning situation". Two reoccurring terms can be identified from the answers—location-independence and didactic relevance—both of which have been fundamental for the description of mobile (collaborative)-learning activities throughout the seminar. Moreover, the change from a thematic to a didactic relevance leads to the conclusion that there has been a change of point of view in the students' minds. An emphasis on didactic relevance suggests that the respondents concentrate more on future learning purposes and less on individual interests on the topics. Although a comparison of the summarized categories in Question Number Seven of both points in time shows some accordance (reduced workload or creativity), it also depicts hitherto unmentioned aspects. The two aspects of autonomous learning and the possibility of new tasks can again be referred to the flow experience in collaborative learning.

The attributes of augmentation, modification, and redefinition of tasks imply new challenges that the learners should be offered. Depending on the level of challenge and skills, the individual could, in return, be in a flow of activity.

Finally, a comparison was made between the answers to Question Number Eight. It can be seen clearly that the attitude toward using mobile devices for learning purposes in their job as future teachers became more positive throughout the semester. Eight students initially disagreed on this statement, while six had no clear view and only four agreed or fully agreed with this statement.

5. Conclusion

As Lee and Ryu (2013: 201) state, collaborative learning is not a panacea. The aim of this article was to show the benefits that can be achieved for both the individual learner and the group if collaborative activities are embedded in mobile learning scenarios. This paper, therefore, sheds light on the unique characteristics of mobile learning such as the role of learning spaces and the self-management/self-determination of the learner. These two basic concepts again become evident in the notion of social flow. By presenting a small study conducted in a foreign language didactic seminar and discussing the results of the data analysis, I intended to show that raising the students' awareness of new forms of learning spaces, combined with theoretical input during the sessions, leads to a more positive attitude toward collaboration. The analysis of the results confirmed these assumptions to some extent. However, it is delusional to think that one seminar on digital media could be a panacea. Owing to the rapidly evolving field of technology, teachers and learners should regularly be trained to work in collaborative multimedia environments.

Welchen Mehrwert haben digitale Medien für das Lehren und Lernen? Dieser Frage geht man seit geraumer Zeit im Bildungs-und Erziehungswesen nach und stößt dabei häufig auf kontroverse Ansichten. Es finden sich hierzu Aussagen, dass Smartphones und Co. als Ablenkungen oder gar Hindernisse für die kognitive oder soziale Entwicklung von Kindern und Jugendlichen zu sehen sind. Auf der anderen Seite belegen jährliche Erhebungen, dass die Nutzung mobiler, digitaler Geräte durch eben jene Gruppen weiter ansteigt und so zu einem festen Bestandteil jugendlicher Lebenswelten wird. Kommunikation findet häufiger virtuell statt. Chats ersetzen Telefonate, Kurznachrichtendienste transportieren emotionale Aspekte von Sprache in Form vom Emoticons/Emojis, und Foren werden zu Lernumgebungen, die durch ihre Nutzer/-innen kontinuierlich wachsen und sich verändern. Ist es demnach gerechtfertigt, digitale, mobile Geräte aus dem Bildungs-und Erziehungswesen fernzuhalten, obgleich es dort auch heißt, man solle einen starken Lebensweltbezug zu den Lernenden herstellen? Der Beitrag fokussiert hierbei einen besonderen Aspekt, der die Möglichkeit zur Kollaboration mit mobilen Geräten umfasst. Zunächst soll dafür der

Begriff der Kollaboration vor dem Hintergrund technologischer Entwicklungen betrachtet werden, um dann genauer auf die kollaborativen Prinzipen des multimedialen Lernens einzugehen (Abschnitt 1/1.1). Mögliche Konzepte von Lernumgebungen bzw. –räumen werden im darauffolgenden Abschnitt im Rahmen kollaborativen Lernens erläutert. Hervorgehoben werden dabei insbesondere die Rollen der Lernenden sowie die der Lehrenden (Abschnitte 1.2.1/1.2.2). Den theoretischen Teil abschließend werden im Abschnitt 1.3 Formen der Leistungsbewertung vorgestellt. Im zweiten Teil des Beitrags werden Ergebnisse einer Studie präsentiert, die im Rahmen eines (fremdsprachen)didaktischen Seminars mit Studierenden einer Hochschule durchgeführt wurden. Ziel ist es, einen Einblick in die individuellen Konzepte von Lernumgebungen bzw. –räumen zu zwei verschiedenen Zeitpunkten zu erhalten: zu Beginn des Seminars (erste Sitzung) sowie gegen Ende des Seminars (letzte Sitzung). Mithilfe von anonymisierten Fragebögen wurden auf diese Weise sowohl die private Nutzung digitaler, mobiler Geräte also auch deren wahrgenommener Mehrwert für das Lernen erhoben, um schließlich herausfinden zu können, ob die inhaltliche Vermittlung hinsichtlich der Konzepte von Lehr-und Lernmöglichkeiten mit den Geräten zu einer veränderten Wahrnehmung führt. Die Ergebnisse zeigen dabei deutlich, dass Lernumgebungen bzw. –räume stärker mit Medien in Verbindung gebracht werden und dass sich der Fokus vermehrt auf Kollaborationen im virtuellen Raum verschiebt. Weiterhin rücken in diesem Kontext zunehmend ausdifferenzierte Ideen zur Aufgabengestaltung bei den Studierenden in den Vordergrund.

Bert Van Poeck
University of Antwerp, Belgium

Critical Perspectives on the Collaborative Learning Potential of Digital Game-Based Learning in the Foreign Language Classroom

The present article explores the learning potential of video games in the foreign language classroom; focusing especially on the use of Massive Online Multiplayer Games (MMOs). Three landmark studies are used to illustrate some of the desiderata in the field of digital game-based learning. Drawing on the major findings of the studies, a framework for the use of video games in the classroom is presented. Moreover, this contribution suggests incorporating game mechanics, i.e. the underlying rules and principles of video games, in task design to create spaces for collaborative endeavors of learners.

1. Introduction

Over the past several decades the idea of using playful media, such as video games, as instruments for learning has intrigued educators and researchers alike. This article supports the idea that video games can enhance the collaborative foreign language learning experience. To this aim, three exemplifying studies on the collaborative potential of Massive Multiplayer Online Games (MMOs) will be analyzed in order to identify strengths and weaknesses in the methodological approaches commonly used in Digital Game-Based Language Learning (DGBLL) (Cornilie/Thorne/Desmet 2012) research. The analysis provides suggestions for an effective implementation of video games in the foreign language learning classroom and recommendations for improving DGBLL research and methodology.

This article situates itself in the domain of the educational usage of ludic entertainment, more specifically video games, for language learning (e.g. Mawer/Stanley 2011; Reinders 2012) commonly known as DGBLL (Cornilie/Thorne/Desmet 2012) situated in the broader field of Digital Game-Based learning (DGBL). Here, researchers such as Paul Gee (2003) have discussed the potential of video games on cognitive development. Gee (2003) extracted learning principles from video games illustrating that they contain powerful learning mechanisms which could be applied to education. Others, such as Marc Prensky (2001), focus on the implications of the digital age for education. Several years ago, Prensky argued that today's learners are 'Digital Natives', born in a digital age, for whom the current state of education is 'a bit outdated' as they have different needs compared to previous generations of learners. Thus, he claimed that 'digital natives' require a 'different' educational approach, one that utilizes, or at least refers to, new media, such as video games (see also Palfrey/Gasser 2008). Nowadays the term 'Digital Natives' has been replaced with the more specific definitions 'Digital Resident' and 'Digital Visitor' which situate users of the 'Digital' on a spectrum ranging from a 'Resident', whose identity often interacts and even relies on digital and online applications, to a 'Visitor', who occasionally utilizes the 'Digital', yet does not actively participate in online culture on a regular basis.

Gradually, educators and researchers have started exploring new and innovative ways to apply new media in educational contexts. This article focuses on how video games create collaborative learning contexts. Collaborative learning has been defined in several ways. In its broadest sense, it refers to a context or situation where two or more learners work together (collaboration) in order to (attempt) to learn something through a joint effort (Dillenbourg 1999: 1). Collaboration in foreign language learning guides and encourages students towards teamwork, problem-solving and even metalinguistic reflections (cf. *ibid.*). For the purpose of this article, collaborative learning is defined as a collective of situations where learners "work together towards a common goal, sharing and constructing a certain level of common knowledge, understanding and expertise" (Romero *et al.* 2012: 1).

In short, this article provides a critical analysis of the usability of video games as tools for collaborative foreign language learning. After a brief introduction to the concept of video games, we will elaborate on one genre in particular, namely the Massive Multiplayer Online game, and consider its potential for collaborative foreign language learning by reviewing three studies indicative of the current state of DGBLL research. Following, a rudimentary framework for applying games in education is offered. Finally, we will present some critical considerations pertaining to the studies and the state of DGBLL research as a whole.

2. The allure of video games

Why video games? Video games are in right now. In its latest annual publication, the Entertainment Software Association (ESA 2015) reports that there are currently 155 million American gamers. In 2014 alone, video game sales reached 15.4 billion dollars in America (*ibid.*: 12). A similar study in Europe, Gametrack, surveyed the video game market in four European countries: the United Kingdom, France, Spain, and Germany. Results reveal that about 20 million people in the UK (29%), 29 million in France (50%), 26 million in Germany (40%) and 14 million in Spain (40%) play video games (ISFE 2012: 53). Without a doubt, video games are popular. Although video games are traditionally seen as a medium for entertainment, increasingly more researchers are exploring their educational potential (e.g. Gee 2003; Cornilie *et al.* 2012; Vandercruysse/Vandewaetere/Clarebout 2012).

When exploring the potential of video games, researchers should be aware of their diversity. On a purely physical level, video games differ in shape and size from the small, rectangular Nintendo 3DS cartridges to the medium-sized Playstation 4 discs. Game content can be vastly different as well. For example, there are role-playing games (RPGs), such as *Final Fantasy* or *Pokémon*, where the player embarks on an epic adventure while immersed in a fantastical world; puzzle games, such as *Bejeweled* or *Candy Crush* where the player needs to solve progressively more intricate puzzles; racing games, where players race against either other players or a computer; and so on. The sheer multitude of game genres as well as describing and examining the pedagogical potential of each one would provide enough material for an entire book. Although different genres exist, DGBLL makes a relatively simple, yet broad distinction between different kinds of games, namely COTS (Commercial-Off-The-Shelf) games and serious games. COTS games are commercial games that can be found in any video game store and have not been developed with any explicit educational goal in mind. Serious games, on the other hand, borrow concepts of COTS games, yet primarily focus on teaching and learning (Cornilie/Thorne/Desmet 2012: 244–247). This article focuses on the educational merit of COTS games in language learning. More specifically, massive multiplayer online games (MMOs), as this specific genre contains characteristics that complement the core concept of collaborative (language) learning (cf. *ibid*.). Studies on serious games will be occasionally referred to as both research directions have influenced and affected one another.

MMOs are online video games where players are immersed in a 3D, or sometimes 2D, virtual environment where they can interact with the digital environment itself, PCs (Playable Characters), and NPCs (Non-Playable Characters). Players can engage with other players through synchronous chat systems or, in some cases, third party software such as TeamSpeak, Discord, or Mumble, which allow players to speak to one another via microphone. In MMOs, the goal is to complete quests and tasks in order to progress the narrative. MMOs' quests are often designed in such a way that they promote and facilitate interacting with other players and, perhaps even more importantly, collaborating with others. In doing so, players can complete these quests and clear objectives. Other objectives in MMOs include, but are not limited to, gathering raw materials used in crafting activities, crafting weapons and armor, and mini games. MMOs also include social-oriented components, such as guilds, a narrow-knit network, a private community within the larger game community that facilitates helping each other as to fully experience the game. In other words, interacting and collaborating are important elements of MMOs (Peterson 2010; Childress/Braswell 2006; Rama et al. 2012; Suh Kim/Kim 2010). In the following we will discuss the pedagogical value of MMOs.

Figure 1: A screenshot of the popular MMO, Guild Wars 2, illustrating the HUD of the game.

3. Video games as a pedagogical resource

The previously mentioned communicative aspects of MMOs are greatly valued in foreign language learning theories. Based on sociocultural theory, interactionist researchers argue that social factors greatly affect language acquisition and many second and foreign language learning acquisition theories stress the importance of (social) interaction during the learning process (Cook 2002; Gass 2000; Long 1996; Lantolf 2000). Additionally, through collaboration students can achieve more than they would on their own. Another faction of pedagogical researchers has investigated the learning mechanism behind video games. For example, Gee (2003) analysed games and their mechanics. He argues that games are *de facto* quite challenging and require a certain proficiency in order to complete the game. Although certain tasks given in-game are quite daunting, players often have little trouble with completing them as they are able to master the required skills for playing the game swiftly. Therefore, Gee argues that video games contain powerful learning mechanisms and principles which certainly should be explored in education.

Furthermore, MMOs can satisfy the need for authentic language materials defined as language produced within an 'authentic', 'real', or non-scripted context (Morrow 1977; Gilmore 2007). Additionally, the abundance of native speakers online provides learners with the unique opportunity to engage with native speakers, who can help in communication and the negotiation of meaning (e.g. Zheng *et al.* 2009; Rama *et al.* 2012). Thus, MMOs can form interesting supplementary language learning materials, inciting researchers to study the potential merits of using MMOs in FLL.

The following explores three studies focusing on MMOs' collaborative FLL potential. These studies are representative of the current state of affairs in DGBLL research with a focus on collaborative learning and should provide a clear overview of what currently is being done in DGBLL.

Suh, Kim and Kim (2010) contrasted traditional FLL instructions with MMORPG[1]-based instructions to test whether an MMORPG could be a more effective language teaching and learning setting than the traditional classroom. Their subjects consisted of 220 Korean elementary students (grade 5 and 6). Students were placed randomly in one of two groups: the MMORPG-group in which learners used an MMORPG for two months to learn English and the control group where the pupils were taught by traditional means. In order to eliminate the course materials and teacher variables, course materials between the two groups were matched and a researcher led the classes with the teacher present in the background (*ibid.*: 372). In the MMORPG group, pupils first engaged with a traditional MMORPG (hunting monsters, gathering materials and treasures, etc.) and afterwards engaged with in-game exercises for speaking, listening, writing and reading. Important to note here is that pupils were encouraged to collaborate by the game. The control group received the same materials but within the context of the traditional foreign language classroom. In traditional lessons, students also sang, performed scenarios/skits and played 'regular' (non-video) games (*ibid.*: 373–374). Results of five tests and one post-test survey showed that the MMORPG group scored significantly higher for listening, reading and writing. However, they did

---

1   MMORPG: Massive Multiplayer Online Role-Playing Game. Although Suh, Kim, and Kim define their game as an MMORPG, the game is best defined as a hybrid between a COTS game and a serious game.

not outperform the control group on the speaking component. Overall, Suh *et al.* concluded that the MMORPG was a useful tool for FL teaching and learning as the MMORPG learners outperformed the control group on three out of four tested FL competencies (*ibid.*: 375–377). In their survey, Suh *et al.* examined variables that might influence language learning, such as motivation, prior knowledge and network speed. While those aspects were perceived as important, network speed was rated to be more important than motivation by learners: a poor network connection could interfere with the MMORPG thus interrupting the 'flow' of the game (*ibid.*: 377).

Another study examining the potential of a COTS MMORPG as a pedagogical tool within a collaborative context was Peterson's (2012). He examined learners' social and linguistic interaction in the MMORPG *Wonderland* to evaluate the potential uses of the game in education and gauge the user experience of DGBLL. In this qualitative study, four intermediate EFL learners were instructed to play *Wonderland*, a prototypical anime-based 2D MMORPG, for four sessions of 70 minutes spread over the course of one month. No explicit educational instructions were given. By collecting chat log data, pre- and post-study questionnaires and post-study interviews, Peterson examined how learners, through collaboration with other players, viewed MMORPG-provided language learning opportunities and their attitudes towards DGBLL, thus gauging if students are open to the idea of using MMOs as pedagogical tools (*ibid.*: 366–367). Data showed that the learners were more comfortable with their language skills (e.g. greeting, turn-taking, small talk, etc.) after the course of the experiment. Overall, the students evaluated their experience as very positive, leading Peterson to conclude that the study "established viability of MMORPGs as venues for for CALL projects involving intermediate learners" (*ibid.*: 377–378).

In that same year, Rama and his colleagues conducted a similar experiment. In this qualitative study, Rama *et al.* (2012) studied the educational value and the potential language learning affordances for Spanish in the popular MMORPG *World of Warcraft (WoW)*. In *WoW*, players level up by slaying monsters, completing quests, and completing so-called dungeon runs. Players can also engage in crafting professions to create new armor and weapons as well as gathering materials for crafting activities. With 5.6 million subscribers as of the end of June 2015. *World of Warcraft* is currently the world's most-subscribed to MMORPG (Activision/Blizzard 2014). The study was conducted by examining chat logs, personal journal entries and feedback from interviews with four undergraduate students over a duration of seven weeks with an average of five hours of playing per week. The three examined affordances were: a safe and low-anxiety learning environment, a focus on communicative competence and the potential collaboration between novice and advanced speakers and gamers. Although four participants were selected, Rama *et al.* focused on the data of two participants in particular: a male participant (Emilio) and a female participant (Silvania) (Rama *et al.* 2012: 327). The researchers drew attention to the profiles of both participants as Emilio was a veteran gamer, but a beginning speaker of Spanish, whereas Silvania was an advanced Spanish speaker yet had little gaming experience. Their rationale was that by focusing on Emilio, they could 'focus on the participant's struggles with L2 rather than the mechanics of the game' and that Silvania could provide insights into how gaming affordances were experienced by a non- gamer. Similarly to Peterson's study (*ibid.*), participants were not given explicit instructions that directed their behaviour toward learning a language. Instead, they were encouraged to play the game to their liking (*ibid.*: 326).

The data showed positive results for all three investigated affordances: participants experienced the game as a safe learning environment. In relation to communicative competence, the results indicated that although games like *WoW* have an 'explicit focus on communicative competence, [the game and its players] allow time for reflection on language and a significant margin for error' (*ibid*: 335). The collaborative variable also showed promise: for both game mechanics and language, players could count on each other to collaborate and attain set goals (i.e. using correct grammar, help with vocabulary, but also with experiencing the game and completing in-game objectives, such as raids or quests) (*ibid*: 332–335). Rama *et al.*, however, formulate several critical remarks. Emilio, the 'expert' gamer, was able to utilise the collaborative component of *WoW* to its full extent as he could rely on his game knowledge in order to collaborate with others eventually leading to language proficiency gains through the collaboration. Silvania, on the other hand, a beginning gamer, yet high level learner of Spanish, could not take full advantage of collaborations as her lack of game knowledge hampered her communications at times. In order to avoid such situations, the authors suggest that learners undergo a mandatory introduction course to the game (mechanics). Another possible problematic feature is the relatively high language level in the game making it unsuitable for beginning learners of a foreign language. Third party software that implement auxiliary tools such as built-in dictionaries are suggested as possible solutions (*ibid*: 336).

3.1 Applying video games in the classroom: developing a framework

The research discussed in this article presents an overview of the state of affairs in DGBLL research. These studies focus on whether or not video games *can* be used in the classroom for FLL rather than on *how* video games can be applied to the FLL context. Due to the constant emphasis on the potential viability of video games, researchers have seemingly abandoned aspirations to develop a framework for effectively applying video games in the classroom. Naturally, being able to prove whether video games can be useful for FLL takes priority, yet in order to systematically test the feasibility of video games in the classroom, a basic framework is fundamental for investigating DGBLL's usefulness for (F)LL. Currently, no framework of any sorts is available for this purpose. The following will provide an outline and suggest several pivotal elements.

3.2 Outline of a DGBLL for FLL purposes framework

The following checklist provides an outline for the proposed framework:

A. Framework's Basis
   a. Concepts
   b. Definitions
B. Users
   a. Teachers
   b. Learners
C. Didactics
   a. Curriculum/Pedagogical Content of Classes
   b. Materials Available
   c. Language Skills – listening, reading, speaking, writing
D. Games
   a. Taxonomy of Genres
   b. Taxonomy of Types

The framework's basis consists of clear, well-defined concepts for DGBLL and video games for educational usage. By defining these notions within the framework no confusion can arise concerning the exact nature and goals of defined concepts (cf. Vandercruysse *et al.* 2012 for a critical review on serious games).

Next, the framework needs to consider and inform its users, teachers and, to a certain extent, learners. Teachers need to be aware of the exact nature of DGBLL and its potential, the "do's and don'ts" of using games for FLL and how games can potentially supplement (F)LL. Challenges concerning learners are addressed as well. What is the background of the learners? Are they familiar with video games? Are they aware of the potential benefits of video gaming? Do they require introductory classes? Are there games that stimulate their interests?

In relation to interaction are learners to engage alone with the games or will they collaboratively learn with other students?

The didactic aspect of the framework, relating to the art of teaching and learning with DGBLL, addresses how games could be implemented and used, as well as when and why. Which language skill(s) (speaking, listening, writing, and reading) are (or can be) targeted? Where does DGBLL provide benefits for language learning? How can DGBLL effectively supplement the curriculum? In order to utilise video games' potential effectively, the didactic facet should consider the potential media used (computers or other consoles) and possible supplementary materials against the background of video game type and genre, discussed separately in the framework.

Closely intertwined and pivotal to the didactic facet of the framework is an exposition of different game types (COTS, Hybrid, or Serious) and game genres (RPG, Action, Puzzle, Strategy, et cetera). By developing these taxonomies relating to both game types and genres, insight about which genre and type are best suited for (F)LL can be attained.

4. Critical considerations

Whereas the previous sections attempted to present a solution for a current deficit in the DGBLL literature, namely a framework for applied DGBLL research, the following deals with more specific deficits in the DGBLL literature and methodology.

The studies discussed in this article present great promise for using video games as pedagogical tools for collaborative foreign language learning. Nevertheless, many gaps in the literature remain, making it currently rather difficult to effectively implement and operationalise MMOs as a pedagogical tool. At least three challenges arise when trying to implement video games in a foreign language learning curriculum. Firstly, when using video games in classes, time and materials should be available. However, the curriculum allows little room or time for 'extracurricular' activities such as video games. In order to implement 'video game classes', schools need to have access to the necessary materials, such as ample computers and a good network connection (if online games are used) (Suh/Kim/Kim 2010). Moreover, the computers need to be advanced enough to be able to run the chosen video game.

Secondly, an important question poses itself in this educational context: which game should be used and why? Which game is best suited to achieve set goals? There are many games available, yet no framework providing teachers with a guide to which game is best suited for the desired learning goal or outcome. This is especially troublesome if the educator has no knowledge about the different kinds of games available which is why collaboration with senior students may be advisable.

Thirdly, educators should consider the potential effectiveness of the game in relation to the learners: Rama *et al.* (2012) showed that Silvania, an inexperienced gamer, was unable to take (full) advantage of the language learning affordances provided in *World of Warcraft* because of her unfamiliarity with video games. An educator cannot expect all learners to be proficient gamers. Therefore, if it is going to be used as a learning tool, an introductory class to playing video game is a necessity (see also Rama *et al.* 2012: 335). This also implies that the educator be knowledgeable enough about the video game to provide clear instructions for successful engagement with the game or teams of learners to collaborate. Not every teacher will have an affinity for teaching with video games, resulting in a time-consuming reflection process for the teacher compared to the amount of time students will engage with video games in the classroom.

Moving away from potential problems when applying DGBLL in the classroom, there are also several problems or 'gaps' in the literature. The first and most critical gap is the lack of studies focusing on the collaborative potential of MMOs. Currently only a handful of studies focus on MMOs' untapped potential on how they can contribute to collaborative learning. Secondly, studies such as Peterson (2012) and Rama *et al.* (2012) 'observe' positive language learning gains when using MMORPGs as a tool for language learning and only report user feedback. While these are by no means invalid or unimportant, they do not compensate for the lack of statistically significant data (see also Peterson 2012: 366). Further, the conclusions come dangerously close to overgeneralization and ambitious suggestions of effectiveness without empirical support.

Although several studies report positive language learning gains, others report inconclusive or even negative results (Vandercruysse *et al.* 2012: 13). A common methodological flaw in these experiments is that they have a relatively short time span and therefore cannot exclude the Hawthorne or novelty effect when using video games as learning/teaching tools (see also Vandercruysse *et al.* 2012: 13).

Thirdly, most of these studies have small focus groups which automatically results in a lack of representative empirical data (Suh/Kim/Kim 2010 being a notable exception). This alone is not a methodological concern. However, the ambitious conclusions and overgeneralisations that accompany the limited results are (e.g. Peterson 2012; *Rama et al.* 2012).

Another issue concerns the choice of the MMO used in the studies. Little attention is given to the description of the chosen game and its potential as a learning tool. Additionally, little to no justification is given for the game chosen. Why did Peterson (2012) use the MMORPG *Wonderland*, and not an English version of *World of Warcraft* (Rama *et al.* 2012)? The chosen games seem to have been selected based on the personal preference of the researcher(s) as no explanation for the choice is provided.

Finally, collaboration in MMOs is largely dependent on the gamer community. While Rama *et al.* (2012) and Peterson (2012) praise MMOs for their collaborative potential, a critical remark should be made: will MMO-players take the time, especially in a COTS game where there is no explicit focus on educating, to collaborate on meta linguistic issues? Furthermore, due to the informal context of MMOs, it is possible that grammatically incorrect forms could be used without consequence and that learners would (involuntarily) pick up the incorrect forms making the close observation and possible intervention of a language instructor (or fellow player/students) a necessity (see also Peterson 2012: 378). In other words, the gaming experience serves fluency more than it will serve accuracy. Finally, all these studies share the same critical flaw: a lack of defining and situating concepts within a broader framework. As Vandercruysse *et al.* (2012) aptly observed '[there is] no univocal or shared framework to talk about educational games' (2012: 13). Although their research focus is on educational games, their conclusions apply to COTS games as well.

Next there is the (unanswered) question of what exactly makes (some) MMOs and games effective learning tools or supplements. Few studies address the different game mechanics, (e.g. the chat function, graphics, story, rewards, etc.) and their effect on the learner's proficiency development. Instead, researchers refer to the accumulation of game mechanics (i.e. the entire game) and state that learners perceive language gains. This is problematic as multiple (game) variables go unaccounted for and no to little empirical data have been collected. One study, for example, using an MMO as a learning platform could conclude that MMOs are an effective language learning platform, while yet another study with a similar MMO and experimental design could present different results. This is likely due to different unaccounted variables inherently linked to the game and test setting used yet not mentioned and calculated within these experiments as well as a lack of a 'univocal framework' (cf. supra). More often than not these studies fail to address exactly why the game could supplement language learning. Instead, they rely on user feedback and little statistically significant data to back their claim (Vandercruysse *et al.* 2012: 13–14). As a result, research on DGBLL remains vague, tentative, and inconclusive.

Two solutions are possible. First, the methodological flaws that currently plague DGBLL research have to be addressed and a common framework for DGBLL needs to be established. A second solution will be to change the course of DGBLL studies and instead focus on the individual game mechanics and principles that make games effective and implement those in language education. We suggest that

DGBLL researchers move the focus from games themselves to their core elements and principles. In other words, it is perhaps time to switch the focus from DGBLL to gamification the study of game mechanics. Instead of focusing on games as wholes, researchers need to look at the game mechanics themselves, extract them out of the game context and then study each mechanic individually applied in an educational context (Deterding *et al.* 2011).

In DGBLL (all game genres included –not just MMOs), many pilot studies report positive trends, yet follow-up studies are either absent or methodologically flawed due to the myriad of variables that are not considered. The mixture of different game mechanics (variables) and the interaction between those mechanics within one game make it challenging for researchers to extract the precise mechanics responsible for potential positive learning gains. Therefore, we suggest that researchers carefully review DGBLL studies and take note of all the potential game mechanics available, extracting those mechanics and examining them individually within the context of gamification to gauge their individual effectiveness. Once that effectiveness has been established, researchers can study the interaction between game mechanics and subsequent results of interaction on learning and, more in particular, on collaborative language learning.

Intrinsically, gamification research and DGBLL research are the same: both experimental discourses focus on how game (mechanics) can improve and enhance the learning and teaching experience. The question then rises whether or not the difference between gamification and DGBLL is too large a leap. It remains to be seen what can be transposed from DGBLL research to gamification research.

5. Conclusion

Although games as pedagogical tools show promise according to research, little effective studies have been carried out. Plagued by a myriad of methodological issues and barriers as well as the lack of a common framework, DGBLL research brings forth tentative conclusions about whether games should be used within an educational context. It seems that even now DGBLL researchers are still busy initiating observations and pilot studies and formulating the potentials of MMOs in a foreign language learning (collaborative) context rather than designing actual experiments in order to gauge its effectiveness. As solutions to this problem, we propose two ideas. The first being a skeleton for a DGBLL framework which aims to bring forth more consistently applied DGBLL research. The second, a marriage between DGBLL and gamification. While retaining most characteristics of DGBLL, gamification is a unique research approach that transposes individual game mechanics to a non-gaming context resulting in less uncontrollable and hard-to-identify variables which plague current DGBLL research. Learning from the methodological malaises in DGBLL research, gamification is perhaps the solution for integrating the essence of video games in contemporary education, and in language learning in particular.

Videospiele stellen nicht nur einen Reflexionsgegenstand von Fremdsprachenunterricht dar, sondern kommen auch als Lernressource selbst zum Einsatz, die jedoch immer wieder auch kritisch hinterfragt wird. Ziel dieses Beitrages ist es zu untersuchen, ob Videospiele kollaborative Lernprozesse im Fremdsprachenunterricht fördern können und, wenn ja, wie. Zur Beantwortung dieser Frage, werden die Ergebnisse dreier ausgewählter Studien herangezogen. Gegenstand der Studien war es, das kollaborative Lernpotential von Massive Multiplayer Online Games (MMOs) näher zu beleuchten. Die Ergebnisse der vorgestellten Studien sind aus verschiedenen Gründen aber auch durchaus kritisch zu sehen, da sie nur auf dem Feedback der Spieler beruhen und somit keine statistisch belastbaren Daten liefern. Hinzukommt, dass weitere Studien keinen positiven Effekt von Videospieleinsatz feststellen konnten und teilweise sogar zu negativen Ergebnissen gekommen sind (vgl. Vandercruysse *et al.* 2012: 13). Zuletzt bleibt festzustellen, dass die Zeitspanne des Videospieleinsatzes eher kurz war und somit der Neuigkeitseffekt als Faktor nicht auszuschließen ist. Im weiteren Verlauf des Beitrages werden unterschiedliche methodische Herangehensweisen näher betrachtet, die im Zusammenhang mit Videospielen als Unterrichtsgegenstand im Sinne des Digital Game-Based Language Learning (DGBLL) Ansatzes Verwendung finden. Während die vorgestellten Studien vielsprechende Ergebnisse hervorgebracht haben, ist der Einsatz von Videospielen im Fremdsprachenunterricht nicht unproblematisch. Abgesehen von curricularen Vorgaben ist vor allem die Ausstattung vieler Schulen als Hindernis zu sehen. Die in diesem Zusammenhang von Gee (2003) herausgearbeiteten Prinzipien (*gamification principles*), auf denen die meisten Videospiele beruhen, werden zum Aufgabendesign herangezogen, ohne jedoch den Einsatz von Videospielen selbst unbedingt zu befürworten. Hierauf aufbauend werden abschließend Vorschläge gemacht, wie Videospiele im Fremdsprachenunterricht zum Einsatz gebracht werden können und Forschungsdesiderate im Bereich DGBLL herausgearbeitet.

Dominik Rumlich & Sabine Ahlers
University of Münster, Germany
Heinrich-Heine-Gymnasium Oberhausen, Germany

The Rich Environment of CLIL Classes as an Ideal Setting for Collaborative Learning

A contextualised outline of CLIL (content and language integrated learning) as a teaching principle will provide the theoretical backbone for our main argument that CLIL teachers should adopt a learner-centred, collaborative approach if they want to achieve the required curricular aims and make the most of a rich CLIL learning environment. The main part of the article puts theory into practice as it is dedicated to possible realisations of collaborative methods that have been successfully used in the context of CLIL geography classes (but could also be employed in other CLIL subjects).

1. CLIL and collaborative learning: two sides of the same coin

Content and language integrated learning (CLIL) is a form of content-based teaching, which denotes "instructional approaches that make a dual, though not necessarily equal, commitment to language and content-learning objectives" (Stoller 2008: 59). The acronym CLIL was coined in the 1990s with a similarly broad denotation:

> Content and language integrated learning (CLIL) is a generic term and refers to any educational situation in which an additional language and therefore not the most widely used language of the environment is used for the teaching and learning of subjects other than the language itself (Marsh/Langé 2000: iii).

CLIL has come to be used as a unifying, somewhat neutral umbrella term covering more than 30 designations of what is often called "bilingual education" in academic and non-academic contexts across Europe and beyond (Baetens Beardsmore 2009: 208; list of designations provided by Marsh 2002: 57f). All of them have in common that they refer to non-language content subject teaching (e.g., geography, chemistry, music or sports) that takes place through a (second or) foreign language with dual-focused educational aims (Coyle/Hood/Marsh 2010: 1; cf. Dalton-Puffer/Smit 2013: 546 for further important criteria).[1]

---

1 Owing to the scope of the article, it is only possible to supply a simplified theoretical account of the concept of CLIL. See, e.g., Wolff 2009, Coyle/Hood/Marsh 2010 or Rumlich 2016 for further details.

After an "explosion of interest" (Coyle 2006: 2) in the 1990s, CLIL has been implemented and established on all levels of education from preschool to tertiary institutions in the majority of European countries (Marsh 2002) and is praised as an "effective means of improving language learning provision" (Council of the European Union 2008: 22), "adding a European dimension to the curriculum" (Fruhauf 1996: 8). In 2009, García (2009: 5, her emphasis) confidently states that "bilingual education is the *only* way to educate children in the twenty-first century."

Such strong views are based on the conviction that, apart from creating favourable content and language learning conditions, CLIL classes are an ideal environment for fostering a broad range of other important competences that students are supposed to develop (e.g., Wolff 1997) as a result of ongoing societal, political, technological and economic developments such as inter-/transcultural (communicative) competences, learner autonomy and self-regulated learning skills, methodological skills, learning strategies, language (learning) awareness as well as other key competences that students need to develop for their professional and private life as responsible citizens in the global village of the twenty-first century.

It has been shown across all of the contributions in this volume that communicative-collaborative learning (in a Vygotskyan sense) in order to scaffold students' advancement in their zone of proximal development (Lee/Smagorinsky 2000) –also in view of their heterogeneity and the necessity for individualised learner-centred teaching– lies at the very heart of modern (post-) communicative language teaching. Furthermore, content-based language teaching is said to be the logical conclusion deriving from the central demands of communicative language teaching (Richards 2006: 3; 26). CLIL could hence be regarded as "the implementation of the principles of the communicative approach on a grand scale" (Dalton-Puffer/Smit 2007: 8) or "the next phase of the 1970s' communicative revolution" (Marsh 2005). As a result, collaborative (language) leaning should, by default, represent a core feature and natural concomitant of CLIL. The contextualised illustration of this will be the main focus of the remaining theoretical part.

2. (Collaborative) Learning in CLIL classes: Contextualisation and potentials

As has been illustrated above, conceptual pluralism is regarded as a hallmark of CLIL (Gießing 2005; Lamsfuß-Schenk/Wolff 1999), yet, its all-embracing nature also represents a major weakness. The term as such is vague (Cenoz/Genesee/Gorter 2014; Wolff 2001) and denotes a teaching principle, i.e. that language and content be taught best in an integrated way, rather than a concrete realisation (Rumlich 2016). Since there are multiple ways of realising CLIL, which then also vary across and even within national education systems, the specification of a concrete educational context is of pivotal importance in any account of CLIL that is supposed to go beyond general remarks about the teaching principle *per se*. Therefore, the following sub-sections are meant to exemplify a concrete educational context (English CLIL geography classes in a CLIL stream at *Gymnasium* in North-Rhine Westphalia, Germany) on the basis of which it will be depicted why (collaborative) learning is a valuable asset to CLIL classes.

2.1 CLIL geography classes within CLIL streams in Germany

In Germany in general and in North-Rhine Westphalia in particular, the most intense form of CLIL takes place in so-called CLIL streams or strands at *Gymnasium*: As of year 7 on the lower secondary level (school Years 5–9 or 5–10, which roughly corresponds to ages 10–15 or 10–16 years), up to three content subjects are taught through a foreign language (usually English or French; cf. Kultusministerium des Landes Nordrhein-Westfalen 1995 or MSW NRW 2007 for the legal requirements of CLIL at secondary schools). Beforehand, future CLIL students receive one or two additional lessons of the CLIL language during the preparation phase in Years 5 and 6 (five or six instead of four lessons per week). This measure is supposed to prepare them for the language demands of CLIL classes. The enhancement of the usual number of content-subject lessons by one lesson per week as of Year 7 (e.g., German geography classes timetabled with two lessons per week, CLIL geography classes with three) is meant to cover language demands and the additional aims of CLIL classes.[2]

Bilingualer Sachfachunterricht (bilingual content-subject teaching) is the equivalent academic term for CLIL in German. The expression itself already implies that CLIL classes in Germany are considered and timetabled as content subject lessons, which signifies that content-related aims clearly prevail. Consequently, there are no special curricula for CLIL classes and the general content-subject curriculum is legally binding. It is merely supplemented by recommendations outlining (additional) aims and principles of learning in CLIL classes (cf. Kultusministerium des Landes Nordrhein-Westfalen 1995). Overarching additional aims include, among others,

- preparing young people for the linguistic and cultural reality of Europe within a world whose citizens are closer together than ever.

---

2   See Breidbach and Viebrock 2012 or Rumlich 2016 for further details on (forms of) CLIL in Germany and the German education system.

- the development of intercultural knowledge, skills and know-how.
- the development of competences in order to learn and communicate about subject-specific issues in a foreign language (subject-specific literacy; analysing, arguing, depicting cause-effect relationships, evaluating, synthesising).
- the development of learning skills, strategies and techniques for increasingly independent, self-regulated learning.

Due to the focus of this article and the fact that many publications have already dealt with the question of why CLIL classes represent a particularly beneficial environment for the development of these skills and competences (e.g., Coyle/Hood/Marsh 2010; Mehisto/Marsh/Frigols 2008; Wolff 2009), we will not go into further detail on the aims of CLIL, but rather focus on the way these aims are to be accomplished.

2.2 (The promises of collaborative) Learning in CLIL classes

Following the ministerial recommendations –and in accordance with a range of publications (see preceding paragraph)– CLIL classes naturally lend themselves to the implementation of modern principles of learning and teaching, such as

- a strong focus on learner-centredness and can-do/action-oriented empowerment approaches,
- the application of authentic subject-specific methods and techniques, and
- the use of inductive approaches and discovery-based learning.

Collaborative settings represent the core of all of these principles, which also play a pivotal role in modern language teaching: Language is the backbone of ideas and (internal) thinking processes, representing *the* means to exchange and create information in interaction (Vollmer 2010: 59). Vygotsky's socio-cultural theory is also rooted in this "interdependence of social and individual processes in the coconstruction of knowledge" (John-Steiner/Mahn 2011: 191). Hence, (language) learning is an active process facilitated by communication and interaction, preferably in a rich learning environment that offers diverse sensual experiences, mental anchors and mnemonic devices.

Since CLIL is a "value-added approach […] that seeks to *enrich* the learning environment" (Mehisto/Marsh/Frigols 2008: 27; emphasis added), CLIL classes virtually *demand* a collaborative approach. They represent a rich(er), yet also highly complex learning environment that challenges students to learn new *subject-matter* through a language they have limited competence in. At the same time, CLIL is based on the "seemingly paradoxical endeavour of learning and teaching *language* through non-linguistic curricular content" (Lyster/Ballinger 2011: 282) with "learners struggling to master academic concepts and skills through a language in which they have limited proficiency, while at the same time striving to improve that proficiency" (Wesche 2001: 201; cf. Coyle/Hood/Marsh 2010: 35; see also Rumlich 2016, Vollmer 2010 or Wolff 1997 for a detailed theoretical account of learning in CLIL classes).

As the learners' construction of language and content knowledge goes hand in hand and (interrelated) difficulties in both domains abound, the need for scaffolding is omnipresent.[3] Scaffolding represents a prerequisite to learning when students encounter difficulties they cannot solve on their own, which renders scaffolding an individual requirement that invokes tailor-made support helping students to advance (within their zone of proximal development). This signifies that an increasing demand for scaffolding needs to be satisfied by increasingly individualized, learner-centred teaching. Collaborative settings empower learners to scaffold each other and self-regulate their learning while freeing teacher capacities and allowing them to provide additional support where needed. At the same time, discovery-based methods, e.g., those that involve experiments/trials and visual teaching materials, e.g., pictures, charts, maps, etc. can reduce students' dependence on language (scaffolding) in order to understand content matter. Even though these are important assents to all language learning classes, they play an even more important role in highly demanding CLIL environments.

3. Putting collaborative learning in a CLIL geography classroom into practice

Students working together in small groups for mutual support of all group members represents the predominant social setting of collaborative learning environments (Jolliffe 2007: 39). The following sections will exemplify three cooperative CLIL geography learning episodes involving detective stories, mini books and experiments. All of the three episodes enable the development of subject-matter competence (*Sachkompetenz*), methodological competence (*Methodenkompetenz*) and language competence (*Sprachkompetenz*) as demanded by the curriculum (MSW NRW 2012: 10).

---

3   Constructivist (language) learning goes back to, among others, Dewey (e.g. 1916 and 1933) and Vygotsky (1930–1934/1978); even though the notion of scaffolding is frequently mentioned in this context and attributed to Vygotsky, the term itself was coined much later by Wood, Bruner, and Ross (1976: 90).

3.1 Detective stories

Detective stories, yes/no stories or lateral stories are also known as "Black Stories" in Germany. A preferably short and explicit, yet at the same time startling statement is provided on the front side of an index card; the complete story can be found on the back. The guessers' task is to uncover the background of the story by asking appropriate questions. The only rule is that the detective may only ask questions that can be answered with yes or no; the only other permissible answer is "unimportant" or "irrelevant" in order to guide the detectives and avoid their going astray. When a question is answered with "no", the next guesser takes over (Becker 2015). One major advantage of this method is that several groups can work simultaneously so that the whole class is involved at once (Storozenko 2015: 277) and student talking time is enhanced.

3.1.1 Theoretical aspects of detective stories in CLIL classes

Becker points out that a synonym for *detective story* is *lateral story*; the learners are intended to think laterally, i.e. outside the box. This encourages the reorganisation of patterns of thoughts (Becker 2015) and the intuitive selection of information is responsible for the generation of new patterns (Kilian/Krismer/Loreck/ et al. 2007: 143). This increases the flexibility in the learners' way of thinking and enhances their curiosity, interest and commitment. Communicative competences are practised by venturing guesses, testing hypotheses, pondering logical connections and analysing new and existing knowledge. Students learn to base their assumptions on logical arguments and exercise their reasoning skills. At the same time, they are required to be creative and original. While listening to the detective story when it is someone else's turn, the students not only train their listening comprehension skills, but, as they need to rely on the information that others have found out, they are required to collaborate and find the solution together, which trains social competences and, in particular, team-working skills. This creates positive interdependence among the students as the cases can only be solved with the help of classmates. In addition, students are encouraged to expand their vocabulary as they are likely to encounter unknown words and phrases, which might be relevant for the solution of the case.

Inventing their own detective story enhances students' creativity, involves subject matter competence and geographical expertise, as well as the competence to transfer factual knowledge to similar phenomena (Braun et al. 2013: 71). Furthermore, the playful atmosphere allows students to use the second language in a pleasant learning setting, which is bound to encourage them to take risks and, in case of success, also enhance their self-confidence. Detective stories provide rich opportunities for face-to-face interaction among peers in pairs or smaller groups. Each student creates their own story and is therefore responsible for the quality of their final result, yet, at the same time, they help each other to improve their stories.

Detective stories can be used in every CLIL subject, as long as the students can ask specific questions about a predetermined topic, are able to synthesise transferred knowledge from previous units and have the means to depict somewhat complex issues in the second language and support them with arguments. In beginners' classes, detective stories can be employed in the context of a clearly defined subject-matter area; with more advanced students, they are also a suitable approach when wrapping up a broad topic within a wide subject-matter area. In those cases, detective stories can be used for a contextualised summary or repetition of the most important aspects in an integrated way. Regarding the social setting, the students start working alone while preparing the stories. Students S1 and S2 each create a detective story on a predetermined topic, afterwards they present the results to each other and guess the solution. Potential mistakes can be corrected and the story as a whole can be made smooth. For a final presentation in class, several arrangements can be chosen, e.g. "one stay, rest stray": From each dyad (A1/A2, B1/B2, C1/C2, etc.), student 1 moves to another table, at which student 2 has remained seated; this procedure leads to new pairs (A1/B2, B1/C2, etc.) who do not know each other's story yet. After they have solved one or both of the stories, student 1 returns to their original table and student 2 strays (cf. Heartland Area Education Agency 2006: 17). The detective stories can also be presented in class and the team whose story needs the largest number of questions before it could be solved wins (alternative: the team with the smallest number of positive (yes) answers).

3.1.2 *Practical examples of detective stories*

The following examples were created by CLIL students from the *Heinrich-Heine-Gymnasium* in Oberhausen, Germany. At this particular school, students start in year 7 with geography and politics as CLIL subjects. In year 8, history is also taught through the medium of English.

> **Tom wanted to go home, but that day there was no train.**
>
> Because of mining subsidence damages there was a washout underneath the rail track. Therefore, there were no trains that day.
>
> Anna, year 9 (The Ruhr Area – Mining in Germany)

> **Otto wanted to see fire, but he only saw water.**
> Otto wanted to visit his former workplace, the blast furnace in Dortmund Hörde. After structural changes in the Ruhr Area, there is the PHOENIX area with a big lake today.
> Maurice, year 9 (The Ruhr Area – Structural changes)

> **Klaudia saw many animals and because of that Amaru learned a lot.**
> Klaudia was on holiday in Kenya on an ecotourism tour. This form of sustainable tourism distributes the profits from tourism among social or ecological projects, for example, Amaru's newly built school.
> Luisa, year 9 (Ecotourism in Kenya)

> **It was burning as Jacob stilled his hunger.**
> Jacob ate a burger at McDonald's. The beef is produced in areas of the tropical rainforest. To get pasture area for the cattle, the rainforest is burned down.
> Ben, year 7 (Destruction of the Tropical Rainforest)

> **Because Luise sat down on her chair, living beings lost their home.**
> Luise sat on a chair made of tropical timber. To harvest this timber the tropical rainforest is destroyed and animals lose their home.
> Annika, year 7 (Destruction of the Tropical Rainforest)

3.2 Mini books

A mini book, also known as a "buddy book" (Stangl 2015), is a small booklet made of one sheet of paper, which, when folded accordingly, makes eight individual pages. Without any major effort, it can easily be created by students of all ages. Originally, the mini-book was used for the purpose of exam preparation similar to a cheat slip, but it can also be employed in numerous ways for collaborative learning activities (*ibid.*).

3.2.1 Theoretical aspects of mini-books in CLIL classes

The use of mini-books is manifold and extends from the above-mentioned cheat slips as a preparation for class tests, vocabulary and pocket books to a replacement for file cards for presentations. Mini-books can be used to foster the skills of structuring and presenting information, summarizing facts and focusing on the essentials as the space on each page is limited. Allowing students to come up with their own designs also possesses the potential of fostering motivation and creativity.

The following example of the use of mini-books in a CLIL classroom is from the beginning of a unit under the heading of "China – a regional analysis". The mini-book is imbedded into the method of jigsaw puzzle/expert groups (e.g., Aronson 1978). In a first step, students come together in expert groups-to-be, each of which works with different materials and on different sub-topics. "This has the benefit of making the experts possessors of unique information, and thus makes the teams value each member's contribution more highly" (Slavin 1995: 126). In the above mentioned unit on China, each expert group works on different landscapes of China under the headlines of Yellow, Green, Cold, and Dry China. The groups obtain information on relief, climate, soil, water supply and land use on the basis of different types of material (e.g. maps, climate graphs, photos, texts, diagrams). Hence, they become experts on their region, but do not know anything about the other regions yet, which is to be addressed in the second phase. Here, students form new groups consisting of at least one expert from each of the different expert groups so that each region is represented in each group. In this phase, each expert teaches the others in his or her group, i.e. the students must rely on their classmates to find out about the regions they do not know. At this stage, it is very important to emphasize that the students "have a responsibility to their teammates to be good teachers as well as good listeners" (Slavin 1995: 125). After all of the experts have presented their topic to their group members (or while they are presenting), the students fill in the pages of their mini-book together. Using mini-books together with a jigsaw puzzle, the teacher achieves individual accountability and positive mutual dependence within the classroom.

In CLIL classes, it is of major importance to prepare the material for each expert group according to the students' level of language and subject-matter competence. Therefore, a topic such as China's landscapes is ideal for a CLIL class as the comprehension of visuals (pictures, maps and diagrams) only requires minimal amounts of linguistic knowledge. Hence, they can also be used as a means of scaffolding and supporting learners' subject-matter comprehension independently of their language competence. Additional language support could be given by providing a framework for writing, explanations of key vocabulary or chunks of sentences.

3.2.2 How to create a mini-book

A mini-book requires one sheet of paper. Take an A4 sheet in portrait format and fold it three times:

1) Horizontally from the bottom to the top.
2) Vertically from the right to the left.
3) Again, horizontally from the bottom to the top.

Unfold it twice, so that you have one horizontal crease in the middle of your paper with its opening at the top. Now cut along the vertical crease from the bottom to the middle of the paper until you reach the horizontal crease. After fully unfolding the paper, there should be a cut in the middle of the sheet. Take the paper in landscape format and fold it along the horizontal line (middle crease) from the top to the bottom. For the final step, hold the paper at the right and the left-hand side and turn it towards you, so that you can look into the hole in the middle. Now push inward, and strengthen the central crease to end up with an A7-size mini-book consisting of eight pages (including front and back cover). A model worksheet is shown in Fig. 1 (see https://www.youtube.com/watch?v=21qi9ZcQVto for a visual demonstration). In this example, Dry China consists of only one page, because this expert group has less material than the others as part of an internal differentiation process.

Figure 1: How to create a mini-book, cf. Fileccia 2015.

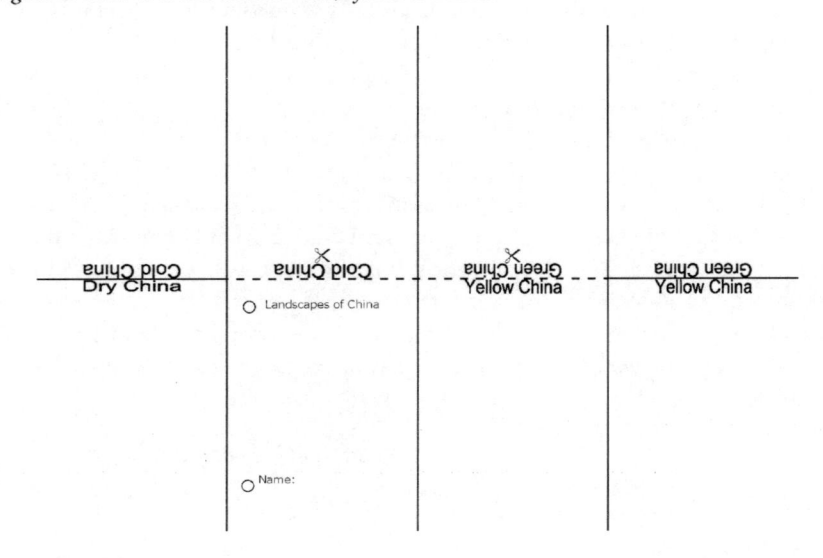

3.3 Experiments

In geography, experiments are not as widespread as they are in other subjects, e.g., in chemistry or physics. They usually denote an attempt to recreate geographical processes in the form of a smaller model and/or simplified version, often to visualise otherwise obscure mechanisms. The main functions of experiments in geography classes are, *inter alia*, (Zimmermann 2004: 2):

1) the facilitation of clear insights into natural processes (often influenced by humans, which may result in more or less complex interactions);
2) the enhancement of curiosity, interest, motivation, commitment and involvement;
3) the initiation of questions;
4) the introduction to accurate observation as an important tool in geographical (field) research. With the help of experiment, connections between processes can be made visible and learner autonomy is stimulated.

The term "experiment" itself is supposed to underline that there is a certain level of uncertainty as to whether or not the recreation of the real-world situation will be successful.[4] Every experiment should be based on a clearly defined research question that is fixed *a priori*.

3.3.1 Theoretical aspects of experiments in CLIL classes

In each phase, active student involvement and their responsibility for their group experiment should be maximised. The didactic quality of an experiment is proportional to the level of learner activity and involvement. Along this vein, student empowerment in autonomous learning situations on the basis of a can-do approach and successful do-it-yourself episodes are major advantages of collaborative student experiments.

Before conducting an experiment, students should have the opportunity to make predictions about the results that the experiment will produce. In other words, the students are supposed to develop hypotheses and prove them right or wrong with the experiment. This does not only activate prior knowledge to facilitate subsequent learning, but it is also a typical way of working of a geographer.

---

4   This everyday meaning of the term stands in sharp contrast to what it denotes in academic contexts. In academic fields such as medicine or psychology, for instance, "experiment" is a technical term with a very specific meaning referring to the standardised observation of changes in an outcome (dependent variable) when an independent variable is manipulated in a systematic way.

During the experiment, the students are operationally active and conduct the experiment/trial on their own. Experiments can also result in a deeper analysis and examination of a specific topic as insights are not required passively with theoretical constructions, but through active, manual performance (Reich 2008: 5). Even "incorrect" and surprising results can have valuable benefits and lead to a higher level of motivation, while, at the same time, the learners' are encouraged to analyse why they obtained a different result from other groups. Experiments also require problem-solving qualities, creative thinking and evaluation skills. Teamwork is necessary as experiments can usually not be conducted alone; since every individual learner contributes to their success, a natural and positive interdependence among the learners is characteristic of experimental learning.

After the experiment has been completed, students need to systematically evaluate their observations in order to obtain a final answer to their research question(s). In a CLIL classroom, experiments need particular language support and scaffolding, owing to the fact that technical terms and characteristic discourse elements are required to adequately verbalise different steps of the trials.

3.3.2 Practical example of an experiment

The following example is taken from year-seven CLIL students from the *Heinrich-Heine-Gymnasium* in Oberhausen, Germany. At the time of the lessons, they have participated in CLIL geography for about five months.

At the beginning, a photo of an Artesian well (water bubbling out of the ground in the desert) is shown and the students are asked to describe what they can see. This is meant to activate prior knowledge and existing vocabulary as well as catch students' interest. Afterwards, the class is invited to utter questions with regard to the photo. A typical question could be: Why is there water bubbling out of the ground in the desert?

The next step is the experiment itself, which is conducted with the help of the following materials: a bottle of water, a hose pipe (with a tiny hole in the middle), a funnel, a nail and a bowl. To illustrate and clarify what the students have to do, sketches on the board or pictures of students' conducting the experiment can be used (fig. 2; similar to the suggestions made in Willis 1996 or Willis/Willis 2007 concerning the realisation of the pre-task in their framework for task-based learning). The experiment consists of three general phases, which are of key importance for students' understanding of the central mechanisms:

1) The nail blocks the hole in the hose pipe when it is filled with water.
2) The hose pipe is filled with just a little bit of water when the nail is removed.
3) The hose pipe is filled with a lot of water when the nail is removed.

Figure 2: Students conducting the experiment

After having conducted the experiment in groups of three to four students, they are asked to describe their observations in their groups. As the language requirements are quite demanding, a think-pair-share procedure (e.g., Eisenmann 2012: 303f) has proved to yield good results: For the "think" stage, the task could be, for instance, to describe in keywords what they observed during the experiment. Next, they share their observations with a partner and improve their own notes. Finally, they answer the question(s) outlined prior to the experiment by trying to explain the underlying mechanisms they observed.

The most important step in this lesson is the final transfer of the experiment to reality for a correct answer to the final research question. This is very challenging and needs careful assistance and scaffolding if this is to be done by the students themselves on the basis of such a collaborative task. In order to help the students to realise the connection the experiment as a simplified model of reality and reality itself, one can take a drawing or sketch of an Artesian well (cf. Fig. 3), number the relevant elements and ask the students to name the corresponding elements from the experiment. The numbered elements could refer to the

1) inner part of the hose pipe
2) (plastic of the) hose pipe itself
3) bottle of water
4) lowest point of the hose pipe
5) highest point of the hose pipe
6) water in the hose pipe.

The necessary lexical items for an adequate description of the mechanisms involved might be largely unknown to the students as they represent specialised technical terms. Hence, the students need appropriate support. They are supposed to label the elements in the drawing by choosing the correct ones from a list of mixed terms: 1. permeable layer, 2. impermeable layer, 3. rainfall, 4. Artesian well, 5. mountain, 6. underground water. Finally, the class is asked to describe the way an Artesian well works in a short written text as a final research report and answer to the initial research question. For reasons of internal differentiation and scaffolding, the teacher or students can provide language help when necessary in the form of words or collocations/chunks, e.g. "Artesian wells occur when…; The water collects between…; When people drill a hole in the ground…; Because of this…; …leads to…; …is caused by…; as a result, …".

Figure 3: The Artesian Well (authors' drawing)

From a geographical point of view, the students advance with respect to the following four areas: They know one form of water supply in the desert and are able to explain its occurrence invoking the impact of water pressure. Additionally, the students are capable of describing the model of an Artesian well and explain how it works as a basis for the transfer of the model to reality. Problem-solving skills and creative thinking are also fostered through collaborative experiments.

4. Conclusion

CLIL classes represent a rich learning environment with great potential for students to develop fundamental academic, linguistic and social skills required in their lives as responsible citizens in the twenty-first century. As a result, CLIL has boomed across Europe over the last 25 years and educational institutions have been eager to adopt it in a variety of implementations in the wake of a new trend in (language) education. Yet, efficient learning in CLIL classes does not happen automatically and the implementation of learner-centred approaches might be even more decisive for students' success in such a challenging environment than in other language learning contexts.

Collaborative settings appear to be a promising way of realising the demand for differentiated teaching and scaffolding according to students' individual needs.

Emulating typical real-world working environments in which two or more people deal with a particular task, collaborative learning adheres to central principles of constructivism and allows learners to be autonomous in their learning process while developing content and language-related knowledge, skills and know-how.

Nevertheless, it is essential to always adapt methodology to the requirements of CLIL students, since the subject dictates the language demands and, consequently, the language support which is needed to support the achievement of content-related aims (Deller/Price 2007: 9). Therefore, the realisation of collaborative methods in CLIL classes requires additional strategies to corroborate understanding and learning in content-driven classes. Besides peer helping, self-evaluation and group support, cooperative science and subject-based learning models are needed in order to place emphasis on exploring problems or posing solutions in a task-based manner; if the teacher can guide their students on their individual learning paths to realise this in an authentic way "the result will be greater persistence and more self-directed learning" (Adams/Hamm 1996: 121; Adams/Hamm 2015: 110). Positive mutual dependence is another key ingredient in collaborative learning episodes that can strengthen students' perseverance and encourage autonomous learning. At the same time, it should also be noted that the teacher still plays a major role in sparking their students' interest and curiosity, nurturing their enthusiasm and providing judicious, appreciative feedback of their effort and results throughout the entire learning process.

Der vorliegende Artikel thematisiert kollaboratives Lernen im bilingualen Sachfachunterricht (engl. CLIL); dabei argumentieren wir aus lerntheoretischer, curricularer und praktischer Sicht, dass sich die reichhaltige und anspruchsvolle Lernumgebung des bilingualen Sachfachunterrichts besonders für kollaboratives Lernen eignet: Es ermöglicht, die sich bietenden Lerngelegenheiten gut auszuschöpfen und das Erreichen vielfältiger Lernziele angemessen im Unterricht zu fördern.Zu Beginn des Artikels wird aus theoretischen Überlegungen hergeleitet, dass bilingualer Sachfachunterricht und kollaboratives Lernen verschiedene Seiten der gleichen Medaille darstellen. Dies ergibt sich aus der Tatsache, dass moderner Fremdsprachunterricht grundsätzlich auf kooperativen Prinzipien aufbaut und die Integration von Sachfach-und Fremdsprachenlernen gleichzeitig als konsequente Weiterentwicklung modernen, inhaltsorientierten Fremdsprachenunterrichts angesehen wird. Aufgrund der internationalen Ausrichtung des vorliegenden Bandes und der unterschiedlichen Umsetzung des CLIL-Prinzips in europäischen Bildungssystemen ist es aus inhaltlichen Gründen sinnvoll, zunächst eine konkrete Form des bilingualen Sachfachunterrichts als Realisierung des generell unspezifisch-inklusiven CLIL-Prinzips innerhalb eines organisatorischen und curricularen Unterrichtsrahmens näher zu charakterisieren. Dies geschieht am Beispiel bilingualen Geographieunterrichts in bilingualen Bildungsgängen/Zügen in Nordrhein-Westfalen, um theoretische, curriculare und praktische Perspektiven anhand eines spezifischen Kontextes im Folgenden näher ausführen zu können. Die Beschreibung des organisatorisch-curricularen Rahmens mündet in die exemplarische Darstellung ausgesuchter Lernziele des bilingualen Sachfachunterrichts (z.B. doppelte Sprach-und Sachfachliteralität, Lernfähigkeit und-strategien für zunehmend eigenständiges, selbstreguliertes Lernen) sowie einer zusammenfassenden Betrachtung theoretisch-konstruktivistischer Überlegungen zu bilingualem Lernen (in kollaborativen Settings) mit besonderem Fokus auf *scaffolding*. Anschließend werden drei Methoden (detective stories, mini books, experiments) und ihr unterrichtspraktischer Einsatz im Zuge kollaborativen Lernens dargestellt. Der Fokus liegt dabei sowohl auf einer detaillierten theoretischen Beschreibung als auch auf der erfahrungsbasierten unterrichtlichen Umsetzung, um exemplarisch konkrete Implementierungen der anfänglichen theoretisch-curricularen Postulate aufzuzeigen.

Jo Mynard
Kanda University of International Studies, Japan

Investigating Social Presence in a Social Networking Environment

Drawing on the Community of Inquiry model (Garrison/Anderson/Archer 2000; 2001), this research investigates the nature of social presence in an online social networking environment (SNE). Social presence is defined as "the ability of learners to project themselves socially and affectively into a community of inquiry" (Rourke et al. *2001: 51). The SNE used in the present research was Ning (http://www.ning.com/) and complemented a face-to-face classroom environment for a group of university students majoring in English language in Japan. The research investigates the range of social presence indicators observed in the SNE as students completed different kinds of online tasks. The social presence indicators were analysed using a qualitative framework (based on Rourke* et al. *2001). The results show that the students used a limited range of social presence indicators, and these findings suggest that the participants were unfamiliar with the conventions of SNEs and with participating in online discussions. Greater preparation would be necessary to raise awareness of these conventions and to expand the students' range of ways to participate online in order to promote learning in social networking environments such as Ning. Some suggestions for ways in which learners can be prepared for online interactions are given.*

1. Introduction

This paper attempts to contribute to the body of knowledge on the importance of preparing language learners for a social networking environment (SNE). The paper focuses specifically on the social presence aspect by drawing on the Community of Inquiry (CoI) theoretical model (Garrison *et al*. 2000; 2001). Researchers and practitioners suggest that an SNE might enhance learning through community-building opportunities (Cole et al. 1998; Haythornthwaite et al. 2000; Kamhi-Stein 2000; McDonald/Gibson 1998; McKenzie/Murphy 2000; Sengupta 2001), however few studies have focused on the discourse that might contribute to the development of such a community and what kind of training learners might need, if any, in using such discourse.

After giving a description of the CoI theoretical model, the author provides a brief overview of a course offered to third year university students of English in Japan, which introduced them to technology tools and promoted learner autonomy. The paper then turns to the research portion which is an analysis of evidence of social presence exhibited in some of the task-related online interactions occurring within the course SNE (in this case, Ning) and an explanation of the results. Finally, there are some recommendations for practice[1].

2. Theoretical framework

2.1 What is the CoI framework?

To investigate learner interactions in online environments, the researcher drew upon the CoI framework (Garrison/Anderson/Archer 2000; 2001). The CoI framework is based on Dewey's (1933) views of practical inquiry, and learning is viewed as construction of meaningful knowledge (Garrison *et al.* 2000). Within the framework, three elements are considered: the private (cognitive) world of the individual learners, the role of the instructor in providing structure to the environment, and how the learner participates within the community. The three elements are named cognitive presence, teaching presence and social presence respectively.

'Cognitive presence' is "the extent to which the participants in any particular configuration of a community of inquiry are able to construct meaning through sustained communication" (*ibid.*: 89). Cognitive presence is investigated by analyzing evidence of critical thinking and knowledge acquisition.

'Teaching presence' is defined as the role of the teacher in providing, structuring, and maintaining the learning community (Garrison 2004). 'Social presence' is defined as follows:

> [...] the ability of learners to project themselves socially and emotionally in a community of inquiry. The function of this element is to support the cognitive and affective objectives of learning. Social presence supports cognitive objectives through its ability to instigate, sustain, and support critical thinking in a community of learners. (Rourke et al. 2001: 51)

Kehrwald (2008) defines social presence to be how an individual demonstrates willingness and availability for interactive participation in an online environment. This will entail "subjective projections of self [...], subjective assessments of others [...] and assessments of the subject's relations with others" (Kehrwald 2010: 41). Although all three elements of the framework are important, the focus of this paper will be on social presence for reasons which will be explained below.

---

1 The author of this paper is also the researcher and the instructor and these terms are used throughout the paper to indicate the same person in a different role. The term 'instructor' is used when referring to the course and 'researcher' is used when referring to the research.

2.2 Why focus on social presence?

The focus of the present research is on social presence for several reasons. Firstly, social/affective factors are considered to be among the main indicators of language learning success (Oxford 1990) and are seen to be important in all kinds of learning, but particularly in distance learning (Hurd 2007; Hurd 2008; Murphy 2011; White 2003), it is likely that social presence also has a significant role to play in online learning.

Secondly, social presence has been reported to have a positive influence on cognitive processes (Luppicini 2003; McPherson/Nunes 2004; Molinari 2004). Learners interacting in an environment which has a high social presence are more likely to take risks when sharing and commenting, showing a greater degree of critical thinking. Or, as Arnold *et al.* (2005: 540) note: "Social presence makes group interactions engaging, which in turn instigates and sustains critical thinking". Group interactions are likely to be more appealing and engaging in an environment high in social presence (Rourke *et al.* 2001).

Thirdly, social presence might be viewed as the most important dimension of online learning. Hauck/Warnecke (2012: 97) view social presence as a core e-literacy skill; a "*conditio sine qua non* […] skill rather than a facilitating element" (emphasis in original) and central to the learning and teaching process.

Fourthly, the importance of community aspects of online learning has been emphasized in the literature. For example, Garrison and Cleveland-Innes (2005) focused on social presence because of their beliefs that "participation and belonging were to be valued first and foremost" (Garrison/Cleveland-Innes 2005: 134). Gunawardena (1995) noted that participants' perceptions of a text-based medium would be influenced by the relationships that the learners made and the sense of community they felt.

Finally, effective social presence is an indicator and strong predictor of learner satisfaction (Gunawardena/Zittle 1997). Further research by Diaz *et al.* (2010) also indicates that social presence is valued by learners and should be stressed in all language learning environments.

2.3 How to foster social presence

In order to develop social presence, Kehrwald (2008) highlights three conditions that link social presence with interpersonal interaction: *ability*, *opportunity* and *motivation*. Ability relates to whether the participants are able to read and send social presence cues. These cues need to be learned and courses should pay attention to developing ability. This can be done through experiential modeling by instructors who can visibly demonstrate social presence with appropriate online behavior.

Opportunity relates to whether participants can interact with each other in practical terms. Instructors need to structure courses in ways that cultivate social presence.

Motivation relates to whether the interactions are beneficial or purposeful. Motivation can be facilitated by need or interest. *Need* usually means that learners are engaging in a task as part of a course of study. *Interest* motivates ongoing interaction that goes beyond course requirements.

2.4 How to evaluate social presence

Using the template within the CoI framework (Rourke/Garrison/Archer 2001) is one way to investigate social presence in online interactions. Evidence of social presence is explored through the examination of contributions between participants, which are termed 'affective responses', 'interactive responses', and 'cohesive responses' in an online environment.

Affective responses indicate a level of closeness, warmth and openness that encourages high interaction. Affective responses include the use of humor, self-disclosure, emoticons or punctuation to express feelings. *Interactive* responses are indications that someone is 'listening'. Examples include referring to what another participant has written or interlocutors asking each other questions. *Cohesive* responses promote a sense of group commitment such as when participants refer to the group as "we" and "us", when they address members of the group by name, or when they greet the group in a personal way.

Many researchers applying the template for assessment of social presence are likely to make some modifications for several reasons, such as being flexible to the type of environment and group dynamics (Lomicka/Lord 2007), and taking task type into account (Duensing *et al.* 2006). Other researchers, such as Hauck and Warnecke (2012) have used an adapted form of the model such as the one supplied by Swan (2002). Others have used alternative ways to investigate social presence, including questionnaires, interviews and group discussions (Kehrwald 2008), or post-project surveys (Mills 2011).

The social presence template within the CoI framework was chosen by the researcher because of its relative ease and convenience to apply, especially if the research is done retrospectively (as in this case) and the participants are unavailable to participate further in the research. Low levels of social presence (i.e. low frequency of indicators) suggests that an environment is impersonal and participants interact simply because they are required to do so. An environment lacking in social presence may result in a decreased amount of information being shared (Leh 2001). High levels of social presence (i.e. high frequency of indicators) are likely to indicate that an environment is collegial and that participants feel a sense of belonging to the group. In the latter case, participants feel that their contributions are valuable, rewarding, and educational (Garrison *et al.* 2001).

2.5 Learner preparation for online interaction

Although some studies have looked at the importance of learner preparation for online interaction (cf. Hauck/Warnecke 2012; Kehrwald 2010; Pegrum 2009; Pritchard 2013), more research into how learners might be better prepared for online environments is needed. Pegrum (2009) refers to learner preparation as 'participatory literacy' which should be seen as a prerequisite for online interaction. Hauck and Warnecke (2012) suggest that initial preparation could include raising awareness of elements of online participation through task-based training. Explicit instruction and reflection activities related to L2 SNE use could also continue throughout a course (cf. Pritchard 2013).

Kehrwald (2010) notes that learners need to experience and notice how others interact and how a community is fostered. Hauck and Warnecke (2012) further emphasize the importance of "experiential modelling" (Hauck and Warnecke: 110) whereby a member of the online community –usually the instructor– models appropriate behavior within the online environment. Related to this is the notion of facilitator visibility; there are links between online presence of instructors and student satisfaction (Richardson/Swan 2003).

In addition, task design is important for learner preparation for TELL. For example, "tasks designed to spark collaborative reflection on issues related to participation, motivation […] seem particularly well suited […] and should therefore be more systematically trialled and integrated into CALL" (Hauck/Warnecke 2012: 112).

3. Background to the study

3.1 Purpose of the present research

The focus of the study was to evaluate the level and kind of social presence evident in the SNE interactions of a class of learners in Japan. The participants were relatively new to the medium and had not received any training or awareness raising of appropriate interactions in an SNE. The study investigates how learners participate in an SNE and then makes suggestions for ways in which the learners –and their instructors– might be better prepared. The research was unplanned while the course was in progress and data were not analyzed until after the course had finished, but the results could help an instructor to plan future courses which incorporate online communication in SNEs. The research questions were:

Research Question 1: What are the levels of social presence evident in the online tasks among learners unfamiliar with SNEs?

Research Question 2: Which social presence indicators can be observed in the tasks?

4. Learning environments and course design

4.1 Overview of the course

The course in which the research took place was entitled "Computer Assisted Language Learning" (CALL) and was offered to third year students of English at a university in Japan. The course had two main aims; one was to promote learner autonomy, the other was to draw on technology tools to support this development. Autonomous language learners can be defined as learners who have the capacity to take responsibility for all aspects of their language learning (Benson 2011; Little 1991). The course also aimed to encourage the students to explore and experiment with various technology-based language learning tools (TLLTs[2]).

4.2 Blended learning

The course was designed to utilize a blended learning environment, which is "a combination of technology and classroom instruction in a flexible approach to learning" (Banados 2006: 534). The blended learning environment included a face-to-face environment (classroom and self-access centre), and an SNE (Ning).

4.2.1 The Face-to-Face Environment (Classroom and Self-access Centre)

The physical space consisted of a classroom equipped with laptops, Internet access and a printer, as well as an adjacent self-access centre. The class met twice per week, and each session began in the classroom even if learners later made use of other spaces for their self-directed work. The classroom-based time always included face-to-face discussions and opportunities for reflection and sharing of ideas.

---

2   Castellano, Mynard, and Rubesch (2011: 12) define TLLTs as "any piece of hardware or software that can be leveraged for language acquisition regardless of whether or not it was originally designed for that purpose".

4.2.2 *The Social Networking Environment (Ning)*

Ning provided most of the online interaction opportunities, and the management of all of the functions was given to the students via their individual customizable pages. The following functions were available to students: blogs, forums, status updates, photo sharing, comments on photos, video sharing, and file sharing.

4.3 Structure of the Course

The course was 14 weeks long and the class was scheduled for two 90-minute periods per week. The course was divided into two parts; in part one (weeks 1–7), the focus was on discovering, trialing and critically evaluating a range of TLLTs according to their usefulness for language learning. Part one was largely instructor directed, but contained group, pair and individual activities in the physical classroom, as well as online activities such as writing blog posts, commenting on another student's blog post, and contributing to online discussions. Part two (weeks 8–14) was largely student directed and involved designing and implementing a learning plan. The students would also write reflective blog posts each week describing their self-directed work.

5. Methodology

5.1 Participants

The participants were members of a class of students that the author was teaching in the fall semester of 2010. The class contained eight students in their third year of a four-year degree at a university in Japan who were seven females and one male all aged 19 and 20. All of the students were Japanese nationals majoring in English language and were members of the English department. At the end of the course, the students gave written permission for their Ning contributions to be analyzed for the research described in this paper.

5.2 Data sample

Over a one-semester period the SNE showed the following activity: 82 blog posts with 120 replies to those posts in total; five discussion threads with 18 replies in total; 90 photos with three comments on the photos in total; and 16 wall posts. There were no instances of students posting video clips or files, or updating their statuses. The online tasks varied somewhat and are summarized in Table 1.

Table 1: A summary of online course tasks

Task	Weeks	Description of Task
1. Self introduction	1 – 2	The first assignment that the students received which required them to post a contribution on Ning. Reading and responding to another student's post was voluntary.
2. Instructor-initiated online discussion	3 – 4	An assigned homework activity. Questions were posted by the instructor, and students were required to respond within a given timeframe.
3. Blog posts reflecting on class tasks and project work	3 – 7	Students' written reflections on classroom-based activities that had been completed that week. Reading and responding to another student's blog was voluntary.
4. Student-initiated discussions	3 – 7	Part of a classroom activity. Students used the discussion forums in order to gather opinions and input from classmates. Responding to the threads was voluntary.
5. Blog posts reflecting on independent study	8 – 13	Written for homework. Students were required to write summaries of their independent work each week and reflect on what they had learned. Reading and responding to another student's blog was voluntary.
6. Final blog post	14	Started for homework and completed during class time. Students were asked to reflect on the period of independent study and how well they had met their original goals. Responding to at least two other students' posts was required.

The data collected were considerable, and in order for the analysis to be manageable (but still enable the researcher to make useful observations) only data related to required tasks where all learners participated were analyzed for evidence of social presence and these were Task 2 and Task 6. Task 2 was the only instructor-initiated task and occurred near the beginning of the course. It was relatively structured and required participants to reply to given questions. Task 6 was relatively structured for the person contributing the initial post, but the replies were unstructured and participants were invited to respond in any way they wished. It yielded the most participation, had multiple examples of threads with multiple replies, and it occurred during the final week of the semester where students were at their most familiar with Ning and online interaction of this kind. The data analyzed from the two tasks comprised 40 forum and blog posts out of the total 225 produced throughout the course.

6. Data analysis

Within the CoI framework, a text is coded according to the category and indicator which best describes it. After some trials with a similar data set, it was decided that the unit of analysis for coding social presence should be flexible and combine the thematic unit with the syntactical unit so could contain one or more sentences related to a theme. This approach (also adopted by Rourke *et al.* 2001) allows the coders to capture a unit more naturally.

The template for evaluating social presence was modified from the original to incorporate emergent categories and is provided below (Table 2). The examples have been taken from the present research.

Table 2: *Template for assessment of social presence (adapted from Rourke et al. 2001: 59)*

Category	Indicators	Definition	Examples
Affective	Expression of emotions	Conventional expressions of emotion, or unconventional expressions of emotion, includes repetitious punctuation, conspicuous capitalization, emoticons	"If we have a computer, we can learn English easily, ANYTIME, ANYWHERE." "p.s. I love Tokyo Disney Sea and Horizon bay restaurant! xx"
	Use of humor	Teasing, cajoling, irony, understatements, sarcasm	"Personally, I think it is kind of a zest of language learning. lol"
	Self-disclosure	Presents details of life outside class, or expresses vulnerability	"When I was in high school, I loved the U.S. rock music so I always surfed on the Internet to gather information and casually met amazing bands or songs."
	Intuiting (added by the author)	Guessing how another participant feels or what he/she means	"That must be a really effective way to study"

Category	Indicators	Definition	Examples
Interactive	Continuing a thread	Using reply feature of software rather than starting a new thread	(no instances recorded in present data)
	Quoting from others' messages	Using software features to quote others' entire message or cutting and pasting selections of others' messages.	"…as Chika said: … (text pasted)"
	Referring explicitly to others' messages	Direct reference to contents of others' posts.	"Oh, you used the expression which you studied!!"
	Asking questions	Students ask questions of other students or the moderator.	"It's very useful, isn't it?" "How was the reaction of the guests?"
	Complimenting, expressing appreciation	Complimenting others or contents of others' messages.	"I really enjoyed the presentations yesterday – good job everyone!"
	Expressing agreement	Expressing agreement with others or content of others' messages.	"I think I have the same opinions as other members of the class."
	Finding common ground (added by the author)	Students make personal connections with the content expressed in previous posts.	"I am looking for a job as well, so I want to use your way of studying"
Cohesive	Vocatives	Addressing or referring to participants by name.	"As Yayoi says, learners may learn bad words or the grammar is not correct."
	Addresses or refers to the group using inclusive pronouns	Addresses the group as we, us, our, group	"Since we are recognized as non-native speakers"
	Phatics, salutations	Communication that serves a purely social function; greetings, closures.	"Have a great week"
	Ganbatte (added by the author)	Students encourage each other to try harder or keep going.	"Keep goin!"

The original analysis template was used in the present research with three additions as there were a notable number of occurrences in the test data set that could not be adequately categorized in the existing template. The three modifications were: (1) the addition of the affective indicator "intuiting" showing examples where participants were imagining how another learner felt or what was meant and responding accordingly; (2) the addition of the interactive indicator "finding common ground" where participants made connections with each other by finding similarities in some way; and (3) the addition of the cohesive indicator "ganbatte". *Ganbatte* is the imperative form of the Japanese verb *ganbaru*. *Ganbatte* is used when encouraging others to work harder or do their best, or as Hemmi (2006: 5) writes:

> "Ganbaru' means 'to try hard', and endure the hardships. Making an effort despite the pain it may involve […] an in-built aesthetic need fostered at home and in the education system at a very early age in Japan."

The concept "ganbaru" was evident, yet the students actually expressed the concept in English, for example 'keep going!'. In fact, only one instance of the students' L1 was used by the participants in the SNE. Contributions by a group of second language users drawing on the L1 might be interpreted to be evidence of social presence; however, the university which forms the context of the study emphasizes the use of English, and students are unaccustomed to using Japanese in class, even in online interactions. The only instance of Japanese used by any of the participants was "Ostukarasama!" (well done/great job) which is an example of what Arnold *et al.* (2005: 559) term a "cohesive community-building device".

In order to analyze the data for evidence of social presence, all of the Ning interactions were analyzed for tasks 2 and 6 as shown in Table 3. In order to establish the reliability of the data coding, a second coder who was familiar with the model and the indicators, analyzed 13% of the posts in the entire data collected (33 posts out of a possible 225). The inter-rater reliability between the two coders was measured by Cohen's (1968) kappa (k) and was calculated to be 0.60 meaning that the reliability fell within the acceptable range of 0.40 to 0.75 representing fair agreement beyond chance (Capozzoli/McSweeney/Sinha 1999). Once reliability had been established, the remaining analysis was conducted only by the researcher, and this is the only analysis which is shown in this paper. Once the data had been coded, the social presence density was calculated for each student based on all of his or her contributions combined. The social presence density allows researchers to compare the occurrence of social presence between threads of differing lengths (Rourke et al. 2001). It is calculated by counting the number of instances of social presence in a thread and dividing it by the number of words. In order to be able to work more easily with small numbers, this figure is multiplied by 1000. In order to establish whether the social presence density would be considered to be high or low, the author followed the example by Whiteside (2007) and calculated the standard deviation in order to create different levels of social presence.

7. Results and discussion

The combined social presence density for Task 2 and Task 6 was calculated for each participant and the results can be seen in Table 3. The average social presence density was calculated to be 35 with a standard deviation of 20. Based on the SD, the social presence density could be considered to be high or low compared with their classmates as follows:

0–14 = Low level of social presence
15–34 = Below average level of social presence
35 = Average level of social presence
36–55 = Above average level of social presence
56–75 = High level of social presence

However, other studies have shown the average to be higher. For example, results from Whiteside's (2007) study showed an average social presence of 39 with a standard deviation of 11 so that a social presence density of 40 or above would be required to indicate above average or high levels of social presence. In that case, all but two of the students would have a below average or low level of social presence.

Table 3: Social presence density by participant[1] in tasks 2 and 6 combined

Student	Total number of words	Total number of posts	Total number of instances of social presence	Social presence density	Level of social presence compared with classmates	Level of social presence based on Whiteside (2007)
Akemi	486	5	38	78	High	High
Ayaka	721	5	31	43	Above av.	Above av.
Chika	2739	5	48	18	Below av.	Low
Mao	804	4	24	30	Below av.	Below av.
Manami	588	6	21	36	Above av.	Below av.
Ryo	1190	5	12	10	Low	Low
Sayuri	733	3	13	18	Below av.	Low

---

[1] All of the students' names have been changed throughout the paper to preserve confidentiality.

Student	Total number of words	Total number of posts	Total number of instances of social presence	Social presence density	Level of social presence compared with classmates	Level of social presence based on Whiteside (2007)
Yayoi	1205	6	30	25	Below av.	Low
Instructor	75	1	4	53	Above av.	High
Total	8541	40	221	311		
Average (mean)	949	4	25	*35		

*SD=20

In order to answer research question 1, the density figure shown in Table 3 was used to see at a glance the level of social presence overall and for each participant. The intact online interactions were also considered alongside this social presence density figure in order to remain connected to the participants and their original messages. By doing this, a researcher is able to notice potential discrepancies. In this case, there was one instance in the data (Table 3) that might be misleading. Data from one student, Chika, showed a high number of instances of social presence, yet as the student produced more text than the other students, the social presence density figure is relatively low. Chika's contributions contained many examples of expressions of emotion, self-disclosure, vocatives, inclusive pronouns and humor. An impressionistic analysis of extracts might be that Chika is highly present, yet the social density figure for this student was well below average.

7.1 Task and interaction type

Although the data collected from Task 2 and Task 6 were analysed together, it is worth noting that as the tasks were different and took place at different points during the semester, there were differences in the social presence patterns observed. Task 2 was an instructor-initiated task which occurred early in the course. Task 6 contained student-initiated posts occurring later in the course. Table 4 shows the social presence density according to the task.

Table 4: Social presence density by task

Task	Total words	Total posts	Total instances of social presence	Social presence density
Task 2 (posts combined)	3246	13	63	19
Task 2 (initial post)	75	1	4	53
Task 2 (reply posts)	3171	12	59	19
Task 6 (posts combined)	5295	27	158	30
Task 6 (initial posts)	4041	7	36	9
Task 6 (reply posts)	1281	20	122	95

A few things can be observed from the data presented in Table 4. Firstly, the data show that the social density in the initial post does not appear to influence the social density of replies. For example, the social presence density calculated for the initial post in Task 2 was above average (53), yet the average social presence density for replies was well below average (19). The reverse is true for Task 6. The initial post was analyzed to have low social presence density (9), yet the average social presence density of the replies was high (95). The social presence was likely to have been influenced by whether the person who wrote the initial post was the instructor or a student, by when in the course the task occurred, by the nature of the task itself or a combination of all of these things. Task 2 was a relatively formal task and in Task 6, although the initial posts were structured, the replies were unstructured. Arnold *et al.* (2005) also reported differences in the ways in which students participated based on whether the tasks were structured or unstructured; tasks requiring structured contributions tended to contain fewer social presence indicators than less structured tasks.

7.2 Social presence indicators

Another level of analysis was done in order to answer Research Question 2 to ascertain the type of social presence indicators that the students' posts were displaying. The results of this analysis can be seen in Table 5. The categories (affective, interactive, cohesive) are all present. The most common indicators were: expressing emotions (affective), self-disclosure (affective), complimenting (interactive), and inclusive pronouns (cohesive) and. The other indicators were relatively infrequent or completely absent. This suggests that the students had a limited repertoire of responses and might benefit from further preparation in order to expand the ways in which they could respond to others and further increase social presence. Arnold *et al.* (2005) note that some indicators might be more likely to be present in certain tasks than others; however, it is likely that the participants did not usually consider using some of the indicators that could be associated with both structured and unstructured tasks, such as *quoting others* or *continuing a thread*.

Table 5: Categories and indicators found in the data sample

Category	Indicators	Number present	Total per category
Affective			51
	Expression	5	
	Emotions	15	
	Empathy	1	
	Humour	2	
	Punctuation	8	
	Self-disclosure	20	
Cohesive			67
	Complimenting	19	
	Gambatte	1	
	Inclusive pronouns	43	
	Phatics, salutations	17	
	Vocatives	2	
Interactive			55
	Agreement	1	
	Questions	2	
	Common ground	9	
	Direct reference	11	
	Agreement	5	
	Quoting	2	
	Referring explicitly	9	

8. Limitations

There are several limitations associated with this research. One limitation is the fact that data were collected once the course had finished and were analyzed over one year later. This meant that it was not practical to obtain additional insights from the participants in order to attempt to gain a deeper insight into the processes involved when contributing to online discussions. Secondly, as with any interpretative research, the coding and subsequent analysis, although conducted as thoroughly as possible, are subject to the researcher's personal interpretation. Every attempt was made to reduce bias throughout the analysis, and involving a second coder ensured that the coding was reliable. In addition, the retrospective analysis allowed for the separation of the instructor and researcher roles.

9. Discussion

9.1 Limited social presence

The author takes the view that social presence is desirable in online environments for language learners, yet the results showed that for all but three learners the engagement in the tasks –and indeed in the SNE in general– showed relatively low social presence (research question 1) and that the repertoire of indicators used by all of the participants was limited (research question 2). However, it was observed that the different tasks did seem to influence social presence due to reasons that would need further research. These reasons are likely to include the participants' growing familiarity and comfort level with SNEs and the discussion thread, their level of audience awareness, and the degree of freedom given to contribute in a relatively unstructured task. Overall however, learners appeared not to fully appreciate social cues and conventions either as readers or as contributors in the ways suggested by Pegrum (2009) in that threads consisted of a maximum of one post per participant. Although not specifically a research question, it was observed that the participants did not follow the usual practices of SNEs. For example, none of the students used the status update feature of Ning, no students commented on photos that their classmates or instructor posted. There are a number of possible reasons for the findings which will be discussed below.

9.2 Limited *need* and *interest*

Many of the online tasks in the course did not require others to read or respond to them. Whereas it was the instructor's hope that the learners would be naturally curious to read their classmates' blogs, the participants restricted their replies to activities they were specifically required to respond to. The students lacked what Kehrwald (2008) terms *need* or *interest*. There was no requirement to read or reply to others (*need*), and the posts were not engaging enough to naturally draw students to interact with classmates online (*interest*). As a result, most of the participants did not experience enough online interaction to be able to be aware of or to sustain social presence.

9.3 Lack of learner training

Hubbard (2013) notes that learner training for CALL is often not deemed necessary, but as the results of this small study show, the learners lacked an awareness of how to interact in an SNE and could have benefitted from training. Many of the posts consisted of a presentation of ideas with no evidence of audience awareness including few or no social presence indicators. The instructor did not participate frequently enough to be a sufficient model as Hauck and Warnecke (2012) advocate, and there were no awareness-raising activities.

9.4 Limited experience with SNEs

Finally, when the class was in session, no students were engaging in social networking activities in English in their free time. Some students were using the Japanese site Mixi, but were not using Facebook or other SNEs at the time. This meant that the genre of social networking in English was unfamiliar to the students.

10. Conclusions and recommendations

The overall observation is that all of the participants were all able to interact in a limited way and three participants demonstrated an above average or high level of social presence even if their repertoire of responses was limited. In addition (according to their responses on the anonymous end-of-course survey), they all enjoyed the course. However, in order to promote social presence (leading to deeper learning) in future courses, a number of things could be addressed. These will be discussed in the following paragraphs.

10.1 Course design

The course was designed in a way that would facilitate online sharing and interaction and this basic design should be maintained. However, the course did not include ways of familiarizing the students with the genre or discussing the expectations that participants within such an environment usually have. This element needs to be embedded into future courses similar to the approach adopted by Pritchard (2013). The course could contain activities which explicitly teach ways of fostering social presence (cf. Hauck/Warnecke 2012) and include awareness-raising activities to help the learners to notice conventions and how they affect social presence.

10.2 Task design

Tasks could be designed in such a way so that participants are required to expand their repertoire of social presence indicators. For example, participants could be asked to refer to others' posts and reply to posts other than the initial post; they could be asked to support an argument with a personal anecdote which will involve a level of self-disclosure; or they could be asked to include at least one question in each reply in order to foster interactivity.

10.3 Experiential modeling and instructor involvement

The instructor has an important role to play by being fully present in the SNE. The instructor could consciously model certain behaviors such as self-disclosure, humor and asking questions so that the students can observe how this is done appropriately online. Aragon (2003) suggests that instructor feedback to students on the interactions might also be useful to develop students' attention to social presence.

10.4 Increase the number of required replies

Another way to increase social presence is for participants to contribute more to the threads. This is done by developing either need (i.e. increase requirements) or interest (i.e. make the tasks more engaging) (Kehrwald 2008). In the case described in this paper, students could have been expected to post on two other learners' posts each week as a course requirement. In addition, there could have been a specified minimum length and some guidelines.

10.5 Final note

One final point should be stressed here. Although social presence has been the focus of this paper, it is by no means the only factor involved in meaningful online interactions, and attention should also be paid to the content and the opportunities for cognitive development through the interactions. Paying attention exclusively to social presence may lead to rather shallow exchanges, but attending to social factors is likely to create an environment conducive to learners contributing their ideas and thinking critically.

Soziale Netzwerke gewinnen auch im Bildungsbereich immer mehr an Bedeutung. Hierbei wird angenommen, dass soziale Netzwerkumgebungen (*social network environment*, *SNE*) durch ihre Möglichkeiten zur Gemeinschaftsbildung zur Verbesserung von Lernprozessen beitragen können. Häufig außer Acht gelassen wird jedoch, dass Lerner auf den medienspezifischen Diskurs in sozialen Netzwerken vorbereitet werden müssen und genau hier setzt dieser Beitrag an. Unter Bezugnahme auf das Community of Inquiry (CoI) Modell von Garrison, Anderson und Archer (2000; 2001) befasst sich der vorliegende Artikel mit dem Aspekt der sozialen Präsenz (*social presence*) in sozialen Netzwerken. *Social presence* wird hierbei nach Rourke, Anderson, Garrison, und Archer (2001: 51) als "the ability of learners to project themselves socially and affectively into a community of inquiry" verstanden. Im Fokus der Untersuchung standen die folgenden beiden Forschungsfragen:

Forschungsfrage 1: *What are the levels of social presence evident in the online tasks among learners unfamiliar with SNEs?*

Forschungsfrage 2: *Which social presence indicators can be observed in the tasks?*

Das genutzte soziale Netzwerk war Ning (http://www.ning.com/), das im Sinne des Blended-Learning Ansatzes ergänzend zum Präsenzunterricht einer Gruppe von Studierenden mit Englisch als Hauptfach an einer japanischen Universität eingesetzt wurde. Verschiedene Indikatoren sozialer Präsenz wurden bei der Bearbeitung unterschiedlicher Online-Aufgaben untersucht und mithilfe eines auf Rourke *et al.* (2001) basierenden Frameworks analysiert. Die Ergebnisse der Studie zeigen, dass die Teilnehmer nur eine begrenzte Anzahl von *social presence indicators* überhaupt genutzt haben, was wahrscheinlich darauf zurückzuführen ist, dass die Studierenden mit den Konventionen sozialer Netzwerke und der Teilnahme an Online-Diskussionen nur bedingt vertraut sind. Es ist anzunehmen, dass, um einen größeren Erfolg zu erzielen, ein verstärktes Lernertraining nötig wäre. Der Beitrag schließt mit einigen Vorschlägen zur Vorbereitung von Lernern auf ebendiese kollaborativen Lernprozesse in sozialen Netzwerken.

Elke Ruelens, Nick Van deneynde & Dieter Vermandere
University of Antwerp, Belgium

A Preliminary Needs Analysis for Online Collaborative Language Learning

In recent years, courses or course components in higher education have been increasingly offered online. Even though it has been argued that implementing online components in the curriculum has many advantages, the benefits of engaging in online learning activities may be counteracted if the learners do not have the necessary skills or attitudes to successfully complete such activities. Therefore, instructors should be well informed of their learners' characteristics, needs, preferences, and experiences concerning online learning before integrating online components in the curriculum. The present article reports on a needs analysis performed at the University of Antwerp to explore the students' needs, experiences, and preferences concerning online collaborative learning activities. The questionnaire used to collect the data was adapted from the survey designed by Lee and Tsai (2011) by integrating issues raised by students who participated in focus interviews. The results indicate that the students could benefit from support with regards to self-regulating their learning, negotiating authority in collaborative learning contexts, and using information seeking strategies.

1. Introduction

Online learning environments and platforms are increasingly being implemented in the higher education classroom. The benefits of these environments are evident: students can follow personalised learning routes adapted to their specific needs and preferences, they can learn at their own pace and in their own time, there is a variety of resources available online, etc. (cf. Gündüz 2005). Due to these developments, the University of Antwerp (Belgium) has also increased its implementation of online learning components in recent years. For instance, the English majors practise their literacy skills in a blended learning environment (cf. Van de Poel/Brunfaut 2004) and are requested to autonomously enhance their general proficiency skills in an online learning environment.

However, when implementing an online learning environment or introducing an online component in the course, an instructor should be attentive to the learners' characteristics, needs, experiences and preferences (cf. Graham 2005; Liaw/Huang/Chen 2007; Lee/Tsai 2011). They need to be aware of the importance of exploring their learners' characteristics, since the benefits of integrating online (collaborative) learning can be counteracted by not considering whether the students can cope in such learning environments. So far, a needs analysis concerning online learning, or collaborative learning involving new media, has not been performed at the University of Antwerp; this might explain why not all online learning environments were received equally well by the students.

The present study reports on a needs analysis involving the linguistics and literature majors of the University of Antwerp; the students' needs, experiences, and preferences concerning collaborative learning involving new media were examined. The students were invited to participate in focus interviews centering on their experiences with different (formal and informal) forms of collaborative learning and the use of online course components or learning environments. The data collected in these interviews, together with a study by Lee and Tsai (2011), informed the development of a questionnaire which was distributed online. In this article, the participants' (perceived) needs, preferences, and experiences are discussed and implications for the teaching practice are considered.

2. Literature review

In this digital age, learners are confronted with computers and the Internet on a daily basis. In order to help their students cope with the richness of the information and resources available online, and in order to foster autonomy in their students, many teachers and educational institutions are introducing online materials in their lessons and curricula, for instance by implementing virtual learning environments.

In addition to confronting the learners with the multitude of sources of information available on the Internet, online environments enable the instructors to use classroom instruction or coaching for communicative and active learning, because learners can acquire background information at their own pace and in their own time (cf. Graham 2005). Web-based learning (i.e., learning associated with 'learning materials delivered in a Web browser' (Tsai/Machado 2002)), e-learning (i.e., 'activities involving computers and interactive networks simultaneously' (Tsai/Machado 2002)) and blended learning (i.e., 'the integrated combination of traditional learning with web based online approaches' (Oliver/Trigwell qtd. in Sharma 2010: 456)) are modes of instruction which are being implemented increasingly, and students are actively encouraged to engage in online environments. However, many of these environments are implemented without the instructors having examined the students' experiences and preferences concerning online learning. When implementing online or blended learning, it is pivotal that learners' computer-and Internet-related skills, needs, and preferences are being considered, and that specific training is offered to both learners and teachers (cf. Graham 2005; Liaw/Huang/Chen; Lee/Tsai 2011).

2.1 Learners' and instructors' computer-and Internet-related skills

For learners to succeed in engaging in online environments implemented for academic purposes, they are expected to be able to work and study autonomously to a certain extent. Contrary to the popular belief that this implies that learners should be able to study without the help of an instructor or their peers, learner autonomy 'entails a [learner's] capacity and willingness to act independently and in cooperation with others, as a socially responsible person' (see Dam 1995: 1–2). This definition implies that autonomous learners should (1) be able to organise their learning process so as to work independently, and (2) be able to engage purposefully with peers and instructors, thus engaging in collaborative learning. In addition to the skills required to be able to learn autonomously, specific computer-and Internet-related skills are required if the learners are expected to engage in online autonomous or blended learning.

In recent years, multiple studies have examined aspects of online learning, skills and attitudes (of both learners and instructors) that predict successful online learning (cf. Cheng/Tsai 2011; Delialioglu/Yildirim 2007; Graham 2005; Jonassen *et al.* 1995; Liaw 2004; Liaw/Huang/Chen 2007; Reynolds/Greiner 2005). One factor predicting success or failure of e-learning and/or blended learning is the characteristics and attitudes of both learners and instructors (Liaw/Huang/Chen 2007; Liaw 2004); it is indeed often argued that personal attitudes can affect individual usage of information technology. Therefore, it is important to be aware of learners' and instructors' experiences with and attitudes towards learning in online environments. Liaw, Huang and Chen (2007), for instance, examined and related enjoyment, perceived usefulness and self-efficacy, as well as intentional behaviour in instructors. When looking at the learners' attitudes towards e-learning, Liaw and his colleagues looked at self-paced learning, instructor-led learning, and multimedia instruction as predictors of these attitudes. Secondly, a consideration for the development of online learning environments recurrently expressed is that e-learning should be networked and supported (Delialiuglu/Yildirim 2007; Graham 2005; Liaw/Huang/Chen 2007). Finally, it is argued that learner interaction and opportunities for communication are to be considered as well in developing or implementing online learning environments (Graham 2005; Liaw 2004).

Another approach to examining learners' characteristics can be found in Lee and Tsai's (2011) study, in which students' perceptions of three aspects of learning, namely, collaboration, self-regulated learning, and information seeking in both

Internet-based and traditional face-to-face learning contexts are investigated. By using a questionnaire that was completed by 150 students, they analysed differences between two elements: (1) students' perceptions of Internet-based and face-to-face learning environments, and (2) the three aforementioned aspects in relation to learners' attributes and the use of the Internet and enrolment in online courses. Significant differences have been found in this study concerning the three learners' attributes: all of them had higher results for the Internet-based learning environments. Furthermore, Lee and Tsai suggest that these attributes might be improved by offering students the chance to gain more experience in working on the Internet. In the following, the three aforementioned aspects will be elaborated on, since they inform the needs analysis performed for the present study.

2.2 Three aspects of learning: collaboration, self-regulated learning and information seeking

According to Alavi (1994), collaborative learning 'involves social (interpersonal) processes by which a small group of students work together (i.e., cooperate and work as a team) to complete an academic problem-solving task designed to promote learning (i.e., get actively involved and participate in problem solving' (Alavi 1994: 161). Multiple studies have found that collaboration has positive effects on learning (cf. Lee/Tsai 2011; Hernández/González/Muñoz 2014). Lee and Tsai (2011) argued that students who participate in collaborative learning show better engagement in the learning process, retain information for a longer period of time, and gain higher-order skills (Lee/Tsai 2011: 906). Definitions of collaborative learning (cf. Alavi 1994, Veldhuis-Diermanse 2002) emphasise the social aspect of the learning process. It should be noted that these are the positive results of collaboration, not specifically related to the use of the computer or the Internet. When looking at collaboration through the Internet, there appear to be quite mixed results according to the approach adopted in the study. A study on students' achievements showed that a face-to-face environment offered better results (Tutty/Klein 2008), whereas, from a social-cognitive point of view, it was argued that an Internet-based learning environment promotes collaborative inquiry, collaborative knowledge building, negotiations, and argumentation (Hara/Bonk/Angeli 2000). One of the challenges educators face when designing online learning environments is creating activities that are purposeful and give meaning to learning (cf. Reeves/Herrington/Oliver 2002). Instructors should avoid simply 'copying' materials from paper to an online environment. According to Karen Swan (2005), 'our concern should be more focused on the design of learning environments and less on instructional design'. The Internet provides many opportunities to enable authentic tasks for students. Reeves *et al.* have condensed research on the design of authentic activities, suitable for online learning, and provide 10 design principles, as well as specific examples of how online technology can facilitate the operationalisation of these principles.

The second aspect addressed by Lee and Tsai is self-regulated learning (henceforth referred to as SRL), which refers to the ability students have to construct meanings while they are learning and to monitor and control their cognition, motivation and behaviour of learning (Lee/Tsai 2011; Zimmerman 1989). It is generally assumed that using the Internet helps students become more self-regulated with regards to their learning behaviour, since it requires a higher level of autonomy and responsibility. Two outcomes have been discussed concerning the relationship between Internet-based learning activities and SRL. First, students enjoy flexible learning at their own pace in Internet-based learning activities (Tiene 2000). However, SRL can be quite challenging and overwhelming if students have never been prepared for this type of learning (Azevedo/Cromley 2004). Furthermore, it has been stated in several studies that SRL is essential for successful online learning (Williams/Hellman 2004), but that it has not received sufficient attention in educational research (Winters/Greene/Costich 2008).

Finally, Lee and Tsai (2011) emphasise the importance of information seeking. This is a fundamental skill for every student in an academic context. They use databases and online search engines to supplement traditional educational materials, such as textbooks. Furthermore, it is argued that there might be a relationship between searching strategies and Internet use: students with high Internet self-efficacy have better searching strategies, and students who are better at gauging the accuracy of information use more sophisticated strategies. Moreover, students participating in Internet-based learning perceived higher capability, more interest in, and more experience in information seeking than the students participating in traditional face-to-face instruction (Lee/Tsai 2011).

2.3 Computer-supported collaborative learning

Collaborative learning can occur in different styles and by using different media. This study focuses on collaborative learning via online learning platforms, which is one of the conceptualisations of computer-supported collaborative learning (henceforth referred to as CSCL). CSCL is generally used as an umbrella term, covering various ideas relating to ways in which collaborative learning can be supported by computers (cf. Bannon 1995: 268). Stahl, Koschmann, and Suthers (2006) assert that CSCL is based on the vision that (new) technology can be used to engage students in activities that encourage (collaborative) 'intellectual exploration and social interaction' (410). The focus of CSCL is on technology-supported learning and its effects on group learning processes, such as peer interaction and shared knowledge building (cf. Gorghiu *et al.* 2011; Veldhuis-Diermanse 2002). Veldhuis-Diermanse (2002) discusses various issues and characteristics of CSCL, defining collaborative learning as a learning situation in which learners 'exchange ideas, experiences and information to negotiate about knowledge in order to construct personal knowledge that serves as a basis for common understanding and a collective solution to a problem' (Veldhuis-Diermanse 2002: 13). Furthermore, she argues that 'people learn by interaction' (*ibid.*). Thus, learners need social contact to learn, to develop new ideas, and evolve in their experience of critical thinking. CSCL aids group learning processes, not through traditional face-to-face classroom activities, but by using computer software and network computer hardware. It also supports shared knowledge building by learners (*ibid.*: 14).

There are two important components in CSCL: learners and teachers. Introducing CSCL into an educational system causes a lot of change. It has been argued that many students perceive this change as discomforting and even threatening. The problem lies in the fact that they abruptly need to be more autonomous, be able to monitor and assess their own learning, cooperate with other learners who might have different backgrounds, and adapt to a new educational method that demands certain skills (*ibid.*: 17).

Not only learners are affected by the introduction of CSCL. The role of the teacher in the learning process has gradually changed from providing information to (also) facilitating the learning process. In online learning environments, the teacher's role moves even closer to that of a facilitator, since face-to-face instruction is not necessarily part of the educational programme anymore. In other words, in online collaborative learning environments, a teacher facilitates collaboration between students and encourages them to monitor their understanding, communicates with them and examines their produced knowledge (*ibid.*: 25). Teachers are also expected to undertake certain actions when they implement CSCL into their curriculum. For instance, teachers have to trust students' independence and share the responsibilities of the learning process with them, or evaluate, judge, value, and validate not only the product but also the learning process (*ibid.*).

3. Methodology

3.1 Participants

In this study, students in a higher education institute in Belgium were asked to participate voluntarily in research concerning collaborative learning. The participants (n = 50) were recruited from both the Bachelor's and the Master's programme in literature and linguistics at the University of Antwerp. The languages on offer in this discipline are the following: English, French, Dutch, German, Italian, and Spanish. Furthermore, students are also able to combine one language with courses in the domain of theatre, film, and literature (from this point on referred to as TFL). In other words, all participants either study two languages, or one language combined with TFL. Students in each phase of the programme (i.e., from the first Bachelor's to the Master's) have encountered forms of group work or collaborative learning. This differed from pair work where the groups were divided by the professor, to larger groups (up to eleven students in one group for a Bachelor's course on modern literature) where students were allowed to form their own groups.

3.2 Research instruments

In an attempt to get the most reliable results for this study, we triangulated our data. A critical literature review raised questions and challenges relating to the implementation of collaborative learning in which new media (online platforms) are used. These issues formed the basis for focus interviews in which students were encouraged to reflect on forms of collaborative learning they had engaged in, and on their preferences (and dislikes) with regards to collaborative learning and the use of new media in education. Finally, on the basis of both the literature review and the focus interviews, we adapted an existing questionnaire (cf. Lee/Tsai 2011) and distributed it online for the students to complete. The research question we concentrated on, was formulated as follows: 'What are the students' needs, experiences, and preferences concerning online collaborative learning? How can these needs inform the instructor's implementation of collaborative learning activities involving new media?'

3.3 Focus interviews

Focus interviews were used as a method to unearth students' perceived and actual needs with regards to online collaborative learning. The questions were based on Lee and Tsai's (2011) questionnaire, and the needs that were uncovered during these interviews have informed the adaptations we made to the questionnaire.

Students of the University of Antwerp were asked to voluntarily participate in focus interviews about their experiences with and preferences concerning collaborative learning and the use of new media in education. The students were asked to answer a series of open questions on the collaborative learning practices (both online and offline) they had experienced, and were asked to comment on specific issues that had been raised during the interview sessions. 21 students participated in the interviews, which were held in small groups, ranging from three to five students per group. Their answers were recorded, and two or three interviewers took notes during the interviews. Each interview lasted about 70 minutes, the interviewers then individually reported their findings, which were further compared and discussed.

3.4 Questionnaire

The students' input was used to adapt Lee & Tsai's (2011) questionnaire on collaboration, self-regulation, and information seeking; it is subdivided in five subtopics, namely collaboration, self-regulated learning (SRL), information seeking (IS), preferences, and expectations.

The questionnaire consists of 49 statements that the participants rate on a 5-point Likert scale: they received a number of statements ('agree – disagree') that aimed at identifying their actual behaviour during collaborative learning [Topic 01], questions about what they felt mattered most ('important – unimportant') in their individual learning attitudes [Topic 02]; the frequency of information seeking strategies they use ('always – never') [Topic 03]; their preferences on communication and evaluation ('agree – disagree') [Topic 04]; and finally, their needs about self-regulated online collaborative learning ('important – unimportant') [Topic 05] (see appendix). At the end of the questionnaire, the students were given the possibility to comment on the questions or some of the answers they provided.

The questionnaire was distributed online; 50 students completed it voluntarily. Only 38 questionnaires were filled in completely; missing results were excluded on a case-by-case basis, resulting in different sample sizes for different questions.

3.5 Data analysis

First, descriptive statistics were performed on the collected data; for each question, the mean, median, mode and standard deviation were calculated using SPSS. Furthermore, in order to test the internal consistency of the answers on each construct, we performed a Cronbach's Alpha. Given the small sample (n = 38 while the population is over 400) we did not pursue a principal components analysis nor a factor analysis.

4. Results

For each topic, the overall answer to the Likert-scale questions is positive (median is 4, mode is 4); yet, there are questions that score below average. The overall internal consistency of the answers to each topic is relatively low, only topic 2 has a Cronbach's Alpha score of .751 which is a high score for internal consistency with real world data.

We will now briefly present the results for each construct.

Table 1: Topic 01 (1= 'strongly disagree' – 5= 'strongly agree')

		Q1	Q2	Q3	Q4	Q5	Q6	Q7	Q8	Q9
N	Valid	40	40	40	40	40	39	40	40	40
	Missing	10	10	10	10	10	11	10	10	10
Mean		3.75	4.08	3.80	4.13	3.88	3.36	3.73	3.63	3.00
Median		4.00	4.00	4.00	4.00	4.00	4.00	4.00	4.00	3.00
Mode		4	4	4	4	4	4	4	4	3
Std. Deviation		1.032	.859	.823	.791	.648	1.063	.877	.838	1.013
Percentiles	25	3.25	4.00	3.00	4.00	4.00	2.00	3.00	3.00	2.00
	50	4.00	4.00	4.00	4.00	4.00	4.00	4.00	4.00	3.00
	75	4.00	5.00	4.00	5.00	4.00	4.00	4.00	4.00	4.00

While the median and mode generally score '4'[1] for this topic (student's behaviour during collaborative learning), the last question[2] scores only a 3. The question with the highest mean is Q4 (M=4.13), which puts it firmly in the 'agree' appreciation scale; this question is about sharing class notes with the peers during online collaborative learning. This seems to be a more practical aspect of online collaboration that is linked to the task at hand. The question that received the lowest overall score is Q9 (M=3.00) and is about 'leading peers in discussion' during online collaboration. Overall, there are two questions with means higher than 4.00 (Q2 and Q4); both concern specific, task-related aspects, like answering questions and sharing notes, which are part of the 'communicative' aspects of collaboration.

---

1 For an overview of the scales, we refer to the appendix at the end of the article.
2 As for the scales, an overview of the questions is provided at the end of the article, in the appendix.

Table 2: Topic 02 (1='not at all important' – 5= 'extremely important')

		Q1	Q2	Q3	Q4	Q5	Q6	Q7	Q8	Q9	Q10
N	Valid	38	38	38	38	38	38	38	38	38	38
	Missing	12	12	12	12	12	12	12	12	12	12
Mean		3.61	3.92	3.37	3.63	3.82	3.58	3.71	4.08	3.66	3.76
Median		4.00	4.00	3.00	4.00	4.00	4.00	4.00	4.00	4.00	4.00
Mode		4	4	3	4	4	4	4	4	4	4
Std. Deviation		.755	.784	.633	.751	.865	.858	.768	.784	1.021	.913
Percentiles	25	3.00	4.00	3.00	3.00	3.00	3.00	3.00	4.00	3.00	3.00
	50	4.00	4.00	3.00	4.00	4.00	4.00	4.00	4.00	4.00	4.00
	75	4.00	4.00	4.00	4.00	4.00	4.00	4.00	5.00	4.00	4.00

In this topic, only Q3 scores a median of 3 and a mode of 3, while with the other questions the median and mode are at 4. The question with the highest mean score is Q8, where the mean is 4.08; the lowest mean is for Q3 (M=3.37) on exploring further learning contents.

Table 3: Topic 03 (1 = 'never' – 5 = 'always')

		Q1	Q2	Q3	Q4	Q5	Q6	Q7	Q8
N	Valid	38	38	38	38	38	38	38	38
	Missing	12	12	12	12	12	12	12	12
Mean		3.26	3.92	4.26	4.29	3.13	3.71	3.66	3.47
Median		3.00	4.00	4.00	4.00	3.00	4.00	4.00	3.50
Mode		3	4	4	4	3	4	4	4
Std. Deviation		.860	.941	.685	.654	.935	.835	.938	.862
Percentiles	25	3.00	3.00	4.00	4.00	2.00	3.00	3.00	3.00
	50	3.00	4.00	4.00	4.00	3.00	4.00	4.00	3.50
	75	4.00	5.00	5.00	5.00	4.00	4.00	4.00	4.00

For the topic on information seeking, questions 1 and 5 have a lower score (median and mode of 3) than the other questions that score 4.

The question with the highest mean is Q4 on integrating new information (M=4.29); the question with the lowest mean is Q5 (M=3.13) on using different searching strategies to find new materials.

A Preliminary Needs Analysis for Online Collaborative Language Learning   301

Table 4: Topic 04 (1= 'strongly disagree'– 5= 'strongly agree')

		Q1	Q2	Q3	Q4	Q5	Q6	Q7	Q8	Q9	Q10	Q11	Q12	Q13	Q14
N	Valid	38	38	38	38	38	38	38	38	38	37	37	37	37	37
	Missing	12	12	12	12	12	12	12	12	12	13	13	13	13	13
Mean		4.03	4.47	4.18	4.08	3.68	4.47	3.79	4.13	3.13	3.68	3.62	3.84	4.27	4.32
Median		4.00	5.00	4.00	4.00	4.00	4.50	4.00	4.00	3.50	4.00	4.00	4.00	4.00	5.00
Mode		5	5	4	5	4	5	4	4	4	4	4	4	5	5
Std. Deviation		1.026	.725	.730	.969	.933	.557	.905	.704	1.119	.818	.953	.688	.804	.915
Percentiles	25	3.00	4.00	4.00	3.00	3.00	4.00	3.00	4.00	2.00	3.00	3.00	3.00	4.00	4.00
	50	4.00	5.00	4.00	4.00	4.00	4.50	4.00	4.00	3.50	4.00	4.00	4.00	4.00	5.00
	75	5.00	5.00	5.00	5.00	4.00	5.00	4.00	5.00	4.00	4.00	4.00	4.00	5.00	5.00

The fourth topic addressed students' preferences for online collaborative learning, and most questions score a mode of 4, and 6 questions out of 14 even a mode of 5. The questions that have a higher score do not all seem to be related to one another:

- Q1 to be part of small groups (max. 5).
- Q2 to receive specific guidelines for the task (from the instructor).
- Q3 to rely on regular classes for extra information/questions about the task.
- Q6 to be able to communicate spontaneously with my peers (without an instructor).
- Q13 to be evaluated individually on my collaboration.
- Q14 to be evaluated individually on my contribution to the final product.

Questions 2 and 6 score the highest mean (M = 4.47). The lowest mean score is for Q9 (M = 3.13) on seeing the instructor participate actively in the online discussions with the peers. The mean of 3.13 hides the fact that there is a significant group of students (13 %) that answered this question negatively.

Table 5: Topic 05 (1= 'not at all important' – 5= 'extremely important')

		Q1	Q2	Q3	Q4	Q5	Q6	Q7	Q8
N	Valid	38	38	38	38	38	38	38	38
	Missing	12	12	12	12	12	12	12	12
Mean		3.71	3.50	3.87	4.11	4.03	4.03	3.97	4.08
Median		4.00	4.00	4.00	4.00	4.00	4.00	4.00	4.00
Mode		4	4	4	4	4	5	4	4
Std. Deviation		.898	.726	.906	.863	.716	.972	.788	.712
Percentiles	25	3.00	3.00	3.00	4.00	4.00	3.00	3.00	4.00
	50	4.00	4.00	4.00	4.00	4.00	4.00	4.00	4.00
	75	4.00	4.00	4.25	5.00	4.25	5.00	5.00	5.00

The final topic generally shows scores of 4 (median and mode), except for question 6, which has a mode of 5. The highest mean score is attributed to Q4 (M=4.11) and concerns getting an individual score for the final product; the lowest mean score is for Q2 (M=3.50).

5. Discussion

Lee and Tsai (2011) argue that examining learners' characteristics and experiences with regard to Internet-based learning environments can inform instructors of which groups will adapt more easily to these environments (Lee/Tsai 2011: 906). The data collected in this study through the focus interviews and questionnaires were examined in order to identify students' needs which instructors should take into account when implementing Internet-based learning environments in the curriculum. These needs, which are either perceived needs by the students or needs deduced from their responses, will be elaborated on in the following paragraphs.

Something that was noticed immediately in the analysis of the participants' responses was that, in general, the statements which imply a certain initiative or responsibility on the part of the students (e.g. 'During online group sessions, I try different searching strategies/approaches to find new materials/information'; 'During online group sessions, I search for new, additional learning materials and information;' or 'During online group sessions, I lead my peers in discussions'), were rated lower than the statements which include activities that students are supposed to do in any case as part of their studies. This may indicate that these students do not feel the need to engage in study activities outside of the curriculum, which, in turn, may imply that the students are not intrinsically motivated to learn more than what they are required to, or that they are/feel incapable of self-regulating their learning. It could, however, also mean that the collaborative learning activities that they had to engage in so far were not necessarily designed to foster their self-regulation. Consequently, students might not feel 'challenged' and thus tend to concentrate on finishing a task, rather than on developing their knowledge and skills. Implicitly, then, students signal a need to be able to engage in online collaborative tasks that also specifically address self-regulation, rather than faithfully executing a script for a task.

5.1 Self-regulated learning: guidelines and intermediate goals

If we follow Zimmerman's (1989) interpretation of the concept of self-regulation, namely that self-regulated students 'personally initiate and direct their own efforts to acquire knowledge and skill' (Zimmerman 1989: 329) and that they do not rely on teachers, the results suggest that the participants of this study are not yet 'self-regulating' students. In comparing the ratings of the different statements, it becomes apparent that the students prefer to receive specific guidelines from the instructors, outlining what an assignment entails, that they are not particularly interested in further exploring what they want to learn, and that they do not use different searching strategies to find additional, relevant learning materials.

These findings imply that students are as yet not familiar with all aspects of their learning process and with ways in which to take charge of these aspects. If we want learners to engage in Internet-based learning environments, and in the meantime take charge of their learning process by organising their learning environments, regulating their learning pace and monitoring and assessing their progress, it is necessary that instructors, when implementing an online learning environment, provide support that relates not to the content of a task, but to the approach of tackling an assignment and describing the methodology used in each case.

One aspect of learning, namely engaging in self-monitoring and self-assessment, is especially important in online environments, since the instructor cannot set the pace or ascertain that the learners engage in learning activities he deems appropriate. The students in this study, however, express a very strong preference for receiving specific guidelines from their instructor. If we want to foster self-regulation, rather than doing away with instructor scaffolding, we believe that the support provided by an instructor should include an emphasis on setting intermediate goals, which will facilitate self-monitoring and self-assessment during the learning process. One possibility is to provide the learners with a plan of action on how to decompose an assignment into smaller, manageable tasks, and to carry out this approach collectively on one assignment. This makes the assignment look less daunting to students, who are often vulnerable to procrastinating their work because of its work load. Furthermore, learners should be made aware of strategies that will facilitate self-assessing their work, such as finding or developing assessment criteria.

5.2 Collaborative learning: cultivating confidence

The results indicate that the students engage in various online collaborative learning activities in; they discuss problems and ideas, answer each other's questions, exchange learning materials (e.g. class notes), and share and discuss learning experiences. This is not a surprising outcome, having learned from the focus interviews that students spontaneously initiate Facebook groups each year, in which they consult each other when they face challenges, share their experiences, and exchange learning materials. This implies that students believe working collaboratively with peers is beneficial for their own learning process. Strangely enough, students do not make use of the online discussion platforms offered by instructors and prefer to solve problems amongst themselves.

However, at the same time, it seems that these students lack a feeling of confidence when they engage in group work. This is illustrated by their wish to be evaluated individually (Topic 04, Q13 and Q14: median = 4 and 5 respectively). In other words, even though the participants seek to collaborate with their peers outside of the classroom and assert that they consider collaborative learning or working beneficial, because they can achieve more collaboratively than individually (M=3.87), they prefer being evaluated individually. This may indicate that students are not able to communicate appropriately about their preferences and expectations; e.g., some students may expect to receive high marks for their work, while others would just like to pass the course, when partaking in a collaborative learning activity. This is underwritten by some of the assertions made by participants in the focus interviews; several students asserted that it is difficult to motivate peers who are not interested in getting high grades, and that they find it hard to address such issues. Furthermore, these results may indicate that students find it difficult to come to an agreement about the division of the workload. When certain members of the group feel that they took on more work than other group members, they want to get recognition for this by receiving a higher mark.

As Fredrick (2008) argues, students need to negotiate authority for their team work to be effective. She argues that both the classroom hierarchy (with the instructor being more powerful than the students) and the Western education system, which stimulates competition between students, make it difficult for students to negotiate authority. Therefore, the instructor should be aware of these difficulties and provide support in finding strategies to negotiate authority. If students learn to make clear arrangements and can communicate openly about issues such as a fair distribution of the workload, they will have more confidence in a successful completion of group work that is satisfactory to all those involved. This, in turn, can lead to a more positive learning environment (Cho/Kim 2013).

Additionally, these findings suggest that lecturers should give sufficient thought to the assessment of collaborative learning activities. On the one hand, a lecturer may want to encourage the students to explore strategies for negotiating authority by assessing the entire group. However, if some students refuse to be involved in the learning activity as much as their group members, the instructor may choose to differentiate the grades. One possibility would be to train the students in engaging in purposeful and objective self-and peer assessment. If the students are able to provide the instructor with sound, constructive feedback about their own and their peers' contributions, the latter can differentiate the grades accordingly. This coincides with an idea expressed by Bruffee (1973), namely that evaluation is an important aspect in collaborative learning, since students should 'gain increasing confidence and ability in critically evaluating their own work and that of their peers' (Bruffee 1973: 640).

5.3 Information seeking: searching for materials

Tsai and Tsai (2003) argue that students with high Internet self-efficacy are better at making use of different and appropriate strategies for searching materials (qtd. in Lee/Tsai 2011: 907). Even though the participants in this study assessed their information seeking skills quite positively (means ranging from 3.13 to 4.29), which implies that they feel confident about their Internet skills, some of the results indicate that students do not feel entirely comfortable in making use of different information seeking strategies. For instance, the statements which scored lowest in the section on information seeking are those about searching for additional learning materials and about the use of different strategies for searching new information or sources (respectively, the means are 3.26 and 3.13).

This could imply that the students are in need of some guidance in searching for relevant and reliable sources. A manifold of resources (in the library, on the Internet, in databases, etc.) is available to the students, and they may not know how to select the appropriate sources of information. Even though this is a 'technical aspect' of learning, it can bear an influence on how students feel about engaging in collaborative learning, especially in academic group works, and on (the quality of) the products of their collaborative efforts. Again, students might perceive the sheer mass of sources as a daunting element in their assignment. Therefore, it may be advisable for instructors to provide their students with a set of guidelines which deal with searching for, selecting and evaluating information sources. Furthermore, some specific exercises or assignments, focusing on the use of information seeking strategies, could be provided as the lower scores on these questions could also mean that students concentrate on the task at hand and do not feel the need to 'use' the task in order to enhance their learning skills for future tasks. In that sense, once more, tasks should probably be centered more on fostering self-regulation and less on just 'getting things done'.

5.4 Students' preferences and performance

The participants' responses to the questions relating to their preferences and performance mainly reinforce the (perceived) needs discussed in the previous paragraphs. One need that can be added to those mentioned above relates to the role of the lecturer in collaborative learning environments. The participants indicate that they wish to be able to contact the instructor when needed, but that they prefer that the instructor does not exert too much control over their process of collaboration and does not examine their progress closely.

If the instructor wishes to take the students' preferences to heart, the issue of providing guidelines should again be raised. The role of the instructor, in terms of fostering self-regulated learning, therefore, should be to provide clear directions to how students might approach a task, rather than determining the content of the students' output beforehand. In other words, the instructor would then act more as a real 'guide'; this will ensure that the students will only contact their lecturer to ask specific questions and experience more freedom in exploring their own content-related contribution.

6. Limitations of the study

A couple of limitations of this study should be considered. First, a thorough needs analysis requires the examination of the points of views of all stakeholders; in this case, this would mean that the instructors' characteristics, experiences, and attitudes must also be taken into account. However, this study has focused mainly on the characteristics of the students. Furthermore, the sample of students was smaller than could have been expected. This may be due to the timing of the study; the online questionnaire was distributed around the exam period.

This study was a useful first step in analysing the students' needs concerning online collaborative learning and has provided some insight into how instructors can support students when integrating such learning activities in the curriculum. However, these needs should be monitored continuously to ensure successful implementation of collaborative online learning; therefore, follow-up studies are highly recommended.

7. Conclusion

The information that can be garnered from this preliminary needs analysis is twofold. On the one hand, students study and plan/organise their learning in function of the specific tasks and assignments that they have to complete. Fostering self-regulation via online collaborative learning will not come automatically if the tasks and assignments students have to carry out are not also designed for promoting self-regulation. From the present inquiry, we have learned that students still tend to focus on solving 'urgent' matters that relate to the task at hand and are not yet looking forward in terms of developing learning strategies to tackle future tasks. In order to encourage them to make that switch, instructors will also have to focus on designing the tasks for that specific learning outcome (apart from the content-related learning outcomes). Instructor scaffolding, while still very much appreciated, should therefore focus on a different role for the instructor as 'facilitator' and this should then lead to a focus on different aspects of a task or assignment, and preferably, on the process of completing the assignment rather than on the content (cf. Veldhuis-Diermanse 2002).

On the other hand, students indicated that they still rely heavily on their individual contribution to a specific task, and that they expect to be graded individually. From this point of view, group assignments will see more active and less active students, free riders and people who do not share the task's objectives, as much of the grading is done on the final product. Here as well, we believe that students need different forms of assessment (e.g., peer assessment and process evaluation) in order to allow them to change their focus and engage in real collaborative task management.

Appendix 1: The questionnaire
Topic 01 "Collaboration" – What happens when you work in groups?
During online group work sessions, I …
  Q1 discuss problems encountered while learning with my peers.
  Q2 answer study related questions asked by my peers.
  Q3 am motivated by the interaction with my peers.
  Q4 share class notes or materials with my peers.
  Q5 provide feedback to ideas suggested by my peers.
  Q6 review learning materials with my peers prior to the exam.
  Q7 make good use of learning information provided by my peers.
  Q8 share my learning experiences with my peers.
  Q9 lead my peers in discussions.

The scale for this topic ranges from 1 to 5. 1 = 'strongly disagree', 2 = 'disagree', 3 = 'neither agree nor disagree', 4 = 'agree', and 5 = 'strongly agree'

Topic 02 "Self-regulated learning" – How do I behave during my learning experience?
During online group work sessions, I can …
  Q1 set my own learning goals.
  Q2 recognize the inadequacy of my knowledge and/or skills.
  Q3 explore even further what I want to learn.
  Q4 use appropriate learning strategies for the task at hand.
  Q5 learn at my own pace.

Q6 review my learning effectiveness.
Q7 improve my learning approaches when it is needed.
Q8 learn from different opinions.
Q9 understand the benefits of collaboration.
Q10 integrate feedback I receive from my peers into my learning.

The scale for this topic ranges from 1 to 5. 1 = 'not at all important', 2 = 'not important', 3 = 'neutral', 4 = 'important', and 5 = 'extremely important'

Topic 03 "Information seeking" – Do I exploit the co-creation of my learning materials?
During online group work sessions, I …
Q1 search for new, additional learning materials and information.
Q2 judge the trustworthiness of the new information I found.
Q3 judge the quality and usefulness of the searched materials.
Q4 integrate new information into my existing knowledge.
Q5 try different searching strategies/approaches to find new materials/information.
Q6 organize and synthesize the searched materials.
Q7 share the learning materials with others.
Q8 am motivated by the possibility of searching new information.

The scale for this topic ranges from 1 to 5. 1 = 'never', 2 = 'almost never', 3 = 'sometimes', 4 = 'most of the time', and 5 = 'always'

Topic 04 "Preferences" – What is really very important to me during collaborative online learning?
During online group work sessions, I really like …
Q1 to be part of small groups (max. 5).
Q2 to receive specific guidelines for the task (from the instructor).
Q3 to rely on regular classes for extra information/questions about the task.
Q4 to be able to select my fellow group members.
Q5 to discuss progress with the instructor.
Q6 to be able to communicate spontaneously with my peers (without an instructor).
Q7 to be able to communicate directly with the instructor (face-to-face).
Q8 to be able to discuss problems during regular class sessions.
Q9 to see the instructor participate in and monitor online discussions with my peers.
Q10 to be able to select my own tasks.
Q11 to participate in peer assessment.

A Preliminary Needs Analysis for Online Collaborative Language Learning 309

Q12 to make decisions on my own about my learning needs.
Q13 to be evaluated individually on my collaboration.
Q14 to be evaluated individually on my contribution to the final product.

The scale for this topic ranges from 1 to 5. 1 = 'strongly disagree', 2 = 'disagree', 3 = 'neither agree nor disagree', 4 = 'agree', and 5 = 'strongly agree'

Topic 05 "Benefits/expectations" – What do I expect from online collaborative learning?
After completing the online group work session(s), …
Q1 I will have experienced the benefits of collaborative learning.
Q2 I will be aware of the importance of online collaboration.
Q3 I will have achieved more than what I would have done on my own.
Q4 I will be evaluated individually on the final product/outcome.
Q5 I will be evaluated on the process and collaboration.
Q6 I will receive an individual score rather than a group score.
Q7 I will concentrate on communication with the group members.
Q8 I will have achieved my learning goals.

The scale for this topic ranges from 1 to 5. 1 = 'not at all important', 2 = 'not important', 3 = 'neutral', 4 = 'important', and 5 = 'extremely important'

Die Ergänzung von Präsenzveranstaltungen durch Online-Elemente wie zusätzliche Kommunikationsplattformen, das Bearbeiten von Online-Aufgaben oder das Einbinden von kollaborativen Online-Aktivitäten, haben vor allem in der universitären Lehre in den letzten Jahren immer mehr an Bedeutung gewonnen. Abgesehen von den zahlreichen Vorteilen, wie die Unterstützung personalisierter Lernwege oder die zeit-und ortsunabhängige Bearbeitung von Aufgaben, welche die Nutzung von Online-Lernumgebungen mit sich bringt, wird immer wieder hervorgehoben, dass eine Steigerung des Lernerfolgs nicht zuletzt von einer kompetenten Nutzung der Angebote anhängt. Hierbei ist wichtig, dass Lerner Online-Angeboten nicht nur positiv gegen-überstehen und als relevant für ihr eigenes Lernen ansehen, sondern auch die nötigen Fähigkeiten besitzen, um diese kompetent zu nutzen und so ihren Lernerfolg zu steigern. Daher scheint es wichtig, dass Lehrende sich über das Vorwissen ihrer Lerner bewusst werden, bevor sie Online-Elemente in ihr Kursangebot integrieren. Hierbei geht es nicht nur um das nötige technische Know-How, sondern auch um die persönliche Haltung der Lerner gegenüber Online-Lernumgebungen und ihre etwaigen Vorerfahrungen. Die Universität Antwerpen, Belgien, hat ihren Anteil an Online-Lernelementen in den letzten Jahren kontinuierlich gesteigert. So wird von Studierenden, die Englisch als Hauptfach studieren, erwartet, dass sie ihre Fähigkeiten in der englischen Schriftsprache eigenständig online verbessern. Vor diesem Hintergrund berichtet dieser Beitrag über eine an der Universität Antwerpen durchgeführte Bedarfsanalyse unter der bereits erwähnten Studierendengruppe, die in dieser Form erstmalig durchgeführt wurde, was ein möglicher Grund für die gespaltene Haltung der Studierenden gegenüber Blended-Learning Elemente sein könnte. Ziel war es, relevante Daten bezüglich des Bedarfs, der Erfahrungen sowie der Erwartungen der Lerner in Hinblick auf kollaborative Online-Lernaktivitäten zu ermitteln. Der dafür verwendete Fragebogen basiert auf einer von Lee und Tsai im Jahre 2011 durchgeführten Studie. Im Rahmen von Fokusinterviews wurden die Studierenden gebeten, über ihre Erfahrungen mit verschiedenen Formen kollaborativen Lernens und der Anreicherung von Präsensveranstaltungen durch Onlinekurselemente zu berichten. Die Ergebnisse der Interviews wurden, zusammen mit den Daten aus der Lee und Tsai Studie, zur Entwicklung eines Online-Fragebogens herangezogen. Der Beitrag diskutiert die Ergebnisse der Erhebung bezüglich der Erfahrungen der Studierenden und ihren damit verbundenen Erwartungen an Blended-Learning Kurse.

Christian Ludwig & Kris Van de Poel
University of Education Karlsruhe, Germany
University of Antwerp, Belgium

Postscript

> "The computer is the most remarkable tool we have ever come up with.
> It is the equivalent of a bicycle for our minds."
> (Steve Jobs)

The present edited volume examines the diverse ways in which new media shape (collaborative) learning in light of educational standards, and in particular output orientation, as well as current expectations and practices in foreign language classrooms. The different authors have demonstrated in exemplary fashion how using social networking sites, video games, and Internet-based applications like websites, contribute to the development and informed practice of a cornucopia of (foreign language-related) skills, competences, and literacies. When used 'wisely', new media provide endless ways to facilitate collaboration in the foreign language classroom. Collaboration, however, is not just a goal in itself: it is also a precondition for making foreign language learning successful, efficient and effective, as well as genuine.

The permanent and consistent implementation of collaborative learning principles through new media will require the transformation of traditional learning environments in order to embrace new virtual learning spaces. In other words, stakeholders will have to allow learners to move their learning beyond the four walls of the classroom and to collaborate with others, but also to learn on their own if they choose to do so. The examples of and ideas for practice presented in this edited volume are characterised by a readiness to explore new routes in order to find more effective ways of learning and using a foreign language. Learning will be increasingly learner-centred, not simply because the technology is there, but because learners demand it. However, an incremental shift of responsibility from the teacher to the learner can only result in better learning results if teachers and learners after critical evaluation of the process and product, and actively (co-)design their individual educational off- and online, fixed and mobile, environment(s). New media are inherently social and learners are able to collaborate with basically anyone in the virtual world and engage in authentic communication as part of their life-long learning process. Moreover, they have ample opportunity to collaborate with a wide range of 'specialists' in the field who thus become directly involved in the learning process.

The argument we have tried to make in this volume is that while it is impossible to say where exactly we are headed in our rapidly changing modern media world, we know for sure that the path is leading in a direction where no learning has gone before. In other words, technology-supported foreign language learning is no longer just behind our neighbour's garden fence; it is in our backyard and about to enter through our back door. Therefore, the ubiquity of new media in our learners' lives and –to a lesser extent– in educational infrastructure needs to have an incremental impact on teacher education programmes. Training (future) teachers in using specific devices is not enough as technology changes rapidly. Rather, we need to enthuse students and teacher trainees about approaches and methods informed by constructivist principles of learning that emphasize the learner's critical role in constructing meaning from new information and prior experience, and which underpin our understanding of learners-as-researchers not only on the web but also on the move.

New media have the power to transform foreign language learning and improve students' learning and achievement for example by providing opportunities for collaboration. With this edited volume we hope to contribute toward filling the theoretical gap in computer-assisted language learning as well as providing practical suggestions for building collaborative learning environments in the new media age.

Christian Ludwig & Kris Van de Poel
Karlsruhe & Antwerp (2017)

References

Christian Ludwig & Kris Van de Poel
University of Education Karlsruhe, Germany
University of Antwerp, Belgium

Further reading

The following list of references represents a small sample of the plethora of academic publications, reports and examples of good practice available on the topic at hand and should be regarded as an addendum to the references used by the authors in this volume. Not least for reasons of practicability, we made a selection from the available resources and confined ourselves to publications in English; apologising for omitting the outstanding publications in other languages. Given the rapidly increasing number and ever changing nature of online resources, we also deliberately chose not to include websites or other electronic sources, but to limit this list to printed scholarly monographs, edited volumes, and articles directly related to collaborative learning and the new media. Despite these restrictions, we hope that the following selection together with the reference list will encourage you to investigate the topic further.

Alavi, Maryam. "Computer-mediated collaborative learning: An empirical evaluation." *MIS Quarterly* (1994): 159–174.

Alvarez, Claudio, Sadaf Salavati, Miguel Nussbaum and Marcelo Milrad. "Collboard: Fostering new media literacies in the classroom through collaborative problem solving supported by digital pens and interactive whiteboards." *Computers & Education* 63 (2013): 368–379.

Alvarez, Ibis, Anna Espasa and Teresa Guasch. "The value of feedback in improving collaborative writing assignments in an online learning environment." *Studies in Higer Education* 37.4 (2012): 387–400.

Andriessen, Jerry, Michael Baker and Daniel Suthers, *Arguing to learn: Confronting cognitions in computer-supported collaborative learning environments*. Vol. 1. Springer Science & Business Media (2013).

Baker, Michael James and Kristine Lund. "Flexibly structuring the interaction in a CSCL environment." *Proceedings of the EuroAIED Conference*. Lisbon: Colibri (1996): 401–407.

Barron, Brigid. "Achieving coordination in collaborative problem-solving groups." *The Journal of the Learning Sciences* 9.4 (2000): 403–436.

Berry, Landon and Brandy Dieterle. "Group consultations: Developing dedicated, technological spaces for collaborative writing and learning." *Computers and Composition* (2016).

Brindley, Jane, Christine Walti and Lisa Marie Blaschke. "Creating effective collaborative learning groups in an online environment." *International Review of Research in Open and Distance Learning* 10.3 (2009). <http://www.irrodl.org/index.php/irrodl/article/vi.ew/675/1271>.

Butter, Marcelo Careaga, Eileen Sepúlveda Valenzuela and María Graciela Badilla Quintana. "Intercultural talent management model: Virtual communities to promote collaborative learning in indigenous contexts. Teachers' and students' perceptions." *Computers in Human Behavior* 51 (2015): 1191–1197.

Cheng, Kun-Hung and Chin-Chung Tsai. "An investigation of Taiwan university students' perceptions of online academic help seeking, and their web-based learning self-efficacy." *Internet and Higher Education* 14 (2011): 150–157.

Cheung, Ronnie and Doug Vogel. "Predicting user acceptance of collaborative technologies: An extension of the technology acceptance model for e-learning." *Computers & Education* 63 (2013): 160–175.

Chou, Shih-Wei and Hui-Tzu Min. "The impact of media on collaborative learning in virtual settings: The perspective of social construction." *Computers & Education* 52.2 (2009): 417–431.

Coll, César, Maria José Rochera and Ines de Gispert. "Supporting online collaborative learning in small groups: Teacher feedback on learning content, academic task and social participation." *Computers & Education* 75 (2014): 53–64.

Cress, Ulrike, Katrin Wodzicki, Martina Bientzle and Andreas Lingnau. "CSCL for intellectually disabled pupils: Stimulating interaction by using a floor-control mechanism." *International Journal of Computer-Supported Collaborative Learning* 6.2 (2011): 307–321.

Crook, Charles. *Computers and the collaborative experience of learning*. Chatham, UK: Mackays (1994).

Curtis, David D. and Michael J. Lawson. "Exploring collaborative online learning." *Journal of Asynchronous Learning Networks* 5.1 (2001): 21–34.

Dascalu, Maria-Iuliana, Constanta-Nicoleta Bodea, Alin Moldoveanu, Anca Mohora, Miltiadis Lytras and Patricia Ordoñezde Pablos. "A recommender agent based on learning styles for better virtual collaborative learning experiences." *Computers in Human Behavior* 45 (2015): 243–253.

Deejring, Kwanjai. "The design of web-based learning model using collaborative learning techniques and a scaffolding system to enhance learners' competency in higher education." *Procedia – Social and Behavioral Sciences* 116 (2014): 436–441.

—. "The validation of web-based learning using collaborative learning techniques and a scaffolding system to enhance learners' competency in higher education." *Procedia – Social and Behavioral Sciences* 174 (2015): 34–42.

Dillenbourg, Pierre and Michael Evans. "Interactive tabletops in education." *International Journal of Computer-Supported Collaborative Learning* 6.4 (2011): 491–514.

Dillenbourg, Pierre and Michael J. Baker. "Negotiation spaces in human-computer collaboration." *Proceedings of the International Conference on Cooperative Systems*. Juan-les-Pins: INRIA (1996): 187–206.

Dillenbourg, Pierre. *Collaborative learning: Cognitive and computational approaches*. Oxford: Elsevier (1999).

Dillenbourg, Pierre, et al. "The evolution of research on collaborative learning." *Learning in humans and machine: Towards an interdisciplinary learning science*. Ed. E. Spada and P. Reiman. Oxford: Elsevier (1996). 189–211.

Drigas, Athanasios, Georgia Kokkalia and Miltiadis D. Lytras. "ICT and collaborative co-learning in preschool children who face memory difficulties." *Computers in Human Behavior* 51 (2015): 645–651.

Du, Jianxia, Mingming Zhou and Jianzhong Xu. "African American female students in online collaborative learning activities: The role of identity, emotion, and peer support." *Computers in Human Behavior* 63 (2016): 948–958.

Duță, Nicoleta and Oscar Martínez-Rivera. "Between theory and practice: The importance of ICT in higher education as a tool for collaborative learning." *Procedia – Social and Behavioral Sciences* 180 (2015): 1466–1473.

Eneau, Jérôme and Christine Develotte. "Working together online to enhance learner autonomy: Analysis of learners' perceptions of their online learning experience." *ReCALL* 24.1 (2012): 3–19.

Fischer, Frank, Ingo Kollar, Heinz Mandl and Jörg M. Haake. *Scripting computer-supported collaborative learning: Cognitive, computational and educational perspectives*. Vol. 6. Dordrecht: Kluwer Academic Publishers (2006).

Gan, Benjamin, Thomas Menkhoff and Richard Smith. "Enhancing students' learning process through interactive digital media: New opportunities for collaborative learning." *Computers in Human Behavior* 51 (2015): 652–663.

Greenhow, Christine and Brad Belbas. "Using activity-oriented design methods to study collaborative knowledge-building in e-learning courses within higher education." *International Journal of Computer-Supported Collaborative Learning* 2.4 (2007): 363–391.

Guitert, Montse. "Time management in virtual collaborative learning: The case of the Universitat Oberta de Catalunya (UOC)." *eLC Research Paper Series* 2 (2011): 5–16.

Haake, Joerg M. and Hans-Rüdiger Pfister. "Scripting a distance-learning university course: Do students benefit from net-based scripted collaboration?" *International Journal of Computer-Supported Collaborative Learning* 5.2 (2010): 191–210.

Häkkinen, Päivi, Maarit Arvaja and Kati Mäkitalo. "Prerequisites for CSCL: Research approaches, methodological challenges and pedagogical development." Ed. Littleton, Karen, Dorothy Miell and Dorothy Faulkner. New York: Nova (2004): 161–175.

Hämäläinen, Raija, Tony Manninen, Sanna Järvelä and Päivi Häkkinen. "Learning to collaborate: Designing collaboration in a 3-D game environment." *Internet and Higher Education* 9 (2006): 47–61.

Hernández, Nuria, Mercedes González and Pablo Muñoz. "Planning collaborative learning in virtual environments." *Communicar* 21.42 (2014): 25–32.

Janssen, Jeroen and Daniel Bodemer. "Coordinated computer-supported collaborative learning: Awareness and awareness tools." *Educational Psychologist* 48.1 (2013): 40–55.

Jeong, Heisawn, Cindy E. Hmelo-Silver and Yawen Yu. "An examination of CSCL methodological practices and the influence of theoretical frameworks 2005–2009." *International Journal of Computer-Supported Collaborative Learning* 9.3 (2014): 305–334.

Juan, Angel A., ed. *Monitoring and assessment in online collaborative environments: Emergent computational technologies for e-learning support.* Hershey, PA: IGI Global (2009).

Kam, Hwee-Joo and Pairin Katerattanakul. "Structural model of team-based learning using Web 2.0 collaborative software." *Computers & Education* 76 (2014): 1–12.

Ke, Fengfeng and Yu-Chang Hsu. "Mobile augmented-reality artifact creation as a component of mobile computer-supported collaborative learning." *The Internet and Higher Education* 26 (2015): 33–41.

Koschmann, Timothy D., ed. *CSCL: Theory and practice of an emerging paradigm.* New Jersey: Lawrence Erlbaum (1996).

Kreijns, Karel, Paul A. Kirschner and Wim Jochems. "Identifying the pitfalls for social interaction in computer-supported collaborative learning environments." *Computers in Human Behavior* 19.3 (2003): 335–353.

Kumpulainen, Kristiina and Antti Rajala. "Negotiating time-space contexts in students' technology-mediated interaction during a collaborative learning activity." *International Journal of Educational Research* (2016).

Labib, Nevine Makram and Rasha H.A. Mostafa. "Determinants of social networks usage in collaborative learning: Evidence from Egypt." *Procedia Computer Science* 65 (2015): 432–441.

Lampe, Cliff, Donghee Yvette Wohn, Jessica Vitak, Nicole B. Ellison and Rick Wash. "Student use of Facebook for organizing collaborative classroom activities." *International Journal of Computer-Supported Collaborative Learning* 6.3 (2011): 329–347.

Laurillard, Diana. "The pedagogical challenges to collaborative technologies." *International Journal of Computer-Supported Collaborative Learning* 4.1 (2009): 5–20.

Lee, Silvia Wen-Yu and Chin-Chung Tsai. "Students' perceptions of collaboration, self-regulated learning, and information seeking in the context of Internet-based learning and traditional learning." *Computers in Human Behavior* 27 (2011): 905–914.

Leinonen, Teemu and Eva Durall. "Design thinking and collaborative learning." *Communicar* 21.42 (2014): 107–116.

Leow, Fui-Theng and Mai Neo. "Redesigning for collaborative learning evironment: Study on students' perception and interaction in Web 2.0 tools." *Procedia – Social and Behavioral Sciences* 176 (2015): 186–193.

Lin, Chia-Ching. and Chin-Chung Tsai. "Participatory learning through behavioral and cognitive engagements in an online collective information searching activity." *International Journal of Computer-Supported Collaborative Learning* 7.4 (2012): 543–566.

López, Nereida and Patricia González. "Audioblogs and TVblogs, tools for collaborative learning in journalism." *Comunicar* 42 (2014): 45–53.

Lu, Jingyan, Qiang Hao and Mengguo Jing. "Consuming, sharing, and creating content: How young students use new social media in and outside school." *Computers in Human Behavior* 64 (2016): 55–64.

Lu, Jingyan, Susanne P. Lajoie and Jeffrey Wiseman. "Scaffolding problem-based learning with CSCL tools." *International Journal of Computer-Supported Collaborative Learning* 3 (2010): 283–298.

Martín-Gutiérrez, Jorge, Peña Fabiani, Wanda Benesova, María Dolores Meneses and Carlos E. Mora. "Augmented reality to promote collaborative and autonomous learning in higher education." *Computers in Human Behavior* 51 (2015): 752–761.

Miguel, Jorge, Santi Caballé, Fatos Xhafa, Josep Prieto and Leonard Barolli. "A methodological approach for trustworthiness assessment and predication in mobile online collaborative learning." *Computer Standards & Interfaces* 44 (2016): 122–136.

Miyake, Naomi. "Computer supported collaborative learning." *The SAGE handbook of e-learning research*. Ed. Richard Andrews and Caroline Haythornthwaite. Sage (2007): 248–265.

Mondahl, Margrethe and Liana Razmerita. "Social media, collaboration and social learning – A case study of foreign language learning." *Electronic Journal of e-Learning* 12.4 (2014): 339–352.

Nookhong, Jarumon and Panita Wannapiroon. "Development of collaborative learning using case-based learning via cloud technology and social media for enhancing problem-solving skills and ICT literacy within undergraduate students." *Procedia Social and Behavioral Sciences* 174 (2015): 2096–2101.

Noroozi, Omid, Stephanie D. Teasley, Harm J. A. Biemans, Armin Weinberger and Martin Mulder. "Facilitating learning in multidisciplinary groups with transactive CSCL scripts." *International Journal of Computer-Supported Collaborative Learning* 8.2 (2013): 189–223.

O'Malley, Claire, ed. *Computer supported collaborative learning*. Vol. 128. Springer Science & Business Media (2012). <http://www.springer.com/us/book/9783642851001>.

Onrubia, Javier and Anna Engel. "Strategies for collaborative writing and phases of knowledge construction in CSCL environments." *Computers and Education* 53.4 (2009): 1256–1265.

Orvis, Kara L. and Andrea L.R. Lassiter. "Computer-supported collaborative learning." *Teaching and learning with virtual teams*. Ed. Sharmila Pixy Ferris. IGI Global (2006): 158–179.

Pedro, Luís, Carlos Santos and Mónica Aresta. "Peer-supported badge attribution in a collaborative learning platform: The SAPO Campus case." *Computers in Human Behavior* 51 (2015): 562–567.

Rambe, Patient. "Constructive disruptions for effective collaborative learning: Navigating the affordances of social media for meaningful engagement." *Electronic Journal of e-Learning* 10.1 (2012): 132–146.

Resta, Paul and Thérèse Laferrière. "Technology in support of collaborative learning." *Educational Psychology Review* 19 (2007): 65–83.

Reychav, Iris and Dezhi Wu. "Mobile collaborative learning: The role of individual learning in groups through text and video content delivery in tablets." *Computers in Human Behavior* 50 (2015): 520–534.

Roberts, Tim S., ed. *Computer-supported collaborative learning in higher education*. IGI Global (2004).

Rodrigues, Stélio João, Suselei A.B. Affonso, Eliane Quinelato and José M. Montiel. "Distance learning in undergraduate education: The challenges of building a collaborative environment." *Procedia – Social and Behavioral Sciences* 116 (2014): 3499–3501.

Schwarz, Baruch B., Reuma de Groot, Manolis Mavrikis and Toby Dragon. "Learning to learn together with CSCL tools." *International Journal of Computer-Supported Collaborative Learning* 10.3 (2015): 239–271.

Sinha, Suparna, Toni Kempler Rogat, Karlyn R. Adams-Wiggins and Cindy E. Hmelo-Silver. "Collaborative group engagement in a computer-supported inquiry learning environment." *International Journal of Computer-Supported Collaborative Learning* 10.3 (2015): 273–307.

Slakmin, Benzi and Baruch B. Schwarz. "Disengaged students and dialogic learning: The role of CSCL affordances." *International Journal of Computer-Supported Collaborative Learning* 9.2 (2014): 157–183.

Stahl, Gerry. "Meaning and interpretation in collaboration." *Designing for change in networked learning environments*. Ed. B. Wasson, Sten Ludvigsen and Ulrich Hoppe. Springer (2003): 523–532.

Stahl, Gerry, Timothy Koschmann and Dan Suthers. "Computer-supported collaborative learning: An historical perspective." *Cambridge handbook of the learning sciences*. Ed. R. Keith Sawyer. Cambridge, UK: Cambridge University Press (2006): 409–426.

Warschauer, Mark. "Computer-mediated collaborative learning: Theory and practice." *Modern Language Journal* 81.3 (1997): 470–481.

Wasson, Barbara and Vibeke Vold. "Leveraging new media skills in a peer feedback tool." *The Internet and Higher Education* 15.4 (2012): 255–264.

Won, Samantha G.L., Michael A. Evans, Chelsea Carey and Christine G. Schnittka. "Youth appropriation of social media for collaborative and facilitated design-based learning." *Computers in Human Behavior* 50 (2015): 385–391.

Yeh, Shiou-Wen, Jia-Jiunn Lo and Jeng-Jia Huang. "Scaffolding collaborative technical writing with procedural facilitation and synchronous discussion." *International Journal of Computer-Supported Collaborative Learning* 6.3 (2011): 397–419.

Yoosomboon, Sathaporn and Panita Wannapiroon. "Development of a challenge based learning model via cloud technology and social media for enhancing information management skills." *Procedia – Social and Behavioral Sciences* 174 (2015): 2102–2107.

Yücel, Ümmühan Avcı and Yasemin Koçak Usluel. "Knowledge building and the quantity, content and quality of the interaction and participation of students in an online collaborative learning environment." *Computers & Education* 97 (2016): 31–48.

Yukawa, Joyce. "Co-reflection in online learning: Collaborative critical thinking as narrative." *International Journal of Computer-Supported Collaborative Learning* 1.2 (2006): 203–228.

Zahn, Carmen, Karsten Krauskopf, Friedrich W. Hesse and Roy Pea. "How to improve collaborative learning with video tools in the classroom? Social vs. cognitive guidance for student teams." *International Journal of Computer-Supported Collaborative Learning* 7.2 (2012): 256–284.

Zeng, Gang and Shigenobu Takatsuka. "Text-based peer-peer collaborative dialogue in a computer-mediated learning environment in the EFL context." *System* 37 (2009): 434–446.

Zhang, Xi, Weiguang Wang, Patricia Ordóñezde Pablos, Jing Tang and XiangdaYan. "Mapping development of social media research through different disciplines: Collaborative learning in management and computer science." *Computers in Human Behavior* 51 (2015): 1142–1153.

Zhao, Ke and Carol K. K. Chan. "Fostering collective and individual learning through knowledge building." *International Journal of Computer-Supported Collaborative Learning* 9.1 (2014): 63–95.

Zheng, Lanqin and Ronghuai Huang. "The effects of sentiments and co-regulation on group performance in computer supported collaborative learning." *The Internet and Higher Education* 28 (2016): 59–67.

Zheng, Lanqin, Junfeng Yang, Wei Cheng and Ronghuai Huang. "Emerging approaches for supporting easy, engaged and effective collaborative learning." *Journal of King Saud University – Computer and Information Sciences* 26.1 (2014): 11–16.

Zumbach, Jörg and Peter Reimann. "Influence of feedback on distributed problem based learning." *Designing for change in networked learning environments*. Ed. B. Wasson, Sten Ludvigsen and Ulrich Hoppe. Dordrecht: Kluwer (2003): 219–228.

References

Adams, Dennis M. / Hamm, Mary E., 1996: *Cooperative Learning*. Charles C. Thomas: Springfield, IL.

Adams, Dennis M. / Hamm, Mary E., 2015: *Imagine, Inquire, and Create. A STEM-inspired Approach to Cross-curricular Teaching*. Rowman & Littlefield: Lanham, MD.

Abdesslem, Habib, 1993: "Analysing foreign language lesson discourse". *International Review of Applied Linguistics* 31, 221–235.

Alavi, Maryam, 1994: "Computer-mediated collaborative learning: An empirical evaluation". *MIS Quarterly* 18(2), 159–174.

Alcón Soler, Eva, 2008: "Investigating pragmatic language learning in foreign language classrooms". *International Review of Applied Linguistics in Language Teaching (IRAL)* 46(3), 173–195.

Alm, Antonie, 2006: "CALL for autonomy, competence and relatedness: Motivating language learning environments in Web 2.0". *The JALT CALL Journal* 2(3), 29–38.

Alm, Antonie, 2009: "Blogging for self-determination with L2 learner journals". In Thomas, Michael (ed.): *Handbook of Research on Web 2.0 and Second Language Learning*. Information Science Reference: Hershey, PA, 202–212.

Androutsopoulos, Jannis, 2006: "Introduction. sociolinguistics and computer-mediated communication". *Journal of Sociolinguistics* 10(4), 419–438.

Appel, Christine / Gilabert, Roger, 2002: "Motivation and task performance in a task-based web-based tandem project". *ReCALL* 14(1), 16–31.

Aragon, Steven. R., 2003: "Creating social presence in online environments". *New Directions for Adult and Continuing Education* 100, 57–68.

Arich-Gerz, Bruno, 2008: "e-Learning as collaborative effort". In: Donnerstag, Jürgen / Volkmann, Laurenz (eds): *Media and American Studies in the EFL-classroom* (American Studies, 172). Winter: Heidelberg, 157–171.

Arnold, Nike / Ducate, Lara / Lomicka, Lara / Lord, Gillian, 2005: "Using computer-mediated communication to establish social and supportive environments in teacher education". *CALICO Journal* 22(3), 537–566.

Aronson, Elliot, 1978: *The Jigsaw Classroom*. Sage: Beverly Hills, CA.

Aston, Guy, 1986: "Trouble-shooting in interaction with learners: The more the merrier?" *Applied Linguistics* 7, 128–43.

Ashton, Sam, 2010: "Authenticity in adult learning". *International Journal of Lifelong Education* 29(1), 3–19.

Azevedo, Roger / Cromley, Jennifer G., 2004: "Does training on self-regulated learning facilitate students' learning with hypermedia?" *Journal of Educational Psychology* 96(3), 523–535.

Baetens Beardsmore, Hugo, 2009: "Language promotion by European supranational institutions". In: García, Ofelia (ed.): *Bilingual Education in the 21st Century: A Global Perspective*. Wiley-Blackwell: Malden, MA, 197–243.

Banados, Emerita, 2006: "A blended-learning pedagogical model for teaching and learning EFL successfully through an online interactive multimedia environment". *CALICO Journal* 23(3), 533–550.

Bardovi-Harlig, Kathleen /Dörnyei, Zoltán, 1998: "Do language learners recognize pragmatic violations? Pragmatic versus grammatical awareness in instructed L2 learning". *TESOL Quarterly* 32(2), 233–259.

Barkaoui, Khaled, 2007: "Teaching writing to second language learners: Insights from theory and research". *TESL Reporter* 40(1), 35–48.

Barkley, Elizabeth F. / Howell Major, Claire, 2014: *Collaborative Learning Techniques: A Handbook for College Faculty*. John Wiley & Son: New York.

Bates, Anthony William (Tony), 2015: *Teaching in a Digital Age: Guidelines for Designing Teaching and Learning*. Bccampus, e-Textbook.

Bax, Stephen, 2003: "CALL — past, present and future". *System* 31(1), 13–28.

Bax, Stephen, 2011: "Normalisation revisited: The effective use of technology in language education". *International Journal of Computer-Assisted Langauge Learning and Teaching* 1(2), 1–15.

Beatty, Ken, 2010: *Teaching and Researching Computer-Assisted Language Learning*. Pearson Education Limited: London.

Becker, Eckhard, 2015: "Laterale – definition". Retrieved 23.8.2015, from http://www.laterale.de/definition/.

Beldarrain, Yoany, 2006: "Distance education trends: Integrating new technologies to foster student interaction and collaboration". *Distance Education* 27(2), 139–153.

Bell, Allan, 1984: "Language style as audience design". *Language in Society* 13(2), 145–204.

Belz, Julie A., 2002: "Social dimensions of telecollaborative foreign language study". *Language Learning & Technology* 6(1), 60–81.

Belz, Julie A., 2003: "Linguistic perspectives on the development of intercultural competence in telecollaboration". *Language Learning & Technology* 7(2), 68–99.

Benson, Philip, 2011: *Teaching and Researching Autonomy*. Pearson Education: Harlow, UK.

Bereiter, Carl / Scardamalia, Marlene, 1987: *The Psychologoy of Written Composition*. Lawrence Erlbaum: Hillsdale, NJ.

Berger, Pam / Trexler, Sally, 2010: *Choosing Web 2.0 Tools for Learning and Teaching in a Digital World*. Libraries Unlimited: Santa Barbara, CA.

Biebighäuser, Katrin / Schmidt, Torben / Zibelius, Marja, 2012: *Aufgaben 2.0: Konzepte, Materialien und Methoden für das Fremdsprachenlehren und -lernen mit digitalen Medien*. Tübingen: Narr.

Biesenbach-Lucas, Sigrun, 2005: "Communication topics and strategies in e-mail consultations. Comparison between American and international university students". *Language Learning & Technology* 9(2), 24–46.

Biesenbach-Lucas, Sigrun, 2007: "Students writing e-mails to faculty. An examination of e- politeness among native and non-native speakers of English". *Language Learning & Technology* 11(2), 59–81.

Bieswanger, Markus, 2013: "Micro-linguistic structural features of computer-mediated communication". In: Herring, Susan C. / Stein, Dieter / Virtanen, Tuija (eds.): *Pragmatics in Computer-Mediated Communication*. De Gruyter Mouton: Berlin, 463–486.

Blake, Robert, 2000: "Computer mediated communication: A window on L2 Spanish interlanguage". *Language, Learning and Technology* 4(1), 120–136.

Blattner, Geraldine / Fiori, Melissa, 2011: "Virtual social network communities: An investigation of language learners' development of sociopragmatic awareness and multiliteracy skills". *CALICO Journal* 29(1), 24–43.

Blattner, Geraldine / Lomicka, Lara, 2012: "Facebook-ing and the social generation: A new era of language learning". *Alsic (En Ligne)* 15(1), 1–22.

Blell, Gabriele / Kupetz, Rita, 2005: *Fremdsprachenlernen zwischen Medienverwahrlosung und Medienkompetenz: Beiträge zu einer kritisch-reflektierenden Mediendidaktik*. Peter Lang: Frankfurt a.M. et al.

Bloch, Joel, 2002: "Student/teacher interaction via email. The social context of internet discourse". *Journal of Second Language Writing* 11(2), 117–134.

Bloch, Joel, 2008: *Technologies in the Second Language Composition Classroom*. University of Michigan Press: Ann Arbor, MI.

Blood, Rebecca, 2002: "Introduction". In: Rodzvilla, J. (ed.): *We've Got Blog: How Weblogs are Changing Our Culture*. Perseus Publishing: Cambridge, MA, ix–xiii.

Bloom, Melanie, 2008: "Second language acquisition in independent settings: Supporting the writing process with cognitive strategies". In: Hurd, Stella / Lewis, Tim (eds): *Language Learning Strategies in Independent Settings*. Multilingual Matters: Bristol, UK, 103–118.

Bolter, Jay David, 1992: "Literature in the electronic writing space". In: Tumon, Myron C. (ed.): *Literacy Online: The Promise (and Peril) of Reading and Writing with Computers*. University of Pittsburgh Press: Pittsburgh, PA, 19–42.

Bonk, Curtis Jay / King, Kira S., 1995: "Computer conferencing and collaborative writing tools: Starting a dialogue about student dialogue". *CSCL 95 Proceedings*, 22–26.

Börner, Wolfgang, 1989: „Didaktik schriftlicher Textproduktion in der Fremdsprache". In: Antos, Gerd / Krings, Hans P. (eds): *Textproduktion. Ein interdisziplinärer Forschungsüberblick*. Tübingen: Narr, 348–376.

Börner, Wolfgang, 1992: „Das Werkzeug der ‚Textverarbeitung' im fremdsprachlichen Schreiben: Idealkonzeption und Realisierungen". In: Börner, Wolfgang / Vogel, Klaus (eds): *Schreiben in der Fremdsprache: Prozeß und Text, Lehren und Lernen*. Bochum: AKS, 297–313.

Boughey, Chrissie M., 2000: "Multiple metaphors in an understanding of academic literacy". *Teachers and Teaching* 6(3), 279–290.

Bradley, Karen Sue / Bradley, Jack Alden, 2004: "Scaffolding academic learning for second language learners". *The Internet TESL Journal* X(5) May. Retrieved 16.8.2016, from http://iteslj.org/Articles/Bradley-Scaffolding/.

Bradley, Linda, 2014: "Peer-reviewing in an intercultural wiki environment – student interaction and reflections". *Computers and Composition* 34, 80–95.

Brake, David Russell, 2012: "Who do they think they're talking to? Framings of the audience by social media users". *International Journal of Communication* 6, 1056–1076.

Brammerts, Helmut, 1996: "Language learning in tandem using the internet". In: Warschauer, Mark (ed.): *Telecollaboration in Foreign Language Learning. Proceedings of the Hawaii Symposium*. University of Hawaii Press: Honolulu, 121–131.

Braun, Dirk / Heiter, Maria / Speckin, Carmen / Wollmann, Jens, 2013: *Kooperatives Lernen in Fächern der Gesellschaftslehre*. Neue Deutsche Schule: Essen.

Breen, Michael P., 1985: "Authenticity in the language classroom". *Applied Linguistics* 6(1), 60–70.

Breidbach, Stephan / Viebrock, Britta, 2012: "CLIL in Germany: Results from recent research in a contested field of education". *International CLIL Research Journal* 4(1), 5–16. Retrieved 12.10.2015, from http://www.icrj.eu/14/article1.html.

Brinkworth, Russell / McCann, Ben / Matthews, Carol / Nordström, Karin, 2009: "First year expectations and experiences: Student and teacher perspectives". *Higher Education* 58(2): 157–173. Retrieved 12.1.2011, from http://www.springerlink.com/content/j1683741v277j6n2/.

Brookes, Arthur / Grundy, Peter, 1990: *Writing for Study Purposes. A Teacher's Guide to Developing Individual Writing Skills*. Cambridge University Press: Cambridge.

Brookes, Arthur / Grundy, Peter, 1998: *Beginning to Write. Writing Activities for Elementary and Intermediate Learners*. Cambridge University Press: Cambridge.

Bruffee, Kenneth A., 1973: "Collaborative learning: Some practical models". *College English* 634–643.

Bruffee, Kenneth A., 1999: *Collaborative Learning: Higher Education, Interdependence, and the Authority of Knowledge*. Johns Hopkins University Press: Baltimore, MD.

Brügelmann, Hans, 2002: "Heterogenität, Integration, Differenzierung: empirische Befunde, pädagogische Perspektiven". In: Heinzel, Friederike / Prengel, Annedore (eds): *Heterogenität, Integration und Differenzierung in der Primarstufe. Jahrbuch Grundschulforschung 6*. Leske & Budrich: Opladen, 31–43.

Brumfit, Christopher, 1984: *Communicative Methodology in Language Teaching*. Cambridge University Press: Cambridge.

Bruns, Axel, 2008: *Blogs. Wikipedia. Second Life and Beyond*. Peter Lang: London.

Buendgens-Kosten, Judith, 2011: "Blogging in the target language: Review of the 'Lang-8' online community". *Studies in Self-access Learning Journal 2*(2), 97–99. Retrieved from http://sisaljournal.org/archives/june11/Bundgens-Kosten.

Buendgens-Kosten, Judith, 2013: "Authenticity in CALL: Three domains of 'realness'". *ReCALL 25*(2), 272–285.

Buendgens-Kosten, Judith / Brombach, Guido, 2013: "Die Welt zu Besuch im Projektseminar? Studentisches Bloggen und die Rolle von Öffentlichkeit". *Zeitschrift Schreiben*. Retrieved from http://www.zeitschrift-schreiben.eu/cgi-bin/joolma/index.php?option=com_content&task=view&id=97&Itemid=32.

Buendgens-Kosten, Judith, 2014: "The effects and functions of speaker status in CALL-oriented communities". In: Jager, Sake / Bradley, Linda / Meima, Estelle J. / Thouësny, Sylvie (eds): *CALL Design: Principles and Practice; Proceedings of the 2014 EUROCALL Conference, Groningen, The Netherlands*. research-publishing.net: Dublin, 29–34.

Buendgens-Kosten, Judith, Forthcoming: "'Please check for grammar': Code-alternations in a language learning blogging community". *Journal of Language Contact*.

Buendgens-Kosten, Judith [forthcoming 2016] „Das Tagebuch im Internet: Wie Lehrerinnen und Lehrer Blogs im Unterricht einführen". Medienlinguistik 3.0. Formen und Wirkung von Textsorten im Zeitalter des Social Web, edited by Eckkrammer, Eva Martha; Müller-Lancé, Johannes; Thaler, Verena; Baechler, Coline (eds). Berlin: Frank & Timme.

Buendgens-Kosten, Judith (2016) „'Please check for grammar.': Code-alternations in a Language Learning Blogging Community". Journal of Language Contact 9, 1, pp. 71–100.

Bueno-Alastuey, María Camono, 2011: "Perceived benefits and drawbacks of synchronous voice-based computer-mediated communication in the foreign language classroom". *Computer Assisted Language Learning* 24(5), 419–432.

Buller, Mary Klein / Buller, David B., 1987: "Physicians' communication style and patient satisfaction". *Journal of Health and Social Behaviour* 28(4), 375–388.

Byram, Michael / Nichols, Adam / Stevens, David, 2001: *Developing Intercultural Competence in Practice.* Multilingual Matters: Bristol, UK.

Campbell, Aaron Patric, 2004: "Using LiveJournal for authentic communication in EFL classes". *The Internet TESL Journal* X(9).

Campbell, Nick, 2009: "Twitter for education". Retrieved 25.9.2015, from http://www.tienetwork.org/content/view/302/.

Canto, Silvia / De Graadd, Rick / Jauregi, Kristi, 2014: "Collaborative tasks for negotiation of intercultural meaning in virtual worlds and video-web communication". In: Gonzalez-Lloret, Marta / Lourdes, Ortega (eds): *Technology-Mediated Tblt. Researching Technology and Tasks.* John Benjamins B.V.: Amsterdam/Philadelphia, 183–212.

Capozzoli, Michelle / McSweeney, Laura / Sinha, Debajyoti, 1999: "Beyond kappa: A review of interrater agreement measures". *The Canadian Journal of Statistics* 27(1), 3–23.

Castellano, Joachim / Mynard, Jo / Rubesch, Troy, 2011: "Technology use in a self-access centre". *Language Learning and Technology* 15(3), 12–27.

Cattafi, Ricardo / Metzner, Christiane, 2007: "A didactic experience in collaborative learning supported by digital media". *Issues in Informing Science and Information Technology* 4, 15–28.

Cenoz, Jasone / Genesee, Fred / Gorter, Durk, 2014: "Critical analysis of CLIL: Taking stock and looking forward". *Applied Linguistics* 35(3), 243–262. Retrieved 15.1.2015, from DOI 10.1093/applin/amt011.

Charmaz, Kathy, 2014: *Constructing Grounded Theory.* Sage Publications: London.

Chase, Christopher / Paul, Alexander, 2007: "The Japan-Korea culture exchange project". In: O'Dowd, Robert (ed.): *Online Intercultural Exchange: An Introduction for Foreign Language Teachers.* Multilingual Matters Ltd: Bristol, UK, 259–264.

Chejnová, Pavla, 2014: "Expressing politeness in the institutional e-mail communications of university students in the Czech Republic". *Journal of Pragmatics* 60, 175–192.

Chen, Chao-hsiu, 2010: "The implementation and evaluation of a mobile self- and peer-assessment system". *Computers & Education* 55(1), 229–236. Retrieved: from DOI 10.1016/j.compedu.2010.01.008.

Chen, Chi-Fen Emily, 2006: "The development of e-mail literacy. From writing to peers to writing to authority figures". *Language Learning & Technology* 10(2), 35–55.

Chen, Hao-Jan Howard / Yang, Ting-Yu Christine, 2013: "The impact of adventure video games on foreign language learning and the perceptions of learners". *Interactive Learning Environments* 21(2), 129–141.

Chen, Jen Jun / Shu Ching, Yang, 2014: "Fostering foreign language learning through technology-enhanced intercultural projects". *Language Learning & Technology* 18(1), 57–75.

Cheng, Kun-Hung / Tsai, Chin-Chung, 2011: "An investigation of Taiwan University students' perceptions of online academic help seeking, and their web-based learning self-efficacy". *The Internet and Higher Education* 14(3), 150–157.

Chen, Tsai-Yu / Chang, Goretti, B.Y., 2004: "The relationship between foreign language anxiety and learning difficulties". *Foreign Language Annals* 37(2), 279–287.

Childress, Marcus D. / Braswell, Ray, 2006. "Using massively multiplayer online role-playing games for online learning". *Distance Education* 27(2), 187–196.

Cho, Moon-Heum / Kim, B. Joon, 2013: "Students' self-regulation for interaction with others in online learning environments". *Internet and Higher Education* 17, 69–75.

Chun, Dorothy M., 2011: "Developing intercultural communicative competence through online exchanges". *CALICO Journal* 28(2), 392–419.

Chun, Dorothy M., 2011: "Computer-assissted language learning". In: Hinkel, Eli (ed.): *Handbook of Research in Second Language Teaching and Learning* (Vol. 2). Routledge: London, 663–680.

CLEX, 2009: *Higher Education in a Web 2.0 World: Report of an Independent Committee of Inquiry into the Impact on Higher Education of Students' Widespread Use of Web 2.0 Technologies*. Retrieved 25.9.2015, from http://clex.org.uk/CLEX_Report_v1-final.pdf.

Cohen, Jacob, 1968: "Weighted kappa: Nominal scale agreement with provision for scaled disagreement or partial credit". *Psychological Bulletin* 70, 213–220.

Cole, Robert / McCarthy Raffier, Linda / Rogan, Peter / Schleicher, Leigh, 1998: "Interactive group journals: Learning as a dialogue among learners". *TESOL Quarterly* 32(3), 556–568.

Coll, César / Rochera, María J. / De Gispert, Inés, 2014: "Supporting online collaborative learning in small groups: Teacher feedback on learning content, academic task and social participation". *Computers and Education* 75, 53–64.

Colpaert, Jozef, 2010: "Elicitation of language learners' personal goals as design concepts". *Innovation in Language Learning and Teaching* 4(3), 259–274.

Colpaert, Jozef, 2012: "Open educational resources for language teachers: A goal-oriented approach". Paper presented at the Joint CMC and Teacher Education EuroCall SIGS Workshop Bologna, 29–30 March 2012. Retrieved from http://eurocallsigsbologna.weebly.com/papers.html.

Colpaert, Jozef, 2013: "Ontological specification of an authoring interface for creating sustainable language learning content". In: Wong, Lung-Hsiang/Liu, Chen-Chung / Hirashima, Tsukasa / Sumedi, Pudjo / Lukman, Muhammad (eds): *Proceedings of the 21st International Conference on Computers in Education*. Asia-Pacific Society for Computers in Education: Indonesia, 644–653.

Colpaert, Jozef, 2014: "Neither technology nor pedagogy should come first in design". *The Educationist,* 10 December 2014. Retrieved from https://www.openlearning.com/educationist.

Colpaert, Jozef, 2014: "Reflections on present and future: Towards an ontological approach to LMOOCs". In: Martín-Monje, Elena / Bárcena, Elena (eds): *Language MOOCs: Providing Learning, Transcending Boundaries* (Open Series). De Gruyter Mouton: Berlin/New York, 62–173. e-Book Pdf: 978-3-11-042250-4.

Colpaert, Jozef / Aerts, Ann / Oberhofer, Margret / Gutierrez-Colon Plana, Mar (eds), 2015: "Task design and CALL". In: *Proceedings of the 17th International CALL Research Conference, 6–8 July 2016, Universitat Rovira i Virgili, Tarragona*. University of Antwerp: Antwerp.

Cook, Vivian, 2002: *Portraits of the L2 User*. Multilingual Matters Ltd: Bristol, UK.

Corbett, John, 2003: *Intercultural Approach to English Language Teaching*. Multilingual Matters: Bristol, UK.

Cornilie, Frederik / Thorne, Steven L. / Desmet, Piet, 2012: "Digital games for language learning: Challenges and opportunities". *ReCall* 24, 243–256.

Council of Europe, 2001: *Common European Framework of Reference for Languages. Learning, Teaching, Assessment*. Retrieved from http://www.coe.int/t/dg4/linguistic/Source/Framework_EN.pdf.

Council of the European Union, 2008: *2868th Council Meeting: Education, Youth and Culture*. Retrieved 10.10.2015, from http://www.consilium.europa.eu/uedocs/cms_Data/docs/pressdata/ en/educ/100577.pdf.

Coyle, Do, 2006: *Content and Language Integrated Learning. Motivating Learners and Teachers*. Retrieved from http://blocs.xtec.cat/clilpractiques1/files/2008/11/slrcoyle.pdf.

Coyle, Do / Hood, Philip / Marsh, David, 2010: *CLIL: Content and Language Integrated Learning*. Cambridge University Press: Cambridge.

Crystal, David / Davy, Derek, 1975: *Advanced Conversational English*. Longman: Harlow, UK.

Crystal, David, 2006: *Language and the internet* (2nd edition). Cambridge University Press: Cambridge, UK/New York.

Dal-Bianco, Veronica, 2012: "Implementing self-directed learning in higher education". In: *Conference Selections*. Glasgow, Scotland: IATEFL, 49–51.

Dal-Bianco, Veronica / MacSween, Fay, 2008: "Teacher role and online communication during a blended learning Business English course". In: Luca, J. / Weippl, E. (eds): *Proceedings of EdMedia: World Conference on Educational Media and Technology 2008*. Association for the Advancement of Computing in Education (AACE): Jacksonville, FL, 3681–3686.

Dal-Bianco, Veronica / MacSween, Fay, 2010: "Digitising feedback on blended learning language courses". In: *New Technologies – Old Teaching Methods?* 6th Language Teachers' Conference Proceedings, Vienna, Austria, 27–33.

Dalton-Puffer, Christiane/ Smit, Ute, 2007: "Introduction". In: Dalton-Puffer, Christiane / Smit, Ute (eds): *Empirical Perspectives on CLIL Classroom Discourse*. Peter Lang: Frankfurt a.M. et al., 7–23.

Dalton-Puffer, Christiane / Smit, Ute, 2013: "Content and language integrated learning: A research agenda". *Language Teaching* 46(4), 545–559. Retrieved 12.12.2015, from DOI 10.1017/S0261444813000256.

Dam, Leni, 1989: "Word processing in the foreign language classroom". *Die Neueren Sprachen* 88, 77–88.

Dam, Leni, 1995: *Learner Autonomy 3. From Theory to Classroom Practice*. Authentik: Dublin.

Dam, Leni, 2008: "How do we recognize an autonomous classroom? – Revisited". In: *A TESOL Symposium on Learner Autonomy: What Does the Future Hold?*, 13–32. Retrieved from: http://www.tesol.org/docs/default-source/new-resource-library/symposium-on-learner-autonomy.pdf?sfvrsn=0.

Dam, Leni / Legenhausen, Lienhard / Wolff, Dieter, 1990: "Text production in the foreign language classroom and the word processor". *System* 18(3), 325–334.

Danet, Brenda, 2001: *Cyberpl@y. Communicating Online*. Berg: Oxford/New York.

Darlaston-Jones, Dawn / Pike, Lisbeth / Cohen, Lynne / Young, Allison / Haunold, Sue / Drew, Neil, 2003: "Are they being served? Student expectations of higher education". *Issues in Education Research* 13(1), 31–52. Retrieved 10.6.2013, from http://www.iier.org.au/iier13/darlaston-jones.html.

Dechert, Hans-Wilhelm, 1983: "How a story is done in a second language". In: Faerch, Claus / Kasper, Gabriele (eds): *Strategies in Interlanguage Communication*. Longman: London, 175–195.

De Geest, A., 2012: "Freshman year: A discrepancy between social and academic well-being". In: *Papers selected from the Junior Research Meeting – Essen 2011. Language Learning and Language Use – Applied Linguistic Approaches*. Universitätsverlag Rhein-Ruhr: Duisberg, 167–175.

Delialioglu, Omer / Yildirim, Zahide, 2007: "Students' perceptions on effective dimensions of interactive learning in a blended learning environment". *Educational Technology & Society* 10(2), 133–146.

Deller, Seelagh / Price, Christine, 2007: *Teaching Other Subjects Through English*. Oxford University Press: Oxford.

De-Marcos, Luis / Hilera, José Ramón / Barchino, Lourdes Jiménez / Martínez, José Javier / Gutiérrez, José Maria / Otón, Salvador, 2010: "An experiment for improving student's performance in secondary and tertiary education by means of m-learning auto-assessment". *Computers & Education* 55(5), 1069–1079. Retrieved from DOI 10.1016/j.compedu.2010.05.003.

DeNoyelles, Aimee / Zydney, Janet Mannheimer / Seo, Kay Kyeong-Ju, 2015: "Save the last word for me: Encouraging students to engage with complex reading and each other". Retrieved 26.8.2015, from http://www.facultyfocus.com/articles/online-education/save-the-last-word-for-me-encouraging-students-to-engage-with-complex-reading-and-each-other-2/.

Deterding, Sebastian / Dixon, Dan / Khaled, Rilla / Nacke, Lennart, 2011: "From game design elements of gamefulness: Defining 'gamification'". *MindTrek 2011*, Tampere, Finland, 1–7.

Dewey, John, 1916: *Democracy and Education: An Introduction to the Philosophy of Education*. The Macmillan Company: New York. Retrieved 10.10.2015, from http://www.gutenberg.org/files/852/852-h/852-h.htm.

Dewey, John, 1933: *How We Think: A Restatement of the Relation of Reflective Thinking to the Educative Process* (2nd ed.). Heath and Company: Boston.

Diary of a Wimpy Kid (5/5) Movie clip – The Wonderful Wizard of Oz, 2010. Retrieved from https://www.youtube.com/watch?v=ro74_tScvSA.

Diaz, Sebastian. R. /Swan, Karen / Ice, Philip / Kupczynski, Lori, 2010: "Student ratings of the importance of survey items, multiplicative factor analysis, and the validity of the community of inquiry survey". *The Internet and Higher Education* 13(1–2), 22–30.

Dillenbourg, Pierre, 1999: "What do you mean by collaborative learning?" In: Dillenbourg, Pierre (ed.): *Collaborative-learning: Cognitive and Computational Approaches*. Elsevier: Oxford, 1–19.

Dillenbourg, Pierre, 2002: "Over-scripting CSCL: The risks of blending collaborative learning with instructional design". In: Kirschner, Paul A. (ed.): *Three Worlds of CSCL. Can We Support CSCL*. Open Universiteit Nederland: Heerlen, 61–91.

Dobao, Ana Fernández, 2014: "Vocabulary learning in collaborative tasks: A comparison of pair and small group work". *Language Teaching Research* 18(4), 497–520.

Dodd, Clare, 2001: "Working in tandem: An Anglo-French project". In: Byram, Michael / Nichols, Adam / Stevens, David (eds): *Developing Intercultural Competence in Practice*. Multilingual Matters Ltd: Bristol, UK, 162–176.

Dodge, Bernie, 1997: "Some thoughts about WebQuests". Retrieved 25.9.2015, from http://webquest.sdsu.edu/about_webquests.html.

Donath, Reinhard, 1991: "Telekommunikation im Englischunterricht". *Praxis des neusprachlichen Unterrichts* 38, 161–169.

Donato, Richard, 1994: "Collective scaffolding in second language learning". In: Lantolf, James P. / Appel, Gabriela (eds): *Vygotskian Approaches to Second Language Research*. Ablex: Norwood, NJ, 33–56.

Dooly, Melinda, 2007: "Choosing the appropriate communication tools for an online exchange". In: O'Dowd, Robert (ed.): *Online Intercultural Exchange: An Introduction for Foreign Language Teachers*. Multilingual Matters Ltd: Bristol, UK, 213–234.

Dooly, Melinda, 2008: "Constructing knowledge together". In: Dooly, M. (ed.): *Telecollaborative Language Learning. A Guidebook to Moderating Intercultural Collaboration Online*. Peter Lang: Berne, 21–45.

Dooly, Melinda, 2011: "Divergent perceptions of telecollaborative language learning tasks: Task-as-workplan vs. task-as-process". *Language Learning & Technology* 15(2), 69–91.

Dörnyei, Zoltán, 2007: *Research Methods in Applied Linguistics: Quantitative, Qualitative and Mixed Methodologies*. Oxford University Press: Oxford.

Dörnyei, Zoltán / Csizér, Kata, 1998: "Ten commandments for motivating language learners: Results of an empirical study". *Language Teaching Research* 2(3), 203–229.

Doughty, Catherine J. / Long, Michael H., 2003: "Optimal psycholinguistic environments for distance foreign language learning". *Language Learning & Technology* 7(3).

Dron, Jon, 2007: "Designing the undesignable: Social software and control". *Educational Technology & Society* 10(3), 60–71.

Ducate, Lara C. / Lomicka, Lara L., 2005: "Exploring the blogosphere: Use of web logs in the foreign language classroom". *Foreign Language Annals*, 38(3), 410–421.

Dudeney, Gavin / Hockly, Nicky, 2007: *How to Teach English with Technology*. Pearson: Harlow, UK.

Dudeney, Gavin / Hockly, Nicky / Pegrum, Mark, 2013: *Digital Literacies. Research and Resources in Language Teaching*. Pearson Education Limited: Harlow, UK.

Duensing, Annette / Stickler, Ursula / Batstone, Carolyn / Heins, Barbara, 2006: "Face-to-face and online interactions -- is a task a task?" *Journal of Learning Design* 1(2), 35–45.

Dunn, William E. / Lantolf, James P., 1998: "Vygotsky's zone of proximal development and Krashen's i+1. Incommensurable constructs; incommensurable theories". *Language Learning* 48(3), 411–442.

Dürscheid, Christa, 2004: "Netzsprache – ein neuer Mythos". In: Beißwenger, Michael / Hoffmann, Ludger / Storrer, Angelika (eds): *Internetbasierte Kommunikation (Osnabrücker Beiträge zur Sprachtheorie 68)*. Gilles & Francke: Osnabrück, 141–157.

Dürscheid, Christa / Frehner, Carmen, 2013: "Email communication". In: Herring, Susan C. / Stein, Dieter / Virtanen, Tuija (eds): *Pragmatics of Computer-Mediated Communication*. De Gruyter Mouton: Berlin, 35–54.

Eck, Andreas / Legenhausen, Lienhard / Wolff, Dieter, 1994: "Der Einsatz der Telekommunikation in einem lernerorientierten Fremdsprachenunterricht". In: Gienow, Wilfried / Hellwig, Karlheinz (eds). *Interkulturelle Kommunikation und prozeßorientierte Medienpraxis im Fremdsprachenunterricht*. Friedrich: Seelze, 43–57.

Eck, Andreas / Legenhausen, Lienhard / Wolff, Dieter, 1995: *Telekommunikation und Fremdsprachenunterricht: Informationen, Projekte, Ergebnisse*. AKS: Bochum.

Eckert, Penelope / McConnell-Ginet, Sally, 1992: "Think practically and look locally. Language and gender as community-based practice". *Annual Review of Anthropology* 21, 461–490.

Economidou-Kogetsidis, Maria, 2011: "'Please answer me as soon as possible'. Pragmatic failure in non-native speakers' e-mail requests to faculty". *Journal of Pragmatics* 43(13), 3193–3215.

Economidou-Kogetsidis, Maria, 2015: "Teaching email politeness in the EFL/ESL classroom". *ELT Journal* 69(4), 415–424.

Egbert, Joy, 2015: "Engagement principles and practice in classroom learning, language and technology". Plenary talk at 49th IATEFL Conference, Manchester, UK.

Egbert, Joy / Hanson-Smith, Elizabeth (eds), 1999: *CALL environments: Research, Practice and Critical Issues*. Teachers of English to Speakers of Other Languages: Alexandria, VA.

Eisenmann, Maria, 2012: "Introduction: Heterogeneity and differentiation". In: Eisenmann, Maria / Summer, Teresa (eds): *Basic Issues in EFL-teaching and Learning*. Winter: Heidelberg, 297–311.

Eisenmann, Maria / Ludwig, Christian, 2014: "Classroom 2.0 – the use of CALL in developing learner autonomy". In: Mynard, Jo / Ludwig, Christian (eds): *Autonomy in Language Learning: Tools, Tasks and Environments*. IATEFL: Kent, UK, 27–41.

Eisenmann, Maria / Strohn, Meike, 2012: "Promoting learner autonomy in mixed-ability classes by using webquests and weblogs". In: Heim, Katja / Rüschoff, Bernd (eds): *Involving Language Learners: Success Stories and Constraints*. Universitätsverlag Rhein Ruhr: Duisberg, 145–158.

Eisenmann, Maria / Ludwig, Christian, 2016: "Authentische Lernprozesse in komplexen Web 2.0-basierten Kompetenzaufgaben zur Förderung von Lernerautonomie". In: Becker, Carmen / Blell, Gabriele / Rössler, Andrea (eds): *Web 2.0 und komplexe Kompetenzaufgaben im Fremdsprachenunterricht*. Pädagogische Hochschule: Karlsruhe, 89–108.

Ekoc, A., 2014: Facebook groups as a supporting tool for language classrooms". *Turkish Online Journal of Distance Education – TOJDE* 5(3), 18–26.

Ellis, Rod, 1984: *Classroom Second Language Development*. Pergamon Press, Oxford.

Ellis, Rod, 1994: *The Study of Second Language Acquisition*. Oxford University Press, Oxford.

Ellis, Rod, 1999: "Theoretical perspectives on interaction and language learning". In: Ellis, Rod (ed.): *Learning a Second Language Through Interaction*. John Benjamins B.V.: Amsterdam, 3–32.

Ellis, Rod, 2003: *Task-based Language Learning and Teaching*. Oxford University Press: Oxford.

Ellison, Nicole B. / Yuehua, Wu, 2008: "Blogging in the classroom: A preliminary exploration of student attitudes and impact on comprehension". *Journal of Educational Multimedia and Hypermedia* 17(1), 99–122.

Elola, Idoia / Oskoz, Ana, 2010: "Collaborative writing: Fostering foreign language and writing conventions development". *Language Learning and Technology* 14(3), 51–71.

Elsner, Daniela / Viebrock, Britta, 2013: "Developing multiliteracies in the 21st century: Motives for new approaches of teaching and learning foreign languages". In: Elsner, Daniela / Helff, Sissy / Viebrock, Britta (eds): *Films, Graphic*

Novels & Visuals: Developing Multiliteracies in Foreign Language Education – An Interdisciplinary Approach. LIT Verlag: Wien, 17–32.

Entertainment Software Association (ESA), 2015. *Essential Facts About the Computer and Video Game Industry 2015: Sales, Demographic and Usage Data*. Retrieved 30.9.2015, from http://www.theesa.com/wp-content/uploads/2015/04/ESA-Essential-Facts-2015.pdf.

Evans, Michael, 2009: "Engaging pupils in bilingual, cross-cultural online discourse". In: Evans, Michael (ed.): *Foreign-Language Learning with Digital Technology*. Continuum: London/New York, 104–130.

Evans, Michael, 2012: "Traditional and modern media". In: Eisenmann, Maria / Summer, Theresa (eds): *Basic Issues in EFL Teaching and Learning*. Winter: Heidelberg, 217–228.

Facebook. n.d. Retrieved 2014, from www.facebook.com.

Facebook Newsroom Statistics, 2015: "Press statistics". Retrieved 3.8.2015, from http://newsroom.fb.com/company-info/.

Falk, Simon / Gerlach, David, 2016: "'We don't need no education' – Die Fremdsprachenlehrerbildung im Spannungsfeld von Lernerautonomie und technologischem Fortschritt". In: Kreyer, Rolf / Schaub, Steffen / Güldenring, Barbara Ann (eds.): *Angewandte Linguistik in Schule und Hochschule. Neue Wege für Sprachunterricht und Ausbildung*. Peter Lang: Frankfurt a.M. et al., 17–39.

Fileccia, Marco, 2015: "Goodschool: Die gute Schule im Internet". Retrieved 2.9.2015, from http://www.goodschool.de/cms/front_content.php?idcat=83&lang=1&client=1.

Findley, Charles A., 1987: *Collaborative Networked Learning: Technology and Opportunities*. Digital Equipment Corp: Burlington, MA.

Flavell, John H., 1979: "Metacognition and cognitive monitoring: A new area of cognitive-developmental inquiry". *American Psychologist* 34(10), 906–911.

Flower, Linda / Hayes, John R, 1981: "A cognitive process theory of writing". *College Composition and Communication* 32, 365–387.

Foster, Pauline, 1998: "A classroom perspective on the negotiation of meaning". *Applied Linguistics* 19, 1–23.

Fourie, Christine., 2015: "Raising awareness about the real task of learning". *Dutch Journal of Applied Linguistics*.

Fredrick, Terri A., 2008: "Facilitating better team work: Analysing the challenges and strategies of classroom-based collaboration". *Business Communication Quarterly* 71, 439–455.

Freiermuth, Mark, 2002: "Internet chat: Collaborating and learning via e-conversations". *TESOL Journal* 11(3), 36–40.

Freiermuth, Mark / Douglas, Jarrell, 2006: "Willingness to communicate: Can online chat help?" *International Journal of Applied Linguistics* 16(2), 189–212.

Fruhauf, Gianna, 1996: "Introduction". In: Fruhauf, Gianna / Coyle, Do /Christ, Ingeborg (eds): *Teaching Content in a Foreign Language*. Alkmaar Stichting Europees Platform voor het Nederlandse Onderwijs: Alkmaar, The Netherlands, 7–11.

García, Ofelia, 2009: *Bilingual Education in the 21st Century: A Global Perspective*. Wiley-Blackwell: Malden, MA.

Garrison, D. Randy, 2004: "Cognitive presence in online learning". *Journal of Computing in Higher Education* 15(2), 30–48.

Garrison, D. Randy / Anderson, Terry / Archer, Walter, 2000: "Critical inquiry in a text-based environment: Computer conferencing in higher education". *Internet and Higher Education* 2(2–3), 87–105.

Garrison, D. Randy / Anderson, Terry / Archer, Walter, 2001: "Critical thinking, cognitive presence, and computer conferencing in distance education". *American Journal of Distance Education* 15(1), 7–23.

Garrison, D. Randy / Cleveland-Innes, Martha, 2005: "Facilitating cognitive presence in online learning: Interaction is not enough". *The American Journal of Distance Education* 19(3), 133–148.

Gasiorek, Jessica / Van de Poel, Kris, 2012: "Divergent perspectives on language-discordant mobile medical professionals' communication with colleagues: An exploratory study". *Journal of Applied Communication Research* 40(August), 368–383.

Gass, Susan M., 2000: "Changing views of language learning". In: Trappes-Lomax, Hugh R. (ed.): *Change and Continuity in Applied Linguistics: Selected Papers from the Annual Meeting of the British Association of Applied Linguistics Edinburgh*. Baal: Edinburgh, 51–67.

Gebhard, Jerry G., 1996: *Teaching English as a Second or Foreign Language*. University of Michigan Press: Ann Arbor, MI.

Gee, James Paul, 2003: *What Video Games have to Teach Us about Learning and Literacy*. Palgrave Macmillan: New York.

Geest, Dirk de / Gorp, Hendrik van, 1999: "Literary genres from a systematic-functionalist approach". *European Journal of English Studies* 3(1), 33–50.

Gerlach, Jeanne Marcum, 1994: "Is this collaboration?" In: Bosworth, Kris / Hamilton, Sharon J. (eds): *Collaborative Learning: Underlying Processes and Effective Techniques, New Directions for Teaching and Learning, No. 59*. Jossey-Bass: San Francisco, CA.

Gerstein, Jackie, 2013: "Team and community building using mobile devices". In: Berge, Zane L. / Muilenburg, Lin Y. (eds): *Handbook of Mobile Learning*. Routledge: New York, 268–284.

Gießing, Jürgen, 2005: "Acht Thesen zum bilingualen Unterricht". *Praxis Fremdsprachenunterricht* 2(1), 33.

Gilmore, Alex, 2007: "Authentic materials and authenticity in foreign language learning". *Language Teaching* 40, 97–118.

Gimenez, Julio C., 2002: "New media and conflicting realities in multinational corporate communication. A case study". *IRAL: International Review of Applied Linguistics in Language Teaching* 40(4), 323–343.

Gläsman, Sabine, 2004: "Communication online". In: Hewer, Sue (ed.): *Infotech*. CILT: Bedfordbury, UK.

Goffman, Erving, 1981: *Forms of Talk. University of Pennsylvania Publications in Conduct and Communication*. University of Pennsylvania Press: Philadelphia, PA.

González-Lloret, Marta, 2014: "The need for needs analysis in technology-mediated TBLT". In: González-Lloret, Marta / Ortega, Lourdes (eds): *Technology-Mediated TBLT: Research technology and tasks*. John Benjamins B.V.: Amsterdam, 23–50.

González-Lloret, Marta / Ortega, Lourdes, 2014: *Technology-mediated TBLT: Researching Technology and Tasks*. John Benjamins B.V.: Amsterdam.

González-Lloret, Marta / Ortega, Lourdes, 2014: "Towards technology-mediated TBLT. An introduction". In: González-Lloret, Marta / Ortega, Lourdes (eds): *Technology-Mediated TBLT: Research Technology and Tasks*. John Benjamins B.V.: Amsterdam, 1– 22.

Godwin-Jones, Robert 2003. "Blogs and wikis: Environments for on-line collaboration". *Language Learning and Technology* 7(2), 12–16.

Gordon, Louise, 2008: "Writing and good language learners". In: Griffiths, Carol (ed.): *Lessons from Good Language Learners*. Cambridge University Press: Cambridge, 244–254.

Görtler, Senta 2009. "Using computer-mediated communication (CMC) in language teaching". *Die Unterrichtspraxis/Teaching German* 42(1), 74–83.

Government of United Kingdom, n.d.: "Ethnographic research". Retrieved 4.7.2014, from https://www.gov.uk/service-manual/user-centred-design/user-research/ethnographic-research.html.

Grabe, William / Kaplan, Robert B., 1996: *Theory and Practice of Writing*. Longman: London.

Graham, Charles R., 2005: "Blended learning systems: Definition, current trends, and future directions". In: Bonk, Curtis. J. / Graham, Charles R. (eds): *The Handbook of Blended Learning: Global Perspectives, Local Designs.* John Wiley & Sons: Hoboken, NJ, 3–19.

Grimm, Nancy, 2013: "Digital media: Promise for or threat to education?" In: Eisenmann, Maria / Summer, Theresa (eds): *Basic Issues in EFL Teaching and Learning.* Winter: Heidelberg, 229–239.

Grimm, Nancy / Hammer, Julia, 2014: "Now, here, and everywhere. Mit Edu-Apps blended learning/Szenarien gestalten und mobil lernen". *Der fremdsprachliche Unterricht Englisch* 128, 2–7.

Groundwater-Smith, S., 1993: "Beyond the individual: Collaborative writing and the microcomputer". In: Monteith, Moira (ed.): *Computers and Language.* Intellect Books: Oxford, 9–20.

Grünewald, Andreas, 2006: *Multimedia im Fremdsprachenunterricht: Motivationsverlauf und Selbsteinschätzung des Lernfortschritts im computergestützten Spanischunterricht.* Peter Lang: Frankfurt a.M.

Grünewald, Andreas, 2010: "e-Learning". In: Surkamp, Carola (ed.): *Metzlers Lexikon Fremdsprachendidaktik.* J.B. Metzler: Suttgart, 41–45.

Guichon, Nicolas / Hauck, Mirjam 2011: "Editorial: Teacher education research in CALL and CMC: more in demand than ever". *ReCALL* 23(3), 187–199.

Gunawardena, Charlotte. N., 1995: "Social presence theory and implications for interaction and collaborative learning in computer conferences". *International Journal of Educational Telecommunications* 1(2–3), 147–166.

Gunawardena, Charlotte. N. / Zittle, Frank, 1997: "Social presence as a predictor of satisfaction within a computer mediated conferencing environment". *American Journal of Distance Education* 11(3), 8–25.

Gündüz, Nanzli, 2005: "Computer assisted language learning". *Journal of Language and Linguistic Studies* 1(2), 193–214.

Guth, Sarah / Helm, Francesca, 2011: *Developing Multiliteracies in ELT through Telecollaboration.* Oxford University Press: Oxford.

Haas, Christophe, 1989: "How the writing medium shapes the writing process: Effects of word processing on planning". *Research in the Teaching of English* 23, 181–207.

Hafner, Christoph A. / Miller, Lindsay, 2011: "Fostering learner autonomy in English for science – a collaborative digital video project in a technological learning environment". *Language Learning and Technology* 15(3), 68–86.

Hamilton, Miranda, 2013: *Autonomy and Foreign Language Learning in a Virtual Learning Environment.* Bloomsbury: London.

Hara, Noriko / Bonk, Curtis J. / Angeli, Charoula, 2000: "Content analysis of online discussion in an applied educational psychology course". *Instructional Science* 25(2), 115–152.

Harklau, Linda, 2002: "The role of writing in classroom second language acquisition". *Journal of Second Language Writing* 11, 329–350.

Harmer, Jeremy, 2004: *How to Teach Writing*. Pearson: Harlow, UK.

Harmer, Jeremy, 2007: *How to Teach English*. Longman: London.

Hatch, Evelyn M., 1978: "Discourse analysis and second language acquisition". In: Hatch, Evelyn M. (ed.): *Second Language Acquisition – a Book of Readings*. Newbury House: Rowley, MA, 401–435.

Hathorn, Lesley G. / Ingram, Albert L., 2002: "Cooperation and collaboration using computer-mediated communication". *Journal of Educational Computing Research* 26(3), 325–347.

Hauck, Mirjam / Lewis, Tim, 2007: "The tridem project". In: O'Dowd, Robert (ed.) *Online Intercultural Exchange: An Introduction for Foreign Language Teachers*. Multilingual Matters Ltd: Bristol, UK, 250–259.

Hauck, Mirjam / Youngs, Bonny L., 2008: "Telecollaboration in multimodal environments: The impact on task design and learner interaction". *Computer Assisted Language Learning* 21(2), 87–124.

Hauck, Mirjam / Warnecke, Sylvia, 2012: "Materials design in CALL: Social presence in online environments". In: Thomas, Michael / Reinders, Hayo / Warschauer, Mark (eds): *Contemporary Computer-assisted Language Learning*. Continuum: London/New York, 95–116.

Haythornthwaite, Caroline / Kazmer, Michelle M. / Robins, Jennifer / Shoemaker, Susan, 2000: "Community development among distance learners: Temporal and technological dimensions". *Journal of Computer Mediated Communication* 6(1), 211–226.

Heacox, Diane, 2012: *Differentiating Instruction in the Regular Classroom. How to Reach and Teach All Learners*. Free Spirit: Minneapolis, IL.

Heartland Area Education Agency, 2006: "Strategies and tools for group processing". Retrieved 23.8.2015, from http://learningteams.pbworks.com/f/Facilitation+Tools+%26+Strategies.pdf.

Hellekjær, Glenn Ole, 2009: Academic English reading proficiency at the university level: A Norwegian case study". *Reading in a Foreign Language* 21(2), 198–222.

Hemmi, Chantal, 2006: "'Ganbarism', an art in the craft of collaborative learning". *IATEFL Voices* 187, 5–6.

Henri, France / Rigault, Claude Ricciardi, 1996: "Collaborative distance learning and computer conferencing". In: Laio, Thomas (ed.): *Advanced Educational Technology: Research Issues and Future Potential*. Springer: Berlin/Heidelberg, 45–76.

Hernández, Nuria / González, Mercedes / Muñoz, Pablo 2014: "Planning collaborative learning in virtual environments". *Comunicar* 21(42), 25–32.

Herring, Susan C., 2007: "A faceted classification scheme for computer-mediated discourse". *Language@Internet* 4(1).

Herring, Susan C. / Kouper, Inna / Scheidt, Lois Ann / Wright, Elijah L., 2004: "Women and children last: The discursive construction of weblogs". In: Gurak, Laura /Antonijevic, Smiljana / Johnson, Laurie / Ratliff, Clancy / Reyman, Jessica (eds): *Into the Blogosphere: Rhetoric, Community, and Culture of Weblogs*. Retrieved 31.1.2010, from http://blog.lib.umn.edu/blogosphere/.

Hine, Christine, 2000: *Virtual Ethnography*. Sage: London.

Hockly, Nicky, 2013: "Mobile learning". *English Language Teaching Journal* 67(1), 80–84.

Hockly, Nicky, 2015: "Online intercultural exchanges". *ELT Journal* 69(1), 81–85.

Holliday, Adrian, 2013: "Authenticity, communities and hidden potentials". Paper presented at the British Council International English Language Teacher Educator Conference, Hyderabad, India.

Hornby, Albert Sydney / Cowie, Anthony Paul / Lewis, Jack Windsor, 1974: *Oxford Advanced Learner's Dictionary of Current English*. Oxford University Press: London.

Hsin-chou, Huang / Chiou-lan, Chern / Chih-cheng, Lin, 2009: "EFL learners' use of online reading strategies and comprehension of texts: An exploratory study". *Computers & Education* 52(1), 13–26.

Hu, Long, 2001: *Computer Assisted Language Learning: Multimedia and Networking Applications*. Shanghai Foreign Language Education Press: Shanghai.

Huang, Heng-Tsung Danny / Shao-Ting, Alan Hung, 2013: "Exploring the utility of a video-based online EFL discussion forum". *British Journal of Educational Technology* 44(3), E90–E94.

Hubbard, Philip, 2013: "Making a case for learner training in technology enhanced language learning environments". *CALICO Journal* 30(2), 163–178.

Hudelson, Sarah, 1988: "Writing in a second language". *Annual Review of Applied Linguistics* 9, 210–222.

Horwitz, Elaine K. / Horwitz, Michael B. / Cope, Joann, 1986. "Foreign language classroom anxiety". *The Modern Language Journal* 70(2), 125–132.

Hurd, Stella, 2007: "Distant voices: Learners' stories about the affective side of learning a language at a distance". *Innovation in Language Learning and Teaching* 1(2), 242–259.

Hurd, Stella, 2008: "Affect and strategy use in independent language learning". In: Hurd, Stella / Lewis, Tim (eds): *Language Learning Strategies in Independent Settings*. Multilingual Matters: Bristol, UK, 218–236.

Hyland, Ken, 2002: *Teaching and Researching Writing*. Longman: London.

Hyland, Ken, 2003: *Second Language Writing*. Cambridge University Press: Cambridge.

Hyland, Ken, 2006: "The 'other' English: Thoughts on EAP and academic writing". *The European English Messenger* 15(2), 34–38.

Hyland, Ken, 2009: *Academic Discourse: English in a Global Context*. Continuum: London.

Hyland, Ken / Hyland, Fiona, 2006: "Feedback on second language students' writing". *Language Teaching* 39(2), 83–101.

Illés, Éva, 2012: "Learner autonomy revisited". *English Language Teaching Journal* 66(4), 505–513.

Inkelas, Karen Kurotsuchi / Weisman, Jennifer L., 2003: "Different by design: An examination of student outcomes among participants in three types of living-learning programs". *Journal of College Student Development* 44, 335–368.

Interactive Software Federation of Europe (ISFE), 2012: *Videogames in Europe: Consumer Study. European Summary Report: November 2012*. Retrieved 30.9.2015, from http://www.isfe.eu/sites/isfe.eu/files/attachments/euro_summary_-_isfe_consumer_study.pdf.

Jauregi, Kristi / De Graaff, Rick / Van den Bergh, Huub / Kriz, Milan, 2011: "Native/non-native speaker interactions through video-web communication: A clue for enhancing motivation?" *Computer Assisted Language Learning* 25(1), 1–19.

Jenkins, Henry, 2009: *Confronting the Challenges of Participatory Culture: Media Education for the 21st Century*. The MIT Press: Cambridge, MA.

Jenkins, Jennifer, 1998: "Which pronunciation norms and models for English as an international language?" *English Language Teaching Journal* 52(2), 119–126.

Jepson, Kevin, 2005: "Conversations – and negotiated interaction – in text and voice chat rooms". *Language Learning & Technology* 9(3), 79–98.

Jessmer, Sherri L. / Anderson, David, 2001: "The effect of politeness and grammar on user perceptions of electronic mail". *North American Journal of Psychology* 3(2), 331–346.

Jin, Li / Erben, Tony, 2007: "Intercultural learning via instant messenger interaction". *CALICO Journal* 24(2), 291–311.

Jin, Seunghee, 2015: "Using facebook to promote Korean EFL learners' intercultural competence". *Language Learning & Technology* 19(3), 38–51.

Johns, Ann M., 1997: *Text, Role, and Context: Developing Academic Literacies*. Cambridge University Press: Cambridge.

Johns, Tim, 1994: "From printout to handout: Grammar and vocabulary teaching in the context of John-Steiner, Vera / Mahn, Holbrook, 2011: Sociocultural approaches to learning and development: A Vygotskian framework". *Educational Psychologist* 31(3–4), 191–206. Retrieved 12.10.2015, from DOI 10.1080/00461520.1996.9653266.

Johns, Tim. 1994: "From printout to handout: Grammar and vocabulary teaching in the context of data-driven learning". In: Odlin, Terence (ed.): *Perspectives on Pedagogical Grammar*. Cambridge University Press: Cambridge, 293–313.

John-Steiner, Vera / Mahn, Holbrook, 2011: "Sociocultural approaches to learning and development: A Vygotskian framework". *Educational Psychologist* 31(3–4), 191–206. Retrieved 12.10.2015, from DOI 10.1080/00461520.1996.9653266.

Johnston, Bill, 1999: "Theory and research: Audience, language use, and language learning". In: Egbert, Joy / Hanson-Smith, Elizabeth (eds): *CALL Environments: Research, Practice, and Critical Issues*. Teachers of English to Speakers of Other Languages: Alexandria, VA, 55–78.

Johnson, David W. / Johnson, Roger T. / Holubec, Edythe J., 1991: *Cooperation in the Classroom*. Interaction Book Company: Edina, MN.

Johnson, David W. / Johnson, Roger T. / Holubec, Edythe J., 1993: *Circles of Learning: Cooperation in the Classroom*. Interaction: Edina, MN.

Jolliffe, Wendy, 2007: *Cooperative Learning in the Classroom*. Paul Chapman: London.

Jonassen, David / Davidson, Mark / Collins, Mauri / Campbell, John / Haag, Brenda B., 1995: "Constructivism and computer-mediated communication in distance education". *American Journal of Distance Education*, 7–26.

Jones, Christopher, 1986: "It's not so much the program, more what you do with it". *System* 14(2), 171–178.

Kabata, Kaori / Edasawa, Yasuyo, 2011: "Tandem language learning through a cross-cultural keypal project". *Language Learning & Technology* 15(1), 104–121.

Kafai, Yasmin B. / Fields, Deborah A., 2013: "Collaboration in informal learning environments: Access and participation in youth virtual communities". In: Hmelo-Silver, Cindy E. / Chinn, Clark A. / Chan, Carol / O'Donnell, Angela M. (eds): *The International Handbook of Collaborative Learning*. Routledge: New York, 480–494.

Kamhi-Stein, Lía D., 2000: "Looking to the future of TESOL teacher education: Web-based bulletin board discussions in a methods course". *TESOL Quarterly* 34(3), 423–455.

Kankaanranta, Anne, 2005: "'Hej Seppo, could you pls comment on this!' Internal email communication in lingua franca English in a multinational company". Jyväskylä University Printing House: Centre for Applied Language Studies, Jyväskylä, Finland.

Kankaanranta, Anne, 2006: "'Hej Seppo, could you pls comment on this!' – Internal email communication in lingua franca English in a multinational company". *Business Communication Quarterly* 69(2), 216–225.

Kaplan, Andreas M. / Haenlein, Michael, 2010: "Users of the world, unite! The challenges and opportunities of social media". *Business Horizons* 53(1), 59–68. Retrieved 1.8.2016, from http://michaelhaenlein.eu/Publications/Kaplan,%20Andreas%20-%20Users%20of%20the%20world,%20unite.pdf.

Kaplan, Andreas M. / Haenlein, Michael, 2011: "The early bird catches the news: Nine things you should know about micro-blogging". *Business Horizons* 54(2).

Kashiwagi, Harumi / Kang, M. / Kato, Masayuki / Sekiguchi, Sachiyo, 2006: "Effects of various communication tools on foreign language learners". 7th International Conference on Information Technology Based Higher Education and Training (ITHET), 10–13 July 2006, Sydney, Australia.

Kehrwald, Ben, 2008: "Understanding social presence in text-based online learning environments". *Distance Education* 29(1), 89–106.

Kehrwald, Ben, 2010: "Being online: Social presence and subjectivity in online learning". *London Review of Education* 8(1), 39–50.

Keller, Stefan, 2013: *Integrative Schreibdidaktik Englisch für die Sekundarstufe*. Narr: Tübingen.

Kern, Richard / Warschauer, Mark, 2000: "Theory and practice of network-based language teaching". In: Kern, Richard / Warschauer, Mark (eds): *Network-based Language Teaching*. Cambridge University Press: Cambridge.

Kessler, Greg, 2009: "Student-initiated attention to form in wiki-based collaborative writing". *Language Learning and Technology* 13(1), 79–95.

Kilian, Dietmar / Krismer, Robert / Loreck, Stefan / Sagmeister, Andreas, 2007: *Wissensmanagement: Werkzeuge für Praktiker*. Linde: Wien.

Kinney, Jeff, 2011: *Diary of a Wimpy Kid: A Novel in Cartoons*. Klett: Stuttgart.

Kirschner, Paul A. / Kirschner, Femke / Janssen, Jeroen, 2014: "The collaboration principle in multimedia learning". In: Mayer, Richard E. (ed.): *The Cambridge Handbook of Multimedia Learning*. Cambridge University Press: Cambridge, 547–575.

Kitade, Keiko, 2002: "L2 Learners' discourse and Sla theories in Cmc: Collaborative interaction in internet chat". *Computer Assisted Language Learning* 13(2), 143–166.

Kitzinger, Jenny, 1999: *A Sociology of Media Power: Key Issues in Audience Reception Research. Message Received.* Longman: Harlow, UK, 207–243.

Klemm, Uwe., 2008: "Weblog 'a long way down'". *Praxis Fremdsprachenunterricht* 1, 37–40.

Knupsky, Aimee C. / Nagy-Bell, Natalie M., 2011: "Dear Professor. The influence of recipient sex and status on personalization and politeness in e-mail". *Journal of Language and Social Psychology* 30(1), 103–113.

Koch, Peter / Oesterreicher, Wulff, 1994: "Schriftlichkeit und Sprache". In: Günther, Hartmut / Ludwig, Otto (eds): *Schrift und Schriftlichkeit/Writing and Its Use. Ein interdisziplinäres Handbuch internationaler Forschung/An Interdisciplinary Handbook of International Research.* De Gruyter Mouton: Berlin/New York, 587–604.

Koen, Billy Vaughn, 1985: *Definition of the Engineering Method* (Monograph of the American Society for Engineering Education). ASEE: Washington, DC.

Koen, Billy Vaughn, 2003: *Discussion of the Method: Conducting the Engineer's Approach to Problem Solving.* Oxford University Press: New York.

Kongmee, Isara / Strachan, Rebecca / Montgomery, Catherine / Pickard, Alison, 2011. "Using massively multiplayer online role playing games (MMORPGs) to support second language learning: Action research in the real and virtual world". Second Annual IVERG Conference: Immersive Technologies for Learning: Virtual Implementation, Real Outcomes, 27–28 June 2011, Middlesbrough, United Kingdom.

Königs, Frank G., 2015: "Ortstermin. Beobachtungen zur Bedeutung der Lernorte für das Lehren und Lernen von Fremdsprachen". In: Burwitz-Melzer, Eva / Königs, Frank G. / Riemer, Claudia (eds): *Lernen an allen Orten? Die Rolle der Lernorte beim Lehren und Lernen von Fremdsprachen. Arbeitspapiere der 35. Frühjahrskonferenz zur Erforschung des Fremdsprachenunterrichts.* Narr Francke Attempto (Giessener Beiträge zur Fremdsprachendidaktik): Tübingen, 90–97.

Kötter, Markus, 2001: "MOOrituri te salutant? Language learning through MOO-based synchronous exchanges between learner tandems". *CALL* 14(3–4), 289–304.

Kötter, Markus, 2002: "Tandem learning on the internet. Learner interactions in virtual online environments (Moos)". In: Faber, Pamela, *et al.* (eds): *Foreign Language Teaching in Europe* (Vol. 6). Peter Lang: Frankfurt a.M. *et al.*

Kötter, Markus, 2003: "Negotiation of meaning and codeswitching in online tandems". *Language Learning & Technology* 7(2), 145–172.

Krashen, Stephen, 1981: *Second Language Acquisition and Second Language Learning*. Pergamon Press: Oxford.

Krings, Hans P., 1989: "Schreiben in der Fremdsprache – Prozessanalysen zum 'vierten Skill'". In: Antos, Gerd / Krings, Hans P. (eds): *Textproduktion. Ein interdisziplinärer Forschungsüberblick*. Narr: Tübingen, 377–436.

Krings, Hans P., 1992: "Empirische Untersuchungen zu fremdsprachlichen Schreibprozessen – Ein Forschungsüberblick". In: Börner, W. / Vogel, K. (eds): *Schreiben in der Fremdsprache: Prozeß und Text, Lehren und Lernen*. AKS: Bochum, 47–77.

Kultusministerium des Landes Nordrhein-Westfalen, 1995: *Empfehlungen für den bilingualen deutsch-englischen Sachfachunterricht. Sekundarstufe I: Erdkunde*. Ritterbach: Frechen.

Kuropatwa, Darren, 2007: "Twitter: Ephemeral learning tool". Retrieved 25.9.2015, from http://adifference.blogspot.com/2007/07/twitter-ephemeral-learning-tool.html.

Kurtz, Jürgen, 2015: "Dimensionen einer fremdsprachendidaktischen Theorie der Lernorte". In: Burwitz-Melzer, Eva / Königs, Frank G. / Riemer, Claudia (eds): *Lernen an allen Orten? Die Rolle der Lernorte beim Lehren und Lernen von Fremdsprachen. Arbeitspapiere der 35. Frühjahrskonferenz zur Erforschung des Fremdsprachenunterrichts*. Narr Francke Attempto (Giessener Beiträge zur Fremdsprachendidaktik): Tübingen, 106–116.

Laal, Marjan / Laal, Mozhgan / Khattami-Kermanshahi, Zhina, 2012: "21st century learning; learning in collaboration". *Procedia – Social and Behavioral Sciences* 47, 1696–1701. Retrieved from DOI 10.1016/j.sbspro.2012.06.885.

Laal, Marjan / Naseri, Azadeh S. / Laal, Mozhgan / Khattami-Kermanshahi, Zhina, 2013: "What do we achieve from learning in collaboration?" *Procedia – Social and Behavioral Sciences* 93, 1427–1432. Retrieved from DOI: 10.1016/j.sbspro.2013.10.057.

Laat, Maarten de / Lally, Vic / Lipponen, Lasse / Simons, Robert-Jan, 2007: "Investigating patterns of interaction in networked learning and computer-supported collaborative learning: A role for social network analysis". *International Journal of Computer-Supported Collaborative Learning* 2(1), 87–103. Retrieved from DOI 10.1007/s11412-007-9006-4.

Lampa, Graham, 2004: "Imagining the blogosphere: An introduction to the imagined community of instant publishing". In: Gurak, Laura / Antonijevic, Smiljana / Johnson, Lurie / Ratliff, Clancy / Reyman, Jessica (eds): *Into the*

Blogosphere: Rhetoric, Community, and Culture of Weblogs. Retrieved 31.1.2010, from http://blog.lib.umn.edu/blogosphere/imagining_the_blogosphere.html.

Lamsfuß-Schenk, Stefanie / Wolff, Dieter, 1999: Bilingualer Sachfachunterricht: Fünf kritische Anmerkungen zum state of the art. *Zeitschrift für Interkulturellen Fremdsprachenunterricht* 4(2). Retrieved 10.10.2015, from https://zif.spz.tu-darmstadt.de/jg-04-2/beitrag/lamsfus2.htm.

Lamy, Marie-Noelle /Hampel, Regine, 2007: *Online Communication in Language Learning and Teaching.* Palgrave Macmillan: Hampshire, UK/New York.

Langellier, Kristin / Peterson, Eric E. (eds), 2004: *Storytelling in Daily Life: Performing Narrative.* Temple University Press: Philadelphia.

Language Test Report 2010–2013, 2013: *Internal Report.* University of Antwerp, Faculty of Arts, OCTLET-Teaching Council: Antwerp.

Lantolf, James P., 2000. *Sociocultural Theory and Second Language Learning.* Oxford University Press: Oxford.

Lantz-Andersson, Annika / Vigmo, Sylvi / Bowen, Rhonwen, 2013: "Crossing boundaries in Facebook: Students' framing of language learning activities as extended spaces". *International Journal of Computer-Supported Collaborative Learning* 8(3), 293–312.

Laursen, Katja Årosin / Frederiksen, Karen-Margrete, 2015: *The Notion of Authenticity in the Context of the Course: Danish for Knowledge Workers. Task Design and CALL.* Universitat Rovira Virgili: Tarragona, Spain, 61–65.

Leander, Kevin M., 2008: "Toward a connective ethnography of online/offline literacy networks". In: Leu, Donald J. / Cairo, Julie / Knobel, Michele / Lankshear, Colin (eds): *Handbook of Research on New Literacies.* Erlbaum: New York, 33–65.

Lee, Ahreum / Ryu, Hokyoung, 2013: "Social versus individual flow in mobile learning". In: Berge, Zane L. / Muilenburg, Lin Y. (eds): *Handbook of Mobile Learning.* Routledge: New York, 196–208.

Lee, Carol D. / Smagorinsky, Peter (eds), 2000: *Vygotskian Perspectives on Literacy Research: Constructing Meaning Through Collaborative Inquiry.* Cambridge University Press: Cambridge.

Lee, Lina, 2002: "Enhancing learners' communication skills through synchronous electronic interaction and task-based instruction". *Foreign Language Annals* 35(1), 16–24.

Lee, Lina, 2004: "Learners' perspectives on net-worked collaborative interaction with native speakers of Spanish in the US". *Language Learning & Technology* 8(2), 81–100.

Lee, Lina, 2007: "One-to-one desktop videoconferencing for developing oral skills: Prospects in perspective". In: O'Dowd, Robert (ed.): *Online Intercultural*

Exchange: An Introduction for Foreign Language Teachers. Multilingual Matters Ltd: Bristol, UK, 281–286.

Lee, Lina, 2009: "Promoting intercultural exchanges with blogs and podcasting: A study of Spanish-American telecollaboration". Computer Assisted Language Learning 22(5), 425–443.

Lee, Lina, 2010: "Exploring wiki-mediated collaborative writing: A case study in an elementary Spanish course". CALICO Journal 27(2), 260–276.

Lee, Lina / Markey, Alfred, 2014: "A study of learners' perceptions of online intercultural exchange through Web 2.0 technologies". ReCALL 26(3), 281–297.

Lee, Silvia W.-Y. / Tsai, Chin-Chung, 2011: "Students' perception of collaboration, self-regulated learning, and information seeking in the context of internet-based learning and traditional learning". Computers in Human Behavior 27, 905–914.

Legenhausen, Lienhard, 1996: "Cooperative writing and the computer". In: Legenhausen, L. (ed.): Computers in the Foreign Language Classroom. Workshop Report No. 2/96. Council of Europe: Graz, 86–91.

Legenhausen, Lienhard, 2001: "Discourse behaviour in an autonomous learning environment". AILA Review 15, 65–69.

Legenhausen, Lienhard, 2003: "Second language acquisition in an autonomous learning environment". In: Little, David / Ridley, Jennifer / Ushioda, Ema (eds): Learner Autonomy in the Foreign Language Classroom – Teacher, Learner, Curriculum and Assessment. Authentik: Dublin, 65–77.

Legenhausen, Lienhard, 2009: "Autonomous language learning". In: Knapp, Karlfried /Seidlhofer, Barbara (eds): Handbook of Applied Linguistics (Vol. 6: Foreign Language Communication and Learning). De Gruyter Mouton: Berlin, 373–400.

Legenhausen, Lienhard / Kötter, Markus, 2005: "Virtual classrooms in foreign language learning – MOOs as rich learning environments". Humanising Language Teaching 7(1). Retrieved 25.6.2016, from http://hltmag.co.uk/jan05/mart02.htm.

Legenhausen, Lienhard / Wolff, Dieter, 1991: "Der Micro-Computer als Hilfsmittel beim Sprachenlernen: Schreiben als Gruppenaktivität". Praxis des neusprachlichen Unterrichts 4, 346–356.

Legutke, Michael K. / Rösler, Dietmar, 2005: "Enhancing collaborative work by integrating digital media into foreign language teacher education". Fremdsprachen Lehren und Lernen 34, 174–191.

Legutke, Michael K. / Thiel, Wolfgang, 1983: "Airport. Ein Projekt für den Englischunterricht in Klasse 6". Hessisches Institut für Bildungsplanung und Schulentwicklung: Wiesbaden.

Leh, Amy S.C., 2001: "Computer-mediated communication and social presence in a distance learning environment". *International Journal of Educational Telecommunications* 7(2), 109–128.

Leki, Ilona, 2006: "Negotiating socioacademic relations: English learners' reception by and reaction to college faculty". *Journal of English for Academic Purposes* 5(2), 136–152.

Levy, Michael, 1997: *Computer-Assisted Language Learning*. Clarendon: Oxford.

Levy, Michael, 1997: *CALL: Context and Conceptualisation*. Oxford University Press: Oxford.

Levy, Mike /Stockwell, Glenn, 2006: *Call Dimensions. Options and Issues in Computer Assisted Language Learning*. L. Erbaum Associates: Mahwah, NJ.

Lewin-Jones, Jenny / Mason, Victoria, 2014: "Understanding style, language and etiquette in email communication in higher education: a survey". *Research in Post-Compulsory Education* 19(1), 75–90.

Liang, Mei-Ya, 2010: "Using synchronous online peer response groups in EFL writing: Revision-related discourse". *Language Learning and Technology* 14(1), 45–64.

Liaw, M.-L., & English, K. (2013). Online and offsite: Student-driven development of the Taiwan-France telecollaborative project Beyond these walls. In M.-N. Lamy, & K. Zourou (Eds.), Social Networking for Language Education (pp. 158–176). Basingstoke, UK: Palgrave Macmillan.

Liaw, Shu-Sheng, 2004: "Considerations for dveloping constructivist web-based learning". *International Journal of Instructional Media* 31, 309–319.

Liaw, Shu-Sheng / Huang, Hsiu-Mei / Chen, Gwo-Dong, 2007: "Surveying instructor and learner attitudes toward e-learning". *Computers & Education* 49, 1066–1080.

Limberg, Holger, 2015: "Principles for pragmatics teaching: Apologies in the EFL classroom". *ELT Journal* 69(3), 275–285.

Lin, Ming Huei / Li, Ji-Jhen / Hung, Po Yi / Huamg, Hui-Wen, 2014: "Blogging a journal: Changing students' writing skills and perceptions". *ELT Journal* 68(4), 422–431.

Little, David, 1991: *Learner Autonomy, 1: Definitions, Issues and Problems*. Authentik: Dublin.

Little, David, 1995: "Learning as dialogue: The dependence of learner autonomy on teacher autonomy". *System* 23, 175–181.

Little, David, 1996: "Freedom to learn and compulsion to interact: Promoting learner autonomy through the use of information systems and information technologies". In: Pemberton, Richard / Li, Edward S.L. /Or, Winnie, W.F. /

Pierson, Herbert, D (eds): *Taking Control – Autonomy in Language Learning*. Hong Kong University Press: Hong Kong, 203–218.

Little, David, 2004: "Democracy, discourse and learner autonomy in the foreign language classroom". *Utbildning & Demokrati* 13(3), 105–126.

Little, David / Dam, Leni / Legenhausen, Lienhard, forthcoming: *Towards Language Learner Autonomy – Theory and Practice*. Multilingual Matters: Bristol, UK.

Liu, Min, et al., 2013: "A study of the use of social network sites for language learning by university ESL students". In: Lamy, Marie-Noelle / Zourou, Katerina (eds): *Social Networking for Language Education*. Palgrave Macmillan: Basingstoke, UK, 137–158.

Liu, M., Evans, M. K., Horowitz, E., Lee, S., McCrory, M., Park, J., & Parrish, C. M. (2013). A study on the use of social network sites for language learning by university ESL students. In M.-N. Lamy, & K. Zourou (Eds.), Social Networking for Language Education (pp. 137–157). Basingstoke, UK: Palgrave Macmillan.

Lloyd, Elwyn, 2012: "Language learners' 'willingness to communicate' through Livemocha.com". *Apprentissage des Langues et Systèmes d'Information et de Communication* 15(1). Retrieved from alsic.revues.org/2437.

Locke, John, 1693 [1989]: *Some Thoughts Concerning Education*. Clarendon: Oxford.

Logan, Robert K., 2010: *Understanding New Media: Extending Marshall McLuhan*. Peter Lang: Franfurt a.M. et al.

Lomicka, Lara / Lord, Gillian, 2007: "Social presence in virtual communities of FL teachers". *System* 35, 208–228.

Long, Michael H., 1980: *Input, Interaction, and Second Language Acquisition*. Doctoral thesis, University of California: Los Angeles, CA.

Long, Michael H., 1996: "The role of the linguistic environment in second language acquisition". In: Ritchie, William C. / Bhatia, Tej K. (eds): *Handbook of Language Acquisition* (Vol. 2). Academic Press: New York, 413–468.

Lotherington, Heather / Jenson, Jennifer, 2011: "Teaching multimodal and digital literacy in L2 settings. New literacies, new basics, new pedagogies". *Annual Review of Applied Linguistics*, 226.

Lowry, Paul Benjamin / Curtis, Aaron / Lowry, Michelle René, 2004: "Building a taxonomy and nomenclature of collaborative writing to improve interdisciplinary research and practice". *Journal of Business Communication* 41(1), 66–99.

Luppicini, Rocci, 2003: "Categories of virtual learning communities for educational design". *The Quarterly Review of Distance Education* 4(4), 409–416.

Luzzatto, Edda / Di Marco, Giordano (eds), 2010: *Collaborative Learning, Methodology, Types of Interactions and Techniques*. Nova Science Publishers: New York.

Lynch, Tony, 2012: "Traditional and modern skills". In: Eisenmann, Maria / Summer, Theresa (eds): *Basic Issues in EFL Teaching and Learning*. Winter: Heidlberg, 69–81.

Lyster, Roy / Ballinger, Susan, 2011: "Content-based language teaching: Convergent concerns across divergent contexts". *Language Teaching Research* 15(3), 279–288. Retrieved 12.12.2015, from DOI 10.1177/1362168811401150.

Macaro, Ernesto, 1997: *Target Language, Collaborative Learning and Autonomy*. Multilingual Matters Ltd: Bristol, UK.

McBrien, J. Lynn / Cheng, Rui / Jones, Phyllis, 2009: "Virtual spaces: Employing a synchronous online classroom to facilitate student engagement in online learning". *The International Review of Research in Open and Distance Learning* 10(3.

McCarthy, Michael, 1991: *Discourse Analysis for Language Teachers*. Cambridge University Press: Cambridge.

Macdonald, Janet, 2008: *Blended Learning and Online Tutoring*. Gower Publishing Limited: Farnham, UK, 115.

McDonald, Jeanette / Gibson, Chère C., 1998: "Interpersonal dynamics and group development in computer conferencing". *The American Journal of Distance Education* 12(1), 7–25.

McDonald, Joseph P. / Zydney, Janet Mannheimer / Dichter, Alan / McDonald, Elizabeth C., 2012: *Going Online with Protocols: New Tools for Teaching and Learning*. Teachers College Press: New York.

MacGregor, Jean / Smith, Barbara Leigh, 1992: "What is collaborative learning?" In: Goodsell, Anne / Maher, Michelle / Tinto, Vincent / Smith, Barbara Leigh / MacGregor, Jean (eds): *Collaborative Learning: A Sourcebook for Higher Education*. National Center on Postsecondary Teaching, Learning, and Assessment, Pennsylvania State University: Pennsylvania, PA.

McKenzie, Wendy / Murphy, David, 2000: "'I hope this goes somewhere': Evaluation of an online discussion group". *Australasian Journal of Educational Technology* 16(3), 239–257.

McLuhan, Marshall, 2003 (1964): *Understanding Media*. Gingko Press: Berkeley, CA.

McPherson, Maggie / Nunes, Miguel B., 2004: "The failure of a virtual social space (VSS) designed to create a learning community: Lessons learned". *British Journal of Educational Technology* 35(3), 305–321.

Manovich, Lev, 2001: *The Language of New Media*. The MIT Press: Cambridge, MA.

Mansor, Noraien, 2007: "Collaborative learning via email discussion: Strategies for ESL writing classroom". *The Internet TESL Journal* XIII(3). Retrieved 17.8.2015, from http://iteslj.org/Techniques/Mansor-EmailDiscussion/.

Marsh, David (ed.), 2002: *CLIL/EMILE – the European Dimension: Actions, Trends and Foresight Potential*. UniCOM, Continuing Education Centre: Jyväskylä, Finland. Retrieved 10.10.2015, from https://jyx.jyu.fi/dspace/bitstream/handle/123456789/47616/david_marsh-report.pdf?sequence=1.

Marsh, David, 2005: Adding language without taking away. *Guardian Weekly* 8.4.2005. Retrieved 10.10.2015, from http://www.theguardian.com/guardianweekly/story/0,12674,1464367,00.html.

Marsh, David / Langé, Gisella (eds), 2000: *Using Languages to Learn and Learning to Use Languages*. University of Jyväskylä: Jyväskylä, Finland.

Martinez, Hélène, 2008: "The subjective theories of student teachers: Implications for teacher education and research on learner autonomy". In: Lamb, Terry / Reinders, Hayo (eds.): *Learner and Teacher Autonomy: Concepts, Realities, and Responses*. John Benjamins B.V.: Amsterdam, 103–124.

Matz, Frauke, 2014: "Schreiben". In: Lütge, Christiane (ed.): *Englischmethodik. Handbuch für die Sekundarstufe I und II*. Cornelsen: Berlin, 33–50.

Mayer, Richard E., 2014: "Introduction to multimedia learning". In: Mayer, Richard E. (ed.): *The Cambridge Handbook of Multimedia Learning*. Cambridge University Press: Cambridge, 1–24.

Medics on the Move (MoM), 2014: "Language solutions where and when you need them". Retrieved from www.medicsmove.eu.

Mehisto, Peeter / Marsh, David / Frigols, María J., 2008: *Uncovering CLIL – Content and Language Integrated Learning in Bilingual and Multilingual Education*. Macmillan Education: Oxford.

Melouk, Mohamed, 2013: "Some practical implications to students writing failure". *Journal of Literature, Culture/Media Studies* 9(10), 213–221.

Merriam-Webster, n.d. Retrieved 8.8.2015, from http://www.merriam-webster.com/dictionary/authentic.

Merrison, Andrew John / Wilson, Jack J. / Davies, Bethan J. / Haugh, Michael, 2012: "Getting stuff done. Comparing e-mail requests from students in higher education in Britain and Australia". *Journal of Pragmatics* 44(9), 1077–1098.

Merse, Thorsten / Schmidt, Jochen, 2014: "Internet-Medien und Web 2.0". In: Lütge, Christane (ed.): *Englischmethodik. Handbuch für die Sekundarstufe I und II*. Cornelsen: Berlin, 155–175.

Mills, Nicole, 2011: "Situated learning through social networking communities: The development of joint enterprise, mutual engagement, and a shared repertoire". *CALICO Journal* 28(2), 345–368.

Ministerium für Schule und Weiterbildung des Landes Nordrhein-Westfalen (MSW NRW), 2007: *Zu BASS 13–21: Bilingualer Unterricht in der Sekundarstufe I. Runderlass des Ministeriums für Schule und Weiterbildung vom 15.4.2007.* Retrieved 10.10.2015, from http://www.bilingual-ag-nrw.de/Runderlass.pdf.

Ministerium für Schule und Weiterbildung des Landes Nordrhein-Westfalen (MSW NRW), 2012: *Bilingualer Unterricht: Erdkunde deutsch – englisch in der Sekundarstufe.* Retrieved 3.10.2015, from http://www.schulentwicklung.nrw.de/cms/upload/bilingualer_Unterricht/documents/ HR_BU_EkE_SekI_0912.pdf.

Mitchell. Rosamond / Myles, Florence, 1998: *Second Language Learning Theories.* Arnold: London.

Mitnik, Ruben / Recabarren, Matias / Nussbaum, Miguel / Soto, Alvaro, 2009: "Collaborative robotic instruction: A graph teaching experience". *Computers & Education* 53(2), 330–342.

Miyazoe, Terumi / Anderson, Terry, 2010: "Learning outcomes and students' perceptions of online writing: Simultaneous implementation of a forum, blog, and wiki in an EFL blended learning setting". *System* 38(2), 185–199.

Molinari, Deana L, 2004: "The role of social comments in problem-solving groups in an on- line class". *The American Journal of Distance Education* 18(2), 89–101.

Moore-Walter, Lawrie / Dal-Bianco, Veronica, 2015: *Collaborative Language Learning and New Media* (Survey). University of Applied Sciences Burgenland: Eisenstadt, Austria.

Morgan, David L., 2008: "Emergent design". In: Given, Lisa M. (ed.): *The SAGE Encyclopedia of Qualitative Research Methods.* SAGE Publications: London.

Morgan, Siân, 2005: "Peer review". *English Teaching Professional* 38, 29–31.

Morrow, Keith, 1977. "Authentic texts and ESP". In: Holden, Susan (ed.): *English for Specific Purposes.* Modern English Publications: London.

Moser, Heinz, 2008: *Abenteuer Internet. Lernen mit WebQuests.* Pestalozzianum Verlag: Zürich.

Moskaliuk, Johannes, 2010: *Individuelles Lernen und kollaborative Wissenskonstruktion mit Wikis: Ko-Evolution zwischen kognitiven und sozialen Systemen.* Meidenbauer: München.

Motteram, Gary, 2013: "Introduction". In: Motteram, Gary (ed.): *Innovations in Learning Technologies for English Language Teaching.* British Council: London, 5–14.

Mourlas, Constantinos / Tsianos, Nikos / Germanakos, Panagiotis, 2009: "Collaborative learning in a web-based environment". In: Mourlas, Constantinos (ed.): *Cognitive and Emotional Processes in Web-based Education: Integrating Human Factors and Personalization.* Information Science Reference: Hershey, PA.

Müge, Satar H. / Özdener, Nesrin, 2008: "The effects of synchronous CMC on speaking proficiency and anxiety: Text versus voice chat". *The Modern Language Journal* 92(4), 595–613.

Müller-Hartmann, Andreas, 2006: "Learning how to teach intercultural communicative competence via telecollaboration: A model for language teacher education". In: Belz, Julie A. / Thorne, Steven L. (eds): *Internet-Mediated Intercultural Foreign Language Education*. Heinle & Heinle: Boston, 63–83.

Mulligan, Christopher / Garofaro, Russell, 2011: "A collaborative writing approach: Methodology and student assessment". *The Language Teacher* 35(3), 5–10.

Munro, Murray J., 2010: "Intelligibility: Buzzword or buzzworthy?". In: Levis, John / LeVelle, Kimberly (eds): *Proceedings of the 2nd Pronunciation in Second Language Learning and Teaching Conference, September 2010*. Iowa State University: Ames, IA, 7–16.

Murphy, Linda, 2011: "I'm not giving up! Motivation maintenance in independent language learning". In: Morrison, Bruce (ed.): *Independent Learning: Building on Experience, Seeking New Perspectives*. Hong Kong University Press: Hong Kong, 73–86.

Murray, Garold, 2014: *Social Dimensions of Autonomy*. Palgrave Macmillan: Basingstoke, UK.

Nguyen, Le Thi Cam / Gu, Yongqi, 2013: "Strategy-based instruction: A learner-focused approach to developing learner autonomy". *Language Teaching Research* 17(1), 9–30.

Nikou, Stavros A. / Economides, Anastatios A., 2013: "Mobile assessment. State of the art". In: Berge, Zane L. / Muilenburg, Lin Y. (eds): *Handbook of Mobile Learning*. Routledge: New York, 346–355.

O'Brien, Teresa, 2004: "Writing in a foreign language: Teaching and learning". *Language Teaching* 37(1), 1–28.

O'Bryan, Anne / Hegelheimer, Volker, 2007: "Integrating CALL into the classroom: The role of podcasting in an ESL listening strategies course". *ReCALL* 19(2), 162–180.

O'Dell, Charlotte, n.d. "Blog". Retrieved from http://westmore-blog.blogspot.de/.

O'Dowd, Robert, 2003: "Understanding the 'other side': Intercultural learning in a Spanish-English e-mail exchange". *Language Learning & Technology* 7(2), 118–144.

O'Dowd, Robert, 2006: "The use of videoconferencing and e-mail as mediators of intercultural student ethnography". In: Belz, Julie A. / Thorne, Steven L. (eds): *Internet-Mediated Intercultural Foreign Language Education*. Thomson Heinle: Boston, 86–121.

O'Dowd, Robert, 2006: "Telecollaboration and the development of intercultural communicative competence". In: Klippel, Friederike (ed.): *Münchener Arbeiten Zur Fremdsprachen-Forschung* (Vol. 13). Langenscheidt: München.

O'Dowd, Robert / Ware, Paige, 2009: "Critical issues in telecollaborative task design". *Computer Assisted Language Learning* 22(2), 173–188.

O'Dowd, Robert, 2007: "Evaluating the outcomes of online intercultural exchange". *ELT Journal* 61(2), 144–152.

O'Dowd, Robert, 2007: "Foreign language education and the rise of online communication: A review of promises and realities". In: O'Dowd, Robert (ed.): *Online Intercultural Exchange: An Introduction for Foreign Language Teachers.* Multilingual Matters Ltd: Bristol, UK, 17–37.

O'Dowd, Robert, 2010: "Issues in the assessment of online interaction and exchange". In: Guth, Sarah / Helm, Francesca (eds): *Telecollaboration 2.0: Language and Intercultural Learning in the 21st Century.* Peter Lang Verlag: Berne, 2, 337–360.

O'Dowd, Robert / Ritter, Markus, 2006: "Understanding and working with 'failed communication' in telecollaborative exchanges". *CALICO Journal* 23(3), 623–642.

Ohta, Amy Snyder / Foster, Pauline, 2005: "Negotiation for meaning and peer assistance in second language classrooms". *Applied* **Linguistics** 26(3), 402–430.

Oliver, Beverley / Goerke, Veronica, 2007: "Australian undergraduates' use and ownership of emerging technologies: Implications and opportunities for creating engaging learning experiences for the Net Generation". *Australasian Journal of Educational Technology* 23(2), 171–186.

Oliver, Martin / Trigwell, Keith, 2005: "Can 'blended learning' be redeemed?" *e-Learning* 2, 17–26.

Ong, Walter J., 1975: "The writer's audience is always a fiction". *PMLA* 90(1), 9–21.

O'Reilly, Tim, 2005: "What Is Web 2.0: Design patterns and business models for the next generation of software". Retrieved from http://oreilly.com/web2/archive/what-is-web-20.html.

O'Reilly, Tim, 2005: "What Is Web 2.0?: Blogging and the wisdom of crowds". Retrieved 20.8.2016, from http://www.oreilly.com/pub/a/web2/archive/what-is-web-20.html?page=3.

O'Reilly, Tim, 2005: "Web 2.0: Compact definition". Retrieved 5.9.2015, from http://radar.oreilly.com/archives/2005/10/web_20_compact_definition.

Oxford, Rebecca L., 1990: "Missing link: Evidence from research on language learning styles and strategies". In: Alatis, James E. (ed.): *Georgetown University Round Table on Languages and Linguistics. The Interdependence of Theory, Practice and Research.* Georgetown University Press: Washington, DC, 439–456.

Oxford, Rebecca. L., 1990: *Language Learning Strategies: What Every Teacher should Know*. Newbury House: Englewood Cliffs, NJ.

Oxford University Press ELT, n.d: "The language legacy of the olympics". Retrieved 20.8.2016, from https://oupeltglobalblog.com/2013/01/08/the-language-legacy-of-the-olympics/.

Palme, Jacob, 1995: *Electronic Mail*. Artech House: Boston.

Panitz, Ted, 1997: "Collaborative versus cooperative learning: Comparing the two definitions helps understand the nature of interactive learning". *Cooperative Learning and College Teaching* 8(2), 5.

Paramskas, Dana, 1993: "Computer-assisted language learning (CALL): Increasingly integrated into an ever more electronic world". *Canadian Modern Language Review* 50, 124–143.

Peterson, Mark, 2010: "Massively multiplayer online role-playing games as arenas for second language learning". *Computer-Assisted Language Learning* 23(5), 429–439.

Peterson, Mark, 2012: "Learner interaction in a massive multiplayer role-playing game (MMORPG): A sociocultural analysis". *ReCall* 24(3), 361–380.

Paulus, Trena M., 2005: "Collaboration or cooperation? Analysing small group interactions in educational environments". In: Roberts, Tim S. (ed.): *Computer-Supported Collaborative Learning in Higher Education*. Idea Group Publishing: London, 100–124.

Pegrum, Mark, 2009: "Communicative networking and linguistic mashups on Web 2.0". In: Thomas, Michael (ed.): *Handbook of Research on Web 2.0 and Second Language Learning. Information Science Reference* (Vol 2). Hershey, PA, 20–41.

Pellettieri, Jill, 2000: "Negotiation in cyberspace: The role of chatting in the development of grammatical competence". In: Warschauer, Mark / Kern, Richard (eds): *Network-Based Language Teaching: Concepts and Practice* (The Cambridge Applied Linguistics Series). Cambridge University Press: Cambridge, 59–87.

Pennington, Martha C., 1992: "Beyond off-the-shelf computer remedies for student writers: Alternatives to canned feedback". *System* 20(4), 423–437.

Peregoy, Suzanne F. / Boyle, Owen F., 1997: *Reading, Writing & Learning in ESL: A Resource Book for K-12 Teachers* (2nd ed.). Longman: New York.

Perez, Luisa C., 2003: "Foreign language productivity in synchronous versus asynchronous computer-mediated communication". *CALICO Journal* 21(1), 89–104.

Peters, Martine / Weinberg, Alysse / Sarma, Nandini, 2009: "To like or not to like! Student perceptions of technological activities for learning French as a second language at five Canadian universities". *Canadian Modern Language Review* 65(5), 869–896.

Peeters, W. (2015). Tapping into the educational potential of Facebook: Encouraging out-of-class peer collaboration in foreign language learning. Studies in Self-Access Learning Journal, 6(2), 176–190.

Pica, Teresa / Doughty, Catherine, 1985: "Input and interaction in the communicative language classroom: A comparison of teacher-fronted and group activities". In: Gass, Susan M. / Madden, Carolyn G. (eds): *Input in Second Language Acquisition*. Newbury House: Rowley, MA, 115–132.

Pihkala-Posti, Laura, 2015: "Spielerische Kollaboration und kommunikative Authentizität mit Minecraft". *GFL – German as a Foreign Language* 2, 99–132.

Pike, Gary R. / Kuh, George D. / McCormick, Alexander C., 2010: "An investigation of the contingent relationships between learning community participation and student engagement". *Research in Higher Education*, 52, 300–322.

Pinner, Richard, 2014: "The authenticity continuum: Towards a definition incorporating international voices". *English Today* 30, 22–27.

Pontes, Catarina / Shimazumi, Marilisa, 2015: "Learning-to-learn with ourselves and with our peers through technology". In: Nunan, David / Richards, Jack C. (eds): *Language Learning Beyond the Classroom* (ESL & Applied Linguistics Professional Series). Routledge: New York, 180–189.

Prabhu, N.S., 1987: *Second Language Pedagogy*. Oxford University Press: Oxford.

Prensky, Marc, 2001: "Digital natives, digital Immigrants, Part 1". *On the Horizon* 9(5), 1–6. Retrieved 1.8.2016, from DOI http://dx.doi.org/10.1108/10748120110424816.

Prensky, M., 2005: "Engage me or enrage me. What today's learners demand". *EDUCAUSE* S, 60–64.

Pritchard, Caleb, 2013: "Training L2 learners to use Facebook". *CALICO Journal* 30(2), 204–225.

Pugliese, Rossella, 2011: "Vom traditionellen Sprachportfolio zum E-Portfolio. Wege zur Autonomie beim Erwerb der deutschen Sprache". In: Arntz, Reiner / Krings, Hans Peter / Kühn, Bärbel (eds): *Autonomie und Motivation. Erträge des 2. Bremer Symposiums zum Autonomen Fremdsprachenlernen*. AKS: Bochum, 195–209.

Rafaeli, Sheizaf, 1988: "Interactivity: From new media to communication". *Sage Annual Review of Communication Research: Advancing Communication Science* 16, 110–134.

Rafieyan, Vahid / Sharafi-Nejad, Maryam / Khavari, Zahra / Eng, Lin Siew / Mohamed, Abdul Rashid, 2014: "Pragmatic comprehension development through telecollaboration". *English Language Teaching* 7(2), 11–19.

Raith, Thomas, 2006: "Lesegepräche im Weblog: Aufgabenorientierte Arbeit mit dem Jugendroman *If You Come Softly*". *Der Fremdsprachliche Unterricht English* 84, 28–31.

Raith, Thomas, 2009: "The use of weblogs in language education". In: Thomas, M. (ed.): *Handbook of Research on Web 2.0 and Second Language Learning*. Information Science Reference: Hershey, PA, 274–291.

Rama, Paul / Black, Rebecca / Van Es, Elizabeth / Warschauer, Mark, 2012: "Affordances for second language learning in world of warcraft". *ReCall* 24(3), 322–338.

Ranalli, Jim, 2008: "Learning English with the Sims: Exploiting authentic computer simulation games for L2 learning". *Computer Assisted Language Learning* 21(5), 441–455.

Reich, Kersten, 2008: *Methodenpool Uni Köln – Experiment*. Retrieved 2.9.2015, from http://methodenpool.uni-koeln.de/download/experiment.pdf.

Reinfried, Marcus / Volkmann, Laurenz, 2012: *Medien im neokommunikativen Fremdsprachenunterricht: Einsatzformen, Inhalte, Lernerkompetenzen; Beiträge zum IX. Mediendidaktischen Kolloquium an der Friedrich-Schiller-Universität Jena*. Peter Lang: Frankfurt a.M. et al.

Reinders, Hayo / Hubbard, Philip, 2013: "CALL and learner autonomy: Affordances and constraints". In: Thomas, Michael / Reinders, Hayo / Warschauer, Mark (eds): *Contemporary Computer-Assisted Language Learning*. Continuum: New York, 359–375.

Reuven, Aviv / Zippy, Erlich / Gilad, Ravid / Aviva, Geva, 2003: "Network analysis of knowledge construction in asynchronous learning networks". *Journal of Asynchronous Learning Networks* 7(3), 1–23.

Reynolds, Thomas / Greiner, Cathleen, 2005: "Integrated field experiences in online teacher education: A natural blend". In: Bonk, Curtis J. / Graham, Charles R. (eds): *The Handbook of Blended Learning: Global Perspectives, Local Designs*. Pfeiffer Publishing: San Francisco, CA.

Rivers, Wilga M., 1968: *Teaching Foreign Language Skills*. University of Chicago Press: Chicago, IL.

Robinson, Peter, 2011: *Second Language Task Complexity: Researching the Cognition Hypothesis of Language Learning and Performance*. John Benjamins B.V.: Amsterdam.

Roen, Duane H., 1989: "Developing effective assignments for second language writers". In: Johnson, Donna M. / Roen, DuaneH. (eds): *Richness in Writing. Empowering ESL students*. Longman: New York, 193–206.

Romero Margarida / Usart Mireia / Ott Michaela / Earp Jeffrey, de Freitas S., 2012: "Learning Through Playing for or Against Each Other? Promoting Collaborative

Learning Learning in Digital Game Based Learning." ECIS 2012 Proceedings. Paper 93. Retrieved 6.2.2017, from http://aisel.aisnet.org/ecis2012/93.

Rourke, Liam / Anderson, Terry / Garrison, Randy D. / Archer, Walter, 2001: "Assessing social presence in asynchronous text-based computer conferencing". Journal of Distance Education 14(3), 51–70.

Roschelle, Jeremy / Teasley, Stephanie D., 1995: "The construction of shared knowledge in collaborative problem solving". In: O'Malley, Claire (ed.): *Computer Supported Collaborative Learning*. Springer Verlag: Berlin/Heidelberg, 69, 97.

Rose, Heath / Elliott, Roxanne, 2010: "An investigation of student use of a self-access English-only speaking area". *Studies in Self-Access Learning Journal* 1(1), 32–46.

Rosenberg, Scott, 2009: *Say Everything: How Blogging Began, What It's Becoming, and Why It Matters*. Three Rivers Press: New York.

Rösler, Dietmar, 2007: *E-Learning Fremdsprachen – Eine Kritische Einführung* (2nd ed.). Stauffenburg: Tübingen.

Rowe Krapels, Alexandra, 1990: "An overview of second language writing process research". In: Kroll, Barbara (ed.): *Second Language Writing. Research Insights for the Classroom*. Cambridge University Press: Cambridge, 37–56.

Rubrico, Jessie Grace U. / Hashim, Fatimah, 2014: "Facebook-Photovoice interface: Empowering non-native pre-service English language teachers". *Language Learning & Technology* 18(3), 16–34.

Rumlich, Dominik, 2016: *Evaluating Bilingual Education in Germany. CLIL Students' General English Proficiency, EFL Self-concept and Interest*. Peter Lang: Frankfurt a.M. et al.

Rüschoff, Bernd, 2009: "Output-oriented language learning with digital media". In: Thomas, Michael (ed.): *Handbook of Research on Web 2.0 and Second Language Learning*. Information Science Reference: Hershey, PA, 42–59.

Rystedt, Hans / Sjöblom, Björn, 2012: "Realism, authenticity, and learning in healthcare simulations: Rules of relevance as interactive achievements". *Instructional Science* 40(5), 785–798.

Sadler, Randall, 2007: "Computer-mediated communication and a cautionary tale of two cities". *CALICO Journal* 25(1), 11–30.

Salaberry, Rafael, 2000: "L2 morphosyntactic development in text-based computer-mediated communication". *Computer Assisted Language Learning* 13(1), 5–27.

Salmon, Gilly / Ross, Bella / Pechenkina, Ekaterina / Chase, Anne-Marie, 2015: "The space for social media in structured online learning". *Research in Learning Technology* 23, 28507.

Sato, Charlene J., 1986: "Conversation and development: Rethinking the connection". In: Day, Richard R. (ed.): *"Talking to Learn": Conversation in Second Language Acquisition*. Newbury House: Rowley, MS, 23–45.

Sauro, Shannon / Smith, Bryan, 2010: "Investigating L2 performance in text chat". *Applied Linguistics* 31(4), 554–577.

Scardamalia, Marlene / Bereiter, Carl, 1986: "Research on written composition". In: Wittrock, Merlin C. (ed.). *Handbook of Research on Teaching* (3rd ed.). McMillan: New York, 778–803.

Schauer, Gila A., 2006: "Pragmatic awareness in ESL and EFL contexts. Contrast and development". *Language Learning* 56(2), 269–318.

Scheidt, Lois Ann, 2006: "Adolescent diary weblogs and the unseen audience". In: Buckingham, David / Willett, Rebekah (eds): *Digital Generations: Children, Young People, and New Media*. Lawrence Erlbaum Associates: Mahwah, NJ, 193–210.

Schenker, Theresa, 2012: "Intercultural competence and cultural learning through telecollaboration". *CALICO Journal* 29(3), 449–470.

Schenker, Theresa, 2015: "Telecollaboration for novice language learners – negotiation of meaning in text chats between nonnative and native speakers". In: Dixon, Edward / Thomas, Michael (eds): *Researching Language Learner Interaction Online: From Social Media to Moocs* (Calico Monograph Series). CALICO, San Marcos, CA.

Schrage, Michael, 1990: *Shared Minds: The New Technologies of Collaboration*. John Brockman: New York.

Schraw, Gregory, 1998: "Promoting general metacognitive awareness". *Instructional Science* 26, 113–125.

Schwartz, Linda / Clark, Sharon / Cossarin, Mary / Rudolph, Jim, 2004: "Educational wikis: Features and selection criteria". *The International Review of Research in Open and Distributed Learning* 5(1). Retrieved 9.4.2015, from http://www.irrodl.org/index.php/irrodl/article/viewArticle/163/244.

Schwienhorst, Klaus, 2002: "Evaluating tandem language learning in the Moo: Discourse repair strategies in a bilingual internet project". *Computer Assisted Language Learning* 15(2), 135–145.

Scrimshaw, Peter, 1993: "Cooperative writing with computers". In: Scrimshaw, Peter (ed.): *Language, Classrooms and Computers*. Routledge: London, 100–110.

Seburn, Tyson, 2015: *Academic Reading Circles*. The Round (e-Book).

Seedhouse, Paul, 2004: *The Interactional Architecture of the Language Classroom: A Conversation Analysis Perspective*. Blackwell Publishing: Maiden, MA.

Sengupta, Sima, 2001: "Exchanging ideas with peers in network-based classrooms: An aid or a pain?" *Language Learning and Technology* 5(1), 103–134.

Sharma, Pete, 2010: "Blended learning". *ELTJournal* 64, 456–458.

Shea, Nicholas / Boldt, Annika / Bang, Dan / Yeung, Nick / Heyes, Cecilia / Frith, Chris D., 2014: "Supra-personal cognitive control and metacognition". *Trends in Cognitive Sciences* 18(4), 186–193.

Shekary, Moozeh / Tahririan, Mohammad Hasan, 2006: "Negotiation of meaning and noticing in text-based online chat". *The Modern Language Journal* 90(4), 557–573.

Shetzer, Heidi / Warschauer, Mark, 2000: "An electronic literacy approach to network-based language teaching". In: Warschauer, Mark / Kern, Richard (eds): *Netword-based Language Teaching: Concepts and Practice*. Cambridge University Press: Cambridge, 171–185.

Silberstein, Sandra, 1994: *Techniques and Resources in Teaching Reading*. Oxford: Oxford University Press, 110–112.

Simpson, Ormond, 2000: *Supporting Students in Online, Open and Distance Learning*. RoutledgeFalmer: Oxford, 9.

Silva, Tony, 1990: "Second language composition instruction: Developments, issues and directions in ESL". In: Kroll, Barbara (ed.): *Second Language Writing. Research Insights for the Classroom*. Cambridge University Press: Cambridge, 11–23.

Skehan, Peter, 1998: "Task-based instruction". *Annual Review of Applied Linguistics* 18, 268–286.

Skovholt, Karianne / Grønning, Anette / Kankaanranta, Anne, 2014: "The communicative functions of emoticons in workplace e-mails". *Journal of Computer-Mediated Communication* 19(4), 780–797.

Slavin, Robert, 1995: *Cooperative Learning*. Allyn and Bacon: Boston, MASS.

Smith, Barbara Leigh / MacGregor, Jean T., 1992: "What is collaborative learning?" In: Goodsell, Anne S. / Maher, Michelle R. / Tinto, Vincent (eds): *Collaborative Learning: A Sourcebook for Higher Education*. National Center on Postsecondary Teaching, Learning, & Assessment, Syracuse University, New York. Retrieved 26.8.2016, from http://evergreen.edu/facultydevelopment/docs/WhatisCollaborativeLearning.pdf.

Snow, Marguerite Ann, 2005: "A model of academic literacy for integrated language and content instruction". In: Hinkel, Eli (ed.): *Handbook of Research in Second Language Teaching and Learning*. Erlbaum: Mahwah, NJ/New York, 693–712.

Socha, Bailey / Eber-Schmid, Barbara, n.d.: "What is new media? Defining new media isn't easy". Retrieved 1.8.2016, from http://www.newmedia.org/what-is-new-media.html.

Solomon, Gwen / Schrum, Lynne, 2007: *Web 2.0: New Tools, New Schools*. International Society for Technology in Education: Washington, DC.

Solomon, Gwen / Schrum, Lynne, 2010: *Web 2.0 How-to for Educators*. ISTE: Eugene, OR.

Sotillo, Susana M., 2009: "Learner noticing, negative feedback, and uptake in synchronous computer-mediated environments". In: Abraham, Lee B. / Williams, Lawrence (eds): *Electronic Discourse in Language Learning and Language Teaching*. John Benjamins B.V.: Amsterdam/Philadelphia, 87–110.

South Africa Government, 2014: "Department of Arts and Culture official language policy". Retrieved 23.1.2015, from http://www.gov.za/documents/department-arts-and-culture-official-language-policy.

Spitzer, Manfred, 2012: *Digitale Demenz: Wie wir uns und unsere Kinder um den Verstand bringen*. München: Drömer.

Stangl, Werner, 2015: *Lerntipps: Buddy Book*. Retrieved 2.9.2015, from http://lerntipps.lerntipp.at/buddy-book/.

Stanley, Graham / Thornbury, Scott, 2013: *Language Learning with Technology. Ideas for Integrating Technology in the Language Classroom* (Cambridge Handbooks for Language Teachers). Cambridge University Press: Cambridge/New York.

Stephens, Keri K. / Houser, Marian L. / Cowan, Renee L., 2009: "R U able to meat me? The impact of students' overly casual email messages to instructors". *Communication Education* 58(3), 303–326.

Stepp-Greany, Jonita, 2002: "Student perceptions on language learning in a technological environment: Implications for the new millenium". *Language Learning & Technology* 6(1), 165–180.

Stewart, Moira A., 1995: "Effective physician-patient communication and health outcomes: A review". *Canadian Medical Association Journal* 152(9), 1423–1433.

Stockwell, Glenn, 2012: *Computer-Assisted Language Learning: Diversity in Research and Practice*. Cambridge University Press: Cambridge.

Stockwell, Glenn / Harrington, Michael, 2003: "The incidental development of L2 proficiency in ns-nns email interactions". *CALICO Journal* 20(2), 337–359.

Stoller, Fredericka L., 2008: "Content-based instruction". In: Van Deusen-Scholl, Nina / Hornberger, Nancy H. (eds): *Encyclopedia of Language and Education*. (Vol. 4: Second and Foreign Language Education, 2nd ed.). Springer: New York, 59–70.

Storch, Neomy, 2011: "Collaborative writing in L2 contexts. Processes, outcomes, and future directions". *Annual Review of Applied Linguistics*, 275.

Storch, Neomy, 2013: *Collaborative Writing in L2 Classrooms*. Multilingual Matters: Bristol, UK, 2–3.

Storozenko, Victoria, 2015: "Tatort Fremdsprachenunterricht: Fremdsprachenlernen mit Krimis". In: Hoffmann, Sabine / Stork, Antje (eds): *Lernerorientierte Fremdsprachenforschung und -didaktik*. Tübingen: Narr Francke Attempto, 273–282.

Stracke, Christian M., 2007: "Quality standards for quality development in e-learning: Adoption, implementation, and adaptation of ISO/IEC 19796-1". Retrieved 11.3.2016, from http://www.qed-info.de/downloads.

Street, Brian, 1999: "Academic literacies". In: Jones, Carys / Turner, Joan / Street, Brian (eds): *Student Writing in the University: Cultural and Epistemological Issues*. John Benjamins B.V.: Amsterdam, 193–199.

Stubbs, Michael, 1992: "English teaching, information technology and critical language awareness". In: Fairclough, Norman (ed.): *Critical Language Awareness*. Longman: London, 203–222.

Suh, Soonshik / Kim, Sug-Whan / Kim N.J., 2010: "Effectiveness of MMORPG-based Instruction in elementary English education in Korea". *Journal of Computer Assisted Learning* 26, 370–378.

Sundqvist, Pia / Sylvén, Liss Kerstin, 2016: *Extramural English in Teaching and Learning*. Palgrave MacMillan, UK. e-Book.

Survey Monkey Gold, n.d. Retrieved 2014, from www.surveymonkey.net.

Swain, Merrill, 1995: "Three functions of output in second language learning". In: Cook, Guy / Seidlhofer, Barbara (eds): *Principle and Practice in Applied Linguistics: Studies in Honor of H.G. Widdowson*. Oxford University Press: Oxford, 125–144.

Swain, Merrill, 1997: "Collaborative dialogue: Its contribution to second language learning". *Revista Canaria de Estudios Ingleses* 34, 115–132.

Swain, Merrill, 2000: "The output hypothesis and beyond: Mediating acquisition through collaborative dialogue". In: Lantolf, James P. (ed.): *Sociocultural Theory and Second Language Learning*. Oxford University Press: Oxford, 97–114.

Swain, Merrill / Lapkin, Sharon, 1998: "Interaction and second language learning: Two adolescent French immersion students working together". *The Modern Language Journal* 82, 320–337.

Swan, Karen, 2002: "Building communities in online courses: The importance of interaction". *Education, Communication and Information* 2(1), 23–49.

Taki, Saeed / Ramazani, Zarha, 2011: "Improving reading skills through e-mail: The case of Iranian EFL students". *International Journal of Instructional Technology & Distance Learning* 8(4).

Tapscott, Don, 1998: "Growing up digital. The rise of the Net Generation". *Education and Information Technologies* 4(2), 203–205. Retrieved 21.8.2016, from https://www.ncsu.edu/meridian/jan98/feat_6/digital.html.

Tarricone, Pina, 2011: *The Taxonomy of Metacognition*. Psychology Press: Hove, UK.

Terantino, Joseph M., 2013: "Facebook comparison research: Faculty and student perceptions of social media for foreign language courses". In: Zou, Bin, *et al.* (eds): *Computer-Assisted Foreign Language Teaching and Learning: Technological Advances*. Information Science Reference: Hershey, PA, 91–103.

The New London Group, 1996: "A pedagogy of multiliteracies: Designing social futures". *Harvard Educational Review* 66(1), 60–92.

Thaler, Engelbert., 2012: *Englisch unterrichten. Grundlagen, Kompetenzen, Methoden*. Cornelsen: Berlin.

Thomas, Michael / Reinders, Hayo (eds), 2010: *Task-Based Language Learning and Teaching with Technology*. Bloomsbury Publishing: London.

Thomas, Michael / Reinders, Hayo /Warschauer, Mark, 2012: "Contemporary computer-assisted language learning: The role of digital media and incremental change". In: Thomas, Michael / Reinders, Hayo / Warschauer, Mark (eds): *Contemporary Computer-Assisted Language Learning*. Bloomsbury Academic: London.

Thorne, Steven L., 2003: "Artifacts and cultures-of-use in intercultural communication". *Language, Learning & Technology* 7(2), 38.

Thorne, Steven L., 2006: "Pedagogical and praxiological lessons from internet-mediated intercultural foreign language education research". In: Belz, Julie A. / Thorne, Steven L. (eds): *Internet-Mediated Intercultural Foreign Language Education* (Aausc Issues in Language Program Direction). Thomson Heinle: Boston, 2–31.

Thornbury, Scott, 2002: *How to Teach Vocabulary*. Pearson Education Limited: Harlow, UK, 14.

Tiene, Drew, 2000: "Online discussion: A survey of advantages and disadvantages compared to face-to-face discussions". *Journal of Educational Multimedia and Hypermedia* 9(4), 371–384.

Tomlinson, Carol A., 2014: *The Differentiated Classroom. Responding to the Needs of all Learners*. Association for Supervision and Curriculum Development: Alexandria, VA.

Tomlinson, Brian / Ávila, Javier, 2011: "Web 2.0. a vehicle for humanizing FLL". *Anglistik* 22(1), 137–151.

Toyoda, Etsuko / Harrison, Richard, 2002: "Categorization of text chat communication between learners and native speakers of Japanese". *Language Learning & Technology* 6(1), 82–99.

Trang, Thi T. / Moni, Karen, 2015. "Management of foreign language anxiety: Insiders' awareness and experiences". *Cogent Education* 2, 1–20.

Tsai, Susanna / Machado, Paulo, 2002: "e-Learning basics: Essay: e-Learning, online learning, web-based learning or distance learning. Unveiling the ambiguity in current terminology". Retrieved 14.7.2006, from http://elearnmag.acm.org/archive.cfm?aid=568597.

Tsai, Meng-Jung / Tsai, Chin.-Chung, 2003: "Information searching strategies in web-based science learning: The role of internet self-efficacy". *Innovations in Education and Teaching International* 40(1), 43–50.

Tudini, Vincenza, 2003: "Using native speakers in chat". *Language Learning & Technology* 7(3), 141–159.

Tudini, Vincenza, 2007: "Negotiation and intercultural learning in Italian native speaker chat rooms". *Modern Language Journal* 91(4), 577–601.

Turner, Rebecca, 2013: *English for Emails* (Short Course Series). Cornelsen: Berlin.

Tutty, Jeremy I. / Klein, James D., 2008: "Computer-mediated instruction: A comparison of online and face-to-face collaboration". *Educational Technology Research and Development* 56, 101–124.

Uhlírová, Ludmila, 1994: "E-mail as a new subvariety of medium and its effects upon the message". In: Cmejrkova, Svetla / Sticha, Frantisek (eds): *The Syntax of Sentence and Text: A Festschrift for Frantisek Danes*. John Benjamins B.V.: Amsterdam/Philadelphia, PA, 273–282.

Van de Poel, Kris / Brunfaut, Tineke, 2004: "Bridging the gap between staff expectations and student interpretations of academic writing: The case of Scribende". *Belgian Journal of English Language and Literatures*, 329–335.

Van de Poel, Kris / Gasiorek, Jessica, 2007: *All Write. An Introduction to Writing in an Academic Context*. ACCO: Leuven/Voorburg.

Van de Poel, K. / Gasiorek, Jessica, 2009a: "Language awareness raising in academic writing: Evaluating an online writing programme". Education et diversité Linguistique et Culturelle (EDILIC) Publications. Retrieved from http://www.edilic.org/fr/fr_publications.php?congres=2006.

Van de Poel, Kris / Gasiorek, Jessica, 2009b: "Effects and effectiveness of language course evaluation: A case study". International Council for Open and Distance Education (ICDE). Retrieved from http://www.ou.nl/eCache/DEF/2/11/519.html.

Van de Poel, Kris / Gasiorek, Jessica, 2010: "Evaluation in the course development process: A learner centred approach". *English Text Construction (ETC)* 3(1)(April), 120–140.

Van de Poel, Kris / Gasiorek, Jessica, 2012a: "Effects of an efficacy-focused approach to academic writing on students' perceptions of themselves as writers. Original research article". *Journal of English for Academic Purposes* 11(4), 294–303. Retrieved from http://dx.doi.org/10.1016/j.jeap.2012.07.003.

Van de Poel, Kris / Gasiorek, Jessica, 2012b: "Academic acculturation: The case of writing". *Journal for Language Teaching* 46(November), 58–72.

Van de Poel, Kris / Fourie, Christine, 2013: "A critical approach to the development of blended medical communication training materials". *Stellenbosch Papers in Linguistics Plus* 42, 333–351. Retrieved from DOI 10.5842/42-0-146.

Van de Poel, Kris / Fourie, Christine, 2013: "A critical approach to the development of blended medical communication training materials". *Stellenbosch Papers in Linguistics Plus* 42, 1–19.

Van de Poel, Kris / Vanagt, Eddy / Gasiorek, Jessica / Schrimpf, Ulrike, 2013: *Communication Skills for Foreign and Mobile Medical Professionals*. Springer: London.

Van de Poel, Kris / Van Dyk, Tobie, 2015: "Discipline-specific academic literacy and academic integration". In: Wilkinson, Robert / Walsh, Mary Louise (eds): *Integrating Content and Language in Higher Education. From Theory to Practice*. Peter Lang: Frankfurt a.M. et al., 161–180.

Van Dyk, Tobie / Van de Poel, Kris / Van der Slik, Frans, 2013: "Reading ability and academic acculturation: The case of South African students entering higher education". *Stellenbosch Papers in Linguistics Plus* 42, 353–369. Retrieved from DOI 10.5842/42-0-146.

Van Dyk, Tobie / Van de Poel, Kris / Van der Slik, Frans, in prep.: "Raising students' awareness on the impact of academic reading preparedness: A global pedagogical issue".

Van den Branden, Kris, 1997: "Effects of negotiation on language learners' output". *Language Learning* 47, 589–636.

Van den Branden, Kris, 2006: *Task-based Language Education: From Theory to Practice*. Cambridge University Press: Cambridge.

Van den Branden, Kris, 2015: "Opening plenary – author notes". Task-Based Language Teaching (TBLT) Conference, Centre for Language and Education, Faculty of Arts, University of Leuven, 16–18 September 2015.

Van den Branden, Kris / Bygate, Martin / Norris, John M., 2009: *Task-based Language Teaching. A Reader*. John Benjamins B.V.: Amsterdam.

Van den Branden, Kris / Van Gorp, Koen / Verhelst, Machteld, 2007: "Tasks in action: Task-based language education from a classroom-based perspective". In: Van den Branden, Kris /Van Gorp, Koen / Verhelst, Machteld (eds): *Tasks in Action: Task-Based Language Education from a Classroom-Based Perspective.* Cambridge Scholars Publishing: Newcastle, UK, 1–6.

Van der Zwaard, Rose / Bannink, Anne, 2014: "Video call or chat? Negotiation of meaning and issues of face in telecollaboration". *System* 44, 137–148.

Vandercruysse, Sylke / Vandewaetere, Mieke / Clarebout, Geraldine, 2012: "Game-based learning: A review on the effectiveness of educational games". In: Cruz-Cunha, Maria M. (ed.): *Handbook of Research on Serious Games as Educational, Business, and Research Tools.* IGI Global: Hershey, PA.

Van Lier, Leo, 1988: *The Classroom and the Language Learner.* Longman: New York.

Van Lier, Leo 1996. *Interaction in the Language Curriculum: Awareness, Autonomy & Authenticity.* Routledge: New York.

Veenman, Marcel V.J. / Van Hout-Wouters, Bernadette H.A.M. / Afilerbach, Peter, 2006: "Metacognition and learning: Conceptual and methodologial considerations". *Metacognition and Learning* 1, 3–14.

Veldhuis-Diermanse, Anna E., 2002: "CSC learning? Participation, learning activities and knowledge construction in computer-supported collaborative learning in higher education". Doctoral thesis, Wageningen University and Research Centre, Wageningen, The Netherlands.

Vinagre, Margarita, 2005: "Fostering language learning via email: An English-Spanish exchange". *Computer Assisted Language Learning* 18(5), 369–388.

Volkmann, Laurenz, 2010: *Fachdidaktik Englisch: Kultur und Sprache.* Narr: Tübingen.

Vollmer, Helmut J., 2010: "Bilingualer Unterricht als Inhalts- und Sprachenlernen". In: Bach, Gerhard / Niemeier, Susanne (eds): *Bilingualer Unterricht: Grundlagen, Methoden, Praxis, Perspektiven* (5th ed.). Peter Lang: Frankfurt a.M. et al., 47–70.

Vygotsky, Lev S., 1962: *Language and Thought.* Massachusetts Institute of Technology Press: Ontario.

Vygotsky, Lev S., 1978: "Interaction between learning and development". In: Cole, Michael / John-Steiner, Vera / Scribner, Sylvia / Souberman, Ellen (eds): *Mind in Society. The Development of Higher Psychological Processes.* Harvard University Press: Cambridge, MA, 79–91.

Waldvogel, Joan, 2007: "Greetings and closings in workplace email". *Journal of Computer-Mediated Communication* 12(2), 456–477.

Wang, Shenggao / Vásquez, Camilla, 2012: "Web 2.0 and second language learning: What does the research tell us?" *CALICO Journal 29*(3), 412–430.

Wang, Yuping, 2004: "Distance language learning: Interactivity and fourth generation Internet-based video conferencing". *CALICO Journal* 21(2), 373–395.

Ware, Paige, 2005: "'Missed' communication in online communication: Tensions in a German-American telecollaboration". *Language Learning & Technology* 9(2), 64–89.

Ware, Paige / Kramsch, Claire, 2005: "Toward an intercultural stance: Teaching German and English through telecollaboration". *The Modern Language Journal* 89(2), 190–205.

Warschauer, Mark, 1996: "Comparing face-to-face and electronic communication in the second language classroom". *CALICO Journal* 13(2), 7–26.

Warschauer, Mark, 1997: "Computer-mediated collaborative learning: Theory and practice". *The Modern Language Journal* 81(4). Special issue: Interaction, Collaboration, and Cooperation: Learning Languages and Preparing Language Teachers. Winter: Heidelberg, 470–481.

Warschauer, Mark, 2004: "Technological change and the future of CALL". In: Fotos, Sandra / Brown, Charles (eds): *New Perspectives on CALL for Second and Foreign Language Classrooms*. Lawrence Erlbaum Associates: Mahwah, NJ, 15–25.

Waters-Adams, Stephen, 2006: "Action research in education". Retrieved 8.3.2013, from http://www.edu.plymouth.ac.uk/resined/actionresearch/arhome.htm.

Weissberg, Bob, 2000: "Developmental relationships in the acquisition of English syntax: Writing vs. speech". *Learning and Instruction* 10, 37–53.

Wesche, Marjorie B., 2001: "French immersion and content-based language teaching in Canada". *The Canadian Modern Language Review* 58(1), 1–8.

White, David / Le Cornu, Allison, 2010: "Eventedness and disjuncture in virtual worlds". *Educational Research* 52(2), 183–196. Retrieved 1.8.2016, from DOI http://dx.doi.org/10.1080/00131881.2010.482755.

White, Cynthia, 2003: *Language Learning in Distance Education*. Cambridge University Press: Cambridge.

White, Goodith, 2008: "Listening and good language learners". In: Griffiths, Carol (ed.): *Lessons from Good Language Learners*. Cambridge University Press: Cambridge, 208–217.

White, Ron / Arndt, Valerie, 1991: *Process Writing*. London: Longman.

Whiteside, Aimee. L., 2007: "Exploring social presence in communities of practice within a hybrid learning environment: A longitudinal examination of two case studies with the technology leadership graduate-level certificate program". Doctoral dissertation, University of Minnesota: Minnesota.

Williams, James D., 2003: *Preparing to Teach Writing. Research, Theory, and Practice* (3rd ed.). Lawrence Erlbaum: Mahwah NJ.

Williams, Peter E. / Hellman, Chan M., 2004: "Differences in self-regulation for online learning between first- and second-generation college students". *Research in Higher Education* 45(1), 71–82.

Willis, Jane, 1996: *A Framework for Task-based Learning*. Longman: London.

Willis, Dave / Willis, Jane, 2007: *Doing Task-based Teaching*. Oxford University Press: Oxford.

Winters, Fielding I. / Greene, Jeffrey A. / Costich, Claudine M., 2008: "Self-regulation of learning within computer-based learning environments: A critical analysis". *Educational Psychology Review* 20, 429–444.

Wolff, Dieter, 1986: "Some assumptions about second language text comprehension". *Studies in Second Language Acquisition* 9, 307–326.

Wolff, Dieter, 1991: "Lerntechniken und die Förderung der zweitsprachigen Schreibfähigkeit". *Der fremdsprachliche Unterricht Englisch* 25(2), 34–40.

Wolff, Dieter, 1997: "Bilingualer Sachfachunterricht: Versuch einer lernpsychologischen und fachdidaktischen Begründung". In: Vollmer, Helmut J. / Thürmann, Eike (eds): *Englisch als Arbeitssprache im* Fachunterricht*: Begegnungen zwischen Theorie und Praxis. Gemeinsame Fachtagung der Deutschen Gesellschaft für Fremdsprachenforschung und des Landesinstitut für Schule und Weiterbildung, 30 Januar – 1 Februar 1997*. Landesinstitut für Schule und Weiterbildung: Soest, 50–62.

Wolff, Dieter, 2000: "Second language writing: A few remarks on psycholinguistic and instructional issues". *Learning and Instruction* 10, 107–112.

Wolff, Dieter, 2001: *Content and Language Integrated Learning: An Evaluation of the German Approach*. Retrieved 12.10.2015, from http://share.dschola.it/dd4pinerolo/clil/Shared%20 Documents/Theory_strategies/Dieter%20Wolff.pdf.

Wolff, Dieter, 2002: *Fremdsprachen als Konstruktion – Grundlagen für eine konstruktivistische Fremdsprachendidaktik*. Peter Lang: Frankfurt a.M. et al.

Wolff, Dieter, 2009: "Content and language integrated learning". In: Knapp, Karlfried / Seidlhofer, Barbara (eds): *Handbook of Foreign Language Communication*. De Gruyter Mouton: Berlin, 545–572.

Wood, David / Bruner, Jerome S. / Ross, Gail, 1976: "The role of tutoring in problem solving". *Journal of Child Psychology and Psychiatry* 17(2), 89–100. Retrieved 12.10.2015, from DOI 10.1111/j.1469-7610.1976.tb00381.x.

Woodin, Jane, 2001: "Tandem learning as an intercultural activity". In: Byram, Michael / Nichols, Adam / Stevens, David (eds): *Developing Intercultural Competence in Practice*. Multilingual Matters Ltd: Bristol, UK, 189–203.

Wright, Tony / Bolitho, Rod, 1993: "Language awareness: A missing link in language teacher education". *ELT Journal* 47, 292–304.

Xie, Tianwei, 2002: "Using internet relay chat in teaching Chinese". *CALICO Journal* 19(3), 513–524.

Xing, Minjie / Zou, Bin / Wang, Dongshuo, 2013: "A wiki platform for language and intercultural communication". In: Zou, Bin *et al.* (eds): *Computer-Assisted Foreign Language Teaching and Learning: Technological Advances*. Information Science Reference: Hershey, 1–16.

Yang, Shu Ching / Chen, Yi-Ju, 2007: "Technology-enhanced language learning: A case study". *Computers in Human Behavior* 23(1), 860–879.

Yanguas, Inigo, 2012: "Task-based oral computer-mediated communication and L2 vocabulary acquisition". *CALICO Journal* 29(3), 507–531.

Zeni, Jane, 1994: "Oral collaboration, computers and revision". In: Reagan, S.B. / Fox, T. / Bleich, D. (eds): *Writing with: New Directions in Collaborative Teaching, Learning, and Research*. State University of New York: Albany, NY, 213–226.

Zhang, Jianwei, 2013: "Collaboration, technology, and culture". In: Hmelo-Silver, Cindy E. *et al.* (eds): *International Handbook of Collaborative Learning*. Routledge: New York/Abingdon, 1215–1249.

Zhang, Tianyi; Gao, Tianguang; Ring, Gail / Zhang, Wei, 2007: "Using online discussion forums to assist a traditional English class". *International Journal on e-Learning* 6(4), 623–643.

Zheng, Dongping / Young, Michael F. / Wagner, Manuela M. / Brewer, Robert A., 2009: "Negotiation for action: English language learning in game-based virtual worlds". *The Modern Language Journal* 93(4), 489–511.

Zimmerman, Barry J., 1989: "A social cognitive view of self-regulated Academic learning". *Journal of Educational Psychology* 81(3), 329–339.

Zimmerman, Rüdiger, 2000: "L2 writing: Subprocesses, a model of formulating and empirical findings". *Learning and Instruction* 10, 73–99.

Zimmermann, Gisela, 2004: *Fachseminar für Erdkunde: Thema: Experimente im Erdkundeunterricht*. Retrieved 2.9.2015, from http://bildungsserver.berlin-brandenburg.de/fileadmin/bbb/zielgruppen /lehramtsanwaerterinnen/erdkunde/Experimente.pdf.pdf.

https://www.google.co.za/#q=the+most+carefully+structured+end+of+the+collaborative+learning+continuum"+(Smith+and+MacGregor%2C+1992

https://wordpress.com/activity/

http://www.newmedialiteracies.org

Editors/Contributors

Editors/Contributors

Editors

Christian Ludwig is currently substitute professor of American Literature and Culture and TEFL at the University of Education Karlsruhe (Germany) where he is also director of the Self-Access Centre and head of the English department. He earned his PhD *Rites de Passage: The construction of gender identities in Alison Bechdel's (autobio-)graphic writings* from the University of Duisburg-Essen (Germany) in 2015. His research interests include learning with literature, new media and learner autonomy.

Kris Van de Poel is professor of Linguistics at the University of Antwerp (Belgium) where she coordinates applied linguistic research at the Unit for Applied Language Studies. She has a background in teaching and research in Scandinavia, Scotland (where she received her PhD), England and South Africa and is also an extraordinary professor at the School of Languages of North-West University (South Africa). She has been teaching academic literacy courses from undergraduate to doctoral levels for many years. Her scholarly interests lie in data-driven research focusing on foreign language learning needs in academic and professional contexts and she has a keen eye for the nexus research-teaching.

Contributors

Sabine Ahlers, née Drees, studied English and Geography at the University of Duisburg-Essen (Germany), earning her teacher's degree for German secondary schools (*Gymnasium/Gesamtschule*) in 2008. During her time as a student, she received specialised CLIL teacher training (joint programme of the English and Geography departments) and developed rich theoretical expertise in this area; afterwards she remained focused on CLIL in her practical teacher training. Currently, she works as a full-time teacher at Heinrich-Heine-Gymnasium in Oberhausen with a focus on teaching geography bilingually. In 2013, on account of her proficiency and expertise in practical CLIL teaching, she was invited by the Goethe-Institute to deliver a speech and give a workshop for Russian teachers of German in Novosibirsk, Russia.

Judith Buendgens-Kosten holds a Master of Arts and doctorate degree in English Linguistics from RWTH Aachen University (Germany) and a Master's degree in

Online and Distance Education from the Open University (UK). She currently works as a professor pro tem at Göthe University Frankfurt. Her research focuses on computer-assisted language learning (CALL) and multilingualism.

Jozef Colpaert teaches Instructional Design, Educational Technology and Computer Assisted Language Learning at the University of Antwerp, Belgium. Prof. Colpaertt is editor of *Computer Assisted Language Learning* (Taylor and Francis) and organizer of the International CALL Research Conferences. He is currently working on the empirical and theoretical validation of Educational Engineering, a novel instructional design model and research method.

Veronica Dal-Bianco works as a freelance teacher and teacher trainer at various Universities of Applied Sciences in Austria. She teaches English as a foreign language (EFL) and was a member of the teaching staff at the University of Applied Sciences Burgenland (Austria) for many years, where she developed and taught blended language learning courses. Her major interest lies in using new technologies to enhance learning and promote learner autonomy.

Maria Eisenmann is professor of EFL Teaching at Julius-Maximilians-University Würzburg (Germany). She studied English and German at the University of Newcastle upon Tyne (England) and at the University of Würzburg, where she passed state examination and acquired her Master's degree. After earning her PhD and working as a grammar school teacher and a lecturer at the University of Würzburg, she taught at the University of Education in Freiburg, held a deputy professorship for EFL Teaching at the University of Erlangen-Nürnberg and held the chair for EFL Teaching at the University of Duisburg-Essen. Her primary research interests lie in the field of teaching literature, media literacy and inter-/transcultural learning.

Simon Falk studied English and Portuguese linguistics as well as political science at the Philipps University in Marburg. He is a research assistant at the *Information Centre for Foreign Language Research* (IFS) and recently submitted his doctoral thesis on Mobile-Assisted Language Learning in June 2017. The main focus lies on contextual and situational learning with tablets and smartphones. In this regard, he also studies the relationship between formal and informal learning.

Christine Fourie studied Afrikaans Literature and Linguistics as well as English Literature at the University of Stellenbosch, South Africa, where she also acquired her Certificate of Educational Competence for high school teaching.

After returning from teaching assignments in the United States and the UK, she taught academic language courses at the University of Stellenbosch. From November 2013 until June 2016 she worked on her PhD at the University of Antwerp (Belgium). Her thesis focuses on second language communication for specific (medical) purposes and raising students' metacognitive awareness in a blended learning environment, which includes an autonomous online platform and a social network site. Currently she is back in South Africa and in the final stages of finishing her PhD, while she resumed lecturing at the University of Stellenbosch.

Stephan Gabel is a Senior Lecturer at the University of Münster (Germany), where he received his PhD in Applied Linguistics in 2000. His main fields of interest are the investigation of learner language, the use of electronic devices as tools in language learning, the promotion of learner autonomy by means of portfolios, the development of self-access learning centres and of methods for raising young learners' language awareness.

Jessica Gasiorek (PhD University of California, Santa Barbara) is an assistant professor in the Department of Communicology at the University of Hawai'i at Mānoa. Her research addresses message processing, social cognition and intergroup dynamics, particularly perceptions of communication accommodation and non-accommodation. Her published work includes both empirical articles and book chapters on communication accommodation theory, communication in multilingual medical and teaching/learning contexts.

Linda Gijsen is a lecturer of English at Fontys University of Applied Sciences, Tilburg, the Netherlands. She teaches a range of general and applied linguistics subjects. Her research interests include teacher education, the use of technology in the foreign language classroom and more specifically task design for collaboration in online intercultural exchanges. She is currently working on her Ph.D. at the faculty of Social Sciences at the University of Antwerp, Belgium.

Saskia Kersten is currently senior lecturer in English Language & Communication at the School of Humanities, University of Hertfordshire (UK). She obtained her PhD from Hildesheim University (Germany) in 2009. Her research interests encompass computer-mediated communication with a focus on different varieties of English and communicative strategies used in English language tweets, use of computer-mediated communication in EFL and the role of formulaic language in second language development of young learners. Her monograph, *The Mental*

Lexicon and Vocabulary Learning: Implications for the foreign language classroom (a study of L2 vocabulary acquisition in primary school), was published in 2010.

Lienhard Legenhausen is professor emeritus of Language Pedagogy and Applied Linguistics at the University of Münster (Germany). His research interests include the study of learner language, technology-enhanced language learning, as well as learner-centred approaches to classroom learning/teaching. In conjunction with Leni Dam, Denmark, he started the LAALE project (Language Acquisition in an Autonomous Learning Environment) in the early nineteen-nineties in which the language development of a class of mixed ability learners was observed systematically over a period of four years. For the last ten years, he has been a visiting professor to the National University of Cherkasy (Ukraine) and taught linguistic and methodology courses in their English and German departments.

Thorsten Merse is a research assistant in the field of Teaching English as a Foreign Language (TEFL) at the University of Munich, LMU (Germany). He holds teacher training seminars for student teachers in their Bachelor and Master of Education programmes, with a special focus on multiliteracies and media. In his doctoral research, he investigates the application of Queer Theory to TEFL contexts. His other research interests include online media in the EFL classroom, Global Education and diversity education.

Lawrie Moore-Walter, MBA, MA is an American lecturer and teacher trainer who has been living in Austria since 1997. She mainly teaches ESP in both traditional classroom settings as well as in blended learning degree programmes. She is especially interested in encouraging students to collaborate and take responsibility for their learning. Lawrie holds a Cambridge CELTA and DELTA and is currently a Celta Course Tutor where she enjoys supporting new EFL teachers in the use of technology in the classroom.

Jo Mynard is associate professor and director of the Self-Access Learning Centre (SALC) at Kanda University of International Studies (KUIS) in Japan. She advises language learners and oversees academic support, research and the general direction of the SALC. She also teaches an undergraduate course on Effective Language Learning and a graduate course on Learner Autonomy as part of the MA TESOL programme. She has co-edited several books on learner autonomy and on advising in language learning and recently co-authored a book on reflective dialogue advising. She has been the editor of SiSAL (Studies in Self-Access Learning) Journal –a peer review, open access publication– since 2010.

Fiona Heather Poorman, MA, is a research assistant at the University of Education in Karlsruhe and deputy director of the Self-Access Centre. She teaches foreign language teacher preparation courses in the English department and language courses in German as a Foreign Language. She is currently writing her PhD on Using Social Networking Sites to Enhance Communicative Competence in the Foreign Language Classroom.

Elke Ruelens is a PhD researcher at the University of Antwerp. She has a background in tutoring/teaching English and Dutch linguistics and literature. Her main research interest is language learner autonomy, and more specifically, the relationship between self-regulation, self-efficacy and learner autonomy, which she is currently examining in the context of academic literacy development. Additional areas of interest include collaborative learning and e-learning as well as blended learning environments.

Dominik Rumlich studied English and Geography at Waikato University in Hamilton (New Zealand) and at the University of Duisburg-Essen (Germany) where he earned his teacher's degree for German secondary schools in 2009. Afterwards, he worked as a substitute teacher at two secondary schools and pursued his PhD studies as a researcher and lecturer at the University of Duisburg-Essen. His large-scale longitudinal quasi-experimental PhD project DENOCS provided the backbone for his thesis *Evaluating bilingual education in Germany. The development of CLIL students' general English proficiency, academic self-concept and interest* which was published by Lang in 2016. He currently holds a professorship for TEFL at the University of Münster. His areas of expertise include CLIL, assessment, motivation, individual learner characteristics and quantitative research (methods).

Theresa Schenker, PhD, is the language program director and senior lector of German at Yale University (USA). She completed her PhD at Michigan State University. Her research interests include computer-mediated communication, the effects of tele-collaboration and study abroad on language skills and intercultural competence, and mobile-assisted language learning. She is in charge of curriculum development, graduate student training, program administration and study abroad. She was awarded the German Embassy Teacher of Excellence Award in 2014 for her innovative integration of technology into the classroom. She has implemented tele-collaboration at all levels of the German language program at Yale and has published about language learning through telecollaboration in peer-reviewed national and international journals.

Jochen Schmidt has worked as a lecturer in Teaching Englisch as a Foreign Language at the University of Münster (Germany) for several years. He is currently a full time teacher with the subjects English and Protestant Theology in a secondary school in North Rhine-Westphalia. His research interests cover practical teacher training and instruction, second language acquisition in the primary as well as the secondary sector, learner/learning strategies in general but with a keen interest in learner autonomy, intercultural learning with a focus on constructions of alterity and difference, as well as the possibilities of new media and web 2.0 for ELT.

Nick Van deneynde is a postgraduate researcher affiliated with the University of Antwerp (Belgium) and a teacher of English and Spanish. His main areas of interest comprise blended learning, World Englishes and collaborative learning. Additional interest lies in learner Englishes and content and language integrated learning (CLIL). As an educator to Spanish natives, he has taught courses in English and CLIL.

Bert Van Poeck graduated from the University of Antwerp (Belgium) with a Master of Arts in English and Dutch Literature and Linguistics in 2015. He briefly worked at the University of Antwerp as a PhD candidate, researching the pedagogical value of gamification –the use of video game mechanics and principles outside of the gaming environment.

Dieter Vermandere teaches Italian and General Linguistics with a focus on sociolinguistics and dialectology, and Intercultural Business Communication as part of the Master's programme in Multilingual Professional Communication at the University of Antwerp (Belgium). His research interests include Italian linguistics (in which he holds a PhD from the University of Louvain in Belgium), sociolinguistics, syntactic variation in Romance languages and dialects, language policy and diversity, and intercultural communication. Prof. Vermandere is co-director of the series Moving Texts Testi Mobili published by Peter Lang.

Gesellschaft für Angewandte Linguistik e.V.

Die Reihe *Forum Angewandte Linguistik (F.A.L.)*, herausgegeben von der Gesellschaft für Angewandte Linguistik (GAL) e. V., vereint Monografien und Sammelbände zu allen aktuellen Themen der Angewandten Linguistik. Angewandte Linguistik wird hierbei verstanden als wissenschaftliches Betätigungsfeld, das sich in Forschung, Lehre und Weiterbildung mit der Analyse und Lösung von sprach- und kommunikationsbezogenen Problemen auf allen Gebieten menschlicher und gesellschaftlicher Interaktion befasst. Diese Zielsetzung erfordert oftmals eine interdisziplinäre Arbeitsweise sowie eine Vermittlung zwischen Theorie und Praxis. Die Reihe will den Dialog über die Grenzen traditioneller Sprachwissenschaft hinweg und zwischen den verschiedenen Arbeitsfeldern der Angewandten Linguistik fördern. Zu diesen Arbeitsfeldern gehören der Muttersprachen- und Fremdsprachenunterricht ebenso wie die Herausforderungen, die beispielsweise migrationsinduzierte Mehrsprachigkeit und interkulturelle Kommunikation mit sich bringen, Fachkommunikations- und Verständlichkeitsforschung, Gesprächsforschung, Lexikographie, die Kommunikation in und mit neuen Medien sowie die Phonetik und Sprechwissenschaft, um nur einige Beispiele zu nennen.

Die GAL als Herausgeberin der Reihe verfolgt das Ziel, die wissenschaftliche Entwicklung in allen Bereichen der Angewandten Linguistik zu fördern und zu koordinieren, den Austausch wissenschaftlicher Erkenntnisse zu beleben und ihren Transfer in die Praxis zu sichern sowie die Zusammenarbeit der hieran interessierten Personen und Institutionen national und international zu intensivieren. Hierzu gehört auch der Kontakt mit Wirtschaft und Industrie, Behörden, Bildungseinrichtungen sowie Institutionen des öffentlichen Lebens.

Die GAL ist Mitglied der *Association Internationale de Linguistique Appliquée* (AILA), des internationalen Dachverbands der Gesellschaften für Angewandte Linguistik.

Kontaktdaten der GAL: http://www.gal-ev.de/

Forum Angewandte Linguistik

Publikationsreihe der Gesellschaft für Angewandte Linguistik (GAL)

Die Bände 1-17 dieser Reihe sind im Gunter Narr Verlag, Tübingen erschienen.

Band	18	Bernd Spillner (Hrsg.): Sprache und Politik. Kongreßbeiträge zur 19. Jahrestagung der Gesellschaft für Angewandte Linguistik GAL e.V., 1990.
Band	19	Claus Gnutzmann (Hrsg.): Kontrastive Linguistik, 1990.
Band	20	Wolfgang Kühlwein, Albert Raasch (Hrsg.): Angewandte Linguistik heute. Zu einem Jubiläum der Gesellschaft für Angewandte Linguistik, 1990.
Band	21	Bernd Spillner (Hrsg.): Interkulturelle Kommunikation. Kongreßbeiträge zur 20. Jahrestagung der Gesellschaft für Angewandte Linguistik GAL e.V., 1990.
Band	22	Klaus J. Mattheier (Hrsg.): Ein Europa – Viele Sprachen. Kongreßbeiträge zur 21. Jahrestagung der Gesellschaft für Angewandte Linguistik GAL e. V., 1991.
Band	23	Bernd Spillner (Hrsg.): Wirtschaft und Sprache. Kongreßbeiträge zur 22. Jahrestagung der Gesellschaft für Angewandte Linguistik GAL e.V., 1992.
Band	24	Konrad Ehlich (Hrsg.): Diskursanalyse in Europa, 1994.
Band	25	Winfried Lenders (Hrsg.): Computereinsatz in der Angewandten Linguistik, 1993.
Band	26	Bernd Spillner (Hrsg.): Nachbarsprachen in Europa. Kongreßbeiträge zur 23. Jahrestagung der Gesellschaft für Angewandte Linguistik GAL e.V., 1994.
Band	27	Bernd Spillner (Hrsg.): Fachkommunikation. Kongreßbeiträge zur 24. Jahrestagung der Gesellschaft für Angewandte Linguistik GAL e.V., 1994.
Band	28	Bernd Spillner (Hrsg.): Sprache: Verstehen und Verständlichkeit. Kongreßbeiträge zur 25. Jahrestagung der Gesellschaft für Angewandte Linguistik. GAL e.V., 1995.
Band	29	Ernest W.B. Hess-Lüttich, Werner Holly, Ulrich Püschel (Hrsg.): Textstrukturen im Medienwandel, 1996.
Band	30	Bernd Rüschoff, Ulrich Schmitz (Hrsg.): Kommunikation und Lernen mit alten und neuen Medien. Beiträge zum Rahmenthema "Schlagwort Kommunikationsgesellschaft" der 26. Jahrestagung der Gesellschaft für Angewandte Linguistik GAL e.V., 1996.
Band	31	Dietrich Eggers (Hrsg.): Sprachandragogik, 1997.
Band	32	Klaus J. Mattheier (Hrsg.): Norm und Variation, 1997.
Band	33	Margot Heinemann (Hrsg.): Sprachliche und soziale Stereotype, 1998.
Band	34	Hans Strohner, Lorenz Sichelschmidt, Martina Hielscher (Hrsg.): Medium Sprache, 1998.
Band	35	Burkhard Schaeder (Hrsg.): Neuregelung der deutschen Rechtschreibung. Beiträge zu ihrer Geschichte, Diskussion und Umsetzung, 1999.
Band	36	Axel Satzger (Hrsg.): Sprache und Technik, 1999.
Band	37	Michael Becker-Mrotzek, Gisela Brünner, Hermann Cölfen (Hrsg.), unter Mitarbeit von Annette Lepschy: Linguistische Berufe. Ein Ratgeber zu aktuellen linguistischen Berufsfeldern, 2000.
Band	38	Horst Dieter Schlosser (Hrsg.): Sprache und Kultur. 2000.
Band	39	John A. Bateman, Wolfgang Wildgen (Hrsg.): Sprachbewusstheit im schulischen und sozialen Kontext. 2002.

Band	40	Ulla Fix / Kirsten Adamzik / Gerd Antos / Michael Klemm (Hrsg.): Brauchen wir einen neuen Textbegriff? Antworten auf eine Preisfrage. 2002.
Band	41	Rudolf Emons (Hrsg.): Sprache transdisziplinär. 2003.
Band	42	Stephan Habscheid / Ulla Fix (Hrsg.): Gruppenstile. Zur sprachlichen Inszenierung sozialer Zugehörigkeit. 2003.
Band	43	Michael Becker-Mrotzek / Gisela Brünner (Hrsg.): Analyse und Vermittlung von Gesprächskompetenz. 2004. 2. durchgesehene Auflage. 2009.
Band	44	Britta Hufeisen / Nicole Marx (Hrsg.): *Beim Schwedischlernen sind Englisch und Deutsch ganz hilfsvoll.* Untersuchungen zum multiplen Sprachenlernen. 2004.
Band	45	Helmuth Feilke / Regula Schmidlin (Hrsg.): Literale Textentwicklung. Untersuchungen zum Erwerb von Textkompetenz. 2005.
Band	46	Sabine Braun / Kurt Kohn (Hrsg.): Sprache(n) in der Wissensgesellschaft. Proceedings der 34. Jahrestagung der Gesellschaft für Angewande Linguistik. 2005.
Band	47	Dieter Wolff (Hrsg.): Mehrsprachige Individuen – vielsprachige Gesellschaften. 2006.
Band	48	Shinichi Kameyama / Bernd Meyer (Hrsg.): Mehrsprachigkeit am Arbeitsplatz. 2006.
Band	49	Susanne Niemeier / Hajo Diekmannshenke (Hrsg.): Profession & Kommunikation. 2008.
Band	50	Friedrich Lenz (Hrsg.): Schlüsselqualifikation Sprache. Anforderungen – Standards – Vermittlung. 2009.
Band	51	Andreas Krafft / Carmen Spiegel (Hrsg.): Sprachliche Förderung und Weiterbildung – transdisziplinär. 2011.
Band	52	Helmuth Feilke / Katrin Lehnen (Hrsg.): Schreib- und Textroutinen. Theorie, Erwerb und didaktisch-mediale Modellierung. 2012.
Band	53	Iris Rautenberg / Tilo Reißig (Hrsg.): Lesen und Lesedidaktik aus linguistischer Perspektive. 2015.
Band	54	Bernd Rüschoff / Julian Sudhoff / Dieter Wolff (Hrsg.): CLIL Revisited. Eine kritische Analyse zum gegenwärtigen Stand des bilingualen Sachfachunterrichts. 2015.
Band	55	Alexandra Groß / Inga Harren (Hrsg.): Wissen in institutioneller Interaktion. 2016.
Band	56	Susanne Göpferich / Imke Neumann (eds.): Developing and Assessing Academic and Professional Writing Skills. 2016.
Band	57	Anja Steinlen / Thorsten Piske (Hrsg.): Wortschatzlernen in bilingualen Schulen und Kindertagesstätten. 2016.
Band	58	Rolf Kreyer / Steffen Schaub / Barbara Ann Güldenring (Hrsg.): Angewandte Linguistik in Schule und Hochschule. Neue Wege für Sprachunterricht und Ausbildung. 2016.
Band	59	Christian Ludwig / Kris Van de Poel (eds): Collaborative Learning and New Media. New Insights into an Evolving Field. 2017.